UNCONDITIONAL EQUALITY

A CULTURAL CRITIQUE BOOK

Cesare Casarino, John Mowitt, and Simona Sawhney, Editors

Unconditional Equality

. . . .

Gandhi's Religion of Resistance

Ajay Skaria

A Cultural Critique Book

University of Minnesota Press
Minneapolis • London

Portions of the Introduction were previously published as "Gandhi's Radical Conservatism," in "Thinking of Gandhi," special issue of *Seminar India* (October 2014), edited by Tridip Suhrud. Portions of chapter 3 were previously published as "Living by Dying," in *Genealogies of Virtue: Ethical Practice in South Asia,* edited by Anand Pandian and Daud Ali (Bloomington: Indiana University Press, 2010).

Published by the University of Minnesota Press
111 Third Avenue South, Suite 290
Minneapolis, MN 55401-2520
http://www.upress.umn.edu

A Cataloging-in-Publication record for this book is available from the Library of Congress.
ISBN 978-0-8166-9865-3 (hc)
ISBN 978-0-8166-9866-0 (pb)

Printed in the United States of America on acid-free paper

The University of Minnesota is an equal-opportunity educator and employer.

21 20 19 18 17 16   10 9 8 7 6 5 4 3 2 1

Contents

Preface

A Religion of the Question

Somewhere in the early 2000s, while preparing to teach Mohandas Karamchand Gandhi's English translation of *Hind Swaraj* to my undergraduate class, a passage about history in the text intrigued me. Since I happened to have the Gujarati version of that text at hand, I consulted it. The divergence is striking. The Gujarati text criticizes "history" (the English word occurs in the Gujarati text) and contrasts it to *itihaas* [usually translated as "history"]. The English text criticizes "history," but in it there is no equivalent for *itihaas*; the contrast between history and *itihaas* is thus obscured.

The gap between the Gujarati and English texts, I have since come to realize, is symptomatic of Gandhi's struggles to think his politics. What this politics involves is by no means clear to him; perhaps he writes so prolifically and indefatigably (his collected works run to ninety-eight volumes in English) precisely in order to try and understand his own politics. This politics becomes even more intriguing when we attend not only to Gandhi as an author or "intending subject," but to his writing.[1] By dwelling in and on the gaps (between Gujarati and English and also within each of these languages) in his writing, this book tries to draw out his politics.

For me, writing this book has been difficult also because of another gap—that between Gandhi's insistence that there can be "no politics without religion" and the secular inheritance that I have, as far as I know, no desire to abandon. Gandhi repeatedly describes *satyagraha* (his most famous neologism, which he coins initially as a translation of "passive resistance") as his "dharma" or "religion," even as the religion that stays in all religions.[2] Symptomatic of my difficulty with this religious politics was my inability for long to even recognize it. When Vinay Lal first asked me in 2007 to write an essay on Gandhi's religion for a volume he was planning on political Hinduism, I protested that I was not interested in this aspect of Gandhi. But with his characteristic persistence, Vinay did not accept my protests, and I ended up writing that essay, which became a precursor of this book.

In the process, my own understanding of dharma and religion as "concepts" has been transformed.[3]

What is Gandhi's religion? Which, given his remarks, is also to ask: What is the religiosity of his politics? What is the politics of his religion? And what is its universality?

This book is an attempt to address these concerns. In preparation for later chapters, here I would like briefly to attend to an issue that, though not explicitly thematized in the book, is yet perhaps the specter animating it—the relation between Gandhi's religion and secularism, or (to briefly signal the argument about this relation) how Gandhi's satyagraha is a religion of the question.

$\sim$

Hegel notes already in 1802 "the feeling that 'God himself is dead' upon which the religion of more recent times rests."[4] Hegel can assert this partially because, by the time he writes, God-centered ethics are on the decline among philosophers, and many philosophers think morality and ethics in secular terms, without reference to God.

The apprehension of the death of God is not only a characteristic of "more recent times." It is already borne (if only as nonpresence) by the various negative theologies that one finds "in" each of the various "religions," including the Buddhist, Christian, Hindu, Islamic, Jain, and Judaic. But it surely does gather an increasingly inescapable force in "more recent times." Justifiably or not, all modern religions and ideologies share the apprehension about the death of God. This apprehension is the mark of their modernity. It forms these religions and ideologies regardless of whether they accept or deny the death of God, whether they denounce or accept secularism.[5]

Gandhi's writing occurs under the shadow of this apprehension of the death of God. He comes to his religion after crossing the "sahara of atheism." And while he considers "modern civilization" "godless," and thinks of his politics as striving for a godliness, his religion and godliness are themselves marked by reason. Thus, condemning the practice of untouchability, he argues: "Hinduism like every other religion, apart from the sanction of Shastras, has got to submit itself to the test of universal reason. In this age of reason, in this age of universal knowledge, in this age of education and comparative theology, any religion which entrenches itself behind Shastric injunctions and authority is, in my own humble opinion, bound to fail."[6] Moreover, he often stresses his affinities with atheists such as "Bradlaw"

(Charles Bradlaugh, whom he admires greatly, and whose funeral he attends while a student in London), whose "atheism was only so-called. He had faith in the moral government of the world."[7]

Most strikingly perhaps, Gandhi cannot conceive God as a sovereign or kingly being; God becomes a shorthand for *sat* or *satya*—words that can be glossed, respectively, as being and truth in the sense of the realization or accomplishment of being. While he is willing to accept a "personal God for those who need his personal presence," he also insists that it is inadequate to think God in human terms, and treats the very word "God" as an example of such humanization; for him, therefore, "satya is God."[8] Such formulations are symptomatic of how satyagraha is concerned not with the transcendent world, but rather with the immanent one. Even his apparent invocations of a transcendent or sovereign God—as, for example, his claim that the 1934 Bihar earthquake was "a divine chastisement sent by God" for the sin of untouchability, or his claim that he seeks *moksha* ("salvation")—turn out on closer scrutiny to be concerned with the immanent world.[9]

This immanent religion organized around satya is all the more intriguing given how his neologism *satyagraha* conjoins two terms: *satya* and *agraha*—force, firmness, insistence, or even seizing. It is not as though the satyagrahi, the practitioner of satyagraha, already knows or possesses satya and seeks only to enforce or spread it; rather, the satyagrahi is engaged in a "quest for satya." And this quest is also a questioning because satyagrahis do not know what satya is—they are only constantly aware of being part of and yet abysally separated from satya, of striving to be seized by satya.

All of this is symptomatic, I would like to argue, of how in Gandhi's writing at its most intriguing, the apprehension of the death of God is accompanied by satyagraha as a religion of the question.[10]

～

But what is this—a religion of the question? We could perhaps begin with that last sentence of Martin Heidegger's "The Question Concerning Technology," which reads: "For the question is the piety of thought."[11] That sentence condenses within it an immense paradox whose implications were already being thought before Heidegger's forceful formulation. The paradox lies in the conjoining of questioning and piety.

Had Heidegger said that the question, and questioning, is the essence of thought, he would only have succinctly restated a powerful and longstanding tradition. For the privileging of the question is shared across various philosophical traditions, most famously but by no means only in the Socratic tradition, which has resonated across the Arabic world, the Indian subcontinent, and Western Europe. Indeed, one of the ways in which what is as a shorthand called the Enlightenment would distinguish itself would be precisely through the claim that, more thoroughly than any other tradition, it makes the question the essence of thought. This relentless privileging of the question is precisely what anchors secularism, with its commitment to a certain vision of science and the public sphere. Where and when the question is privileged, the death of God becomes an especially potent possibility.

But Heidegger does not simply say that questioning is the essence of thought. He says something quite different: that questioning is the piety, piousness, or devoutness of thought.[12] This formulation presumes that even if the question bears the possibility of the death of God, that death is not a privative one. Rather, the question as a concept conserves something of the spirit or perhaps specter of religion.

What is this piousness? And how would the question as a concept be transformed if it is the piousness of thought?

It could be argued that the piousness of the question has two modalities. First, there are the dominant traditions of the Enlightenment. These traditions usually privilege the question quite emphatically, and apparently accord only a secondary or subordinate place for piousness. These traditions also presume a distinction between the public and the private, where the public is the realm of the question and the private is the realm of faith, where the question is not allowed access. It is in this spirit that Kant famously says: "I have therefore found it necessary to deny knowledge in order to make room for faith."[13]

This opposition between faith and knowledge does not erase piousness (and is not meant to by either Kant or Hegel) from the secular public sphere. Now knowledge provides both an ontology (it grounds the world) and a theology (it names what is highest: as Francis Bacon says in the sixteenth century, "the sovereignty of man lieth hid in knowledge"). Knowledge is here constantly produced, revised, and governed by a certain kind of question—one that from its sovereign and autonomous (giving itself its own law) position seeks to know itself and its object. Knowledge is thus premised on an enshrining of the sovereign question.

In this enshrining, moreover, the question inaugurates modern secularism, for it allows the secular state to claim the grounding and the sovereignty associated with religious authority. Secularism appropriates the very terms of theology: as Karl Marx notes already in the 1840s, "the perfected Christian state" is "the atheist state, the democratic state," the secular state.[14] (Carl Schmitt restates this insight from an idealist perspective in the 1920s, "All significant concepts of the modern theory of the state are secularized theological concepts.")[15] The most powerful of these newly sacralized terms is perhaps "citizen"—the figure who restlessly asks questions of the state, who demands to participate in the state's sovereignty, and who by this very demand already begins participating in at least the form of that sovereignty. Man as citizen worships the sovereign question as the essence of thought, as Being, but this question he worships is himself.

One form of questioning as the piety of thought, then, is this theological secularism.[16] And theological secularism emerges along with the modern concept of religion, which now names the heteronomous realm—the realm of laws given by the other. Hence the challenge that theological secularism formulates for itself: How to limit religion to the private realm? How to sustain an autonomous politics?

Gandhi's religion questions and relinquishes this theological secularism. While he acknowledges the need for a secular state, this is a very different secularism, for he repeatedly insists that there can be "no politics without religion." His "religion" of *satyagraha* or "passive resistance" is equally difficult to understand in the terms provided by theological secularism: it is neither a private religion (for it operates in the secular public sphere) nor a public religion (for it does not seek an institutionalized political or social space for specific religious practices).[17]

In what sense, then, is Gandhi's satyagraha a religion of the question?

～

Even more than the sovereign question, the second sense in which questioning is the piety of thought predates Enlightenment traditions. It receives for example an especially succinct formulation in Saint Augustine's cry, "I have become a question to myself." Here, to become a questioning being is to become bereft of one's own sovereignty. Augustine's question, as Hannah Arendt notes, is indicative of how "man initiates the quest for his own being. . . . This quest for his own being arises from his being created and endowed with a memory that tells him he did not make himself."[18] Many religions respond to this memory by becoming theological—by claiming to ground themselves in either knowledge or revelation. At least at this moment of his anguish, Augustine finds himself unable to do this:

his religion remains a groundless faith, a faith that accepts that it cannot find grounds for itself—this is why he becomes a question to himself.

In one of the few remarks he makes about Augustine, Gandhi's attention is drawn to this absence of sovereignty: "But one thing is sure that the humility which feels itself nothing before God is necessary for mystical experiences, such as those of Saint Francis and Saint Augustine. On the other hand, a Bradlaw [Charles Bradlaugh] or a Marcus Aurelius, though following conscience, felt themselves to be self-made men and not dependent on God, and so they could get no mystical experiences or joy."[19] The contrast here with Bradlaugh, who, recall, has "faith in the moral government of the world," is telling. Unlike Bradlaugh's secular conscience, which retains sovereignty over itself, Gandhi's "mystical experience" or religion involves a surrender of sovereignty.[20] This makes the humility involved in secular conscience very different from that involved in religion in Gandhi's sense. Even where secular conscience humbles itself before the sovereign question, it only humbles itself before man—this is the sense in which secular conscience remains sovereign. By contrast, the question that Gandhi's religious experience humbles or surrenders itself before is the other experienced in groundless faith. But this humbling is also freely offered, and so it is never a subordination to the other. Religion bears always, in however obscured a manner, this surrender without subordination.

Gandhi associates several persons with aspects of the experience of religion in this sense—among them Augustine, Jalaluddin Rumi, Jesus, Mohammed, Narsinh Mehta, Mirabai, Rabia Bibi, and Tulsidas. He claims, moreover, that satyagraha is the way of being most faithful to this experience of religion, that it is most proper to religion, that it is the "religion that stays in all religions."

This claim turns on the distinctive way he conceives satya as "love." Exemplary of this way is his explanation (in the sixth of the Rowlatt Satyagraha pamphlet series, which is written during that movement to explain what satyagraha is): "An axiom of religion [dharma] is that satya itself is religion. Love [prem] itself is religion is a second axiom. But since religion cannot be two, so religion itself is love or love is religion. And if we sit down to reflect further, we shall find that without love, conduct based on truth [satya] is impossible. This is why truth force [satya shakti] is love force [prem shakti]."[21] Religion now becomes "universal love."

As this and other similar formulations unfold, a striking difference opens up between satyagraha and the other conceptions of "universal love." For example, the Augustinian love of the neighbor (of which the twenty-three-year-old Hannah Arendt provides a breathtaking reading in her dissertation) is for a transcendent and sovereign God. Here, first, as Arendt notes, "For the lover who loves as God loves, the neighbor ceases to be anything but a creature of God. All meet in this love, denying themselves and their mutual ties. . . . he loves his neighbor neither for his neighbor's sake, nor for his own sake. Love of neighbor leaves the lover himself in absolute isolation, and the world remains a desert for man's isolated existence."[22] Second, "In the equality of all people before God, which love of neighbor makes thematic," the concretely temporal question of whether my neighbor is my friend or foe, or how my neighbor regards me, becomes a matter of indifference. What matters rather is that "in the being before God all people are equal, that is, equally sinful."[23]

The critique that Arendt makes of Augustine could very easily be made of Gandhi's explicit formulations. Indeed, he never thematizes and is perhaps never even explicitly conscious of his divergences from Augustine. But his writing at its most intriguing is marked by irreconcilable differences from Augustine or other thinkers of a transcendent religion. In contrast to Augustinian Christianity, satyagraha is a religion that becomes immanent because of its apprehension of the death of God. Here the segue from satya and religion to universal love is not mediated through a higher entity such as God. It is rather the very impossibility of God as a sovereign being that sustains the emphasis on a universal love. Because of this very different starting point, even same or similar phrases, such as "universal love" or "equality before God," rotate away on very different trajectories.

For example, even though Gandhi emphasizes universal love, in his writing such love becomes inseparable from *swadeshi* [staying with one's own *desh*—country or place]. He insists:

> One rule of swadeshi is that in serving people we should first serve *[seva]* those who live near us. There is also an opposite rule, that we should first serve those who are distant from us and then those who are near us. Near in the first rule means physically near, and distant in the second rule means distant from us mentally. . . .
>
> The reason behind this rule of swadeshi is that we cannot reach all human beings in this world. If instead of serving the person near you, you ignore your neighbour and seek to serve someone living far away, that would be pride on your part.[24]

"Universal love" is thus reinscribed in the local; it must first take up precisely the local friend or enemy, and from there proceed locally to other
friends and enemies. This extremely local way of proceeding, which loves
the neighbor for the neighbor's and satyagrahi's sake, and then strives to
universalize itself, is quite at odds with Augustinian love.

Equality with and of all beings also undergoes a similar transformation, whose incendiary implications are perhaps even more striking. In
transcendental religions, equality is sustained by a Creator: love of that
Creator, or emergence from that Creator, makes for equality. In satyagraha,
as I will indicate at greater length, we encounter an equality that comes
after the death of God; we now have creatures without a sovereign Creator.
Their absolute equality, moreover, is irreducibly and tumultuously plural
because it must include all being (not only humans but also animals and
things).

This absolute equality of all being, an absolute equality that does not
in his explicit formulations seem to demand any specific political or institutional form (though there is perhaps a hesitant taste for republican
democracy), is the most crucial stake of Gandhi's thinking of religion, of
"no politics without religion."[25]

But even our radical traditions of thinking politics and the political
often quite obscure from us this absolute equality of all being. In order to
indicate how this happens, we could start with another essay by Arendt,
this time the controversial "Reflections on Little Rock."[26] Arendt identifies
three different spheres: the political realm, or the realm of citizens, which
is organized around the principle of equality of "different men"; the realm
of society, "that curious, somewhat hybrid realm between the political and
the private," which has discrimination along various lines (such as "profession, income, and ethnic origin") as its organizing principle; the realm
of privacy, where "our choice is guided, not by likeness or qualities shared
by a group of people—it is not guided, indeed, by any objective standards
or rules—but strikes, inexplicably and unerringly, at one person in his
uniqueness, his unlikeness to all other people we know."[27]

Arendt's essay is not at all tenable as an analysis of school desegregation
(Ralph Ellison powerfully pointed this out at the time).[28] Nor even perhaps is its distinction between the three realms tenable when it is made
so rigidly.[29] The uncanny salience and brilliance of her essay lies rather
in its distinctive double move: on the one hand, it identifies equality as
the principle of the political, and on the other hand, it precisely identifies

some apparently unavoidable restrictions placed on that principle by the other two realms.

This double move has also been found unavoidable by many thinkers whose commitments we might usually consider, unlike Arendt's, to be close to the radical left. Thus Étienne Balibar, in *Equaliberty*, his incisive exploration of how equality and liberty are coeval rather than (as much liberal theory would have it) equality coming after liberty as a way of limiting it, is quite clear that he is concerned with the "trace of equaliberty in the history of modern citizenship."[30] In this formulation, one may say (and I make this point not so much to criticize the book as to bring out its founding presuppositions), equaliberty is restricted to humans. Even if "fraternity" no longer does the work it has since at least the French Revolution of simultaneously repressing sexual difference and mediating equality and liberty, even if "fraternity" is no longer explicitly invoked, it persists now as an anthropology. Implicitly excluded thus from equality are all those incapable of modern citizenship—most evidently, animals and things (though perhaps the lines between humans, animals, and things must always pass through humans).[31]

To offer another example, Jacques Rancière, after identifying politics as "that activity which turns on equality as its principle," goes on to describe politics in terms of disagreement, which is "a determined kind of speech situation: one in which one of the interlocutors at once understands and does not understand what the other is saying"; it is "the conflict between one who says white and another who also says white but does not understand the same thing by it or does not understand that the other is saying the same thing in the name of whiteness."[32] Thus, though Rancière would include the social and the private within the political, his own conception of the political must exclude all those who do not have speech, who do not have the power of agreement or disagreement—most massively, again, animals and things. It is symptomatic of this exclusion and anthropocentrism that Rancière conceives equality in terms of the demand for emancipation—a demand, in other words, that presumes the potential for an everyday exercise of sovereignty, which it would be difficult to attribute not only to animals and things but also, in many situations, to humans.

In a dizzying departure from secular traditions of thinking the political, then, Gandhi insists on the absolute equality of all beings; indeed, this absolute equality is satya or the realization of being. That insistence makes satya synonymous with justice—now the seizure by the demand for equality and against inequality is ownmost to being. To this seizure, Gandhi gives the name *satyagraha*. Gandhi repeatedly describes satyagraha as an "ancient truth." There is of course something new about satyagraha, but "like the name itself," it is only "a new presentation of an old doctrine." Gandhi can make these claims because in his writing satya always already is this absolute equality and absolute plurality, and it bears practices that sustain this equality and plurality, practices condensed especially in the word satyagraha, but also in all those words that Gandhi uses as synonyms for satyagraha and for each other: among them, "pure means," "love," and "pure self-sacrifice." These practices are the originary answer that satya bears.

But that answer, satya, dehisces into many questions, for what satya "is" is constitutively obscured. Justice among such radically different beings cannot be thought in the usual terms; what is now required is a justice without sovereignty. It is only satyagraha as a religion of the question that can apprehend, in trembling and without knowledge, this other justice— satya as the equality of all being. Conversely, it is only as a religion of the question that those of us who find it impossible to abandon their faith in secularism can at all think with—as distinct from think about—Gandhi's religion. *Unconditional Equality* attends to this never-ending dehiscence of the answer, satya, into the question, satyagraha.

Surrender without Subordination

When I think that I cannot express myself well in Gujarati but can do so in English, I tremble.

—Mohandas Gandhi, *Akshardeha*

The more original a thinking, the richer will its unthought be. The unthought is the most precious gift that a thinking has to convey.

—Martin Heidegger, *What Is Called Thinking?*

O N ANOTHER SEPTEMBER 11, this one in 1906, Mohandas Karamchand Gandhi, then a lawyer practicing in South Africa, leads a meeting at the Empire Theater in Johannesburg. The meeting is held to discuss the proposed Asiatic Law Amendment Ordinance in Transvaal, which requires all male Asians to register themselves. Recalling that meeting in 1925, by which time he has emerged as the most prominent leader of the Indian nationalist movement, Gandhi writes that the theater is "wholly destroyed by fire" a day later, on September 12, and that some of his interlocutors treat this as a "good omen," a sign that the Ordinance will "meet the same fate as the Theatre."

At the meeting (conducted in Hindi and Gujarati, with Tamil and Telugu translations), one of the earliest Indian residents in South Africa, Sheth Haji Habib, declares in the name of God that he will not submit to this law and exhorts all others to do likewise. The oath, the invocation of God, initially surprises Gandhi, but soon his "perplexity gave place to enthusiasm." He speaks again, explains how an oath is different from a resolution. "We all believe in one and the same God, the differences of nomenclature in Hinduism and Islam notwithstanding. To pledge ourselves or to take an oath in the name of that God or with Him as witness is not something to be trifled with. If having taken such an oath we violate our pledge we are guilty before God and man." The meeting concludes with "all present, standing with upraised hands" taking "an oath with God as witness not to submit to the Ordinance if it became law."[1]

In Gandhi's Gujarati book *A History of the Satyagraha in South Africa,*
the chapter devoted to the meeting is titled "The birth *[janm]* of satyagraha"; the English translation carries the title "The advent of satyagraha."
But the identification of September 11, 1906, as the date of the birth or
advent of satyagraha is retrospective. In 1906–7, Gandhi resorts to the
phrase "passive resistance" to describe the struggles he leads against the
South African colonial regime. Only by December 1907, dissatisfied with
the use of such English words, does he invite readers of *Indian Opinion*, the
trilingual periodical he edits, to submit "exact Gujarati equivalents."[2]

In a January 1908 issue of the periodical, he writes that a correspondent
(Maganlal Gandhi, his second nephew and close associate) had suggested
the word *sadagraha*. Gandhi replaces the prefix *sad* or "good" with *satya*.
Gandhi is taken with the new word. "I think *satyagraha* is more appropriate
than *sadagraha*. "Resistance" means determined opposition to anything.
The correspondent has rendered it as *agraha*. *Agraha* in a right cause is *sat*
or *satya agraha*. The correspondent therefore has rendered "passive resistance" as firmness in a good cause. Though the phrase does not exhaust
the connotation of the word "passive," we shall use *satyagraha* till a word is
available."[3] Though it begins as a temporary placeholder for passive resistance, the word quickly becomes the most central term in Gandhi's vocabulary. By 1910, in chapter 17 of *Hind Swaraj,* he translates *satyagraha* into
English as "more popularly but less accurately, passive resistance."

"*Satyagraha*" is an immensely freighted neologism. The word *sat* can be
glossed as being, and is predictably one of the most charged and debated
terms in Indian philosophical vocabularies. The suffix *ya* carries the sense
of accomplishment of the word it suffixes. *Satya* can thus be glossed as the
accomplishment of or orientation to *sat*, or even the enactment of *sat* (for
the suffix *ya* usually presumes activity). This may be why *satya* also bears the
sense of "truth"—not in the secondary sense of objective verifiability, but
truth in the sense of fidelity to being.[4] *Satya*, then, is no less charged than *sat*.

But the conceptual power of his neologism lies in the conjoining of *satya*
with the suffix *agraha*, or perhaps *graha*. Gandhi often translates *agraha* as
force (satyagraha is "Truth-force"). But *agraha* is not just any force—it
carries the connotation of overpowering force. *Agraha* is thus the force
that occurs as a seizing, a taking hold, or a firmness. While there is a long
tradition of thinking about *satya*, whether as being or truth, the neologism
satyagraha broaches a new question, perhaps never before asked in quite
this way: How would the force proper to *satya* work? That one query

yields, when we attend to it, a sheaf of searching and scouring questions. These, to begin with: What is satya? What is the force proper to fidelity to satya? What is the proper, what a relation of propriety? And how ever does this word "satyagraha" work, even provisionally, as a translation of passive resistance—what transposition takes place in this strange shuttling?

In order to elicit what satyagraha entails, we could begin by attending to the curious movement in Gandhi's writings between two senses of the word *swaraj*. Consider *Hind Swaraj*, his best-known work, which he wrote in Gujarati in 1909 and then translated into English in 1910.[5] The book is organized as a dialogue between two figures—a Reader and an Editor. The Reader argues for "modern methods of violence," if necessary, to secure swaraj; the English version translates his use of "swaraj" as "Home Rule." Since at least the late nineteenth century, Indian nationalists had been invoking the word "swaraj" to describe their demand for political sovereignty. Continuing this tradition, the Reader imagines a swaraj or Home Rule that will be centered around an Indian nation-state governed by an Indian parliament, and will thus presumably institute among Indians a social order organized around abstract equality and the rights of man and citizen.

The Editor disagrees. He wants swaraj too, but not the swaraj the Reader or mainstream nationalists want. In chapter 14, he says: "It is swaraj when we learn to rule ourselves," and "such swaraj has to be experienced by each one for himself." For this swaraj, moreover, "it is not necessary for us to have as our goal the expulsion of the English." The Editor goes back in effect to the etymology of the word: swa—self, but with connotations of proper and ownmost; and raj—rule. Swaraj here names the rule of the self, and in the process wrestles with the questions: What is proper to rule? What is proper to the self? What would the rule of the ownmost involve? Perhaps because of these unfamiliar senses the word *swaraj* acquires, the Editor's use of the word *swaraj* often remains untranslated in Gandhi's English rendering. This recalcitrance to translation is conserved in the very title of the English version—*Hind Swaraj or Indian Home Rule*.

The Editor describes swaraj by drawing on two words with which Gandhi is inextricably associated—*ahimsa* and *satyagraha*. Ahimsa, etymologically nonviolence [*a*, non; *himsa*, violence], is a storied term with long and complex genealogies in Buddhist, Hindu, and Jain texts. Satyagraha is described also as "love-force" [*prembal*] and "soul-force" [*atmabal*]. While for him satyagraha and ahimsa are synonyms, he seems to prefer his neologism, perhaps because he senses that the active nature of "ahimsa" is not emphasized enough in its customary usage.

His reading of satyagraha is indicative of Gandhi's divergence from the way most liberal thinkers affirm nonviolence and civil disobedience. For these thinkers (to take two recent examples, Jürgen Habermas and John Rawls), civil disobedience is a different means to better secure the same freedom and equality that is institutionalized in republican democracy, or what Gandhi sometime calls *prajasatta* (popular government, though the phrase is sometimes translated as "a republican form of government").[6] The Editor, by contrast, treats satyagraha as opening onto another swaraj—another freedom and equality.

Perhaps we can intensify our sense of this other freedom and equality by noting that Gandhi conceives of satyagraha not only as his "religion" [*dharma*], but as constitutive of religion—as the "religion that stays in all . . . religions." The first explicit reference to religion occurs in chapter 6, when the Editor attacks "modern civilization" or "modern civility."[7]

> In it there is no thought for ethics [*niti;* "morality"] or religion.
> The votaries of modern civility say quite clearly that their job is not
> to teach people religion. So many believe that religion is only a
> superstitious growth. Also, so many wear the mantle of religion;
> they even talk of ethics; nevertheless I tell you after twenty years of
> experience that unethicality [*aniti,* "immorality"] is taught in the
> name of ethics. . . . This civility is irreligion [*adharma*], and it has
> spread to such an extent in Europe that the people who are in it
> appear half-mad.

And the Editor fears the spread of irreligion to Hindustan. In chapter 8, he says: "Religion is dear to me, and so my first reason for grief is this—that Hindustan is becoming ever more irreligious [*dharmabhrasht*]. By religion I do not here mean Hindu or Mussalman or Zorastrian religion. But the religion that stays in all these religions has gone. We are turning our faces away from God."[8] In later years too, he repeatedly invokes the injunction shared across classical Jain, Buddhist, and Hindu texts—*ahimsa paramo dharma,* "non-violence is the highest religion."

The invocation of religion to think another freedom and equality makes little sense from a secular perspective, not even if the religion in question is nonviolence. The Reader voices our secular skepticism and commonsense

when in chapter 8 he says: "In the name of religion Hindus and Mahomed-
ans fought against one another. For the same cause Christians fought
Christians. Thousands of innocent men have been murdered, thousands
have been burned and tortured in its name. Surely, this is much worse than
any civilization." The Reader's dismissal of religion resonates with the way
secular traditions distinguish between a private sphere and a rational public sphere, and try to confine religion to the private sphere. These traditions presume that if religion were introduced in the public sphere, it
would not only cause its adherents to lose their freedom (for they would
behave irrationally and incalculably), but would also threaten the freedom
of others. To fight in the name of religion leads, the Reader suggests, to
"charlatanism."

It is symptomatic of our suspicion—quite justified—of religion that
much scholarship until recently regarded Gandhi's interventions as a roman-
ticism, a critical traditionalism, as symptomatic of the communitarian
ideology of precapitalist agrarian societies, or in the most sophisticated
readings as enabling the "political appropriation of the subaltern classes by
a bourgeoisie aspiring for hegemony in the new nation-state."[9]

However, as the hegemony of secular traditions frays, it becomes possible to reconsider the stakes of Gandhi's emphasis on satyagraha as the
"religion that stays in all these religions."[10] In Gandhi's writing, this book
will argue, satyagraha is the unrepresentable and inexpressible kernel that
constitutes the condition of possibility for any religion as well as for any
conception of the ethical. Symptomatic of this is its vexed relation with
"all . . . religions," which he also sometimes describes as "customary religion" or "formal religion." These religions achieve their most complete
form simultaneously in today's "religious fundamentalisms," and in modern secularisms—despite appearing so opposed to each other, both com-
plexes draw on each other to conceive universality in terms of sovereignty,
whether of divinity or of reason.[11]

Satyagraha, by contrast, involves a "self-surrender" that relinquishes
sovereignty over self and other, as also any universality conceived in terms
of sovereignty. As such, satyagraha is both borne and obscured by "formal
religions." It is borne by them in the sense that all religions are marked by
the surrender, offered in faith, of the self to the sacred. It is obscured by them
in the sense that these religions conceive surrender as subordination to
a sovereign power—God or the divine. In Gandhi's writing, satyagraha is
the struggle of being to emerge from its obscuring in formal or theological

religions, to open instead onto a freedom, equality, and universality organized around what he calls "pure means."

The word *agraha* is indicative of this struggle: while the ownmost orientation of all beings is to attend to satya, it is also obscured from them, so that *agraha* here involves not only insistence and force (the more conventional renderings of the word) but also resistance. This resistance or force is moreover "passive" in the sense that all beings suffer it without having chosen to do so. Satyagraha is the active cultivation of this passive force; this is why Gandhi on occasion describes satyagraha as the most intense activity. (An intense activity, one might add, that must proceed without sovereignty or autonomy.) Offered in this passive sense, resistance becomes religion, even the religion that stays in all religions.

By drawing on a range of terms—among them, pure means, pure gift, pure example, and surrender without subordination—this book explores both what is entailed in satyagraha, and in the liberal and conservative traditions that satyagraha questions and relinquishes.

～

The liberal understanding that Gandhi begins to question from around 1906 is forcefully articulated in his own earlier writings, and in the Reader's arguments in *Hind Swaraj*.[12] Like most liberal theories that conjoin freedom and equality, these writings implicitly presume a human capable of autonomy, the Kantian term for the ability of the "rational being" to exercise a sovereignty over the self that allows it to author a law that is universal in the sense that all rational beings will freely submit to it.[13]

Unlike the liberal theorists he invokes, however, the young Gandhi often considers all humans capable of autonomy or rational freedom. Despite lauding Thomas Babington Macaulay's conception of equality as "the cornerstone of the imperial edifice," his open letter in 1894 to Europeans in Natal and the Legislative Assembly radicalizes that equality (and thinkers from colonized regions repeatedly perform similar maneuvers). "I would ... quote an extract from Macaulay: 'We are free, we are civilized, to little purpose, if we grudge to any portion of the human race an equal measure of freedom and civilization.' ... I have but to refer you to writers like Mill, Burke, Bright, and Fawcett, to further show that they, at any rate, would not give countenance to the treatment accorded to the Indians in the Colony."[14] While colonial thinkers presume that the colonized are still in their "nonage" (to use John Stuart Mill's term in *On Liberty*), and have to wait before they are ready for self-rule, the petition draws on abstract equality to refuse such historicist hierarchies; it presumes that abstract equality requires "self-government" as its form of 'sovereign power" [*rajsatta*].[15] And through his study and practice of law as well as his campaigns in South Africa, Gandhi would have been deeply if perhaps unconsciously aware of how autonomy, and the abstract equality it presumes, is also premised on a certain way of rendering immeasure into measure, or incalculability into the calculable.[16] Citizens are immeasurable because they are imbued with sovereign power. That is why influential liberal traditions have refused to conceive human rationality solely or primarily in terms of the measurable registers of interests and appetites. They have insisted, rather, that citizens are ends (and Kant's writings are again exemplary)—incalculable and immeasurable, sovereign over themselves in their freedom, giving themselves their own law.[17]

Simultaneously, however, citizenly sovereignty also requires measure. For in the world of citizens, sovereignty (which, as Claude Lefort, among others, reminds us, is always both one and divided; this division of the one is the originary moment of the political) must be divided in a new way: it must be equally shared among the vast multiplicity of citizen-sovereigns.[18] So, unlike kingly sovereigns who exercise measure over others but do not and must not themselves submit to measure, here it is necessary to both exercise and submit to a rational measure even in order to sustain the immeasure and autonomy of citizens. In this transaction, not only is immeasure made measurable, but measure is made immeasurable. (Liberal traditions thus already provide the internal resources to question the argument—made by right-wing liberals—that liberty is primary, and names an immeasurable freedom that equality measures only secondarily.)

As this twofold rendering suggests, in the liberal political imagination abstract equality is the hinge that holds together the sovereignty and plurality of citizenship. Such a republican democracy—of formally equal citizens whose difference is rendered into equivalence, who have identical votes, and who are capable of autonomous critique—is the institutional apotheosis of "general responsibility," which Jacques Derrida has described as "an accounting, a general answering for oneself with respect to the general and before the generality."[19]

In *Hind Swaraj*, the Reader's liberalism is evident in his desire for a parliament, and for rights [*hako*]. Where the autonomous reason here ascribed to parliament prevails, relatedly, religion must also be formally confined to the private sphere—religion in the public sphere would make for a heteronomous law. (The abstract equality involved in autonomous reason thus institutes an order very different from that sustained by those religious traditions that may insist on an equality before God.) Indeed, in his insistence on extending abstract equality to the colonized, the Reader could well be said to represent one of the highest and most inclusive moments of the liberal problematic. He seizes upon and transforms its historicist concept of equality, where colonial or imperial rule is an "imaginary waiting room" on the path that leads to equality for the colonized, and where colonial rule can therefore in the long run be a positive force.[20] Thus, he criticizes early nationalists because they presume that petitions without force—that is to say, petitions only appealing to the colonizers' rhetoric about eventual equality—will persuade the British. Nationalists like the Reader want abstract equality now, and as autonomous figures they feel free to import their models of it at will from everywhere. The Reader says of parliament and rights in chapter 4: "What they have done in their own country has not been done in any other country. It is, therefore, proper for us to import their institutions." The Reader's positions exemplify one response to the paradox that Gayatri Chakravorty Spivak has identified—that one "cannot not want" the autonomy and place of the citizen-subject, even after the most searching critique of that subject.[21]

While responses such as the Reader's have been widespread in anticolonial and other modern subaltern moments, they come at a heavy price that Gandhi is all too acutely aware of by the time he writes *Hind Swaraj*. For him, sovereign power is not exemplified only in the state. Rather, every self is deeply fissured, and sovereignty is ubiquitous, always exercised everyday by the self—for example, in the act of eating—in order to persist in its ipseity, to master the other and return to itself. For this everyday sovereign power, Gandhi has several names, including "force of arms" and "attachment" [*asakti*].

Autonomy becomes here one kind of sovereign power—that exercised over the self through the measure and calculation involved in the exercise of reason. And when autonomy is institutionalized as a social order, as it is with parliamentary democracy, the violence of sovereign power is intensified in two ways. First, it grants equality only to those beings presumed to possess the power to reason, and in this way systematizes domination over all other beings (such as animals or the colonized). Second, autonomous beings inflict a massive violence on themselves, for they lose the power to love, which in Gandhi's writings requires the surrender of autonomy, for while even sovereigns can love, purely autonomous beings cannot. (It is because of the prospect of this loss that he says that the English deserve "pity.") In both these ways, the rule of the major that republican democracy institutes is profoundly violent: here the subaltern can refuse subordination only by participating in domination. What is lost is the possibility of an exit from subalternity that does not participate in domination.

⁓

In Gandhi's writing, religion provides another way of thinking freedom and equality, another swaraj. He writes in 1926, for example: "The truth is that my dharma not only permits me to claim but requires me to own kinship [sagpan] with not merely the ape but the horse and the sheep, the lion and the leopard, the snake and the scorpion."[22] As kin, his remarks elsewhere suggest, satyagrahis must strive to be absolutely equal to all beings.

But beings such as the snake or the scorpion can never claim the equality involved in sovereign power. His religion thus requires him to ask: How might a subaltern politics not only refuse subordination, but do so by relinquishing autonomy and even sovereignty?[23] Such a religion must strive for an equality of and with the minor—an equality that does not make the minor into a major, that becomes and remains minor. In chapter 17, the Editor takes issue with the privileging of the majority: "It is a superstition and an ungodly thing to believe that an act of the many [ghana, 'majority'] binds the few [thoda, 'minority']. Many examples can be given in which acts of the many will be found to have been wrong and those of the few to have been right. All reforms owe their origin to the initiative of the few in opposition to the many."[24] Gandhi notes also that his dear friend in South Africa, Simmonds (we do not learn his first name), "had a principle that truth is always with the minor party [nana paksh] or "minority." Simmonds would often playfully tell him that if Gandhi's party ever became big, then he would "withdraw his support of me," for in the hands of the "'majority' (major party) [mota paksh] even truth becomes untruth."[25] Here and elsewhere, minority names not so much a sociological or historical category as a way of being. Relinquishing sovereignty, satyagrahis must strive for an equality of and with the minor. As that phrase suggests, the minor is never simply an individual—minority names here rather the community that perdures without sovereignty, and yet without submitting to majority or sovereignty.[26]

Central to Gandhi's equality of the minor is what could be called surrender without subordination. In chapter 13, for example, the Editor remarks:

"every lover of India" should "keep faith [*shraddha*]," and "cling to Indian civility even as a child clings to the mother." These lovers, thus, do not autonomously and as mature adults arrive at a love for India that makes them stand by India and loyally critique it. Rather, their love makes them minors, surrender as a child would, and in that surrender offer "passive resistance"—here, resistance to the Reader's conception of *swaraj*.

Gandhi's remarks in 1928 during the Bardoli satyagraha indicate how such resistance proceeds: "What comparison can there be between the strength of the people of Bardoli and the might of the British Empire? Whereas the people of Bardoli are like ants, the latter is like an elephant. But when the satyagrahi becomes an ant, only then does God saves him, as He saves the ant which is about to be crushed under the elephant's foot. This is what has happened in Bardoli."[27] "Surrender" or "self-surrender" must thus mark the resistance that satyagrahis offer.[28] Here, to practice satyagraha is not only to refuse to take up arms, but to surrender as a way of refusing subordination, of giving and receiving a freedom and equality that is secreted in the very act of surrender. As subjects, satyagrahis are not agents—they do not exercise autonomy or sovereignty. Rather, they are marked by a constitutive resistance, which is at the same time the most intense passivity and the most intense activity.

Through their surrender without subordination, satyagrahis enact a distinctive swaraj—they relinquish the everyday exercise of sovereignty, and that relinquishment itself opens onto another freedom. Surrender without subordination is the most crucial stake of Gandhi's politics—what it most gives to think, and yet what remains most obscured in this politics. Indeed, religion looms so large in Gandhi's writing because surrender without subordination infects politics by beginning here.

An initial clue to what is at stake in surrender without subordination emerges in a curious divergence on occasion in his translation of the word *vinay*. The word would usually be translated as "humility," and Gandhi does often so render it. In the English *Hind Swaraj*, the Editor says: "When an equal [*barobariya*] petitions, that is a sign of humility [*vinay*]." But in a quietly surprising way, this passage also associates *vinay* with equality; elsewhere, *vinay* is even translated as equity or equality.[29] In infecting the English word "equality" with *vinay*, what usually remains recessive in the conventional English usage is brought to the fore: that here equality involves humility—a surrender to the other. And in infecting the Gujarati word *vinay* with the English word "equality," what usually remains recessive in conventional Gujarati usage is again brought to the fore: that humility can properly be offered only by equals. Such shuttling between *vinay* and equality exemplifies what goes on in surrender without subordination: satyagrahis submit to the other, but in doing so they resist the other and call the other to a similar submission. In this surrender, satyagrahis strive to participate in the other, and by doing so they not only perform a distinctive equality with the other, but also receive, give, and intensify their difference from the other.

This surrender without subordination resonates intriguingly with the "pre-definition" Derrida offers of religion:

> However little may be known of religion in the singular, we do know that it is always a response that is prescribed, not chosen freely in an act of pure and abstractly autonomous will. There is no doubt that it implies freedom, will and responsibility, but let us try to think this: will and freedom without autonomy. Whether it is a question of sacredness, sacrificiality or faith, the other makes the law, the law is other: to give ourselves back, and up, to the other."[30]

Derrida's formulation radically reworks the Kantian inheritance where man's exit from his self-imposed immaturity requires autonomy. Derrida is drawn to religion and faith, to "will and freedom without autonomy," because he shares the trepidation, growing since at least the late nineteenth century, about the Kantian inheritance.

By quite another path, Gandhi too comes to think a will and freedom without autonomy or even sovereignty. In his writing, moreover, satyagraha is the most proper and even the only way to enact such a will and freedom. As he works out what satyagraha involves, uncanny resonances appear between these very different thinkers. The writings of both are seized by questions of sacrifice, the pure gift, the promise, forgiveness, the proper; most broadly, by the concern to think the justice that precedes and exceeds law. But both also remain abysally apart from each other. Later chapters will explore how, in this immense proximity and distance, Derrida's and Gandhi's writings incite each other to both a greater incandescence and a greater darkening.

～

Surrender without subordination, and the equality of the minor it enacts, is necessarily immeasurable: there can be no measure that sustains an equality between beings so different as the ant, scorpion, and human. This is why the equality of the minor is incomprehensible from within a liberal framework, which is premised on some shared measure, such as the concept of autonomy. Gandhi thinks this unconditional equality—the equality of all being, without exception—in terms of what is always immeasurable to oneself—one's own death (and, thus, life). In chapter 10 of *Hind Swaraj*, for example, the Editor discusses what Hindus might do in cases where Muslims might seek to kill a cow: "I should sacrifice my life to save her but not take my brother's. This, I hold, is the religious law." And later: "If I do not obey the law and accept the penalty for its breach, I use soul-force [satyagraha]. It involves sacrifice of self. Everybody admits that sacrifice of self is infinitely superior to sacrifice of others."

But while this epigraphic utterance—religion as the sacrifice of self rather than sacrifice or killing of others—is an unavoidable point of departure for Gandhi, it is also preliminary in that it leads to further conceptual challenges. To begin with, Gandhi encounters this profoundly difficult question: self-sacrifice can also be offered in order to consolidate or claim sovereign power in the name of a greater good (for him, the British exemplify such self-sacrifice). What, then, is the self-sacrifice or self-surrender proper to satyagraha and religion? Or, put differently: given that self-sacrifice is always what is proper to sacrifice, what is the most proper self-sacrifice? What self-sacrifice would relinquish sovereignty over both self and other, and sustain an unconditional equality?[31]

His response emphasizes a self-sacrifice conceived in terms of self-limitation. For him, an emphasis on the limit [*hadh, maryada*] is constitutive of religion. In chapter 10, the Editor says of the railways:

> I will add this, that man [*manas*] is made in such a way that what
> movements and other things are possible for his own hands and
> feet, only that should be done. If we did not at all rush around
> ["from place to place"] by railways and other means [*sadhano*,
> "such other maddening conveniences"], then we would not fall
> into these confusion-filled questions [*guchvaada bharela savaalo;*
> "much of the confusion that arises would be obviated"]. We by our
> own hands wrap ourselves in troubles. Man's limits [*hadh*] were set
> by God [*khuda*] through the very form [*ghaat*] of his body, yet
> man found the means to go beyond that form's limits. Man was

given intellect that he might know God; man used intellect to forget God. . . . By using the railways, man has forgotten God.

The contrast here is between modern civility and "true civilization" or true civility. Modern civility breaches limits and makes finite beings infinite. Indeed, making infinite through measure—specifically, the citizenly measure condensed in autonomous reason—is the violence distinctive to modern civility. To it the Editor opposes self-limitation, which is "true civilization" or true civility. In chapter 8, he says, "Hinduism, Islam, Zoroastrianism, Christianity and all other religions teach that we should remain passive about worldly things and active about religious things, that we should set a limit [hadh] to our worldly ambition and that our religious ambition should be illimitable." And in chapter 10, he says: "God has given us a limited mental capacity, but they [the English] usurp the function of the Godhead."[32]

Such self-limitation, need it be said, does not make sense within the terms of modern civility, which conceptualizes the human through the classical couple of metaphysics that has organized our humanism: infinitude-finitude. Here, finitude is the mark of an inert object, thing, animal, or minor—in sum, of the heteronomous being. Conversely, it is the human power to make infinite that makes humans, uniquely, free; this power is most systematically theorized in the Kantian emphasis on autonomy and the Hegelian emphasis on spirit).[33]

By contrast, the spirit of satyagraha requires dwelling in radical finitude. Thus, Gandhi affirms *aparigraha* or nonpossession. In a speech in 1931 in London, he says, for instance: "possession seems to me to be a crime. I can only possess certain things when I know that others, who also want to possess similar things, are able to do so. But we know—every one of us can speak from experience—that such a thing is an impossibility. Therefore, the only thing that can be possessed by all is non-possession, not to have anything whatsoever. In other words, a willing surrender."[34]

The emphasis on nonpossession plays out in various practices of ascesis that Gandhi observes himself and enjoins on his associates—limiting consumption to the minimum possible, celibacy, control of senses, and so on. But on various occasions, Gandhi acknowledges of each of these practices that they are not essential to satyagraha—what remains always essential is "willing surrender." Such willing surrender, as later chapters will argue, demands self-sacrifice—the nonpossession of one's own life; in this sense, nonpossession is inseparable from a sacrifice of the self, as indeed from satyagraha. And self-sacrifice or willing surrender is not, moreover, to another infinite or sovereign entity such as the nation or even a sovereign God—it must be to finitude itself, to self-sacrifice.

Also, the willing surrender at work in nonpossession must not be a willed surrender. *Satyagrahis* should rather be so possessed by nonpossession as to perform an involuntary surrender—they should surrender so automatically as to not require a conscious act of the will. If the surrender is willing, it is so here in the sense that desire and will converge. Such an automatic surrender requires daya or prem (or, less often, *karuna*)—words that he uses interchangeably and translates as "compassion," "pity," or "love."[35] The emphasis on daya or prem is pervasive: among the synonyms in *Hind Swaraj* for satyagraha is *dayabal* ["love force"] and *prembal* [the force of love]; satyagraha is described as *dayadharma,* the "religion of compassion and love"; and *dayadharma* itself is occasionally described as the religion that stays in all religions.

If daya is so crucial to the experience of nonpossession, perhaps that may be because of its distinctive involuntariness. Daya seizes those who experience it, but it nevertheless cannot subordinate them, for daya can only be experienced by free beings; daya is thus the experience of surrender without subordination. Moreover, daya involves a self-limitation: to experience daya is to give oneself to the limit, and in this limitless sense limit oneself.

〜

But the "religion that stays in all these religions," as also Gandhi's questioning of liberalism, is often obscured not only from us but also from Gandhi. Symptomatic of this is the way his apparently clear and bracing prose becomes marked, on more careful consideration, by tensions and divergences between his Gujarati writings and his own translations of them into English. Entire words and phrases go missing, or carry quite different connotations, when he translates his Gujarati writings into English. We have already encountered this phenomenon with the words *itihaas, swaraj* and *vinay,* and shall encounter more examples: *purushartha* (conventionally, the four classical ends of human life) becomes "immeasurable pity"; *adhunik sudhar* (modern reform? modern civility? transient reform? transient civility?) becomes "modern civilization"; *potey maut mathey lai farey* (conventionally, "carry his own death on his head") becomes "keeps death always as a bosom friend"; *trahit manas* (conventionally, third party) becomes "ordinary man," and is even contrasted to the *treeja manas* ("third party"); eight different words and phrases are translated as "brute force"; some sentences vanish while others are added.[36]

The dissonances are not simply because the original Gujarati is inadequately or unfaithfully translated. Indeed, given Gandhi's bilingual skills, given that he thinks himself more fluent in English than Gujarati, it would even be inappropriate to presume that the Gujarati text is original and the English text secondary. When he writes and reads in Gujarati, he may well be translating crucial concepts and words that he possibly encounters first in English as he works his way through British, Indian, and South African legal systems. When he writes and reads in English, conversely, he does so as a figure already deeply immersed in Gujarati concepts and words.[37] It would be too easy also to presume that the Gujarati texts are addressed to a regional or Indian audience and the English texts are addressed to a Westernized one. As Gandhi is surely aware, the audiences overlap, if only because nationalists elsewhere in India often translate his writings in English into the languages prevalent in these regions.

In the 1910 preface to the English translation of *Hind Swaraj*, Gandhi offers his own reasons for the divergences:

It is not without hesitation that the translation of *Hind Swaraj* is submitted to the public. A European friend [Hermann Kallenbach] with whom I discussed the contents, wanted to see a translation of it and, during our spare moments, I hurriedly dictated and he took it down. It is not a literal translation but a faithful rendering of the original . . . whilst opinions were being invited as to the advisability of publishing the work, news was received that the original was seized in India. This information hastened the decision to publish the translation without a moment's delay. . . .

I am quite aware of the many imperfections in the original. The English rendering, besides sharing these, must naturally exaggerate them, owing to my inability to convey the exact meaning of the original. Some of the friends who have read the translation have objected that the subject-matter has been dealt with in the form of a dialogue. I have no answer to offer to this objection except that the Gujarati language readily lends itself to such treatment and that

it is considered the best method of treating difficult subjects. Had I
written for English readers in the first instance, the subject would
have been handled in a different manner.[38]

The explicit argument here implies that the divergences are an essential
part of good translation itself rather than a failing. Beginning with a hesitation about the inadequacy of the hurried and hasty translation, the passage
goes on to a decisive formulation: if the English translation is defective,
this is primarily because it does not diverge enough from the Gujarati text.
Had there been more time, had there been an even more faithful rendering,
had *Hind Swaraj* been written anew in English, the "form of a dialogue"
would itself have been abandoned.

Most explicitly at work in these remarks is that classical concept of representation where thought exists prior to and guarantees the writing, where
writing secondarily expresses and represents thought, and where good
translation represents the original thought. Here faithful rendering requires
not just a constative correspondence but even more crucially a performative felicity across languages.[39] Writing the same thing from scratch in
English may produce even more divergences, such as the abandonment of
the dialogue form. When we work with such an understanding of Gandhi's
"faithful rendering," we can use the divergences in the Gujarati and English
texts to clear up and throw light upon one another's obscurities.

While not incorrect, that explanation must be supplemented with
another one, borne by the very phrase "faithful rendering." If we operate
with the conventional meaning of rendering as transforming something
so as to transport its essence to another context or changed situation, then
a rendering is by its very nature faithful to what it renders, and "faithful
rendering" is merely a tautology. Could this resort to tautology be symptomatic of an anxiety that the practice of rendering tries to repress?—the
anxiety that the rendering is not faithful simply in the sense of being continuous with the original, the anxiety that something new and different
emerges here, that a rending has taken the place of the rendering?

The divergences are a symptom of the trembling that everywhere marks
Gandhi's texts. Though he starts out to affirm the grounded faith held
in place by a constative-performative continuity, his writing opens onto
another faith—one that is groundless and bare. This other faith sustains
readings that exceed the faithful renderings that Gandhi explicitly endorses;
this other faith is the "religion that stays in all . . . religions."

～

In order to attend to this trembling, *Unconditional Equality* will stress three themes, and also elicit the three divergent ways in which Gandhi thinks the self-sacrifice required by satyagraha. First, it explores his often-inadvertent critique of and departure from liberal traditions. That departure is intimated in his efforts in later years to distinguish between satyagraha and "passive resistance." The latter phrase for him increasingly comes to name liberal forms of civil disobedience. And while both satyagrahis and passive resisters practice "civil disobedience" or (in later years) "civil resistance," he insists that they do so in starkly different ways.[40] His disquiet is perhaps unsurprising, since liberal civil disobedience depends on a hierarchy between speech and voice that does not allow for the absolute or unconditional equality of all being.

Hannah Arendt elegantly reiterates and affirms that hierarchy: "man, to the extent he is a political being, is endowed with the power of speech"; relatedly, violence is "incapable of speech."[41] Arendt dismisses those with only voice; democracy is for her the community of those who have speech. Relatedly, on her reading, civil disobedience belongs to speech—the voice of reason—rather than merely voice. "It is most unfortunate that, in the eyes of many, a 'self-sacrificial element' is the best proof of 'intensity of concern' of 'the disobedient's seriousness and his fidelity to the law,' for single-minded fanaticism is usually the hallmark of a crackpot and, in any case, makes impossible a rational discussion of the issues at stake."[42] She distinguishes between the "conscience of the believer who listens to and obeys the voice of God" and the "strictly secular conscience," and suggests that civil disobedience involves the latter, where conscientious objectors come together as "public opinion."

In Arendt's argument, then, while civil disobedience may involve self-sacrifice, that should be secondary to "rational discussion"; in this spirit, she envisions finding a "constitutional niche for civil disobedience." Here civil disobedience belongs firmly to the sphere of civil society, rather than to the inarticulate and spectral reaches of voice. And by unconditionally submitting to and affirming the laws of a constitutional state, should one say, civil disobedience also institutes a theological secularism?[43]

Within these hierarchies, the colonized usually belong with those who do not have speech, who are limited to voice. In such a context, nonviolent resistance can be a way for the colonized to work their way up these hierarchies, to claim speech by demonstrating that they too are capable of "rational discussion." In the early years, Gandhi's satyagraha often involves such a claim to speech. But in later years, satyagraha questions these hier-archies; it relinquishes the privileging of speech while refusing to simply affirm the converse, voice.

In the process, it departs from the liberal association of violence with un-controlled instrumentality, and nonviolence with right measure or means—with means-ends relations calculated so as to avoid oppression. The Kantian categorical imperative, for example, seeks to install right measure through its insistence that every rational being be treated as an end (i.e., as an autonomous being) rather than only a means to an end. With this, there is an ethical imperative to become major, for only majors can exercise auton-omy and right measure or means.

In Gandhi's writing, by contrast, nonviolence involves a paradoxical relation with sovereignty. Violence is synonymous with sovereign power, which involves a mastery of self and other. "Right means" such as autonomy can only regulate this mastery, not redress or question it. Nonviolence therefore requires that satyagrahis give up sovereignty and autonomy. And while he strives to do so, Gandhi also does the opposite as a leader of the Indian National Congress: he echoes the Reader and demands "parlia-mentary swaraj" or "political swaraj," insisting all the time that this is not the swaraj or "self-rule" he seeks as a satyagrahi.

Gandhi's writing can inhabit and shuttle between these two apparently contradictory positions because it acknowledges the self's complicity in the demand for sovereignty, and strives to discipline and transform the self (which is also, recall, the *swa* of swaraj) so as to allow it to relinquish that demand. Satyagrahis cannot impose this discipline on even themselves, for they would then be sovereign over their own selves. Rather, this discipline must seize them in that automatic surrender described with words and phrases such as "pure means," "religion" "daya," or "satyagraha." Only in this seizure can satyagrahis relinquish sovereignty.

The paradoxical relation with sovereignty at work here is quite at odds with the more common communitarian critique, which often celebrates affective relations as precluding the need for sovereign power (and in that very rejection surreptitiously reinscribes an undivided sovereign power within the body of the community). But the relation articulated here res-onates strikingly with some of the most fascinating interventions in politi-cal thought, which have in very different ways stressed that sovereignty, especially as autonomy, is what the subaltern cannot not want.[44] Through engagements with some of these thinkers, *Unconditional Equality* traces the distinctiveness of Gandhi's paradoxical politics.

⌒

Second, this book elicits how, as Gandhi thinks the difference and relation between immeasurable and absolute or unconditional equality, he forcefully articulates a radical conservatism. We do not know to what extent Gandhi is explicitly familiar with the tradition of modern conservatism. He does invoke Edmund Burke on a few occasions, and in the early years admires John Morley (an admiration that does not survive Morley's stint as secretary of state for India), who is deeply influenced by Burke and even writes a biography of him. But whether he is familiar with conservative traditions or not, his politics develops a very distinctively conservative vocabulary.[45]

In 1790, in what is perhaps the founding text of modern conservatism, *Reflections on the Revolution in France*, Edmund Burke opposes two freedoms: that organized around "abstract principles [such] as the 'rights of men'" or "a geometrical and arithmetical constitution," and that organized around the "rights of Englishmen." The phrase "rights of Englishmen" indicates the way that rights are here sustained by the relations of affect that he describes with the term "inheritance." As an inheritance, the "rights of Englishmen" are constitutively organized not around a calculating and abstract reason, but around an incalculability and finitude organized by faith and affect: Englishmen are bound by traditions they have not chosen, and it is within these traditions that they find their freedom.

This affect and faith is not opposed to reason but is itself a form of reason. Burke thus insists:

> Through the same plan of a conformity to nature in our artificial institutions, and by calling in the aid of her unerring and powerful instincts, to fortify the fallible and feeble contrivances of our reason, we have derived several other, and those no small benefits, from considering our liberties in the light of an inheritance. Always acting as if in the presence of canonized forefathers, the spirit of freedom, leading in itself to misrule and excess, is tempered with an awful gravity. . . . By this means our liberty becomes a noble freedom. . . . All your sophisters cannot produce any thing better adapted to preserve a rational and manly freedom than the course

that we have pursued, who have chosen our nature rather than our speculations, our breasts rather than our inventions, for the great conservatories and magazines of our rights and privileges.[46]

Here equality is quite compatible with and even marked by hierarchy. Burke rejects the abstract equality of the Jacobins as merely a leveling that never succeeds:

> Believe me, Sir, those who attempt to level, never equalize. In all societies, consisting of various descriptions of citizens, some description must be uppermost. The levellers therefore only change and pervert the natural order of things; they load the edifice of society, by setting up in the air what the solidity of the structure requires to be on the ground. (69)

And he offers instead a vision of an equality marked by a "generous loyalty to rank and sex," a "proud submission," "dignified obedience," and "subordination of the heart," which keeps "alive, even in servitude itself, the spirit of an exalted freedom" (98). A "noble equality" accompanies and works across inequalities; this equality consists in the respect that each rank offers the other.

Gandhi's conservatism manifests itself in many ways. He insists, for example, on swadeshi (etymologically, one's own land), of which he offers the following "definition": "swadeshi is that spirit in us which restricts us to the use and service of our immediate surroundings to the exclusion of the more remote." "Hinduism has become a conservative religion and therefore a mighty force because of the Swadeshi spirit underlying it."[47]

Yet his conservatism is at the same time radical. It is radical not in the sense of being to the left or right, but in the etymological sense of *radix* that precedes and gives rise to these senses: it both works to the roots of and uproots the conservatism that it begins from (and conservatism is very much a discourse about roots). That rooting and uprooting occurs most forcefully perhaps when he draws on the figure of the warrior. Thus, this most famous proponent of nonviolence repeatedly describes satyagrahis as "true Kshatriyas" or "true warriors," and calls on Indians to at least conduct themselves as arms-bearing warriors, if not satyagrahis.

What draws Gandhi to the arms-bearing warrior is the latter's immeasurable equality. The warrior lives a life he has received by risking and putting into play what is simultaneously finite and yet immeasurable or incalculable to him—his own death and life. Warriors also conceive their immeasure and finitude in terms of sovereign power: warriors are masters over themselves. They risk their lives, in other words, to seize the last chance before their own death, and they give up even that last chance if an immeasurable or incalculable sovereignty is not possible. When they do submit to others, they do so freely—as sovereigns who in their separateness refuse measure. Moreover, if, as Jacques Rancière suggests, "politics is that activity which turns on equality as its principle," then the warrior exemplifies an especially charged political moment, for here equality becomes incalculable and immeasurable—in other words, a "principle."[48]

Two "principles" of equality, then: while citizens exemplify a measure that has been made immeasurable and thus infinite, warriors exemplify an immeasure that refuses to truck in measure and thus becomes finite. Gandhi senses that warrior's immeasurable equality and finitude allows the arms-bearing warrior to practice what modern civility cannot—trust, forgiveness, or love. But he is also acutely aware that the immeasurable equality of the arms-bearing warrior is also simultaneously an immeasurable inequality—not only with the opponents whom the warrior seeks to kill but also with those who cannot ever be warriors: for example, women and lower castes.

The warrior's incalculable political order is sustained through an economy of the gift. As we know well, the gift is constitutively marked by incalculability—this is what distinguishes it from the commodity. Here the warrior gives what is incalculable to him—his own life. But what is given is an economic gift—he gives with conscious or unconscious expectation of return. It is not only that the warrior offers his life in return for sovereignty at least over himself and potentially over others. Even more crucially, his gift institutes a proper social order, a sovereignty of the proper, a propriety.

This emphasis on propriety is especially evident in the warrior's caste. As a Kshatriya, the warrior himself is one of the four *varnas* or castes, and it is his dharma or religion to uphold both *varnashramdharma* [the fourfold order of castes and stages of life] as well as *stridharma* [the dharma of womanhood].[49] Here each entity limits itself to its religion, and in this sacrificial self-limitation maintains the social order. Each caste and gender is moreover so immeasurably given to what is proper to it that there can be no equality across divisions; they can be equal only in and to their inequality. Even where there is no inequality, there can only be incommensurability across social divisions. To the extent that warriors are presumed to govern a political and social order organized around immeasurable sovereignty, they could well be considered exemplars of the affect and faith that modern conservatism affirms.

Gandhi radicalizes the conservatism he begins from—the arms-bearing warrior's immeasurable equality-inequality—by insisting that the root [mool, jad] of the arms-bearing warrior's power is fearlessness [a-bhay]. He suggests, moreover, that a residual bhay or fear marks the arms-bearing warrior and makes him take up arms, and more broadly makes him seek sovereign power. Satyagrahis, by contrast, are true warriors—so fearless as to never take up arms, as to sacrifice themselves rather than kill their opponents. They work for an absolute or unconditional equality, which requires uprooting the warrior's immeasurable equality-inequality. Through self-sacrifice, satyagrahis offer fearlessness to their opponents and experience it themselves. Their fearlessness differs from that of warriors; while the latter requires a mastery of fear, the former requires a welling of love or compassion (prem, daya).

These opposed forms of fearlessness—one organized around sovereign power, and the other around satyagraha—are, moreover, coeval with each other. "Just as satya is eternal [sanatan], so too is asatya eternal. Light is eternal, and likewise darkness is eternal. The eternal is fit to be conserved [sangharva] only if it is mixed up with satya."[50] This is why satyagraha has to be conceived as the relinquishment of sovereign power, which is in Gandhi's writing inseparable from asatya. It may also be why Gandhi has to activate the word ahimsa or nonviolence rather than work with, say, the other canonical word from Hindu texts, shanti, "peace." More explicitly than the latter, ahimsa thinks nonviolence in terms of a violence that it is coeval with and opposes.

The satyagrahi's fearlessness involves abhaydan, the gift (dana) of fearlessness (abhay) or, in his suggestive translation once, the "gift of life." Gandhi draws this charged word from Jain traditions, where abhaydan names the first and foremost of gifts, even the only gift. For him too, abhaydan is the "greatest of gifts," "the first requisite of true religion."[51] Gandhi, extending Jain traditions, reads satyagraha as the most intense moment of that gift.

∽

But Gandhi's radical conservatism is not one. As he struggles with the question of how to gift fearlessness, his writing comes to be marked by the destruction of conservatism in two divergent senses of the genitive—one where conservatism destroys and sacrifices satyagraha's strivings for absolute equality, and the other where absolute equality destroys and sacrifices the conservative insistence on immeasurable inequalities. Both are radical in the sense that both go to the roots—the first in order to uproot the warrior's equality and reroot it in a fearlessness deeper than the warrior's, the second in order to accomplish the distinctive uprooting and impropriety that turns out to be most proper to conservatism.

Gandhi perhaps never draws a line between the two radical conservatisms; perhaps, indeed, that line cannot be known or knowably drawn. The same sentences, phrases, and even words often accomplish the destruction of conservatism in both senses of the genitive. In the first sense, "destruction of conservatism" means: the conservatism that satyagrahis set out from destroys the absolute equality that they seek to inhabit. Destruction in this sense happens where satyagrahis are driven by their prem or love to exercise so thorough a sovereignty over their own lives that they refuse to seize even the last chance at life before their own death. By doing so, they try to destroy the arms-bearing warrior's immeasurable inequality over self and other, and orient themselves instead toward an absolute and unconditional equality.

Precisely because of the resultant universality, satyagrahis as the true warriors are no longer only male. Here, rather, the gender, caste, and majority of the arms-bearing warrior are thoroughly transformed. It turns out thus as we attend to Gandhi's writings that the exemplary satyagrahis are usually women and children. In these and many other ways, the true warrior is organized around what is made minor in the figure of the arms-bearing warrior.

Nevertheless, this satyagraha becomes as "demonic" and violent as "modern civilization," or the immeasurable sovereignty of the warrior. Even if satyagrahis claim no sovereignty over the other, this is so because they submit to the sovereignty of the proper over the self. That grounding violence also implicitly imposes the sovereignty of the proper over the other, too.

It would be easy enough to indicate the many occasions on which Gandhi's interventions institute such sovereignty over both self and other. His explicit formulations draw heavily on the trope of the thekana [rightful place] in thinking of the role of women or varnadharma [the fourfold caste order]. He cannot envisage any significant role in the Congress for prostitutes—women who exemplify the abandonment of rightful place—and his explicit formulations cannot conceptualize a political role for insurgent untouchables or "Dalits," only for deified untouchables or "Harijans." In all these cases, even though satyagrahis give themselves aneconomically, by doing so they establish only an economy of the proper—a sovereign social order centered on propriety and appropriation. In the process, what is destroyed is Gandhi's insistence on the equality of all being.

To the extent that Gandhi works within the terms of the proper, then even on the most generous reading he can only appear the way he does to Jawaharlal Nehru or, even more, Dr. B. R. Ambedkar—as thoroughly unable to even recognize the demand for equality from the margins. Where caste, gender, or the Indian villages are understood in terms of the sovereignty of the proper, existing relations of power are naturalized. These relations come to be regarded as prepolitical, and their work of domination is glossed over. Such an understanding would also be entirely incapable of responding to the subaltern demand for abstract equality—which Gandhi faces, for example, from Ambedkar.

～

The third and most sustained theme of *Unconditional Equality* is the other and more intriguing radical conservatism, recessive often in Gandhi's explicit formulations, perhaps as untimely now as then, and yet bursting forth from them. Here "destruction of conservatism" means: the conservatism that satyagrahis set out from is destroyed by the absolute equality they seek to inhabit, and this destruction is nevertheless faithful to conservatism. Destruction in this sense happens where satyagraha becomes what Gandhi calls "pure means." Such pure means requires what I have been calling a surrender without subordination, or what could also be called a politics of the pure gift—schematically, the gift that is aneconomic, or given and received without reciprocity. Here satyagrahis no longer practice a greater degree of the same fearlessness as that practiced by arms-bearing warriors; they no longer exercise the immense sovereignty over self that allows them to surrender to their opponent without subordinating themselves. Rather, they surrender by relinquishing sovereign power even over themselves. While the first radical conservatism involves a willed surrender, where satyagrahis exercise their will over themselves, the second radical conservatism involves a surrender where satyagrahis relinquish their will, where they become *shunya* or "ciphers," to use a word that infects his vocabulary from the late 1910s.

What is at stake in becoming a cipher? In one of her essays, Gayatri Spivak notes that "no one can say "I am a subaltern" in whatever language."[52] Put differently, the subaltern as a concept names the being who does not possess being. We usually focus on the subaltern's privative nonbeing— the result of the subaltern being cut off from lines of social mobility. The Reader challenges this nonbeing when he claims nonprivative being— rights and citizenship.

But the privative nonbeing of the subaltern can also be challenged in another way—by claiming nonprivative nonbeing. Spivak's "Can the Subaltern Speak?" implicitly acknowledges this possibility, noting that Derrida "discloses the vulnerability of his own desire to conserve something that is, paradoxically, both ineffable and nontranscendental." In relation to colonialism, Spivak goes on, this ineffable nontranscendental space is "cathected by the subaltern subject."[53]

In Spivak's argument, the figure of the subaltern is to be conserved. But what is conserved (vulnerably) here? Clearly not subordination. What can be conserved rather is only this: the striving for an equality of the minor, an equality where the margin strives to destroy or annihilate the center without then itself becoming the center.

This other equality is perhaps the most crucial stake of both Gyanendra Pandey's "In Defense of the Fragment," and Dipesh Chakrabarty's *Provincializing Europe*. Pandey thus resists the historical discipline's emphasis on writing about the whole, and writes: "Part of the importance of the 'fragmentary point of view is that it resists the drive for a shallow homogenization and struggles for other, potentially richer, definitions of the 'nation' and the future political community."[54] Similarly, Chakrabarty argues: "Provincialising Europe becomes the task of exploring how this [European] thought—which is now everybody's heritage and which affects us all— *may be renewed by and from the margins*" (emphasis added).[55] Europe is renewed in Chakrabarty's formulations, note, precisely by being provincialized. The province provincializes Europe and itself—the effort here is to destroy any center.

How is the center to be destroyed? Chakrabarty's remarks are relevant here: "For at the end of European imperialism, European thought is a gift to us all. We can talk of provincialising it only in an anticolonial spirit of gratitude."[56] The end of European imperialism: to provincialize is to bring about that end in a distinctive way—not by claiming autonomous reason, but by exiting the problematic of that reason. When brought to such an end, the European thought of autonomy and abstract universalism, which was given as anything but a gift, is transformed into a gift.[57] Thus transformed by the gift from the colonies, European thought may exit into a freedom that does not participate in domination, into a will and freedom without autonomy.[58]

~

As *abhaydan* or the offer of fearlessness, satyagraha is also a politics of the pure gift. Marcel Mauss correctly describes the pure gift as impossible. Nevertheless, as I will argue, there can be no gift without at least the impossible specter of the pure gift. Surrender without subordination and freedom without sovereignty, as inseparable as two sides of a coin, strive to accomplish that impossible—the pure gift.

A pure gift can only be given and received freely—it thus presumes a freedom and swaraj for both the giver and the receiver. But this is a strange freedom. On the one hand, to give a gift is always to relinquish sovereignty and agency: a gift is separated from the giver, who cannot and will not control the gift. Indeed, the gift no longer belongs to the giver, for it has come also to be marked by the receiver. On the other hand, the gift does not belong to the receiver, for it is marked by the giver. To accept a gift is again to relinquish agency; the gift seizes the recipient, even though the giver cannot control the recipient. This loss of sovereignty and agency by both giver and receiver, this separation from oneself experienced by both—this is what everywhere marks the pure gift.

To give or receive a pure gift is therefore to simultaneously destroy sovereignty and subordination. Involved in the pure gift is the politics proper to the being who (not that—this is a singularized being) simultaneously refuses privative nonbeing and autonomous being, who is oriented, in other words, toward a freedom without being and sovereignty, without propriety. The pure gift is, moreover, marked by a distinctive purity of means, for this gift is not given or received as a means to an end, however delayed or deferred. In ways both evident and not so evident, satyagraha "is" the politics of pure means, or the pure gift (and those quotes around the "is" are necessary since satyagraha and the satyagrahi do not possess the sovereignty or grounded being that usually make for is-ness).

Abhaydan or the gift of fearlessness, moreover, makes satyagraha the most intense moment of politics, if we recall with Rancière's description of politics as that activity which turns on equality as its principle. In their self-sacrifice, satyagrahis strive to gift the greatest equality to all being and do so, moreover, only by receiving it themselves from all being. Gandhi's aneconomic thinking of the gift of fearlessness perhaps murmurs already in the English translation of *Hind Swaraj*, where the Editor remarks that the satyagrahi "keeps death always as a bosom friend" (there is, as we shall see, no equivalent to this phrase in the Gujarati text). In Gandhi's writing, only in friendship with one's own death is it possible to love at all. Friendship with death names the way that satyagrahis must go to their own deaths, the nonbeing that must mark their being. They cannot go to their death as sovereigns over their lives—if so, they would fight death, and the moment of their death would be the moment that death becomes sovereign over them. Rather, they must gift themselves to their own death and receive their own life as a gift from their own death. This friendship with death is the nonbeing, not-ness, or ciphering proper to satyagraha.

Friendship with one's own death, moreover, sustains a relation of the pure gift with the other. Satyagrahis always offer their own lives to the other, and the life that they lead after so making themselves vulnerable is one that is received from the other.

And yet this surrender is never a subordination; here, rather, submission to the other is the utmost resistance. Put differently, because they give a life that they have received through a friendship with their own death, their submission is at the same time the giving of the not-ness of their being to the other. When they submit, they give to the other only their difference from the other. By so doing, they derange both themselves and the other; this derangement is swaraj.

Swaraj as derangement? If swaraj is the *raj* or rule of the *swa* or proper/ ownmost, then here *swaraj* becomes the impropriety and uprooting proper to being. How does this other *swaraj* work? What is its relation with the *swaraj* of sovereignty? In this book, I will track Gandhi's deeply disturbing and yet compelling responses to these questions.

· I ·

Before Satyagraha

CHAPTER 1

Stumbling on Theological Secularism

This is a religious [dinani, dharmni] *fight. That is to say, of that religion which stays in all religions.*

—Gandhi, Message to Indians in South Africa,
February 25, 1909, *Akshardeha*

Imagine abstract man, without the guidance of myth—abstract education, abstract morality, abstract justice, the abstract state . . .

—Friedrich Nietzsche, *The Birth of Tragedy*

GANDHI WRITES LITTLE about and during his "religious ferment" [*dharmik manthan*, churning] from 1891 to 1903 (the year he founds *Indian Opinion* and begins writing prolifically)—the period when, according to the accounts he provides many decades later in the *Autobiography*, he first engages with categories like daya ["compassion"] and *dharma* ["religion"] and when he commences on his trajectory of confrontation with the state.

But he would certainly have encountered writings about daya. The late nineteenth-century writer Narmad, or Narmadashankar Lalshankar Dave, writes in the preface to his translation of the *Bhagavad Gita* (reproduced in his *Dharmavichar,* a book that Gandhi describes in 1911 as "eminently worth reading") that *swadharma*—for Narmad here, the dharma ordained by one's caste duties—is more important than dayadharma ["religion of compassion"]. In Narmad's *Gita,* the divine Krishna reminds Arjuna of the latter's dharma as a Kshatriya or warrior, and goes on: "Dayadharma is for all, but it is essential for Brahmins, and it is for you too, but when [someone] comes to battle with you, then your primary dharma is to battle that person and in this context you have to consider dayadharma secondary."[1]

A more sympathetic interlocutor is the Jain thinker Raychandbhai Mehta (also known as Shrimad Rajchandra), whom Gandhi first meets in 1891, on the evening he returns from Britain.[2] Raychandbhai emphasizes dayadharma consistently. Gandhi writes in the *Autobiography* that he regards

Raychandbhai as a "real seeker after Truth." Elsewhere he remarks: "Three moderns have left a deep impress on my life, and captivated me: Raychandbhai by his living contact; Tolstoy by his book *The Kingdom of God Is Within You;* and Ruskin by his *Unto This Last.*" Of these three he gives "first place" to Raychandbhai; he also values Raychandbhai's religious understanding more than Tolstoy's and Ruskin's.[3]

The second chapter of Raychandbhai's best-known book, *Mokshamala,* written at the age of fifteen (and the only one we know that he requested Gandhi to read), is titled "A Religion Accepted by All" [*sarvamanya dharma*]. It identifies the "essence of religion" as daya, and repeatedly calls for daya toward all living beings. "There is no religion like daya. Daya is the ownmost form [*swarup*] of religion." "Truth, good conduct and charity are worth the name only where there is daya"; "even religion becomes devilish without compassion."[4]

But until about 1908 Gandhi reads daya and dayadharma in terms of abstract equality—as indeed radicalizing that equality. (Abstract equality, after all, does not disavow love—for example, a certain love is at work in the way fraternity always marks liberty and equality. Similarly, secular religion, or a religion within the limits of reason alone, affirms love.) Thus, he initially understands Jainism as a secular religion, remarking in a lecture in 1905 that Jainism was "the most logical of all faiths," "did not claim for the faith that it was of divine origin," and that "its most remarkable characteristic was its scrupulous regard for all things that lived."[5] The implicit deism of secular religion provides indeed one way of thinking the "religion that stays in all religions," the phrase that he uses later to describe satyagraha.

Yet secular religion is not enough for Gandhi: it limits itself to the private sphere and leaves the public sphere to secularism. And by 1906 Gandhi is already acutely aware of who and what secularism and abstract equality exclude.[6] He is driven therefore to an especially intense and radical form of theological secularism. Secularism, as the preface suggested, is always marked by a certain theology in the way it elevates the question and knowledge to the highest place. What makes theological secularism radical here, even perhaps fragile and autoimmune because of its radicalism, is that now abstract equality is extended even to those who lack autonomous reason. Such secularism is not simply theological: it is religious in the sense that it no longer acts by reason alone (equality could not then be extended to those who lack autonomous reason), but by a certain groundless faith in autonomous reason.

His theological secularism is articulated in the Gujarati serialization, over several weeks from early January 1907 in *Indian Opinion*, of "the substance" of the "teachings" of William Mackintire Salter's book *Ethical Religion*. Gandhi writes in a preface: "A Society [the Society for Ethical Culture] has been founded which has shown, after an investigation of all religions, that all of them teach morality *[niti]*. Not only that, but their basis is for the most part on ethical principles. And whether or not one professes a religion, it is one's duty to obey the laws of ethics." This society identified the "fundamentals of all religions," and "this creed they call Ethical Religion." "Mr Salter," he says, had published an "excellent" book on this creed, and "we shall publish the substance of these teachings each week."[7] With this, he embarks on an abbreviated translation of Salter's book, though after eight issues, less than halfway through the book, he abandons the serialization without giving any reasons.

It is apposite that Gandhi should pick on Salter at this moment when, even as he is increasingly critical of British institutions, he still believes in their essential rationality and justice. Salter critiques abstract equality from within the problematic of that equality; he effectively articulates what Rousseau in *The Social Contract* seems to yearn for—a "civil religion." Salter's term "ethical religion" carries the insistence that all humans are equal to the very limit of what is conceptually possible within the problematic of abstract equality. He insists on the equality of even those normally excluded as minors—in his case, the American Indians. And precisely because abstract equality cannot by its very nature be extended to those deemed incapable of exercising it, this insistence leads him to a somewhat different conception of rights—that exemplified, I shall argue, in the rights that Jeremy Bentham grants to those who can suffer.

Ethical Religion provides the resources for Gandhi's early critique of republican democracy, and his early understanding of religion. But he translates Salter at a time when, quite unknown to himself, he is moving toward more radical readings. The trajectory comes to mark his rendering of Salter in unacknowledged but dramatic ways. And by the time of *Hind Swaraj*, there are signs of an inadvertent dismissal of *Ethical Religion* (though he never disavows the book)—most evidently, as I argue later, in the attack on "immeasurable pity." Salter and *Ethical Religion* disappear from his conversation in later years (unlike, say, Thoreau, Ruskin, Tolstoy, or Raychandbhai). The terms *nitidharma*, *dayadharma*, and *daya*, all of which he first conceptualizes systematically through Salter, remain with him. But for all of them he can claim other genealogies too, and he foregrounds these in later years.

~

After attending divinity school at Yale and Harvard in the 1870s, Salter turns away from Christianity and becomes a close associate of Felix Adler. Adler starts the Ethical Culture movement in the 1870s.[8] It quickly expands, with branches especially in the United States and Germany. The movement seeks to "replace the particularism of prayer, ritual and distinct creeds with a humanistic faith embracing all humanity, while stressing the rights of individuals."[9] Salter co-founds the second branch of the society in Chicago. Like Adler, he is also involved in several profoundly liberal initiatives. Though not himself an anarchist, he tries to secure leniency for the anarchists involved in the Haymarket affair in 1895. As part of the all-white Indian Rights Association, he encourages the adoption of American Indian children and argues that American Indians should be assimilated into white society.

He also keeps up a vigorous interest in philosophy. *Ethical Religion* (originally issued in 1889 by the Rationalist Press Association, though Gandhi possibly worked with a revised edition published in 1905), possibly Salter's first book, is marked by traces of his readings of Immanuel Kant. He follows it up with *First Steps in Philosophy* (1892), a popular introduction to philosophy focusing most of all on intuitionism and utilitarianism. In later years, his works include a study of Friedrich Nietzsche, which is influential at the time.

Ethical Religion assents neither "to theism on the one hand nor to positivism on the other."[10] Claiming descent from Ralph Waldo Emerson (whose writings Gandhi too later finds thought-provoking), Salter suggests: "Theology gathers all our thoughts of the higher and better together, and conceives them in the form of a perfect person who rules and guides the world." He criticizes this theology, and indeed "all the prevailing forms of religion." For him, "not only is the personal deity of theology illusory, but by gathering divine qualities into a form outside of man, it allows us to forget that they are qualities for man, and religion becomes the worship of something already existing, instead of the sense of a burden and a task."[11]

At the same time, he identifies secularism with an "ordinary, everyday life," to which his hostility is even greater. A later essay points out that Nietzsche "writes a notable aphorism 'In honor of *homines religiosi*,'" and suggests that "if we have in mind the essential spirit of religion I think we may call him [Nietzsche] more a religious than an irreligious man. The real antithesis of religion is our ordinary, everyday life with its immediate aims and narrow horizons, and absence of anything begetting awe and reverence—secularism."[12]

Dissatisfied simultaneously with both institutional religion and secularism as profane everyday life, he seeks instead an "ethical religion" that will infuse knowledge with faith. The "noble side of theology," he suggests, can be "easily disengaged from theology itself." Even "when one ceases to believe in God in the ordinary sense," religion can still be affirmed— "not indeed in the common way, as of something additional to morality, but of morality as religion." This morality is both subjective and objective. Thought subjectively, from "the purely human side," religion is "man's supreme interest: whoever has an absorbing interest may be said to have a religion." "If morality then, if the thought of the good . . . masters their life, it becomes their religion."[13] Or as he puts it later in the book, religion involves a "common recognisable attitude": "There is an intentness, a reverential manner, a humility, an awe, that are absolutely characteristic, and that a man shows at no other time than when he is in a religious mood." Indeed, "religion is a general term—it is whatever one holds sacred, whatever one venerates, whatever gives one his supreme rule of life. But what that shall be is another question."[14]

And religion "defined from its objective side" "is man's relation with what is ultimate and supreme in the world. The truest religion would be that one in which the supreme interest gathers about that which is really supreme and ultimate in the world." He describes the "really supreme": "Whenever, wherever, two persons arise and look into each other's faces, the law of mutual reverence and respect—the law of justice, we call it— obtains. . . . If there are other rational beings than men, it applies to them just as truly; the law is a universal law for all rational intelligences." "In this way, morality becomes religion."[15]

"Ethics realized in its meaning is religion; it is the only religion for the rational man." Indeed, "morality is nothing but reason uttering itself; and there are rational ends just as truly as there are rational means of choosing them." "We are to become divine, we are to make this world a scene of justice."

Such a religion for him both exemplifies the nobler strivings of older religions, and yet breaks from their institutional forms and from the fear that marked them. "The old religions leave us on our knees in rapt contemplation and worship; the new will summon us to stand erect, and to believe that all men have worshipped, all that they have dreamed of, all that has seemed so far above them and beyond them, men and women in the future are to become and to realise." Ethical religion is "nothing else than a changed thought of the nature of religion . . . namely that it can be no longer for rational men today to worship or pray; but to have the sense of a task, the sense of somewhat limitless to accomplish, and to accomplish it."[16]

He thus elevates autonomous reason, or the secular equality of rational beings, to a matter of "reverence." "I feel that if I do not honour another I do not honour myself, for I fundamentally am every other: it is one common nature, wherein we all share." Drawing implicitly on Kant, Salter says that the equality he wants is "not indeed similarity of place and function for everyone; not that all should do the same work or get the same returns for their work; but simply that all should be in turn ends as well as means, that no one should dare make of another a mere instrument to his own satisfactions, but should regard him as having an independent worth and dignity of his own." "In the ideal order every man shall be an end as well as a means. I need not point out that this principle has not been generally recognised in the past. . . . The notion of the universal rights of man is a modern one. It is neither in the Old Testament nor in the New. I doubt if it be in the Scriptures of any of the religions of the world."[17] "Ethical religion" infuses reason and abstract equality with what he takes to be the essence of religion—a sense of submission and awe.

Within a shared idealist framework, Salter's moves lead him on a trajectory diametrically opposed to that of Carl Schmitt some decades later, who suggests that "all significant concepts of the modern theory of state are secularized theological concepts."[18] Where Schmitt questions secularism by pointing to how institutional religions and religiosity underpin it, Salter tries to deepen secularism by infusing its abstract equality with a religiosity that does not belong to any institutional religion. In the process, Salter's religion becomes a most radically inclusive form of abstract equality. And yet, in the very way "ethical religion" includes and excludes groups, we encounter the limits of the problematic of abstract equality.

∼

These limits mark his effort to simultaneously critique and justify how American Indians are treated.

And though I grant that civilisation has a perfect right to dispossess barbarism of an exclusive and profitless occupation of the soil, it is nonetheless a crime, and a heinous crime, to do as our country has done—treat the dispossessed barbarians as if they had no claims whatever upon us. The Indians are human beings, they have the rights of human beings; and if they cannot defend those rights, all the more shame on that Government which will wantonly trample upon them. The Indians might have been elevated; they may still be elevated. It may be questioned whether there is a race of men on the earth which, if humanely and wisely treated, may not lose its savagery and take a place in the ranks of civilized peoples. Not all the interests of civilization justify injustice. Rather is it the problem for the superior race to lift the other with it, to use its superiority and its strength for service, and not for oppression.[19]

Most of what Salter says here emphasizes the need to dispossess barbarians. Still, Salter shifts the emphasis to the responsible spirit in which the civilized must dispossess them. "Indians are human beings, they have the rights of human beings." As such, the Indian has "claims upon us."

But if American Indians cannot reason properly, if they cannot share in the sovereignty and equality of autonomous reason, if they cannot exit their state of immaturity, then how and why do they have rights; what authorizes their claims?

To these questions, Salter's book provides no direct answer. But it approvingly invokes two thinkers in the Utilitarian tradition, Jeremy Bentham and James Mill. Both write about the claims and even rights of those who lack reason. Bentham famously suggests: "The day *may* come when the rest of animal creation may acquire those rights which never could have been witholden from them but by the hand of tyranny. . . . The question is not, Can they *reason?* Nor, Can they *talk?* But, can they *suffer?*"[20]

Derrida suggests that Bentham's question breaks from the tradition of defining the animal in terms of its power or capacity to reason. "[T]he form of this question changes everything. . . . The question is disturbed by a certain passivity. "Can they suffer" amounts to asking "Can they not be able?" . . . Being able to suffer is no longer a power; it is a possibility without power, a possibility of the impossible."[21] That phrase, "possibility of the impossible," signals also the invocation of the pure gift, which Derrida describes elsewhere as: "Not impossible but the impossible. The very figure of the impossible. It announces itself, gives itself to be thought as the impossible."

~

And yet, to affirm the Benthamite question as a possibility without power, as a possibility of the impossible, as a moment of the pure gift—would this not be what Derrida, writing of Claude Lévi-Strauss, describes as "an ethnocentrism thinking itself an anti-ethnocentrism"?[22]

The Benthamite question not only reproduces the exclusions of abstract equality (or what Salter describes as "the universal rights of man"); it also gives itself a clear conscience.[23] The animal exemplifies the being who must be excluded from abstract equality—who has voice but no speech (the animal would include usually those humans who cannot reason and talk; historically, massive examples of such animal-humans would include women, slaves, colonized, Salter's American Indians, and terrorists). Animal suffering imposes a special responsibility on those who have speech, and thus bear witness to the suffering. Indeed, bearing witness to the suffering of the animal-human has been central to the civilizing mission. James Mill, a close associate of Bentham (and the other Utilitarian who Salter cites), articulates this mission powerfully in *The History of British India*. As Leela Gandhi observes, the book is a "detailed invective against Indian customs and manners," and "paints a picture of unmitigated barbarism. Mill withholds the prerogatives of civilization from India on familiar utilitarian grounds (the absence of traditions of law, government, and obedience in Indian culture).[24]

This lack, however, never only limits Indians; it also names the suffering of Indians, and especially of ordinary Indians. In the grand narrative that unfolds in Mill's *History*, thus, the suffering of the colonized names their peculiar right—the right to be colonized by the British, and to thus be relieved of their suffering. This responsibility to colonize is precisely what makes Pax Britannica a civilizing mission.

The rights intimated by suffering thus do not involve autonomous reason or any other form of sovereignty. John Stuart Mill, son of James Mill, can thus say: "Despotism is a legitimate system of government in dealing with barbarians, provided that the end be their improvement, and the means justified by actually achieving that end. Liberty, as a principle, has no application to any state of things anterior to the time when mankind have become capable of being improved."[25] Inhabiting this anterior time, the colonized intimate their humanity in a more limited way: by suffering.

Suffering thus names a distinctive realm in the discourse of rights—the rights exercised by those who are not quite human. These rights are never demanded by sufferers (who after all lack the agency that is required to make a demand). The demands are made rather on their behalf—by fully human subjects, and of other such subjects. Surely this sensitivity to the less-than-human is part of what we describe in everyday terms as humane treatment, where "humane" is an attribute not of the less-than-human but of the fully-human. The English translation of *Hind Swaraj*, as we see below, rejects this distinctly colonial sensitivity, calling it "immeasurable pity."

Bentham's suggestion—that we recognize that animals suffer—participates in this colonial structure. The rights of animals are for him emphatically secondary to those of men. Bentham has no objection to any "medical experiment" that is "beneficial to mankind." His objection is to "every act by which, without prospect of preponderant good, pain is knowingly and willingly produced in any being whatsoever"; these for him are acts of cruelty.[26] Thus, while the emphasis on suffering questions gratuitous violence, it allows for instrumental relations with animals and practices that calculated responsibility and peculiar equality known as colonial rule.

This profoundly colonial concept of suffering also organizes the "claims upon us" that Salter's American Indians have. On the one hand, because American Indians lack in reason and speech, it is just to take land away from them. On the other hand, American Indians can still claim equality in the ability to suffer. This equality makes a claim on the more civilized and rational segments of society—the claim to now practice a benevolent colonialism, colonialism as a civilizing mission. By insisting, moreover, on equality in a religious spirit, Salter makes this benevolent colonialism an inescapable responsibility.

This is why there is no contradiction between Salter's presumption that it is just to dispossess Indians and his insistence that "I feel that if I do not honour another I do not honour myself, for I fundamentally am every other," or that "whenever, wherever, two persons arise and look into each other's faces, the law of mutual reverence and respect." This responsibility is perhaps more sensitive to the face of the other than the unapologetic racism with which Emmanuel Levinas, even as he affirms the face, justifies Israeli dispossession of Palestinians. Unlike Levinas, what Salter calls for is for the dispossession to itself be carried out responsibly, in a way that responds to the suffering of Indians because they are in a barbaric state and engaged in profitless occupation."[27] Would the responsibility and equality involved in such colonialism make it more or less intolerable, more or less impossible to forgive?

~

Gandhi sets out, then, to translate and endorse Salter's theological secularism. And there can be no doubt that Gandhi participates in theological secularism's exclusionary and violent hierarchies, perhaps even more so in the early years than Salter. In the 1890s and early 1900s, he seeks vigorously to institute a distinction between "Kaffirs" and "Indians," and regards the "Kaffirs" as inferior to "Indians." He complains in 1894: "A general belief seems to prevail in the Colony that the Indians are little better, if at all, than savages or the Natives of Africa. Even the children are taught to believe in that."[28] At a public meeting in Bombay two years later, he insists: "Ours is one continual struggle against a degradation sought to be inflicted upon us by the Europeans, who desire to degrade us to the level of the raw Kaffir whose occupation is hunting, and whose sole ambition is to collect a certain number of cattle to buy a wife with and, then, pass his life in indolence and nakedness."[29] He seeks through various petitions to ensure that the government treated "Indians" and "Kaffirs" differently. Again in 1906, he complains that "the Boer Government insulted the Indians by classing them with the Kaffirs."[30] He also supports a court decision that "Kaffirs have no legal right to travel by the trams. And, according to tram regulations, those in an unclean dress or in a drunken state are prohibited from boarding a tram. Thanks to the Court's decision, only clean Indians or Coloured people other than Kaffirs can now travel by the trams."[31]

He continues until 1911 to try to persuade the Boers to treat "Kaffirs" and the "Indians" differently because the latter are superior,[32] to protest against the powers given to "every Kaffir policeman" to inspect the permits of "Indians." The contrast with the Kaffirs is central even to his concept of satyagraha during this period: "The British rulers take us to be so lowly and ignorant that they assume that, like the Kaffirs who can be pleased with toys and pins, we can also be fobbed off with trinkets."[33] In the accounts of being imprisoned during the South African struggles, exposure to the "Kaffirs" is one of his complaints. "Kaffirs are as a rule uncivilised—the convicts even more so. They are troublesome, very dirty and live almost like animals. Each ward contains nearly 50 to 60 of them. They often started rows and fought among themselves. The reader can easily imagine the plight of the poor Indian thrown into such company!"[34]

The English account of those experiences in the same issue of *Indian Opinion* is even more emphatic. In jail, he says, the satyagrahis were "classed with the natives.... Degradation underlay the classing of Indians with natives."[35] As Ashwin Desai and Goolam Vahed have pointed out, his notions of racial hierarchy and purity led him to separate the Indian cause from that of Africans. He also consistently "placed African below Indian in racial hierarchy." In the process, he "not only rendered African exploitation and oppression invisible, but was, on occasion, a willing part of their subjugation and racist stereotyping."[36]

And though in the years after his return to India he no longer talks of "Kaffirs" or how uncivilized they are, surely some of that language is transferred to his remarks about and to Dalits. As is well known, while he vigorously criticizes the violence that Dalits face from upper castes, he also believes that Dalits must abandon "evil habits," such as eating beef, and "reform" themselves.[37]

～

However, Gandhi's religious politics while in South Africa not only partakes of Salter's responsible racism; it also articulates an anticolonial racism. Gandhi cannot accept the presumption that the Christianity of the West (or in some arguments the Abrahamic tradition) is the only or first religion where faith in God requires that one live without faith in miracles or without expecting or hoping for God's intervention—where one already lives in an incipiently secular manner, by morality alone, as though God were dead. In narratives that accept this presumption, secularism and modernity comes to the non-West always from the West. And because secularism in such a narrative has not grown out of the indigenous context of the non-West, its practice there is presumed always to be marked by a lack, or conversely by an excess that compensates for the externality of secularism.

Even a thinker as responsible to the other as Derrida often finds it difficult to break from these traditions, presuming, for instance, that modernity emerges from and is articulated in "an Abrahamic language which is not (in the case of Japan or Korea, for example) that of the dominant religion of their society, but which has already become the universal idiom of law, of politics, of the economy, or of diplomacy: at the same time the agent and symptom of this internationalisation." In a related vein, he notes that "the sacredness of the human," central to the concept of human rights, "finds its meaning in the Abrahamic memory of the religions of the Book, and in a Jewish but above all Christian interpretation of the 'neighbour' or the 'fellow man.'"[38]

By contrast, early twentieth-century anticolonial thinkers, even when they begin from (and that they do so is by no means as clear as it is sometimes presumed to be) or traverse a Eurocentric problematic, often move on to reject the Eurocentric founding of secularism on Christianity, and to claim different genealogies for their secularism. Gandhi, for example, claims for his "tolerance" origins in his childhood and youth quite independent of his engagement with European traditions. The *Atmakatha* or *Autobiography*, for instance, says that as a youth he was "taught all sorts of things except religion," "yet I kept on picking up things here and there from my surroundings." And "one thing took deep root in me—the conviction that the world is founded on ethics [*niti*; "that morality is the basis of things"], and that satya ["truth"] is the substance of all ethics. Satya became my sole objective." Given the association of satya with God (an association quite common in South Asian traditions), this remark implies that the young Gandhi by his account already understands dharma in terms of a category of world religion—*niti* or ethics, rather than a specific set of religious beliefs.[39]

And this ethics, he comes to feel very early on, runs through various religions:

> I got an early grounding in toleration [*samaanbhav*] for all branches
> of Hinduism and sister religions [*sampradaya*]. For my father and
> mother would visit the *Haveli* [Vaishnava temple] as also Shiva's
> and Rama's temples, and would take or send us youngsters there.
> Jain monks also would pay frequent visits to my father, and would
> even go out of their way to accept food from us—non-Jains. They
> would have talks with my father on subjects religious and
> mundane. He had, besides, Mussalman and Parsi friends, who
> would talk to him about their own faiths, and he would listen to
> them always with respect, and often with interest. Being his nurse,
> I often had a chance to be present at these talks. These many things
> combined to inculcate in me a toleration for all faiths [*dharma*].[40]

In the early years, his equal respect for all religions "did not mean that I had any living faith in God." His inability to summon enthusiasm for the

Manusmriti inclines him, if anything, "somewhat towards atheism." But this atheist secularism, if that is indeed what it was, does not last for long. The *Autobiography* suggests that by the end of his second year in England, when he would have been around twenty-one, he had "already crossed the Sahara of atheism."[41] And once he does, he returns in a different register to the deist emphasis on ethics as something that is not unique to any one religion.

After his arrival in England, Gandhi works his way through European renderings of Hinduism and "Indian civilization" in order to articulate an anticolonial racism. He writes in the *Autobiography* that he reads the *Bhagavad Gita* for the first time neither in Gujarati nor in Sanskrit but in Edwin Arnold's translation. This is followed by a course of readings about Hinduism, Buddhism, and South Asia. A theme he picks up from these readings is that India had been a civilization comparable to European civilization, and not a "semi-barbarity."[42]

His affirmation of Indian civilization is accompanied by a questioning of the privilege that Christianity claims for itself as a distinctively secular and modern religion. According to the retrospective account provided in the *Autobiography* and elsewhere, in his youth, listening to the missionaries "stand in a corner near the high school and hold forth, pouring abuse on Hindus and their gods," he comes to be convinced of the equality of all religions except Christianity, which because of its intolerance could not be equal to the Indian religions. As we know well, this view changes drastically during his stay in Britain, when he comes to be more admiring of Christianity and especially the New Testament.[43] And at least from the retrospective distance of *Autobiography*, this newfound admiration occurs within a comparative framework within which Christianity does not seem so remarkable:

> The pious lives of Christians did not give me anything that the
> lives of men of other faiths had failed to give. I had seen in other
> lives just the same reformation that I had heard of among
> Christians. Philosophically there was nothing extraordinary in
> Christian principles. From the point of view of sacrifice [*tyag*], it
> seemed to me that the Hindus greatly surpassed the Christians. It
> was impossible for me to regard Christianity as a perfect religion or
> the greatest of all religions.[44]

Nor, however, given untouchability and other Hindu practices, can he think of Hinduism as the "greatest of all religions."

~

Phrases like "other faiths," "all religions" or, most tellingly, "world religions" reveal the comparative framework Gandhi works with. In its nineteenth-century metropolitan usage, "world religion" hierarchizes those "religions" considered closest to Christianity, the pinnacle of religious development. Thus, as Jonathan Smith notes, the 1884 essay by Cornelius Petrus Tiele on "Religion" in *Encyclopaedia Britannica* distinguishes between "nature religions" and "ethical religions"; the latter respond to universal considerations. The highest ethical religions for Tiele are "world religions," a phrase that he deploys to "distinguish the three religions . . . which profess the intention to conquer the world," rather than limiting their law to a given community.[45]

We do not know whether Tiele's classification informs Salter's phrase "ethical religion." However that may be, anticolonial intellectuals often invoke "world religion" to question the Eurocentric privileging of Western European Christianity. Thus, by casting Hinduism as a world religion, nationalists effectively claim that Hinduism too is and has for long been, to invoke a Kantian phrase, a reflecting faith (briefly, a faith that makes a distinction between revelation and knowledge, and posits that what is important is not what God has done for the salvation of the human being, but what the human being has done to be worthy of this assistance). With this move, anticolonial nationalists challenge classical Eurocentrism and claim an indigenous modernity and even secularism for India; other nationalists elsewhere make similar claims for "their" religions.

Gandhi participates in this anticolonial redeployment, insisting quite characteristically in 1936, that "the great world religions other than Christianity professed in India were no less true than Christianity."[46] Similarly, it is in the name of "world religion" that he sometimes evaluates both Hinduism and Islam. Attacking the practice of untouchability, for example, he argues that "in the history of the world religions there is perhaps nothing like our treatment of the suppressed classes."[47] And in questioning the claim that Muslims in India had forcibly converted Hindus, he again argues in terms of world religion: "No Mussulman, to my knowledge, has ever approved of compulsion. Islam would cease to be a world religion if it were to rely upon force for its propagation."[48]

These anticolonial accounts of "world religion" effectively claim a genealogy from outside Europe for a universalist morality and ethics, indeed for a theology that can found modern sovereignty, that can distinguish between public and private, or secular and religious. Here, all world religions, rather than only or primarily Christianity, bear the potential for internally generating secularism and universalizable ethics. Gandhi's moves are thus part the anticolonial pluralization of universalism—the insistence that traditions of universalism and reason are not only Western.[49] This pluralization in Gandhi's case, we may speculate, is sustained and made possible by South Asian universalist traditions, both precolonial and colonial.

But even as the term "world religion" is appropriated for new agendas, it remains constitutively racist. There are always those who do not belong to world religions, as for example, those who practice Tiele's "nature religions." It is as a participant in a world religion—whether Hinduism or Islam—that the Indian is superior to the Kaffir. What the Gandhi of 1894 says could still have perhaps been said by the Gandhi of 1907 or even 1911: that if he objects to the "Indian . . . being dragged down to the position of a raw Kaffir," this is because "Indians were, and are, in no way inferior to their Anglo-Saxon brethren, if I may venture to use the word, in the various departments of life—industrial, intellectual, political, etc."[50]

~

Should the genealogies of satyagraha itself be traced to theological secularism?

Only in July 1907, around ten months after that other September 11, does Gandhi initiate "passive resistance" in opposition to the Transvaal Asiatic Registration Act, which by this time has come into effect. In the interim period, between January 5 and February 23, 1907, just after he returns from a trip to Britain as part of a delegation that sought unsuccessfully to halt the proposed act, he translates *Ethical Religion*. Could *Ethical Religion*, then, be attractive partially because it provides a way in those early years of thinking "passive resistance"?

Gandhi translates the book, recall, at a time when he has not yet arrived at his thinking of satyagraha. After he does, he often reserves the English phrase "passive resistance" for describing the liberal concept of civil disobedience; relatedly, satyagraha becomes the term he draws on to describe his concept of passive resistance. But perhaps at this early stage, Salter's theological secularism still holds out the possibility of a civil disobedience organized and fueled by autonomous love.[51] Indeed, a civil society that limits its dissent to civil disobedience might even be described as the fantasmic apogee of republican democracy (the form of liberalism, "modern civilization," or "modern civility" that Gandhi later attacks most often). It is a liberal injunction that civil society must avoid recourse to arms, that only the state can legitimately exercise armed force; this division is considered just because civil society has legislated the rule of law that the state enforces.

Progressive liberal thinkers effectively defend civil disobedience because it defies the state in a way that remains most faithful to this injunction. Habermas suggests: "every constitutional democracy that is sure of itself considers civil disobedience as a normalized—because necessary—component of its political culture."[52] Similarly, Rawls says of civil disobedience: "This theory is designed only for the special case of a nearly just society, one that is well-ordered for the most part but in which some serious violations of justice nevertheless do occur. Since I assume that a state of near justice requires a democratic regime, the theory concerns the role and the appropriateness of civil disobedience to legitimately established democratic authority."[53]

Practitioners of Habermasian or Rawlsian civil disobedience thus have a theological relation with the democratic authority they affirm. As autonomous beings, they are part of that authority, and when they submit to that authority, they submit only to the higher form they themselves are. By dying without taking another's life, they respect to the utmost the liberal state's injunction against violence by any actor other than itself. Even when faced with repression, they treat this violence as aberrant rather than symptomatic of the nature of the state. So they autonomously submit with nonviolent resistance, and refuse to allow for any exception in which to practice a revolutionary or founding violence that might produce another state order. They seek only the removal of some specific irrationality in the extant rule of law, and by doing so seek to strengthen that law, that republican democracy.

Throughout his life, Gandhi finds such a concept of civil disobedience attractive. And much scholarship today continues to read *Hind Swaraj* as criticizing "modern civilization" primarily for its instrumentality, and as insisting on right means—here, means that respect the nature of both self and other as autonomous ends. Understood this way, Gandhi's "Editor" turns out again to be a radical precursor to Rawls and Habermas—radical in that he does not limit the field of operation for civil disobedience to republican democracies, and radical also in that he pushes the emphasis on civil disobedience to an impractical if admirable point. Here, through their silent suffering, those who are presumed to have only voice burst into speech.

During much of this period, moreover, Gandhi believes—even as his own intellectual and political trajectory has begun to destroy these beliefs—not only that the British Empire is just, but also that he loves it. Thus, as late as 1920, he describes himself as "a devoted well-wisher of the British Empire." It would be quite easy to read civil disobedience in this liberal sense also into Gandhi's famous speech at his 1922 trial, where he states: "I am here to ... submit cheerfully to the highest penalty that can be inflicted upon me for what in law is a deliberate crime and what appears to me to be the highest duty of a citizen."[54]

When Gandhi's politics is understood as primarily one of Habermasian or Rawlsian civil disobedience (as much scholarship has tended to), then liberal thought can regard him as an exemplary political figure. Somewhat impractical perhaps, but still be to regarded with awe, as the finest kind of liberal. Toward such satyagraha, republican democracy can only simultaneously express the deepest respect (for its idealism) and deepest skepticism (for its impracticality)—the combination, strikingly, that often marks Nehru's remarks on Gandhi.

∼

In his account of that other September 11 in that building which is to burn down the next day, Gandhi notes that he could "read in every face the expectation of something strange [*navu,* new] to be done or to happen." That evening, he notes, "some new principle had come into being."[55]

What is the new principle that comes into being that evening, and what is the place in which that new principle comes into being? Reading Nelson Mandela's claim that he admires the Law and Rights, Derrida seems to think of the place where the struggle against apartheid comes into being as the West, and relatedly of the principle involved in that struggle as itself not just of the West, but of the formal universality of the law that belongs to the West:

He admires the law, he says it clearly, which commands constitutions and declarations, essentially a thing of the West? Does its formal universality retain some irreducible link with European or even Anglo-American history? If it were so, we would of course still have to consider this strange possibility: that its formal character would be as essential to the universality of law as the event of its presentation in a determined moment and place in history. How could we conceive of such a history? The struggle

against apartheid, wherever it takes place and such as Mandela
carries it on and reflects it, would this remain a sort of specular
opposition, an internal war that the West would maintain in itself,
in its own name? An internal contradiction that would suffer
neither radical alterity nor true dissymmetry? [56]

Gandhi's arguments would seem to withdraw from such presumptions,
and this in two divergent senses. To begin with, the law and "modern civilization" are not only of the West. For both the Reader and the Editor,
"modern civilization" has genealogies in the premodern pasts of the colonies too: while "modern civilization" and "Western civilization" "have become convertible terms," this for Gandhi is only "for the time being."[57] In
this sense, "fictional equality" is for him neither Western nor Eastern, even
if it is in his historical moment associated with the West, and the struggle
in the name of fictional equality would never be "an internal war that the
West would maintain in itself, in its own name." Gandhi refuses, as do so
many other anticolonial thinkers of the time, the immense conceit that
assumes that the law can only come from the West.[58] Relatedly, within the
terms that Gandhi inhabits, it should not be surprising if the universality
of law (such as fictional equality or civil disobedience) is best realized by
the formerly subaltern or colonized—this has happened time and again,
and is the ironical destiny of liberalism, even perhaps what is most thought-
provoking about it.

   Second, in contrast to Derrida's account of the struggle against apartheid as part of an "internal war that the West would maintain with itself"
as part of the liberal problematic of the law, Gandhi is emphatic, at least
retrospectively, that what happened in the Empire Theatre on that other
September 11 cannot be comprehended even within the most radical or
autoimmune moment of that problematic—civil disobedience or passive
resistance.

   None of us knew what name to give to our movement. I then used
   the term "passive resistance" in describing it. I did not then quite
   understand the implications of "passive resistance" as I called it. I
   only knew that some new principle had come into being. As the
   struggle advanced, the phrase "passive resistance" gave rise to
   confusion and it appeared shameful to permit this great struggle
   to be known only by an English name.[59]

Passive resistance is thus a placeholder within which there murmurs a difference that exceeds the phrase. This is unsurprising. On any rigorous accounting, it is difficult to consider Gandhi (or King or Mandela for that matter) as drawing on the liberal concept of civil disobedience. In both Rawls's and Habermas's formulations, civil disobedience is appropriate only for some situations—the well-working republican democracy, what we saw Rawls calling the "nearly just society." But the three most famous sites commonly associated with civil disobedience (British-ruled India, racially segregated United States, or apartheid South Africa) differ greatly from republican democracies. Born into this difference, even what might start out as liberal civil disobedience or passive resistance can survive only by becoming something else.[60]

Something "strange" (going by the English translation) and "new" (going by the Gujarati text), then, does condense in that hall on that other September 11. This strangeness and newness, however, can only remain obscured as long as we work with the liberal concept of civil disobedience. In order to work our way out of this concept, I would like to attend here to another strange experience that Gandhi has a little before this—his involvement in July 1906 in the British effort to put down the Bhambatha Rebellion. If there were to be the usual attempt to locate a fracture in Gandhi's biography, an epiphany or turning point, it should perhaps be located at least as much here as in the famous incident in 1893 of his being thrown out of that train—while the latter consolidates his anticolonial pacificism, the former rends him into satyagraha.

As the uprising starts, he writes in April 1906: "It is not for us to say whether the revolt of the Kaffirs is justified or not. We are in Natal by virtue of British power. Our very existence depends upon it. It is therefore our duty to render whatever help we can."[61] He goes on, as is well known, to set up an ambulance corps. Writing of the corps later in his *Autobiography,* he remarks: "I bore no grudge against the Zulus, they had harmed no Indian. I had doubts about the 'rebellion' itself, but I then believed that the British Empire existed for the welfare of the world. A genuine sense of loyalty prevented me from even wishing ill to the Empire. The rightness or otherwise of the 'rebellion' was therefore not likely to affect my decision."[62]

But his experience in the corps begins changing those beliefs. This experience is not, of course, the kind of experience had by those subjects, if such exist, who are fully present to themselves. It is rather an experience in the sense of a rending, and it rends Gandhi from both his racism and his faith in the British Empire (and it may not be coincidental that he abandons both at about the same pace). This rending does not occur all at once, nor is it ever completed. His experience of 1906 is not, in other words, only in the calendar year 1906; perhaps it is even least of all in 1906. It unfolds rather in fits and starts over the next few decades, and it never ceases unfolding. He is to refer to it over and again over the ensuing decades. He writes later in the *Autobiography*:

> The Zulu "rebellion" was full of new experiences and gave me much food for thought. The Boer War had not brought home to me the horrors of war with anything like the vividness that the "rebellion" did. This was no war but a man-hunt, not only in my opinion, but also in that of many Englishmen with whom I had occasion to talk. To hear every morning reports of the soldiers' rifles exploding like crackers in innocent hamlets, and to live in the midst of them was a trial. But I swallowed the bitter draught, especially as the work of my Corps consisted only in nursing the wounded Zulus. I could see that but for us the Zulus would have been uncared for. This work, therefore, eased my conscience.[63]

This is a refrain. Participating in an unjust war that he had presumed would be a just war ("I saw that there was nothing there to justify the name of 'rebellion'"), for him in retrospect (though not then) it was the moment when he begins to suspect that a generalized racism is constitutive of the British Empire.

In an interview in 1939, he says,

> I and my companions were privileged to nurse the wounded Zulus back to life. It is reasonable to suggest that but for our services some of them would have died. I cite this experience not to justify my participation however indirect it was. I cite it to show that I came through that experience with greater non-violence and with richer love for the great Zulu race. And I had an insight into what war by white men against coloured races meant.[64]

In the wake of the rending experience of the Bhambatha Rebellion in July 1906, Gandhi increasingly comes to question his racism. The word "Kaffir" itself disappears from his vocabulary by the mid-teens, to be replaced by "Zulu." And by 1939 he is willing to envisage the political submission of Indians to the "indigenous inhabitants."

> The rights and privileges (if any could be so called) of the indige-
> nous inhabitants are different from those of the Indians. So are
> their disabilities and their causes. But if I discovered that our rights
> conflicted with their vital interests, I would advise the forgoing of
> those rights. They are the inhabitants of South Africa as we are
> of India. The Europeans are undoubtedly usurpers, exploiters or
> conquerors or all these rolled into one.[65]

~

In the wake of the meeting on that other September 11 the same year, Gandhi translates Salter over several weeks in *Indian Opinion*. What follows over the next few weeks is, when we compare it with Salter's book, a drastically abridged "adaptation" (to use a word that Gandhi employs later to describe what he had done with Salter's book) that displaces Salter's arguments.[66]

First, the translation understands "religion" differently. In a preface, Gandhi writes that many societies devoted to "ethical religion" [*nitidharma*] have emerged. "It is not among the aims of these societies to criticize any religion. Men professing all religions can, and do, join these societies. The advantage of such a society is that members adhere to their own faith more strictly and pay greater attention to its moral teaching." Unlike Salter, then, Gandhi does not oppose conventional religions to "ethical religion."

In translating the very chapter where Salter attacks the conventional notion of God, Gandhi reintroduces both God and the relation of submission to God that Salter had attacked. "God is omnipotent, He is perfect. There are no limits to His mercy [*daya*], to His goodness and to His justice. If this is so, how can we, His bond slaves, stray at all from the ethical path?"[67] Gandhi thus effectively undoes the Ethical Culture movement's attempt to retain only a rational essence from the concepts of God and traditional religion. Missing also are assertions such as this one by Salter: "The old religions leave us on our knees in rapt contemplation and worship; the new will summon us to stand erect."

Second, Gandhi recasts Salter's arguments about equality. Salter's passage about Native Americans is rendered thus:

Till we have in our minds daya for every human, till then we have
not known or practiced ethical religion [nitidharma]. Now we
know that the higher morality must be inclusive of all [sarvajanik].
In our relations, every man can claim a right over us. That is to say,
it is our duty to always serve him. We should act on the assumption
that we have no claim on others. Somebody might say that the man
acting in this manner will be trampled in the world's scramble, but
such talk is ignorant. For it is a universal experience that God
always saves the man who whole-heartedly devotes himself to the
service of others.

   According to this moral standard all men are equal [sarkha].
This is not to be interpreted to mean that all men hold equal
positions or do identical work. It only means that, if I hold a
high place, I also have the ability to shoulder its responsibility
[javaabdaari]. I should not therefore lose my head and believe
that men with smaller responsibilities are my inferiors. Equality
[eksarkhapan] depends on the state of our mind. Till our mind
reaches that state, we are backward. According to this moral
standard no nation can rule another for selfish ends. It is immoral
of the American people to reduce the real inhabitants to an inferior
status and run the government. A higher people coming into
contact with a lower people [neechi praja] has a duty [farj] to make
the latter like itself. By the same rule, a king is not the sovereign of
his people but their servant.[68]

With this adaptation, Gandhi's displacement of liberal equality gets under
way. There is no mention of Salter's argument that equality is modern,
or that no religion allows for equality. To the contrary, now God saves
those who practice equality. "God-given equality" upturns Salter's arguments about the claims that American Indians have, because of their suffering, claims on the more civilized; now, instead, "every man can claim
a right over us," and "we have no claim on others." Consequently, a "higher
people" has the obligation to make a "lower people" "like itself." Until then
everybody is backward.

   But how would this obligation, which Salter's equality cannot meet,
be fulfilled? The adaptation does not and perhaps cannot yet address this
paralyzing question. Or perhaps it does in an elliptical way?—could the

paralysis be what makes Gandhi abandon the adaptation less than halfway through?

By the time he translates *Ethical Religion*, Gandhi's arguments are without his knowledge shearing and rending away from Salter's. Two years later, in *Hind Swaraj*, the shearing and rending is even more marked. The Editor attacks "modern civilization," which Salter celebrates in distinguishing between civilized and savage, and in claiming a convergence of the religious and the moral. For the Editor, "modern civilization" is irreligious. From such a perspective, a theological secularism such as Salter's would be profoundly violent.

～

Translating *Ethical Religion* in the wake of the Bhambatha Rebellion and that other September 11, it is perhaps unsurprising that Gandhi's attempt to reprise the book's arguments should end up displacing them, that his anticolonial arguments should come to be destroyed by his postcolonial arguments. As I will point out in later chapters, the postcolonial Gandhi too draws on the trope of suffering. But this Gandhi's question is not Salter's and Bentham's objective-subjective one "can *it* suffer." Rather, equality is always an enactment, and to enact it involves the ability to *oneself* suffer. Satyagraha "postulates the conquest of the adversary by suffering in one's own person." What is involved in "suffering in one's own person"?— perhaps this is one way of describing the question that seizes him by the time of *Hind Swaraj*.

Gandhi's unmarked critique (perhaps unnoticed even by him) of Salter's religion occurs in chapter 16 of *Hind Swaraj*, as the Editor responds to the Reader's insinuation that force against the British would be as justified as force to prevent a child from going into the fire. If we are to translate in a way that is close to the Gujarati (though the resultant prose is quite awkward in English):

> Remember that, in thus preventing the child, you are minding
> entirely the child's interest [*swarth*]. The one on whom restraint is
> being placed—the restraint is in the interest of that very one. This
> example does not all apply to the English. In using brute force
> against the English you consult entirely your own, that is to say the
> national [*praja*] interest. There is not the slightest daya in this. If
> you say that the actions of the English, being evil, represent fire,

that they go into the fire out of ignorance, and that out of daya you try to save the ignorant person—the child—, then to carry out this experiment, wherever whichever [jya jya je je] person is doing evil work, you will have to reach each of those places and in each of them instead of taking the life of the one who is in front of you—of the child—you will have to sacrifice your life. If you can do such *purushartha*, then you are a master [*mukhtyaar*]. It is impossible. ["If you are capable of such immeasurable pity, I wish you well in its exercise. It is not going to happen."]

In Indian classical texts, *purushartha* usually names the four ends of life— *dharma* (duty), *artha* (material prosperity), *kama* (pleasure), *moksha* (liberation); etymologically, the meaning or end [*artha*] that is sought by man [*purush*]. The English version glosses this powerfully resonant word as "immeasurable pity." Why this lexically unjustifiable gloss or slippage? Why does the Editor think of "immeasurable pity" as impossible? Gandhi does not explicitly address these questions; they remain ours to address.

Gandhi's translation of *purushartha* as "immeasurable pity" retrospectively opens up the Gujarati text for us. It both acknowledges the legitimacy and persuasiveness of "immeasurable pity" as a way of thinking *purushartha*, and relinquishes that way. Could this relinquishment be because involved in immeasurable pity as *purushartha* is a conception of God as an infinitely purer and more powerful version of the earthly sovereign, or as in Gandhi's Gujarati text, a "master"? Only such an infinite sovereign is capable of encompassing all, and thus also capable of sacrificing itself for all that lives, without affect organizing its decisions. (This conception of God as infinitely sovereign is one that Gandhi would have been familiar with from canonical readings of key texts in the two religious traditions he is familiar with by this time—Hinduism and Christianity.) Putting together the Gujarati and the English versions of the passage above, one might say that the Editor conceives of immeasurable pity/*purushartha* as "impossible" (a word that Gandhi's rendering glosses as "not going to happen")—or more precisely possible only for the one who, having attained salvation, has become godlike.[69] (The use of the word *mukhtyaar*, which is left untranslated in the English rendering, is especially redolent here: it would usually refer to the chief of a village, a sovereign, but also carries connotations of mastery.)

But in what sense is this impossible? It would be quite inadequate to understand the impossibility involved as that of impracticality—both the Editor and Gandhi often affirm goals that are impossible in the practical sense of being easily achievable goals. Gandhi, for example, professes over and again to be seeking moksha or salvation himself; a certain impossible *purushartha* matters to him. And the swaraj the Editor seeks in *Hind Swaraj*—what is this if not impossible? It is thus not every impossibility that Gandhi relinquishes.

But "immeasurable pity" is the impossible as imagined from within the problematic of general responsibility (schematically, responsibility to the whole, to what is most general, such as the laws of the land, or the rights of man and citizen), or more precisely here, autonomy (using that term here as a shorthand—inadequate, I admit, but nevertheless not misplaced— for the exemplarily modern form of general responsibility, for that complex named by the phrase "liberty, equality, fraternity"). However generous and all-encompassing such pity may be, it is profoundly hierarchical— extended downward from the sovereign to all his subjects. As such, it is simultaneously the hyperbolic and unrealizable realization of that problematic, and the most generous way that problematic conceives of absolute responsibility (schematically, the responsibility that is heedless of the law and the whole, that demands all of the one who is seized by it), which is its opposite and outside.[70] Put differently, "immeasurable pity" is how absolute responsibility appears from within the problematic of general responsibility.[71]

From within the problematic of abstract equality, satyagraha and ahimsa often appear as "immeasurable pity"—the greatest and most inclusive radicalism that can be imagined within this problematic. Here satyagraha becomes the most radical form of liberal civil disobedience, and Gandhi becomes the thinker of a utopian to-come. But it is precisely this conception of immeasurable pity that the Editor rejects.

～

What, then, is Gandhi's dharma or religion if not immeasurable pity? Perhaps his thinking of dharma, as well as its stakes, can be brought into greater relief initially by three counterpoints with Derrida's thinking of religion. First, Derrida insists that reason, and the abstraction it entails, is always marked by faith. For him, religion persists in the many secularisms that think that they have founded themselves on a knowledge free of, pure from, religion or faith. And, conversely, knowledge or reason persists in "religion" too:

> In order to think religion today *abstractly*, we will take these powers of abstraction as our point of departure, in order to risk, eventually, the following hypothesis: with respect to all these forces of abstraction and of dissociation . . . , "religion" is at the same time involved in reacting antagonistically and reaffirmatively outbidding itself. *In this very place,* knowledge and faith, technoscience ("capitalist" and fiduciary) and belief, credit, trustworthiness, the act of faith will always have made common cause, bound to one another by the band of their opposition.[72]

But as the very careful formulation above suggests, to insist that reason and faith or religion are marked by each other is not at all to create a zone of indistinction between the two. Rather, it radically reworks the Kantian Enlightenment tradition. As he insists in *Rogues,* deconstruction is commited to reason:

> Deconstruction, if something of the sort exists, would remain above all, in my view, an unconditional rationalism that never renounces—and precisely in the name of the Enlightenment to come, in the space to be opened up of a democracy to come— the possibility of suspending in an argued, deliberated, rational fashion, all conditions, hypotheses, conventions, and presuppositions, and of criticizing unconditionally all conditionalities, including those that still found the critical idea, namely, those of the *krinein,* of the *krisis,* of the binary or dialectical decision or judgment.[73]

Nevertheless, Derrida also engages with faith and religion as a continuation—a continuation otherwise—of the Enlightenment tradition. "We shall doubtless attempt to transpose, here and now, the circumspect and suspensive attitude, a certain epoche that consists—rightly or wrongly, for the matter is serious—in thinking religion or making it appear 'within the limits of reason alone.'" Or again: "How then to think—within the limits of reason alone—a religion which, without again becoming 'natural religion,' would today be effectively universal? And which, for that matter, would no longer be restricted to a paradigm that was Christian or even Abrahamic"?[74]

Derrida transforms that "circumspect and suspensive attitude" that consists in thinking religion within the limits of reason alone by attending to the faith that autonomous reason necessarily requires, and which remains aporetic to it: "It is a matter of thinking reason, of thinking the coming of its future, of its to-come, and of its becoming, as the experience of *what* and *who* comes, of what happens or who arrives—obviously as other, as the absolute exception or singularity of an alterity that is not reappropriable by the ipseity of a sovereign power and a calculable knowledge."[75] It is a reason marked in this sense by a "will and freedom without autonomy" that Derrida affirms. This other reason he describes as a "messianicity without messianism." In a vein that resonates strikingly with his discussion of Kant's definition of "reflecting faith," he describes "messianicity without messianism" as a "faith without dogma" that "is announced wherever, reflecting without flinching, a purely rational analysis brings the following paradox to light: that the foundation of law—law of the law, institution of institutions, origin of the constitution—is a 'performative' event that cannot belong to the set it founds, inaugurates or justifies."[76] Rational analysis, put differently, cannot ground itself, and is in this constitutive sense marked by a messianicity, even if it is not a messianism since it does not strive for a moment where time ends with the messianic event.

Second, this messianicity without messianism is a most rigorous, perhaps even the most rigorous, form of the calculable opening to the incalculable:

> We have to think together two figures of rationality that, on either side of a limit, at once call for and exceed one another. The incalculable unconditionality of hospitality, of the gift of forgiveness, exceeds the calculation of conditions, just as justice exceeds law, the juridical, and the political. . . . The heterogeneity between justice and law does not exclude but, on the contrary, calls for their inseparability: there can be no justice without an appeal to juridical determinations and to the force of law; and there can be no becoming, no transformation, history, or perfectibility of law without an appeal to a justice that will nonetheless always exceed it. . . .
>
> On both sides, then, whether it is a question of singularity or universality, and each time both at once, *both* calculation *and* the

incalculable *are necessary*. This responsibility of reason, this
experience that consists in keeping within reason [*a raison garder*],
in being responsible for a reason of which we are the heirs, could
be situated with only the greatest difficulty. Indeed I would situate
it precisely within this greatest of difficulties or, rather, in truth,
within the autoimmune aporia of this impossible transaction
between the conditional and the unconditional, calculation and
the incalculable. . . . If I had to attribute a meaning, the most
difficult, least mediocre, least moderate meaning, to this well-worn,
indeed long-discredited, word *reasonable*, I would say that what is
"reasonable" is the reasoned and considered wager of a transaction
between these two apparently irreconcilable exigencies of reason,
between calculation and the incalculable.[77]

The incalculable, the realm of faith and religion, must be inhabited and
traversed now by reason. And in that traversal, it becomes possible to
arrive at a hypercritical faith—to distinguish, in howsoever tenuous and
fragile a manner, between faith on the one hand and religion, dogma, or
theocratic institutions on the other:

This hiatus [between the calculable and the incalculable] opens
the rational space of a hypercritical faith, one without dogma and
without religion, irreducible to any and all religions and implicitly
theocratic institutions. It is what I have called elsewhere the await-
ing without horizon of a messsianicity without messianism. It goes
without saying that I do not detect here even the slightest hint or
irrationalism, obscurantism or extravagance. This faith is another
way of keeping within reason [*raison garder*] however mad it
might appear. If the minimal semantic kernel we might retain from
the various lexicons of reason, in every language, is the ultimate
possibility of, if not a consensus, at least an address universally
promised and unconditionally entrusted to the other, then reason
remains the element or very air of a faith without church and
without credulity, the raison d'être of the pledge, of credit, of
testimony beyond proof, the raison d'être of any belief *in* the other,
that is, of their belief and of our belief in them—and thus also of
any perjury.[78]

Third, this most reasonable opening of the calculable to the incalculable involves that distinctive relation to death that Derrida describes as autoimmunity. Because here reason must in the spirit of autonomy give up on autonomy, it exposes itself even to the possibility of its own death. For Derrida, republican democracy is the form of rule that conforms most to this autoimmunity of reason. His preference for republican democracy is already marked in "Faith and Knowledge":

> We also share, it seems to me, something else—let us designate it cautiously—an unreserved taste, if not an unconditional preference, for what, in politics, is called republican democracy as a universalizable model, binding to the public "cause," to the res publica, to "publicness," once again to the light of day, once again to the "lights" of the Enlightenment (aux Lumières), once again to the enlightened virtue of public space, emancipating it from all external power (non-lay, non-secular), for example from religious dogmatism, orthodoxy or authority (that is, from a certain rule of the doxa or of belief, which however does not mean from all faith.[79]

In *Rogues*, he describes at length the autoimmunity that distinguishes this democracy: it "protects itself and maintains itself precisely by limiting and threatening itself." This autoimmunity that marks democracy sets it apart from all other regimes, for it "entails the right to self-critique—another form of autoimmunity—as an essential, original, constitutive and specific possibility of the democratic, indeed as its very historicity, an intrinsic historicity that it shares with no other regime."[80] It is this autoimmunity, rather than some ideal vision of a future democracy, that he describes as "democracy to come."

~

If we are, in Derrida's spirit, to stop following his text in "the style of a commentary" and attend instead to "interpreting [it] from the point of its avenir," then we could begin by noting this: here autoimmunity secretes a certain sovereignty in the very moment of death.[81] For even though the autoimmunity of republican democracy questions its own sovereign power, it nevertheless must continue to affirm that very power. Consider his discussion of "what happened in postcolonial Algeria in 1992. Here the "state and the leading party interrupted a democratic electoral process" because of the fear that the Islamic party, which won the elections, would "abolish the normal functioning of democracy or the very democratization assumed to be in progress."[82] This "suspension of the electoral process in Algeria would be, from almost every perspective, typical of all the assaults on democracy in the name of democracy." "Hence a certain suicide of democracy. Democracy has always been suicidal, and if there is a to-come for it, it is only on the condition of thinking life otherwise, life and the force of life."[83]

But is suicide and autoimmunity too preliminary a way of describing what happens here? As the phrase "leading party" should remind us, what is to begin with distinctive about republican democracy is that it is not the sovereignty of one or the whole alone—it is simultaneously the sovereignty of the one and the many, of the whole and the parts. These parts organize themselves as parties, leading or otherwise; there are also always those who do not have a part but demand a part, who are not a party but seek to be a party. In view of this, would it not be appropriate to say that the suicide of republican democracy always involves a double murder?—one party murders the party (usually a minor, or a party that has no part but seeks a part) that it considers a threat to republican democracy, and in this process murders also republican democracy, for now sovereignty is only one. The murdering party, moreover, does not usually sacrifice itself in the process. To describe this double murder as only suicide: Would this not collude in giving a clear conscience to the murdering party? Would it not collude in the depoliticization and legitimation of the murder? In a profound injustice?

Moreover, this double murder is itself an act of sovereign justice. In the Algerian case, for example, the suspension of republican democracy is carried out by exercising the sovereign exception, where the leading party decides to keep sovereignty to itself by killing republican democracy and the other. And it does so autonomously—by claiming that the other is not autonomous and so might kill republican democracy permanently, and that therefore the leading party's autonomous exercise of the sovereign exception is more likely to conserve the possibility of later reinstituting republican democracy. The autoimmunity of democracy, then, enshrines sovereignty even more firmly in place. In this sense, the resort to the word "suicide" in the translation is suggestive (whether appropriate to the French or not): to commit suicide is to perform the sovereign act of taking one's own life.

Symptomatic again of the persistence of sovereign justice is the hierarchy of the "not yet" that organizes Derrida's writing. The task in Algeria

> would consist in doing everything possible to join forces with all those who, and first of all in the Islamic world, fight not only for the secularization of the political (however ambiguous this secularization remains), for the emergence of a laic subjectivity, but also for an interpretation of the Koranic heritage that privileges, from the inside as it were, the democratic virtualities that are probably not any more apparent and readable at first glance, and readable under this name, than they were in the Old and New Testaments.[84]

Here the "secularization of the political" is a desirable goal, and in the trajectory toward this secularization some groups and societies are unavoidably further along than others. This is why the "democratic virtualities" of the Koran "*are* probably not any more apparent and readable at first glance, and readable under this name, than they *were* in the Old and New Testaments" (emphasis added). This is why, again, for Derrida "a certain Islam," "this particular one and not Islam in general (if such a thing exists), would represent the only religious culture that would have resisted up until now a European (that is, Greco-Christian and globalatinizing) process of secularization, and thus of democratization, and thus, in the strict sense, of politicization."[85]

Where republican democracy (which is always marked not only by the autoimmunity that Derrida notes but also by the double murder) prevails, the democratic sovereign must always decide: Is the other ready for democracy? Can these specific groups or peoples sustain democracy without killing democracy itself? If that question must be answered in the negative, then a rule that presents itself as the suspension of democracy or the wait for democracy is always justifiable and even just. When democratic Britain ruled its colonies, but disallowed democracy in them on the grounds that these colonies were not yet ready for it, and would kill democracy, can it be said with certainty that this just logic was not at work? Indeed, regardless of whether democracy is killed by the other or commits suicide to save itself for another time, in both cases there is an implicit acknowledgment that the other is not capable of the exercise of the autoimmunity of democracy: while democracy can kill itself and in this very killing revive itself, the other can kill democracy but not rescue or revive it. The autoimmunity of republican democracy is in this sense continuous with imperialism, colonialism, or that racism which would designate one section of the *demos* not yet ready to exercise democratic rights; there can be no taste for republican democracy that is not also a taste for imperialism and racism.

Encountering this sovereign autoimmunity, we must say of Derrida what Derrida says of Heidegger: "And there we would have difficulty following him. First along his own path."[86]

$\sim$

Elsewhere in "Faith and Knowledge," however, Derrida thinks autoimmunity not along the suicidal-murderous path of republican democracy but along another path—that constituted by a conjoined emphasis on self-sacrifice and an absolute respect for the life of the other. "The religion of the living—is this not a tautology? Absolute imperative, holy law, law of salvation: saving the living intact." This "intentional attitude," he suggests, involves a "restraint or *holding back [halte]* in general."

> Perhaps they [the various movements of holding back] constitute a sort of universal, not "religion" as such, but a universal structure of religiosity. . . . Such a universal allows perhaps the global translation of *religio*, that is: scruple, respect, restraint, *Verhaltenheit*, reserve, Scheu, shame, discretion, *Gelassenheit*, etc—all stop short of that which must or should remain safe and sound, intact, unscathed, before what must be allowed to be what it ought to be, sometimes even at the cost of sacrificing itself and in prayer: the other.[87]

Ventured here the possibility of a religion that exceeds the respect for and sacralization of only the "anthropo-theological life" of the "rational finite being," that is about restraint and finitude, and that might relatedly practice a self-sacrifice that does not belong to republican democracy. While the potentialities of this other religion are not pursued in "Faith and Knowledge," Derrida's other texts offer a thinking both of absolute respect for the animal (a scrupulous reexamination of the massive distinction between the human and the animal) and of the pure gift, including the gift of death to oneself and the other (or self-sacrifice as a gift that exceeds the autoimmunity of republican democracy). In these other texts, Derrida's deconstruction of sovereignty gathers a force that is perhaps unparalleled in our times.

We encounter thus a strange phenomenon. It is from Derrida's texts that we receive a thinking of religion as a "will and freedom without autonomy" (as also of the doubled axioms of faith and sacrality that organize religion—another theme that marks "Faith and Knowledge"). But in their very taste for republican democracy, these texts also recoil from a thinking of what would be proper to the sacred and to faith. It is thus only by breaking from these texts that what they give us to think be thought. That break, need it be said, must not be a sovereign break that overcomes these texts; it must always be the most faithful surrender to these texts.

And to this break, Gandhi's writing brings us by another path. On each of the three thematics, Gandhi and Derrida are as abysally apart as they are infinitely close. In Gandhi's writings thus, satyagraha suffuses autonomous reason and everyday life, but pure satyagraha starts where autonomous reason fails, and in this sense exceeds the latter; the hypercriticality of satyagraha involves continuously and repeatedly distinguishing between institutionalized or theological religions and the "religion that stays in all religions"; finally, satyagrahis too must relinquish sovereign power, and for this practice a certain self-sacrifice.

For now, that last thematic will suffice to indicate the abyssal apartness and infinite proximity between Derrida's and Gandhi's writing. Autoimmunity is too preliminary a word to describe the self-sacrifice involved in satyagraha. Gandhi will repeatedly insist on a distinction between suicide and self-sacrifice, and will describe the former as *duragraha* (the force of or seizure by evil) and the latter as satyagraha. Yet the line between these two is not at all clear for him—even the satyagrahi's self-sacrifice always risks becoming suicide. The self-sacrifice proper to satyagraha—the self-sacrifice that will be neither suicide, nor murder, nor sublation into a greater entity— he describes sometimes by drawing on the phrase "friendship with death." His writing will arrive at this friendship by a distinctive path: by departing from autonomous sovereignty for the warrior's sovereignty. That departure is necessary because the warrior's sovereignty involves an immeasurable equality and inequality that is quite opposed to the measurable equality and inequality that is involved in autonomous sovereignty. His writing will depart also from the immeasurable equality of the warrior for the absolute equality of the satyagrahi—the equality that strives to destroy every sovereignty.

And yet, nothing is more difficult to think than this trajectory condensed in the phrase "friendship with death." Along the grown-over path—no, paths—of this thinking, not only originary but obscured and obscuring, he remains to be followed.

· CHAPTER 2 ·

Between Two and Three

READER: *"What do you think is the reason that the English people became like this?"*
EDITOR: *It is not due to any peculiar fault of the English people. It is rather the fault of their—rather, Europe's—modern civilization [sudharo, civility]. That civility is kudharo ["destructive of civilization"], and under it the people [praja] of Europe are becoming degraded and ruined day by day."*

—Mohandas Gandhi, *Hind Swaraj*

Just as we call idea of living things biology, just so the presentation and full articulation of all beings, dominated as they now are everywhere by the nature of the technical, may be called technology....
Viewed from the present and drawn from our insight into the present, the step back out of metaphysics into the essential nature of metaphysics is the step out of technology and technological description and interpretation of the age, into the essence of modern technology, which is still to be thought.

—Martin Heidegger, "The Onto-theo-logical Constitution of
Metaphysics," in *Identity and Difference*

IN CHAPTER 4 OF *Hind Swaraj*, the Reader suggests that after the English leave, "we shall still keep their constitution and shall carry on the Government." "We must own our navy, our army, and we must have our own splendor, and then will India's voice ring through the world." The Editor responds: "You have drawn the picture well. In effect it means this: that we want English rule without the Englishman. You want the tiger's nature, but not the tiger; that is to say, you would make India English. And when it becomes English, it will be called not Hindustan but *Englishtan*. This is not the Swaraj that I want."

If the Editor's response is one of the best-known passages in *Hind Swaraj*, this may be because it resonates with the pervasive suspicion in recent decades that every abstract and placeless universal, every pure intelligible, is marked—surreptitiously or not—by a particular or sensible. Derrida writes, for instance, of a dialogue in Anatole France's *The Garden of Epicurus:* "The interlocutors are concerned precisely with that sensible figure which is sheltered, and worn out to the point of seeming to pass unnoticed, in every metaphysical concept. Abstract notions always conceal a sensible figure. It seems that the history of metaphysical language is commingled with the erasing of what is effective in it, and the wearing out of its effigy."[1]

In the colonies, moreover, the sensible or particular always has the same proper name: as Chakrabarty remarks, "For capital or bourgeois, I submit, read 'Europe' or 'European.'"[2] We usually read the phrase "English rule without the Englishman" similarly—as Gandhi pointing to the originarily English or European nature of "modern civility."

But what is named by the phrase "English rule without the Englishman" is not so clear. Toward the end of chapter 6, the Editor says: "Parliaments are really emblems of slavery.... It is not that they [the English] cannot be cured of this disease of civilization, but it should not be forgotten that they are at present afflicted by it." And in chapter 8 he says: "India is being ground down, not under the English heel, but under that of modern civilization. It is groaning under the monster's terrible weight." Here modern civility, exemplified by parliaments, stands apart from and over the English; it has mastered and enslaved them, and may do the same to India. "English rule without the Englishman" only names the rule of modern civility.

And modern civility here is not even originarily European. It is rather a "disease" that has afflicted Europe and England; the Editor suggests therefore that rather than finding fault with the English, they deserve compassion or daya ["pity"].[3] While "modern civility" is especially dominant in England and Europe, they are nevertheless only its somewhat aleatory bearers.[4]

At the same time, "modern civility" is not a placeless universalism that erases every sensible, toward which all cultures converge. Rather, it is a restless potentiality to make humans infinite—a potentiality that is simultaneously absolutely internal and absolutely external to every socius, every time, every historical moment. Thus in chapter 10 the Editor remarks: "Our difficulties are of our own creation. God set a limit to man's locomotive ambition in the construction of his body. Man immediately proceeded to discover means of overriding the limit." And in chapter 13: "our ancestors" "set a limit to our indulgences" because "the mind is a restless bird."

In describing the restless potentiality of modern civility, he draws often on the phrase "third party" or "third person" [*treejo manas*]. "Third party" is here no longer just any phrase. In Gandhi's writing, that phrase condenses within it an axiomatics of modern civility: the axiomatics shared by the judge, the law court, and the sovereign who works by the principle of general responsibility (autonomy could well be described as the exemplarily democratic form of that principle); by "machinery" or technology; shared also by measure in both its forms—on the one hand, instrumentality, and, on the other hand, calculability, or the calibration of instrumentality into "right means," which is required for citizenship.

He contrasts the third party to the finitude of two-ness; this finitude is signaled often by the phrase "each other" or one another [*ekbeeja*]. "Third party" and "each other": these provide two ways in Gandhi's writings of conceptualizing nonviolence, equality, and even being. By exploring the contrasting tropes of three-ness and two-ness in Gandhi's writing, as this chapter will, we can begin moving toward a more nuanced understanding of how, in the years after abandoning the problematic of "immeasurable pity," Gandhi questions modern civility and thinks satyagraha.

What makes the work of these tropes in Gandhi's writing all the more intriguing is that he finds it difficult to think two-ness, and relatedly his critique of three-ness. In his explicit formulations, two-ness often becomes indistinguishable from European romantic and communitarian traditions, which have often questioned the concept of the third by invoking the unity of two. The commonsensical force of these traditions has to do with what is thinkable in the vocabulary of "modern civilization." This vocabulary, to put it briefly for now, has a concept of one and of three, but can conceive two only as romantic unity—in other words, as one.

But Gandhi's writing also secretes another kind of disquiet with the "third party." In the process, like those few other texts that question every form of sovereign power, it thinks anew that which is never new—limit, finitude, two, all interchangeable words here.[5] In the rest of this chapter (and indeed, the rest of the book), I shall explore the struggles in his writing with the questions that emerge in the process: How does sharing occur in relations of the limit or finitude? How can relations of two-ness sustain multiplicity—more than two? What is the relation between the limit and three—the infinitude of "modern civility" or autonomy? How can the absolute equality proper to two-ness be conceptualized and sustained?

∼

One of the earliest sustained discussions in *Hind Swaraj* of three-neess and two-ness occurs in chapter 8. As the Editor attacks "modern civilization," the Reader asks: "Then you will contend that Pax Britannica is a useless encumbrance." For the Reader, law exemplifies a juridical and state-centered order, and even if some laws may be unjust, law is in principle nonviolent because it is infused with justice. He is willing to reject English courts, but not the rule of law. And for him, Pax Britannica imposed the rule of law, and put an end to "the terror that the Thugs, the Pindaris and the Bhils were to the country"; the British have brought "peace" to the country. The Editor responds:

> You may see peace *[shanti]* if you like; I do not see peace and contentment. . . .
>
> Moreover, today's peace is only nominal. We have through this peace become unmanly, effeminate, and cowardly. We should not assume that the British have changed the nature *[swabhav;* habits, ownmost orientation] of the Pindaris and Bhils. If there are such perils, then they are worth suffering. But if a second person *[beeja manas,* "someone else"] rescues us from that torment, this will produce utter baseness. Rather than have us become without strength, I would prefer to be killed by the arrow of a Bhil.

A further dimension emerges in chapter 10, when the Editor suggests that law is "another form of the exhibition of brute force." He suggests that even when Hindus and Muslims fight, "we certainly do not want to engage counsel and resort to English or any law courts."

> I do not suggest that Hindus and Mussalmans will never fight. When two brothers live together, then clashes happen. We shall sometimes have our heads broken. Such a thing ought not be necessary, but all men are not equi-minded *[sarkhimati,* "equitable"]. When people are in a rage, they do many foolish things. These we have to put up with. But we should not take clashes to big lawyers, or English courts. Two persons fight, one or both of them have their heads broken. What justice can a third party do in this *[tema trijo manas shu nyaya kari shakaye]?* Those who fight may expect to be injured. When body hits body, there will necessarily be a wound *[nishani].* In this, how can there be justice?[6]

The next chapter opens with the Reader's response: "You tell me that when two men quarrel they should not go to a law court. This is astonishing." The Editor says: "Whether you call it astonishing or not, it is the truth. . . . My firm opinion is that the lawyers have enslaved India, have accentuated Hindu-Mahomedan dissensions [kajiya] and have confirmed English authority." "I only wish to show you that the profession [law] teaches the unethical [aniti]." The Editor goes on:

> Do you think that if English courts were not there, the English could continue their rule? Courts are not for the benefit of the people. Those who want to perpetuate their power, they subdue people through courts. If people were to fight amongst themselves, then a third party [treejo manas] could not institute his power. Truly, when men fought with their own hands or by instituting their kin as arbiters, they remained men. When courts came, then they became effeminate. To fight with one another and die was considered a sign of savagery [janglipan]. Now that a third party ends my quarrels, is it any less savagery? Can anybody say that the decision [tharaav] of a third party is always right? Who is right, that both partisans [bane pakshkar; "parties alone"] know. We in our simplicity and ignorance assume that a third party [treejo manas, "stranger"] takes our money and gives us justice.

It is unsurprising that the Editor attacks the third party by questioning Pax Britannica. Colonial officials celebrate Pax Britannica as the cornerstone of British rule. In colonial narratives, Pax Britannica keeps the "weaker races" from fighting one another, rendering justice among these races while remaining outside and above them. Pax Britannica is just because it seeks a proportionate equality; it institutes a general responsibility, or a responsibility to the whole, which works through measure. As that ur-text of European traditions of justice, Aristotle's *Nicomachean Ethics* (which Gandhi and other Indians studying law in England would likely have encountered in some form), remarks: "If what is unjust is what is unequal, what is just is equal . . . what the judge does is to restore equality."[7] In proportionate equality, rather than everybody receiving equal shares, the unequal receive shares equal to their inequality. If the colonized do not have the same rights as the rulers, this follows from different levels of ability and evolution. Pax Britannica also reveals thus the essential affinity

between British rule in the metropole and the colonies—the same calculability, the same justice, the same general responsibility, is at work in both
places.

In sustaining its justice, Pax Britannica works as the third party, correctly measuring and comparing the two parties before it. The third party
does not just deploy measure; the third party constitutes measure. It is
instructive here to recall Heidegger, who argues that three is not the third
number but the first *number*. Only when we perceive the first and the second from the perspective of the third do they become numbers—only
then does there arise the possibility of a series.[8] Without such a series
there can be no measure. Pax Britannica involves a justice of the third, or
the third party, which allows two to be compared and judged.

This distinguishes the work of Pax Britannica from that done by two
other colonial categories—those of primitive violence and arbitrary rule
or despotism. The latter, in colonial accounts usually the characteristic of
most precolonial regimes, is a derangement of justice because it measures
wrongly. Primitive violence, by contrast, belongs to the prehistory of justice; it is before the emergence of a third party as judge.

It is so, first, as a boyishness, as the violence of those who are not yet
capable of either being brought before or administering justice. (Symptomatically, to recall an example, one Bhil revolt in colonial western India
is described as "a regular case of naughty boys making a disturbance in the
school-room when they believed the school-master's attention was
momentarily diverted.") Colonial officials celebrate this boyishness, which
prefigures the adulthood needed for justice.[9] It is so, second, as the originary moment of measure and reciprocity. Feuds and vengeance intimate
a reciprocity between the two that makes them one, that enables disputes
to be conducted without the third, without justice. And yet, when guided
by a firm and considerate hand, such as that provided by colonial officers,
feuds and vengeance can be transmuted into the legal order. "Primitive
violence" thus sustains the fantasy that the three of justice and number
is not external but an elaboration of this internal measure; it sustains the
thought of a one that is originarily three, and a three that is originarily one.

Colonial officials see themselves as putting in place, through their deployment of a regular and proportionate measure, the rule of law. Indeed,
rule of law is for them the crux of Pax Britannica. More generally in the
self-congratulatory veins of European thought, rule of law has often been
regarded as the incalculable gift that Europe has given to its colonies, which

have received it with greater or lesser alacrity. Only by ensuring the prevalence of the rule of law can the natives be prepared for self-rule or, even better, republican democracy.

And while the Reader refuses to accept the colonial celebration of Pax Britannica, he also sees it as enabling. Like many prominent Indian nationalists of the time, he affirms the calculable form of general responsibility—its third party, its rule of law. If in the passage above he wants the two men to go to a law court, this is because he conceives justice and even everyday being in terms of measure. He questions only the wrong measure of the British, exemplified in the different way British and Indians were treated, and even more in the absence of swaraj. Wrong measure makes the British Empire a despotism rather than the true measure required by general responsibility. He will follow therefore the example of the English parliament and arrive at his own sovereign measure—an Indian parliament. If he is willing to resort to "any means whatsoever" to drive out the British, this is so only as a founding exception or revolutionary violence necessary to establish an institutional order organized around right means—"parliamentary swaraj" or, more broadly, the autonomous order of republican democracy.[10]

A suggestive exchange occurs in chapter 9, when he dismisses the Editor's charge that "if there had been no railways, the English could not have such a hold [kaabu] on Hindustan." For the Reader, "all the disadvantages of railways are more than counterbalanced by the fact that it is due to them that we see in Hindustan the spirit of one people [ek praja, new spirit of nationalism]." Indians demand "national independence" because of this "new spirit." Remarks such as the Reader's are replete in nationalism's autobiographies, where national independence does not simply establish a sovereign state, but more importantly infuses the state with liberty and equality. Now the people themselves participate in the sovereignty of the state; they are the state and they partake of its divinity. Thus Nehru's often-quoted speech to a gathering of Jat peasants: "You are parts of this Bharat Mata, I told them, you are in a manner yourselves Bharat Mata, and as this idea slowly soaked into their brains, their eyes would light up as if they had made a great discovery."[11]

Put differently, the British have an external or transcendent relation with India: they hold India as something finite, something subordinated to and subsumed within them as a third party. In contrast, the nationalists' India is suffused by the abstract equality of all its citizens; here, the third party is theologized, or becomes a simultaneously immanent and transcendent end.

Within this tradition, then, the phrase "rights of man and of the citizen," which the nationalists would have received from the French Revolution, names a necessary togetherness because the autonomy of man requires the rights of citizen as a guarantee. At the time of *Hind Swaraj,* Gandhi does not distinguish between imperial and national citizenship. But by the time of the Great Trial in 1922, he recognizes what the Reader had more than a decade earlier, and what Arendt was to stress around three decades later in *The Origins of Totalitarianism,* after the Holocaust brought home to Europeans the violence they had long practiced in the colonies—that abstract equality requires national citizenship to guarantee it: "I discovered that as a man and an Indian I had no rights. More correctly, I discovered that I had no rights as a man because I was an Indian." Republican democracy can in other words only be realized within a nation-state.[12]

Nor can the tension between man and citizen be contained within the nationalist resolution. Indeed, if abstract equality has been adopted so enthusiastically in so many places across the world (and emphatically not just by elites), surely this is because the concept of the third party organizes general responsibility in an especially forceful way—one that leaves open in principle, which is to say in its very abstraction, the equality of what is marginal to what is dominant and universal.

~

In the very dialogue form of *Hind Swaraj,* the relinquishment of general responsibility begins. Etymologically, the word *samvaad,* translated as "dialogue," decomposes most intriguingly: *sam*—simultaneously equality and togetherness, and *vaad*—talk. In a *samvaad,* equals talk together. *Hind Swaraj* is a dialogue between two "forms" of responsibility—general responsibility and absolute responsibility, named in his writings by the concept-metaphors of three and two (though "two" refers in his writing to the responsibility not only of the satyagrahi but also of the conservative sovereign, to introduce a figure who will gather force only in the next chapter).

Hind Swaraj may be organized as a dialogue because of Gandhi's familiarity with Plato—he translates the "Apology" just the year before he writes *Hind Swaraj.* But recall he also remarks in the English preface: "Some of the friends who have read the translation have objected that the subject-matter has been dealt with in the form of a dialogue. I have no answer to offer to this objection except that the Gujarati language readily lends itself to such treatment and that it is considered the best method of treating difficult subjects."[13] Considered by whom? This remains unclear. Not much of the literature of the period adopts the dialogue form (though Raychandbhai's writings occasionally do). Could he be referring to Gujarati translations of the *Bhagavad Gita,* organized as a dialogue between Arjuna and Krishna, which he has been immersed in since the early 1890s? Both the *Gita* and Plato's dialogues could well be read as dialogues of general responsibility. Deleuze and Guattari indicate how the dialogue initiated by Plato's Socrates institutes the dominance of the single concept.[14] Similarly, if we read the *Gita* along the lines Simona Sawhney suggests, then Arjuna is subordinate to Krishna, with his actions done as a sacrifice to the godhead Krishna.[15]

Because he affirms abstract equality, the Reader conducts a dialogue (which he initiates, asking the question that opens the book) of the third party. The third party provides a most intense way to think an abstract commonality and universalism, and therefore can be more inclusive than the forms of general responsibility that precede it—Arjuna's *kuladharma* [duty to his clan], Krishna's *nishkamakarma* [disinterested action] or Plato's ethics.

Relatedly, from the perspective of general responsibility and the third party, absolute responsibility can only be conceived negatively. From this perspective, the cardinal mark of absolute responsibility—indeed, the mark of its absoluteness—is its groundlessness. It is absolute: here, this also says—it is not amenable to reason, it is marked by faith alone, it has no further form or entailments. Consequently, it must be kept out of the mainstream secular public sphere and transformed into a secular religion or a religion within the limits of reason alone; general responsibility must not be contaminated by it.

If the Reader attacks religion so vehemently, then, this is because for him the relinquishment of general responsibility in the name of religion or absolute responsibility would be the greatest violence. Where there cannot be the dialogue organized by general responsibility, there can only be irrational relations that are always likely to topple over into violence in at least two senses. First, how will absolute responsibility be responsible to—dialogue with—what it is not in an absolute relation with? Will not this relation always be absolutely irresponsible? Second, how will absolute responsibility ever ensure the justice of its relation with what or who it claims absolute responsibility toward? When Rama banishes Sita, or Harishchandra raises his sword on Taramati (two examples that Gandhi discusses obsessively in later years)—how can these acts of absolute responsibility ever be just? For those like the Reader, these insuperable objections make it imperative that absolute responsibility always be limited and confined to the private sphere, or in other words not be allowed to be absolute.

When the Reader seeks a dialogue, then, he seeks one that is conducted within the terms of general responsibility. Such dialogue may not lead to resolution. It may even acknowledge that disagreement can never be overcome, that politics is disagreement (to use a word that we have come to associate with Jacques Rancière, among the most radical thinkers of general responsibility). But it does at least presume address as its horizon—that each can address the other within the dialogue, and that even where such address fails, the most responsible response would be to continue to speak to each other. To abandon the address involved in dialogue—this for the Reader, as more broadly for those committed to general responsibility, would be to lapse into irrationalism. If he is willing to use force with the British, it is precisely because by their refusal to heed the nationalist demand for swaraj, they have revealed their fundamental irrationality.

⌣

While *Hind Swaraj* breaks with the figure of the third party, and relatedly with dialogue understood in terms of the third party, the nature of this break is often obscured from Gandhi as an intending subject. In questioning the third party, the Editor often draws on the romantic and communitarian register internal to "modern civilization"—that register where two is one, or the originary moment of unity.

Thus, to recall the passages this chapter began with, he uses the phrase *beeja manas* (another or second person/party) to describe the third party who intervenes between the Editor and the Bhils or Pindaris. Here, the two that is the Editor and the Bhils or Pindaris have become one. Hence it becomes possible to describe the figure who intervenes (who would number as the third person) as the second person. This second person continues to be thought in terms of three-ness and one-ness (and this simultaneity is not accidental, since "one" and "three" as concepts here segue into each other, precluding two-ness). Not only does Gandhi's English translation render *beeja manas* as "someone else," but elsewhere in the same chapter this same *beeja manas* is described as the *treejo manas*, or third man. The phrase *beeja manas* or second man thus conceptualizes two as one and three; it remains silent about two-ness.

Symptomatic of the communitarian way of thinking two is the remark in Gandhi's English translation, "The parties *alone* know who is right" (my emphasis). Here, on the most obvious reading, the constative truth of the known secret—who (and also what) is right—sustains the relationship of the partisans. Their lonesome intimacy unites the antagonists against the judge. To know the secret as a secret—this would be to become of the structure of the one, even if the empirical number of knowers is more than one or two. Such a concept of the two claims an intimacy so strong as to make the two into a one that can settle its own disputes, that has no parts distinct enough from each other to need a third party.

The logic of two-as-one here is not, however, as antinomic to the three as might appear, since the one-ness of this two again enables a shift directly to three. For the judge, the two is constituted by a secret that makes them one. His task is to excavate this secret, make it public. Through a measure of this no-longer-secret constative knowledge, the judge dispenses a justice that ensures proportionality, whether geometric or arithmetic, between offense and penalty. Knowing the two as one, the judge transforms it into the order of three so that there can be justice within the one. In this conceptual order, the one and the three segue from each to the other without ever encountering the otherness and multiplicity of the two.

~

It is unsurprising that *Hind Swaraj* should fall back upon a communitarian and romantic thinking of two-ness, upon the very concept of the third it sets out to question. Thought that strains at available conceptual vocabularies always runs the risk of falling back on, and being taken back by, these very vocabularies. More intriguing are the moments when that strain can no longer be contained within these vocabularies, and when *Hind Swaraj* ventures a thinking of the very distinctive politics and justice of two-ness.

In a way, the rest of the book is about Gandhi's thinking of two-ness, about the backtrackings, twists, and turns that mark it. A passage in chapter 13 of *Hind Swaraj* can ease us into this thinking:

We have seen that man's mind is fickle. His mind keeps moving restlessly ["is a restless bird"]. The more we give to his body the more it asks for. Even after taking more it is not satisfied. Enjoying pleasure, the desire for pleasure keeps increasing [*bhog bhogavta bhogni iccha vadhti jaye;* "The more we indulge our passions, the more unbridled they become."] This is why ancestors put limits

["Our ancestors, therefore, set a limit to our indulgences."]. . . .
Seeing this, they made us leave the desire for pleasure [*bhog,*
"luxuries and indulgences"]. The plough that we had thousands
of years back we have continued with. Our huts we have kept
forever like they were thousands of years back. The education that
we had thousands of years back has continued. . . . It is not that we
did not know how to invent machines [*sancha*]; but our ancestors
saw that if man fell into the entanglement of machines etc., then
he would become a slave and give up his own ethics [*potani niti
tajshe,* "lose our moral fiber"]. They thoughtfully said that we
should do only what can be done with hands and feet. Only in
the use of hands and feet is there true contentment, only in it
health ["happiness and health consisted in a proper use of hands
and feet"]. . . .

This people had courts, had lawyers, had doctors. But all were
within proper limits [*reethsar niyam,* "all within bounds"]. . . .
Justice was about right [*theek theek,* "tolerably fair"]. People
preferred to avoid going to courts. . . . Ordinary people lived in
an independent manner and did their agricultural occupation.
They enjoyed true *swaraj.*[16]

Two complementary elements are especially intriguing in this passage.
First, there is the emphasis on *bhog,* the word translated variously as "luxuries and indulgences," "pleasure," "passions." Etymologically, *bhog* is associated with the Sanskrit *bhaj,* or breaking. The words describe the pleasure,
desire, and enjoyment involved in the double movement of a breaking or
fracturing of the self to encounter another, *and* a return to the self by and
after that encounter with the other.

But here the focus is on the distinctiveness of the bhog that marks
"modern civilization." *Bhog bhogavta bhogni iccha vadhti jaye:* one sentence
repeats bhog thrice over in two grammatical forms. In these grammatical
forms, bhog becomes both means *(bhogavta)* and end or goal *(bhog).* In
the bhog that marks "modern civilization," bhog itself is aggrandized: it
returns to itself and takes over the self.

This *bhog* that is "modern civilization" works through and in a distinctive modality—that of *sancha* or "machine/s." Later in the book, chapter 19
is titled "Sanchakam" (in English, "machinery") and it indicts machinery
as "the chief symbol of modern civilization" and as a "great sin." The Editor

suggests: "It is machinery that has impoverished India. We cannot draw a limit to the harm ["measure the harm"] that Manchester has done to us."

Gandhi, like other nationalists, is critical of the deindustrialization that he believes has been wreaked on India by the British through machinery. But the word *sanchakam* also works on another register. *Sancha,* "machine," carries connotations of a contrivance, and presumes that what defines a machine is its "in-order-to": the machine is a means directed at achieving an end. The word *sanchakam* is related—*sancha,* machine and *kam,* work: the work of the machine.[17] *Sanchakam* (and by extension "modern civilization"), it is tempting to speculate, names the possession of human beings by means as an abstract force, or what could be described in Nietzsche's terms as a doing that stands apart from the doer, a doing that has taken over both subject and object.[18]

The Reader finds this abstraction empowering and seeks to institutionalize it through that order of right means called parliamentary swaraj. The injunction to treat every person as an end in himself or herself (which the Reader's republican democracy would perhaps institute in order to guard against instrumentality, in order to safeguard, in the form of "rights of man and citizen," the incalculability and infinitude of citizen-sovereigns) institutes right means as the only way to abide by it.

In the Editor's writing, by contrast, such abstract means cannot be accepted, for they cannot by their very nature be singular. What is made into such means comes to be infused with an abstract effectivity that makes it fungible across what is different from it—abstract means can only be specific, particular, or general, never singular.[19] This making into means is the force of *sanchakam,* where machinicity works by a mastery, consumption, and subsumption within itself not only of the other that is its object, but also of the figure that deploys it. To this machinicity and repetition, Gandhi also gives the name bhog. Here bhog becomes infinite, and there is little possibility for the difference of either the other or the self.

The Editor suggests moreover that "our ancestors" were already putting in place injunctions that guard against "modern civilization." Here the adjective "modern" in the phrase "modern civilization" or "modern civility" refers not to the "modern" in a chronological sense, but rather to the modern in the conceptual sense of the dominance of an order of abstract means: "modern civilization" is the reform that allows only for the present that is itself, that cannot allow for the otherness of the past or a future, that seeks to reduce all to calculation, and thus erases difference. Here present, past, and future can only be calculable or, more precisely, marked with the immeasurable measure that, as the introduction suggested, distinguishes liberalism.

This making into means is also the death that marks "modern civilization." As the Editor criticizes the third party, a distinction creeps into the text between two deaths, between the violence of law or three and the violence of finitude or two. Recall: "To fight with one another and die was considered a sign of savagery [*janglipan*]. Now that a third person ends my quarrels [*kajiyo patave*], is it any less savagery? Can anybody say that the decision of a third party is always right?" Recall also: "Rather than have us become without strength [*abada*, 'effeminate'], I would prefer to be killed by the arrow of a Bhil."[20]

Here death in a relation of two-ness is affirmed over the life given by law [*kayada*], by the third party. The latter life, the passage seems to argue, will make us *abada*, without strength. And if we attend to the murmurings of the text, it turns out that three-ness, the life of *kayda* or law, also involves a certain kind of death—the death that comes as a cessation. Thus the words and phrases used to describe the work of justice. *Kajiyo patave*— usually, end a quarrel. The word *patavu* carries connotations of ceasing; it can even be an allusive way of referring to killing. Justice, going by this formulation, kills the quarrel. And it kills, moreover, in a distinctive way. *Tharaav*, the term for decision that occurs in the very next sentence, similarly carries connotations not only of judgment, but of a stopping, a cessation, a solidifying, of a death that comes as an end. Two words in quick succession, then, suggest that the justice of law involves a cessation. (The sense of cessation is missing in the English version, which goes: "Is it any the less so, if I ask a third party to decide between you and me? Surely, the decision of a third party is not always right.")

Cessation or ending: from the perspective of colonial law, among the problems with primitive violence is that it cannot bring about a cessation. Its reciprocity is not quite general responsibility but only the prehistory of such responsibility. As such, it is inconclusive in its very finitude: when one killing is met by retaliation, this does not necessarily end matters but leads to escalation, and other deaths. In opposition to this, the justice of law seeks to practice a general responsibility where violence is met by its proper measure, neither less nor excessive. It seeks, put differently, justice conceived in terms of reciprocity, as bringing to an end. After the just violence of law, the wound or grief can remain only as a private matter; there can be no legitimate space for the wound to fester in the public sphere.

Cessation or ending: by contrast, from the perspective that the Editor puts forth here, the reciprocity of the justice of law only makes the third party infinite. It renders all calculable, including the judge. True, this justice would save the life of all the three parties. But what is saved is only a certain kind of life—a life constituted by measure, where measure is made immeasurable, theologized.[21] This life—which prevails in the making infinite of means, or the third party—the Editor refuses.

~

The second element I want to stress is the striking emphasis on limits. What is distinctive for the Editor about "true swaraj" is that bhog is kept within "proper limits." To begin with, "ancestors put limits," they "thoughtfully said that we should do only what can be done with hands and feet." By doing so, they bring courts, lawyers, and doctors within "proper limits."

The emphasis on limits presumes a distinctive concept of violence. Recall the passage also from chapter 10: "all men are not similar or equivalent . . . two persons fight, one or both of them have their heads broken. What justice can a third party do in this?" The next sentence, which is also the final sentence of the chapter in the English version, is: "Those who fight may expect to be injured." Two more sentences, missing from the English, follow in the Gujarati chapter. "When body hits body, there will necessarily be a wound (*nishani*, lit. mark). In this, how can there be justice [*nyaya*]?"

These formulations say: the wound remains, and the justice of the third party cannot erase or resolve it. *Sarkhi mati. Sarkhi:* both equal, and similar. *Mati:* understanding, or even orientation. *Sarkhi mati:* usually, of similar orientation, but potentially, also of equivalent orientation. Between two who cannot depend on similarity or equivalence to settle their disputes, how can there be the justice of the third party?

The incalculable nature of the wound, the way it is inscribed on the body, requires another justice (though justice is a severely inadequate word here). How this other justice must begin is indicated in Gandhi's response to the "Malabar happenings":

What the truth is no one knows. The Hindus say that the Moplah atrocities were indescribable. Dr Mahmud tells me that these have been grossly exaggerated, that the Moplahs too had a grievance

against the Hindus. . . . I merely mention the two versions to ask
the public to conclude with me that it is impossible to arrive at the
exact truth, and that it is unnecessary for the purpose of regulating
our future conduct.

"No one knows"; furthermore, such knowledge is "unnecessary for the
purpose of regulating our future conduct." The impossibility of arriving at
the truth is not only an empirical one, as would have been the case with a
secret truth that, even if not knowable to "Hindus" and "Moplahs" because
of obfuscatory passions, even if not knowable to the public because of
lack of evidence, nevertheless would possess a constative and even performative structure that in principle makes it knowable. Here, by contrast, the impossibility of knowing is of the very structure of the dispute.
There remain two versions, incapable of forming one shared knowledge
that the judge or nationalist public can excavate and pronounce on. "Future
conduct," whatever it be, will have to take this two-ness as its point of
departure.

Moreover, as these formulations also insinuate, relinquishing the third
party does not in itself lead to nonviolence—those who fight may still
"expect to be injured." The remarks on the Bhils and Pindaris also refer
to the unavoidability of violence. To be with the Bhil or Pindari: this is
to accept the possibility of even death at their hands, and to envision a
community and justice that begins from that acceptance. While it is originary, two-ness or finitude can be as violent as nonviolent. This impossibility of justice or nonviolence may be why "true civility" is not portrayed in
utopian terms—fights still take place, justice is only "theek theek" or about
right, and courts, lawyers, and doctor will also not be erased, only brought
within proper limits.

The *nishani*—mark or "wound"—names the way being in its two-ness
or finitude experiences the refusal of equality—whether that refusal comes
in the form of the justice of measure, or killing at the hands of the Bhil. The
wound remains because the refusal of equality is incalculable—the measure of the third party cannot provide recompense for it. This incalculable
refusal of equality, in all its two-ness, constitutes the moment of violence,
and it is intensified when a third party intervenes.

As he emphasizes the incalculability or immeasurability of violence,
two words become ubiquitous in his vocabulary: *rakshasi* and *asuri*, both
of which he usually translates as monstrous, demonic, or evil. The *rakshas*

names, of course, a monstrosity that is opposed to the godly or divine, that is the condensation of the irreligious; hence also perhaps the translation of *rakshasi* as evil. (As the distinctly precolonial and premodern provenance of these two words again suggests, there is nothing necessarily chronologically modern about "modern civility.")[22]

Even satyagraha becomes monstrous when it generates fear as a response rather than surrender without subordination. After Chauri Chauri, thus, Gandhi says: "I know the only thing that the government fears is this monstrous majority that I appear to command. They do not know that I fear it still more than they do themselves. I am literally sick over it. I would feel myself on surer ground if I were spit upon by them."

The terms *rakshasi* and *asuri* are, however, applied especially to that moment of the greatest calculability—"modern civilization." In *Hind Swaraj,* the Editor already describes "modern civilization" as monstrous (though there is no equivalent for this in the Gujarati). From around the mid-teens, and especially after Jallianwala Bagh, he uses the adjectives *rakshasi* and *asuri* quite consistently to describe British rule too.

In Gandhi's writing, then, what is especially terrifying about "modern civilization" is precisely its reluctance to even recognize the incalculable and ineffaceable nature of all violence, including its own. By attempting to respond to the wound with a justice based on measure, it multiplies violence. "Modern civilization" is in this sense marked by the incalculable violence of treating both violence and justice as calculable. Perhaps this is why he can say: "England is not free, but only powerful. . . . To a slave, his master seems free, and he strives to be like the latter. . . . Such a slave never really becomes free."[23]

~

The distinctiveness of Gandhi's emphasis on the limit can be indicated by contrasting it with Emmanuel Levinas's arguments about two-ness. Levinas insists both on a two-ness that does not belong to measure and on the complex relation that this two-ness nevertheless has with three-ness or measure, which the former cannot simply negate or overcome:

> From the first: that is, the self answers "gratuitously," without worrying about reciprocity. This is the gratuitousness of the for-the-other. . . .
>   But now the simplicity of this primary obedience is upset by the third person emerging next to the other; the third person is himself

also a neighbor, and also falls within the purview of the *I's* responsibility. Here, beginning with this third person, is the proximity of a
human plurality. Who, in this plurality, comes first? This is the time
and place of the birth of the question: of the demand for justice!
This is the obligation to compare unique and incomparable others;
this is the moment of *knowledge* and henceforth, of an objectivity
beyond on the hither side of the nakedness of the face; this is the
moment of consciousness and intentionality. An objectivity born
of justice and founded on justice and thus required by the for-the-
other, which is the alterity of the face, commands the *I* . . . .
      Extra-ordinary exteriority of the face. Extra-ordinary, for order
is justice: extra-ordinary or absolute in the etymological sense of
that adjective by virtue of its always being separable from every
relation and synthesis, extricating itself from the very justice in
which that exteriority is involved.[24]

Note the work of two and three here. Levinas's two, the moment of the for-
the-Other, involves an absolute responsibility and allegiance that defies
reciprocity. The encounter of the two with multiplicity produces a third
quite distinct from the juridical third. There are two threes then—those of
the Other, and of law.

And yet here responsibility to the nonjuridical third itself leads to general responsibility or the juridical third. In the face of the originary multiplicity of the Others, of the nonjuridical third, absolute responsibility
leads to the "obligation to compare"—to the reciprocity of general responsibility, the position of the judge. Justice as three follows from the absolute
obligation to the Other. Law itself responds to absolute responsibility: "An
objectivity born of justice and founded on justice . . . commands the I."
Consequently, to affirm only a nonjuridical third would be irresponsible.
This is why Levinas must insist, along with his affirmation of two and the
Other, on the centrality of law, and especially a law that remains open to
absolute responsibility. For him, the liberal state embodies such a law:

> I've told you that justice is always a justice which desires a better
> justice. This is the way that I will characterize the liberal state. The
> liberal state is a state which holds justice as the absolutely desirable
> end and hence as a perfection. Concretely, the liberal state has
> always admitted—alongside the written law—human rights as a

parallel institution. It continues to preach that within its justice there are always improvements to be made in human rights. Human rights are the reminder that there is no justice yet.[25]

Gandhi's way of thinking two-ness suggests two sets of questions for Levinas. First, while the justice of the Other sets the justice of law going, it remains heterogeneous to law, unerased by law's reciprocity. Even after the encounter with the third, the originary two remains—"the extra-ordinary exteriority of the face." Levinas's passage gives a name to that extraordinary exteriority: human rights, or the rights of man. But to conceive of human rights as absolute responsibility—would this not be the "immeasurable pity" the Editor attacks?

Second, in formulations such as these, Levinas no longer regards law as a wound. Where measure springs from absolute responsibility, it becomes the most responsible form of that responsibility. Would not such a defense of law produce the most systematic kind of racism? A racism as or more unforgivable than those that mark classical colonialism, or Heidegger's collusion with Nazism (which so troubles Levinas)? Does this defense allow Levinas by his silence to collude and participate over many decades in Israeli apartheid—a collusion made all the more unforgivable by the fact of his intense awareness of the Nazi genocide?[26] Is Levinas's profound racism a necessary part of his ethics rather than an error or misstep on his part?

~

Because of Gandhi's emphasis on a wound that resists all measure, he has a more critical relation with general responsibility even in its most radically open and cosmopolitan forms, such as that which Levinas discerns in the liberal state and human rights. We received a sense of this already in the previous chapter, in the discussion of the Editor's refusal to admire the "immeasurable pity" that the Reader will practice. A related dimension of that critical relation emerges in his discussion of the railways in chapter 10 of *Hind Swaraj*:

> Man was given intellect that he might know God; man used intellect to forget God. Going by my natural limits, I can serve only those people who stay in nearness to me [*aaspaas vasta manaso*], but I quickly in my conceit discovered that I must with my body serve the whole world [*duniya*]. In doing this, people of many religions and types come together. This burden cannot at all be

lifted by humanity and so it is confounded. By this thinking, you will understand that railways are a destructive means. By using the railways, man [*manas*] has forgotten God. ["I am so constructed that I can only serve my immediate neighbors, but in my conceit I pretend to have discovered that I must with my body serve every individual in the Universe. In thus attempting the impossible, man comes in contact with different natures, different religions, and is utterly confounded. According to this reasoning, it must be apparent to you that railways are a most dangerous institution. Owing to them, man has gone further away from his Maker."]

Here the Editor opposes "thus attempting the impossible" and advocates something apparently limited and even parochial—serving "only those people who stay in nearness to me," or as the English rendering says, "my immediate neighbors." And he attacks as a "conceit" the effort to be responsible "for every individual in the Universe" (as succinct description of the concept of human rights as possible).

Why is this immense responsibility a "conceit"? In what sense is it "the impossible?" And why and how is the apparently parochial responsibility of serving the neighbor preferable? The first question may be rephrased by attending to a suggestive gap between the Gujarati and the English versions. The Gujarati text says: "serve the whole world." Such cosmopolitanism extends the Reader's general responsibility beyond national boundaries to an even larger totality or greater end—"humanity." The English translation says: "serve *every individual* in the Universe." To serve "every individual" would radicalize general responsibility: now violence against an individual or minority can no longer be justified in the name of a greater end, whether humanity or the state.

To rephrase, then: this way of thinking responsibility to every other through measure/law, this way of conceptualizing calculation or measure to the immeasurable or incalculable, why should the Editor describe even such a radicalized general responsibility as a "conceit"?

Here we run up against an ellipsis. Beyond his terse description of its folly ("in thus attempting the impossible"), the Editor says nothing. Again, it remains our task to elicit what happens in the ellipsis. We could start by noting once again that satyagraha and ahimsa are themselves impossible. He objects, then, not to attempting the *impossible*, but to *thus* attempting the impossible.

Thus?—by going beyond the immediate neighbor, by making the body infinite. Perhaps the Editor senses that here a break with general responsibility is impossible. To reprise Levinas, in serving "every individual" we encounter always the problem of multiplicity. Even where justice is immeasurably given to serving "every individual," it must in order to deal with the multiplicity of individuals call forth measure and law. When humans in their immeasurability suffer injustice, not to measure out justice between victims and aggressors would effectively be to authorize and accept violence. Despite its questioning of totality, the practice of responsibility for "every individual in the Universe" must nevertheless measure out its in/finitude among the various calls on it; it cannot give up the making infinite of means that for Gandhi marks "modern civilization." Once again, the very practice of absolute responsibility requires making general responsibility infinite, adopting the measure of the judge.

A further profound irony: the judge, let us not forget, is not merely powerful; he exemplifies the sovereign; he occupies a position inseparable from measure, domination, privilege, and general responsibility. This is why the subaltern, as subaltern, cannot be a judge. Subalterns can be judges only by assuming the powers of those whom they challenge—by becoming like the dominant. In the figure of the judge, responsibility and domination go hand in hand—the only way to be responsible, it turns out, is to dominate, even maybe to colonize.

Also, to adopt the position of the judge is to obscure from oneself several questions: What would be an immeasurability that does not either control or let itself be controlled? That can claim an equality other than that of sovereignty? Any affirmation of responsibility to "every individual in the world" leaves these questions abyssally obscured. Here the "impossible" is conceived from within the problematic of sovereignty.

Put differently, from the perspective enabled by *Hind Swaraj*, to "serve every individual" would be to misunderstand the equality of measure with the immeasurable. Though such service seeks to measure up to and with the immeasurable, it conceptualizes the immeasurable in terms of measure; it is thus marked by "immeasurable pity." And to calculate to or with the incalculable, to measure to or with the immeasurable, would be to obscure two-ness by understanding it in terms of the sovereign third party.

Therefore, satyagrahis strive to inhabit two-ness without resorting to measure or calculation. To do so, they strive to relinquish every form of sovereign power; they cannot become judges. Consequently, they become homeless to every state and sovereign order. "A true pacifist refuses to use the fruit of arms—peace and order. So long as we eat a single grain of wheat grown under the protection of arms we participate in violence. When one realizes this one has to be an exile in one's own country and a rebel."[27]

⌒

But absolute responsibility is homeless in a strange way: though satyagrahis cannot find a home in general responsibility, they do not and cannot reject, overcome, or even disavow it. As is already implicit in his demand for "political swaraj," and as he comes to acknowledge more explicitly by the 1920s, machines, measure, and law too belong to "own hands and feet."[28] In the 1920s, an interviewer asks Gandhi whether he is against machinery. "How can I be when I know that even this body is a most delicate piece of machinery. . . . Ideally, I would rule out all machinery, even as I would reject the very body, which is not helpful to salvation, and seek the absolute liberation of the soul. . . . but machines will remain because, like the body, they are inevitable."[29]

His acknowledgment flows from the very nature of absolute responsibility. In order to surrender to the limit, absolute responsibility must desist from overcoming or mastering that which it confronts. If it did, it would no longer "be" absolute responsibility; rather it would make itself into a sovereign power.

How, then, would satyagraha as an absolute responsibility relate to general responsibility? On the one hand, it must provincialize or more precisely relinquish general responsibility. In other words, satyagraha involves a nonpassage or aporia between absolute and general responsibility.[30] Satyagrahis cannot inhabit general responsibility—they cannot demand political swaraj, machines, or persistence in the body. And yet they do. How? They do so to the extent that they are not satyagrahis, or have not been seized by satyagraha. And they must constantly work to relinquish the being who makes those demands. Indeed, the aporetic relation can be sustained only by making religion an absolute responsibility: where there is general responsibility, then as with Levinas or the Reader, a passage springs up between the two, and the aporia dissolves.

⌒

On the other hand, to relinquish general responsibility is also to simultaneously supplement it with absolute responsibility. Gandhi thus traverses the same terms he questions, imbuing them with an absolute responsibility.

The concept of three now names a multiplicity outside the third party; bhog names the difference proper to satyagraha; the machine now names the repetition proper to satyagraha. Each of these concepts turn out thus have two sources, one general and the other absolute.

The supplementary relation of absolute responsibility with general responsibility is exemplified in the way that Gandhi inflects the word *bhog* with quite another sense. In chapter 1 of *Hind Swaraj*, the Reader criticizes early Congress leaders for being too sympathetic to the British. Disagreeing, the Editor defends Dadabhai Naoroji and other early Congress leaders: "A people who desire to experience swaraj [*swaraj bhogav-va*] cannot afford to despise their elders. When the practice of giving respect goes from us, then we will become useless. *Swaraj* can be experienced [*bhogvi*] only by matured [*peedh*] men, not by frivolous men." Bhog now names, in a sense, the experience of swaraj—the experience of respect for elders in their separation and singularity rather than their specificity. Here the encounter with the other involved in bhog plays out differently: it is no longer about subsumption or consumption.

The very practice of satyagraha involves *bhog* in this other sense. In chapter 17, the Editor remarks:

> That word [*satyagraha*] has come to be applied to the way in
> which, to get their own rights, people have themselves borne
> suffering.... If I do not accept ... [a] law and suffer [*bhogvi*] the
> penalty for breaking it, then I have used soul-force or satyagraha.
> In satyagraha, I give myself in sacrifice [*aapbhog aapu chhu*]. To give
> oneself in sacrifice [*aapbhog aapvo*] is better than giving the other
> in sacrifice [*par-bhog*], this all say. Besides, if the satyagrahi's fight is
> wrong, then only he who fights suffers [*dukh bhogvey chhe*]. So for
> his own error, he himself suffers.... No man can say with certainty
> that a certain activity is bad. But when he thinks it bad, then for
> him it is bad. In such a situation, he should not do it, and should
> suffer the consequences of this. This is the key to satyagraha.

Aapbhog, a phrase that he translates as self-sacrifice, is thus the key to satyagraha. *Aapbhog aapvu chhu:* there is an *aapvu* (etymologically associated with the Sanskrit *arp*, give) of the *aap* (etymologically associated with *atman*, soul) as a sacrifice. Here there occurs a giving of the self to the other as a breaking of the self into two, a break after which there can be no measured return of either the self or the other to themselves. Because of this radical difference that perdures in it, satyagraha is justice.

Two "forms," then, of bhog. The bhog of general responsibility, in its abstraction and care for the whole, immunizes itself against vulnerability, and consumes not only the other but also the self. This bhog, in Gandhi's writings, shears humans away from animals, plants, and things, and places them on the side of machinicity and infinite repetition. The bhog of satya-graha involves a responsibility marked by finitude, or by an openness to and even acceptation of vulnerability. When humans practice this bhog, they are for Gandhi closer to plants and animals, who unlike humans are inescapably marked by finitude.

This bhog of satyagraha, as chapter 7 will argue, involves also a distinc-tive machinicity, because of which Gandhi will enjoin satyagrahis to cipher themselves and behave as machines. For now, I only wish to stress how this other bhog and machinicity also invokes another three-ness. That invoca-tion occurs in a curious way in the Gujarati text of chapter 11 of *Hind Swaraj* and more mutedly in the English version. "The Hindus and Musalmans have fought ['quarreled']. A *trahit manas* ['ordinary man'] will say: now forget about it *[bhooli jao]*; both must be at fault, live in togetherness with each other *[ekbijane sampine rahejo;* 'he will tell them that both must be more or less at fault, and will advise them no longer to quarrel']." The Edi-tor contrasts the behavior of the *trahit manas* with that of lawyers, who would further the fight and take it to the court of law. The most evident etymology for *trahit* would be: *tra* (three) *aahit* (place): the place of the third. And not untypically, the wonderfully idiosyncratic 1904 Gujarati English dictionary by M. B. Belasare (which Gandhi could have had access to while translating *Hind Swaraj*) has the following entry: "A disinterested person; a third party. 2. an umpire; an arbitrator. 3. A stranger. 4.adj. dis-interested; unconcerned. 5. unacquainted; unknown." *Trahit manas,* thus, cannot immediately be lexically distinguished from the *trijo manas* or third party attacked in passages both before and after this one. If at all it can be distinguished, this is in terms of its suggestive etymology: as Tridip Suhrud points out (and Belasare's etymologies support this reading), "*trahit* comes from Sanskrit Tirohita which means among other things concealed, disap-peared; what has disappeared is self hence [*trahit* is also] selfless."[31] There is a resonance between "*trahit*" and the self-less-ness involved in satyagraha (about which more in later chapters).

The chapter on lawyers, then, has two threes, one attacked (*trija manas,* third party) and the other affirmed (*trahit manas,* "ordinary man"). The other three becomes invisible in the English text (through the leap, un-authorized by any dictionaries, which translates *trahit* as "ordinary").[32] The other three does some crucial work: the *trahit manas* says: *ekbijane samp-ine rahejo,* stay in togetherness with each other. Instead of the measure that produces abstract equality and an essential oneness (where "people of many religions and types come together"), broached here is the thought of a multiplicity that remains two, that does not belong to the concept of the third party.

Named in this two and togetherness of *"trahit"* is the challenge of thinking relations across abyssal difference. Where threeness or abstract equality and oneness or substantive commonality are both relinquished as insensitive to abyssal difference, as indifferent so to speak, then that challenge becomes especially vexing. How is justice to be thought here? More-over, how does the satyagrahi enact the aporetic relation of this two, this *trahit* of selflessness, with one and three—with the universalism involved in general responsibility and the third party?

And what is the other universalism (which must struggle to "be" the other of the universalism involved in every ontotheology and logocen-trism) involved in the togetherness of two? How is it nonviolent? If the violence of the wound is pervasive, then what is the difference between the wounds inflicted in and by "true civility" and "modern civility"? Why does Gandhi find the latter wound especially heinous and terrifying? And if "true civility" or two-ness too is marked by the persistence of a wound, when, then, is the sense in which ahimsa is nonviolent?

In responding to these questions, his thinking comes to be marked by a trembling, itself splits into two, and also into three.

CHAPTER 3

The Warrior's Sovereign Gift

I have not got rid of the fear of death, despite much thinking.

—Mohandas Gandhi, "Letter to Raojibhai Patel," March 7, 1914

It individuates in such a way that it makes everyone equal. In being together with death everyone is brought into the "how" that each can be in equal measure; into a possibility with respect to which no one is distinguished; into the "how" in which all "what" dissolves into dust.

—Martin Heidegger, *The Concept of Time*

L ONG BEFORE HE COMES UP with the neologism *satyagraha,* Gandhi is drawn to a complex of related terms, among them, *aapbhog, arpan, balidan, kurbani, tyag,* and *yajna.* He translates all these hardly interchange-able words often as "self-sacrifice." Some of these terms usually refer to sacrifice rather than self-sacrifice, but he insists that while yajna [sacrifice] can have many meanings, "as one's own religion *[swadharma]*" it "has only one meaning," "and that is to be willing to offer one's life for true welfare."[1]

He invokes these terms already in the 1890s, though the earliest sus-tained engagement comes in an essay titled "Self-Sacrifice" in *Indian Opin-ion* in January 1904, which says: "Sacrifice is the law of life. It runs through and governs every walk of life." The essay goes on to cite many cases of "true sacrifice" (Christ, Joan of Arc, the Americans who "bled for their indepen-dence"), and to urge the Indians in South Africa to prepare for self-sacrifice as they launched their struggles.[2]

By the time of *Hind Swaraj,* self-sacrifice has come even more to the fore. In chapter 17, the Editor says: "That people ['nation'] is great which sleeps always with death as its pillow. They have left fear of death, which means they have left fear of everything."[3] Around a decade later, in 1918, when Gandhi's controversial attempts in Kheda district to recruit farm-ers for the British Army meet with little success, he writes to C. F. Andrews: "I find great difficulties in recruiting but do you know that not one man has yet objected because he would not kill. They object because they fear to die. This unnatural fear of death is ruining the nation."[4] And writing in 1921, he remarks: "I have been collecting descriptions of swaraj. One of these would be: swaraj is the abandonment of the fear of death. A nation which allows itself to be influenced by the fear of death cannot attain swaraj, and cannot retain it if somehow attained."[5] Swaraj requires "dying willingly."

It is only to be expected that a thinker of finitude and two-ness should be fascinated by the question of "dying willingly." Self-sacrifice, after all, involves entering into an active relation with the death that is always inescapably one's own finitude; it involves appropriating that death in the way the sacrificer thinks fit—whether by negating, defying, or loving one's own death. And self-sacrifice is for him not only about abandoning fear of one's own death; it is even more about the very distinctive life that emerges from that embrace of death. Here death is no longer a nullity that comes only at the end of life; now it marks life from the beginning.

Indeed, self-sacrifice is universal and profoundly democratic in the sense that not only all humans but all being can offer it. What the Editor says of satyagraha in chapter 17 of *Hind Swaraj* could be said of all self-sacrifice: "Even a man weak in body is capable of offering this resistance. One man can offer it just as well as millions. Both men and women can indulge in it. It does not require the training of an army; it needs no Jiu-Jitsu. Control over the mind is alone necessary." Self-sacrifice, in other words, works with the only "possession," so to speak, that even the most powerless "have"— their own being (though this having occurs in the mode of not having— the converse in other words of Lockean possession and more broadly of agency, which have as their point of departure the assertion that "every man has property in his own person").[6] Nor is self-sacrifice limited to humans: he stresses also the sacrifice of the seed involved in the birth of the plant, the sacrifice of animals to protect their young, and so on.

As Gandhi writes about self-sacrifice, another term comes into play— *abhay* or "fearlessness." In 1916, soon after his return to India, he becomes convinced that abhay is India's most "immediate need." While "in general terms, a proper religious spirit is the greatest and most immediate need," Indians "live in a state of perpetual fear" because this religious spirit is "dormant." Therefore the "spirit of fearlessness" is "the first thing indispensable before we could achieve anything permanent and real."[7] In this striking association, only in the not-ness of putting one's own being at stake is it possible to achieve "anything permanent and real." He notes shortly afterward that when the *Gita* lists the various attributes of the divine heritage, then "among the qualities that make for the religious way of life, this [*abhay*] occupies almost the first place."[8]

But what would be the self-sacrifice required for a life and death that dwells in finitude and two-ness?

The question presses in on Gandhi very forcefully because he is acutely aware that it is not only satyagrahis who practice *aapbhog* or self-sacrifice. In an essay in 1920 titled "The dharma of *aapbhog*," he writes: "Without yajna [sacrifice] this earth cannot exist even for a moment. Before the Turks could conquer Constantinople, they sacrificed innumerable troops and used the corpses as a bridge."[9] Self-sacrifice constitutes modern civility: the British live by it, as do the revolutionary nationalists who are willing to die and kill for their cause; "there is one thing in common between him [the revolutionary] and me—the ability to suffer."[10]

But precisely because self-sacrifice is so pervasive, Gandhi dwells almost obsessively on the question of what is distinctive about the satyagrahi's self-sacrifice. And one key term he draws on is "purity." "Sacrifice to be effective must be backed by the uttermost external and internal purity . . . without the requisite purity sacrifice is no better than a desperate self-annihilation devoid of any merit. Sacrifice must, further, be willing and it should be made in faith and hope."[11] Pure self-sacrifice is again universal, a potentiality borne by all being—plant, animal, human, even perhaps things. In January 1921, for example, he writes: "We have to learn the *mantra* ["secret"] of 'living by dying' [*mariney jivavano*]. The world exists by this mantra. The corn grows only when the seed dies. The child lives only because the mother suffers for it even to the point of death. We eat stolen property if we eat without offering sacrifice. Swaraj can be won only through sacrifice and that sacrifice, that martyrdom, can be acceptable to God only if it is pure [*pavitra*]."[12]

A mantra is both an answer and a question. As an answer, it says: living by dying requires pure sacrifice. Pure sacrifice is the religion that stays in all religions, it is "one's own religion"; it does not only require but is ahimsa and satyagraha. But despite the ubiquity of pure sacrifice, the answer is also a question, since a mantra remains secret, even and especially perhaps from those who offer pure sacrifice. So he always finds himself answering the questions (for himself to begin with, because he does not know): What is this pure self-sacrifice and fearlessness? Why is it synonymous with ahimsa and satyagraha? How to practice it?

∼

His answers repeatedly draw on the figure of the warrior. Indeed, the smell of blood and war hangs heavy over Gandhi's discussions of self-sacrifice. The *Gita,* the text he draws on most, is itself set on the battlefield, with Krishna the charioteer speaking to Arjuna the warrior; any thinking of the sacrifice of the *Gita* is also a thinking of the sacrifice of the warrior. And then, Gandhi himself draws repeatedly on the figures of war and the warrior. He sometimes describes the human body as a "little Kurukshetra" (the battlefield where the war described in the *Mahabharata* takes place), and refers repeatedly to satyagraha against the British as a *dharmayudh* (usually translated as "religious battle"), or writes of the "war of satyagraha."

Almost as soon as Gandhi invents the neologism "satyagraha," he casts the satyagrahi as a warrior. The introduction to his fascinating rendering in 1908 of Plato's "Apology" into Gujarati under the title *Ek Satyavirni Katha* [Story of a Warrior for Truth] describes Socrates (or "Sukrit," as Gandhi writes his name, in keeping with precolonial traditions) as a satyagrahi who "adopted satyagraha against his own people." The title of the translation back into English from Gujarati, possibly given by Gandhi, goes: "The Story of a True Warrior."[13] In this rendering, we can see a new thinking emerge. Whereas in the Gujarati title the warrior fights for truth, in the English title *satyagraha* is the truth of the concept of the warrior.

The warrior is even more prominent in *Hind Swaraj.* In chapter 17 of the English version, responding to a remark from the Reader that satyagraha seems a "splendid weapon of the weak, but that when they are strong they may take up arms," the Editor says: "What do you think? Wherein is courage required—in blowing others to pieces from behind a cannon, or with a smiling face to approach a cannon and be blown to pieces? Who is the true warrior *[ranvir]*—he who keeps death always as a bosom-friend, or he who controls the death of others?"

And from around April 1918, as he gets involved in the satyagraha in Kheda (where many villagers could claim to be Kshatriya—the warrior caste), he comes to describe the satyagrahi as the true warrior, and even to assert a Kshatriya genealogy for ahimsa.[14] In 1920, he asserts: "I claim to be one of the greatest Kshatriyas of India."[15] Also: "nonviolence was taught by a Kshatriya [Krishna?] to a Kshatriya [Arjuna?].[16] "Ahimsa is the religion of a Kshatriya. Mahavira was a Kshatriya, Buddha was a Kshatriya, Rama and Krishna were Kshatriyas and all of them were votaries of ahimsa. We want to propagate ahimsa in their name. But today ahimsa has become the monopoly of timid Vaisyas and that is why it has been besmirched."[17]

"The nonviolence of my conception is the weapon of the strong, of the true Kshatriya."[18]

He even prefers the violence and killing done by warriors to the non-violence of those who are afraid to die. "I want both the Hindus and Mus-sulmans to cultivate the cool courage to die without killing. But if one has not that courage, I want him to cultivate the art of killing and being killed, rather than in a cowardly manner flee from danger. For the latter in spite of his flight does commit mental himsa. He flees because he has not the courage to be killed in the act of killing."[19]

And he dwells on the affinity between the self-sacrifice of two figures— the satyagrahi and the *duragrahi* or arms-bearing warrior. In 1917, in the context of his efforts to recruit soldiers for the war, he explains why he asks the government to give military training. Such training, he explains, is meant for those who do not believe in satyagraha. "The satyagrahi and the *duragrahi* are both warriors. The latter, bereft of his arms, acknowledges defeat, the former never. . . . Anyone who is neither of the two is not a man, for he does not recognize the *atman*. . . . Like a miser his wealth, he tries to save his body and loses all. Such a one does not know how to die. But the armored soldier always has death by him as a companion. There is the possibility of his becoming one day a satyagrahi."[20]

In conjoining self-sacrifice and the warrior, these passages implicitly make two intriguing presumptions. First, abhay or fearlessness works here as the criterion of the political. Writing around the same time, Carl Schmitt locates the criterion of the political in the most intense and extreme rela-tionship, which for him is the friend–enemy distinction. In Gandhi's writ-ing, however, the most intense relationship is abhay, best exemplified in self-sacrifice, and in the relation between oneself and the other that emerges in this moment. Abhay does not allow for subordination—the ones who experience it give up their being rather than accept inequality. In some of Gandhi's formulations at least, the potentiality for abhay marks all being—equally the *duragrahi* and the *satyagrahi,* equally the human and animal. (Schmitt's criterion of the political could well be regarded as a secondary to and derivative of abhay: How can an antagonism be the "most intense and extreme" save in willingness to practice self-sacrifice rather than accept subordination?)

Second, abhay or fearlessness secretes always also the potentiality for sovereign power. The criterion of sovereign power is a fearlessness that sac-rifices the self only in order to better conserve itself, whether by securing its own being or by securing domination over the other. The *duragrahi* or arms-bearing warrior exemplifies this criterion. (If we extend Gandhi's terms, Schmitt's criterion of sovereignty—that the sovereign is he who decides on the exception—would follow from the sovereignty already exercised in securing itself through self-sacrifice.)

Politicalness is perhaps never innocent of sovereign power—in the remarks above for example, *duragrahis* have the potential to become satyagrahi. Indeed, if Gandhi finds the warrior—satyagrahi or *duragrahi*—so unavoidable, that is because condensed in this figure is the fraught and originary co-implication (never identity) of politicalness and sovereignty—a co-implication intimated already in the very word *swaraj*.

This chapter explores how Gandhi thinks the self-sacrifice of the warrior in two ways that shear and rend away from each other. Sometimes he renders it in sublative terms, where the warrior masters his fear of his own death, subsumes within himself without remainder the beings that he dominates in order to secure his own being. At other times he renders it in more intriguing terms—as marked by finitude and two-ness, and relatedly by an economy of the gift, by an immeasurable equality and inequality.

Gandhi's sublative thinking of satyagraha emerges forcefully in his translation of Plato's "Apology." The translation foregrounds, even more than its English source, Socrates' insistence that he has no "fear of death": "to fear death is equal to [*barobar*] claiming the pomp of knowledge. For who has discovered for certain that death is a thing to be afraid of? Why should we not believe that death is the greatest good that can happen to men [*manas*]? ... If I have any wisdom, it is this: I claim to know nothing about death."[21]

Socrates' absence of fear of death follows from his questioning. This questioning, this principle of the question, is the wisdom that sets him apart from everyone else. When the question becomes a principle in this manner, then it does not simply desire answers, or a positive knowledge that dispels ignorance. Rather than seeking the truth, here the question is itself the truth, always dispelling the "pomp of knowledge." If Socrates does not fear the nonbeing that death usually symbolizes, this is because the being of the question sublates into it even the apparent nonbeing of death.

The fearlessness of the question exemplifies here the self-sacrifice of the warrior. And such fearlessness also springs from a love—in the *Phaedo*, the other dialogue in the volume from which Gandhi likely translates the

"Apology," their love of wisdom *(philo-sophia)* makes philosophers fearless. (The subsequent history of fear and fearlessness overlaps with the history of Western philosophy itself: Kant in "What Is Enlightenment?" describes "Dare to know" as the motto of the Enlightenment; Hegel, that last great metaphysician, associates the emergence of the master-slave dialectic, and for that matter of conceptuality itself, with the slave consciousness experiencing a fearlessness that comes from being "seized with dread; for it has experienced the fear of death," and then shedding that fear (this distinguishes the slave from the master, who is fearless in the sense of not having experienced fear);[22] Arendt, reflecting on the totalitarian regimes that were quite the equal of British colonialism in their violence, writes: "Fear and the impotence from which fear springs are antipolitical principles and throw men into a situation contrary to political action."[23]

If Gandhi finds his Socrates' fearlessness so attractive, this may have been because he too often yearns for a similar fearlessness—one that denies the nonbeing of death, that practices a self-sacrifice marked by the sublation of death. In a speech he gives on the *shradh* [death anniversary] of the Indian nationalist "Deshbandhu" C. R. Das, for instance, he draws on the *Gita* and remarks:

> But what I want to do is to explain to you the meaning of death. If you believe with me that the *Gita* is an allegory *[rupak]*, you will also be able to understand the meaning of death as explained in it:
>
>> What is nonbeing is never known to have been, and what is being *[sat]* is never known not to have been. Of both these the secret has been seen by the seers of the truth.
>
> This verse contains the whole meaning. Verse after verse states that the body is *asat* [untruth/nonbeing]. . . . But there are probably no other people who fear death and cry and grieve over it as much as we do. In the *Mahabharata*, in fact, it is stated that lamentation after someone's death gives pain to the departed soul, and the *Gita*, too, was composed to remove the fear of death. . . . The more I think about the ceaselessly active life of Deshbandhu, the more I feel that he is alive today. While he lived in the body, he was not fully alive, but he is so today. In our selfishness, we believed that his body was all that mattered, whereas the *Gita*

teaches—and I understand the truth of this more clearly as days pass—that all worry about a perishable thing is meaningless, is so much waste of time.

Nonbeing simply does not exist, and Being never ceases to exist.[24]

Both arguments—his own, and those made by his Socrates—reject the association of death with nonbeing in the sense of privative nullity. Both arguments also respond by insisting that being persists even beyond death; both share an emphasis, organized quite differently of course, on the transcending of finite life by the infinitude proper to the human. Within this problematic, if swaraj is the abandonment of the fear of death, this is so because only by dying for a larger entity can these transcendent and infinite entities like the nation live; here the nationalist dies into the nation. Thus, during his campaigns in 1918, soon after the first Kheda satyagraha, to recruit soldiers for the British Indian Army, he tells peasants that "soldiers' death on the battle-field makes them immortal, if the scriptures are right, and becomes a source of joy and pride to those left behind."[25] At work here, indeed, is what in Bataille's terms could be described as a restricted economy—an economy where all exchange is productive, including death.[26]

Such sublative self-sacrifice is at work in the bravery of both the English and the revolutionaries. Of course, Gandhi does distinguish between the two. "The English are both a timid and a brave nation," the Editor says in chapter 15 of Hind Swaraj. The description is symptomatic of Gandhi's skepticism about the ubiquitous ontotheology that he would have unsystematically encountered in European literature of the time. That ontotheology assumes that there is a Western tradition of self-sacrifice, of which modern Western European polities are the latest exemplifications. In these modern polities, it is assumed, self-sacrifice founds the political, if necessary through revolution, and also saves it in moments of danger. In the process, self-sacrifice is sublated and spiritualized into a distinctive order of everyday life—one organized around the interdependence between political society or the public realm where the rights of citizen and self-sacrifice prevail, and civil society or the social and private realms where the rights of man and self-interest prevail.[27]

Gandhi is critical of such narratives about a modern public sphere organized around self-sacrifice. Symptomatic of this is the Editor's scathing dismissal of English newspapers, English public opinion, and the English parliament. As we might extrapolate from that dismissal, Gandhi finds it evident that a politics of self-interest has come to dominate the public realm. And the dominance of self-interests, which are organized by prudent calculation and recoil from self-sacrifice, makes the English timid.

By contrast, though the revolutionary is part of "modern civility," he is constituted—like the satyagrahi—by the demand for a constant self-sacrifice and fearlessness. Disagreeing with a correspondent who attributes cowardice to the Indian nationalists who espoused violence, Gandhi writes: "The writer pays poor compliment to the party of violence or by whatever name it may be called, when he imputes to them fear of death. They forfeited their lives when they dedicated themselves to their creed. That they keep themselves in hiding does not mean that they fear death, but it means that they want to hang on to life as long as possible so as to carry out their project."[28] In other words, the heroic nationalists also live a life that is after death. Though they evade capture by hiding and so on, they do so in the spirit of self-sacrifice—so as to better serve their cause. Even those nationalists who renounce violence may still live this sublative life. He cites Tilak and Gokhale as "instances of non-revolutionary patriots who gave their lives for the country.... [They] died for their country. They worked in almost total disregard of their health and died much earlier than they need have. There is no necessary charm about death on the gallows; often such death is easier than a life of drudgery and toil in malarious tracts."[29] Here, even if he questions the death involved going to gallows, the life he contrasts to it is not necessarily less sublative.

～

Some of his readings of *brahmacharya* (conventionally "celibacy") indicate how Gandhi conceives the satyagrahi's self-sacrifice in terms of this restricted and sublative economy. Already while in South Africa, he comes to realize "how indispensable it *[brahmacharya]* was to self-realization [*ishwardarshan,* vision of God]."[30] He continues in later years to describe it as "the royal road to self-realization or attainment of Brahman."

Brahmacharya for him is more than the practice of celibacy. "Let us remember the root meaning [*mool arth*] of 'brahmacharya.' *Charya* means 'course of conduct'; *brahmacharya,* 'conduct adapted to the search of Brahman, that is, Truth.' From this root meaning arises the special meaning, viz., control of all the senses. We must entirely forget the incomplete definition which restricts itself to the sexual aspect only."[31] Here *brahmacharya* comes to name the state of being "free from desire," which leads to moksha conventionally, spiritual liberation from the mortal cycle of birth, death, and rebirth).

In the canonical texts that Gandhi relies on, moreover, *brahmacharya* involves a mastery of the self so as to be free from desire. Conceived this way, it is quite assimilable to the being after death sought by Gandhi's Socrates, or the Gandhi of the *shradh* speech for the Deshbandhu. The *brahmachari* does not fear death because he gives himself to Brahman; death is only a "portal to life eternal"—the English translation in one case of the Gujarati phrase "mantra of living by dying."[32]

Similarly, the Editor remarks in chapter 17: "To become a warrior [*ranvir*]—it is not as though everybody can do so as soon as they wish to. A warrior [*ladvaiya*] will have to observe *brahmacharya*." Indian classical traditions certainly support this argument. It may even resonate etymologically. The Editor uses the word *vir* by itself to refer to the warrior but also as a suffix in the words *satyavir* and *ranvir*. And the *brahmachari* is one who retains his *virya* (semen). Gandhi writes in 1913: "He who has conserved his generative fluid is known as *viryavan*, man of strength."[33] In many of his writings, he reverts to the need to "conserve the vital fluid." In making these remarks, he draws on the many Hindu texts which insist that it requires enormous male energy to produce semen, and that to expend it is to lose that energy, or "lose stamina"—Gandhi's translation of the word *avirya*. Also, to conserve semen is to be sublated into a larger spiritual and social order, where the warrior dies for a cause larger than himself.

When conceived this way as sublative self-sacrifice, satyagraha once again becomes indistinguishable from the liberal concept of passive resistance. Gandhi tries in later years to maintain the distinction by suggesting that passive resistance is a "weapon of the weak or the voteless," used only because of the pragmatic recognition that they are too weak to used armed force.[34] Thus, while passive resistance "may be offered side by side with the use of arms" and involves the idea of "harassing the other party," satyagraha is opposed to harassment and the force of arms. Relatedly, "while there is no scope for love in passive resistance, satyagraha does not have any place for hatred."[35]

But as the discussion of Habermas and Rawls in chapter 1 should remind us, this is an inadequate description of passive resistance. Passive resisters also radicalize self-sacrifice by dying themselves instead of killing their opponents, by affirming not only their but also their opponents' agency and rights—they practice an autoimmunity that is no longer either suicide or murder. They are impelled, even compelled, to do so by their love of republican democracy. And in dying for republican democracy this way, passive resisters exemplify the most democratic moment of republican democracy.

Could it be this Socratic Gandhi who suggests that the *Gita* is written to remove fear of death and that the *Mahabharata* does not allow for lamentation? Where self-sacrifice is part of such a restricted and sublative economy, death becomes the opening onto a higher life, and there is no place or need for grief. There is thus the constant insistence, in almost all his explicit formulations about grief and lamentation, on the need to overcome them and make them external. As in the speech at the Deshbandhu's *shraddh,* he dismisses grief for "this mortal body" insisting that what is eternal survives death.

~

By the time of *Hind Swaraj,* Gandhi inadvertently displaces this sublative understanding of *brahmacharya* and satyagraha with a conservative understanding. This latter understanding too draws on the figure of the *brahmachari* and is, without the slightest doubt, as profoundly masculine as the concept of the transcendent *brahmachari* that it displaces. Nevertheless, a significant shift takes place here: now it turns out that the warrior has his own nonsublative encounter with death, one marked by conservatism (including the conserving of semen) rather than sublation.

This second concept of the warrior—the warrior as the truth of *brahmacharya,* rather than the other way round—organizes his later affirmation of the satyagrahi as the true warrior. In order to elicit its distinctiveness, perhaps we can take some initial cues from his discussions of *dharmayudh*—a word often used to describe the battle at Kurukshetra in the *Mahabharata,* and which can only very poorly be translated as "righteous war." Such a word can only be misunderstood within a liberal problematic (as indeed a comparable term, *jihad,* has been) to mean the pursuit of an end authorized by religion or duty (that is, by a force not amenable to reason) and that may therefore be pursued religiously (here, by any means possible, since the end is unconditionally important). This misunderstanding is not merely an error. It occurs because liberalism encounters a strangeness it cannot fathom when evaluating *dharmayudh* in its terms—those of a calculable general responsibility, of rule-bound means and autonomous ends.

Gandhi's understanding of *dharmayudh* emerges especially forcefully in 1928, when he compares two alternative translations (made presumably by associates) of an article title, "*Nidaan dharmayudh karo.*" He suggests that the translation "Fight Square If You Must" is superior to the one in the authorized translation, "At Least Fight a Religious Battle."[36] The basic rule of conduct of a *dharmayudh*, then, is to "fight square," or to practice an equality with the enemy. He could possibly have found many passages in the *Mahabharata* to support his reading. In the opening passages of the *Bhishma Parva* (the sixth book of the *Mahabharata*), before the battle begins, the commanders meet and agree on several battle codes. These provide the necessary equality required of combatants, stating that those engaged in combat will only fight their equals and will never engage in combat against unequal opponents. Though even the most virtuous go on to violate these codes (as, for example, Yudhisthira, who as Gandhi notes tells a lie to win a crucial battle), nevertheless in Gandhi's concept of *dharmayudh*, this intimation of equality sets the life and death of the warrior apart from all privative or sublative forms of dying.[37]

What can equality among warriors mean here when there is no common measure? Three arguments run through Gandhi's remarks about the warrior or the Kshatriya.

First, the warrior is fearless not in the sense that death sublates him into a being beyond death (that is, nation, salvation, and so on), but in the sense that he practices an equality with his own death. The very dharma of the warrior is to give himself to his own death, to keep his death as a constant prospect. Contrast this argument with that ventured, for example, by Levinas, who suggests: "Prior to death there is always a last chance; this is what heroes seize, not death. . . . Death is thus never assumed, it comes."[38] Gandhi's readings suggest that though the warrior does seek to survive the battle, and in this sense embraces not death but the last chance before death, such a correct statement would gloss over what is constitutive of the warrior. It would continue to think death privatively or sublatively—as that finitude which takes life away, or as that which has to be transcended for a being beyond it. (I do not speak here in an anthropological or sociological spirit. If that were the case, it would be easy enough to multiply examples of South Asian warrior cultures around both a transcendental afterlife and a privative death.)

Rather, what constitutes the warrior is that he assumes his own death. The warrior lives only after having given himself to his own death; the warrior "is" the one who has received himself back from his own death.[39]

Unlike the *brahmachari*, who surrenders his life as a sublation to a greater cause (whose life is not valuable compared to this greater cause, in which he can live), the warrior loves his life. But the life he loves is marked by sovereign freedom. In order to *secure*—and that word is very appropriate here—this life, he must give himself to his own death. As such, what is thought here is not only the proper death but, more important, a distinctive life, marked by a freedom that calls for more thought.

What is this life the warrior receives? The warrior has received himself back from death. But death is a peculiar limit. Given to his own death, the warrior no longer "is." In this life, perseverance in being is no longer dominant. Being a warrior is no longer about being, and above all not about mastering death so as to allow a being to exist beyond death. The warrior has been separated from his being in the most radical manner possible—by giving himself to his nonbeing.

Of this radical separation, there can be no measure, for there no longer "is" something substantive to be measured. (Hence also the centrality of finitude in Gandhi's writing—only in finitude can this separation be suffered: what is infinite will transcend this separation.) The warrior's life is immeasurable not because his life has been objectively promulgated as an infinite end (as in the case of human rights), or because he is subsumed within a transcendent and infinite end (such as the nation), but because he receives life from and through an equality with his own death, which is always immeasurable to him. The warrior lives thus a life of immeasurable equality.

By doing so, moreover, he breaks with the problematic of instrumental or (in the case of autonomy) calculable means and ends. Because he no longer seeks to be, the warrior is not either an end who masters the means or a cause that effects the end. Marked by sacrifice, he is immeasurably given to the tasks he seeks to accomplish.

Second, the warrior's immeasurable equality is organized always as a gift—and more precisely as the gift of sovereign power, if one may resort to a profoundly paradoxical locution. The gift, as a vast literature has taught us, is quite different from a commodity: while transactions around the latter involve calculable goods and power, transactions around the former involve incalculable goods and power. (This can of course only be said schematically: there is no purely calculable commodity, as the phenomenon of commodity fetishism should suffice to remind us.) And this incalculability takes two forms—those of the pure gift and the sovereign gift.

The pure or free gift, as Derrida points out, "interrupts economy." It "opens the circle so as to defy reciprocity or symmetry, the common measure." "If the figure of the circle is essential to economics, the gift must remain *aneconomic*. Not that it remains foreign to the circle, but that it *keeps* a relation of foreignness to the circle." "For there to be a gift, there must be no reciprocity, return, exchange, countergift, or debt. If the other *gives* me *back* or *owes* me or has to give me back what I give him or her, there will not have been a gift, whether this restitution is immediate or whether it is programmed by a complex calculation of a long-term deferral or differance." The donee thus cannot give back anything to the donor.[40] At its purest, I will be suggesting throughout the book, the unconditional gift requires the relinquishment and forgetting of domination and subordination—of sovereign power in both its statist and everyday forms; it keeps in a relation of foreignness to sovereign power.

But a crucial strand in Marcel Mauss's argument is that the sovereign gift usually dominates the pure gift: "Prestations which are in theory voluntary, disinterested and spontaneous" "are in fact obligatory and interested. The form usually taken is that of the gift generously offered; but the accompanying behavior is formal pretence and social deception, while the transaction itself is based on obligation and economic self-interest."[41]

Bataille's discussion of the potlatch indicates how the sovereign gift creates and sustains power. While the potlatch involves excess and is "useless," the excess and uselessness he identifies is not nothing. Rather, it initiates a reciprocity outside calculation. "But the gift would be senseless (and so we would never decide to give) if it did not take on the meaning of an acquisition. Hence giving must become *acquiring* a power. Gift-giving has the virtue of a surpassing of the subject who gives, but in exchange for the object given the subject appropriates the surpassing." "Potlatch is, like commerce, a means of circulating wealth, but it excludes bargaining. More often than not it is the solemn giving of considerable riches, offered by a chief to his rival for the purpose of humiliating, challenging and obligating him." The potlatch is in this sense the "gift of rivalry."[42]

In the South Asian traditions that Gandhi works with, similarly, the gift is central to the constitution and exercise of sovereign power. We could multiply examples of this, but suffice for now to recall the many Indian narratives where kings give and receive gifts. Through the gift, might one say, sovereign power is made more than calculable—it comes to be imbued with its profoundly violent incalculability. Here the gift organizes the conservative thinking of the proper. The king's gifts not only consolidate his power but uphold varnadharma as the dharma or law-duty-religion that assigns people to their *varna* or caste and its associated obligations. And the sovereign is the first giver in a reciprocal order: recipients recognize the gift as such, and the resultant obligation keeps them in their place; the donor recognizes himself in the gift and gives back to himself symbolically what he thinks he has given. (This is why subordinate groups must, when they question authority, also refuse gifts from the dominant.)[43]

The warrior is an exemplary bearer of the sovereign gift. In order to practice his equality with death, he must fight and kill only equals. By doing so, by fighting in a way that makes his opponents equal, he makes his own death a constant prospect. This is a repeated theme in Gandhi's remarks. In chapter 15 of *Hind Swaraj*, the Editor criticizes the extremists who call for the assassination of key Englishmen as a way of securing swaraj. Speaking of Madan Lal Dhingra, the revolutionary who in 1909 shoots and kills a British official, the Editor says:

> The murders that Dhingra did, the murders that have happened in Hindustan—it is a big mistake [*bhool*] to believe that there will be any benefit from them. I do consider Dhingra to be a patriot, but his love was blind. He sacrificed [*bhog*, "gave'] his own body in the wrong way. So there can only be loss of benefit."

What is the "wrong way" in which Dhingra gives his body? For Gandhi, Dhingra is violent not because he uses arms, but because he does not treat his opponents as equals:

> If I kill someone in my own house without a warning—someone who has done me no harm—I cannot but be called a coward. There is an ancient custom among the Arabs that they would not kill anyone in their own house, even if the person be their enemy. They would kill him after he had left the house and after he had been given time to arm himself. Those who believe in violence ["that violence will lead to good"] would be brave men if they observe these rules when killing anyone. Otherwise, they must be looked upon as cowards. It may be said that what Mr. Dhingra did, publicly and knowing full well that he himself would have to die, argues courage of no mean order on his part. But as I have said

above, men can do these things in a state of intoxication, and can
also banish the fear of death. Whatever courage there is in this is
the result of intoxication, not a quality of the man himself. A man's
own courage consists in suffering deeply and over a long period.
That alone is a brave act which is preceded by careful reflection.[44]

"In this the courage is that of the intoxication, not of the man." Gandhi's
warrior seeks a death quite distinct from the death of the one who dies
fearlessly in the name of a cause. In intoxication, force may directed at an
unequal—here, for example, an unarmed opponent.

But what does equality with the opponent or enemy mean here? We
often read equality in terms of common measure, where equal warriors
would be those with equal power. We could, for example, so read the
Bhishma Parva, where equals are understood as those with comparable
weapons and equipment. But the passages above suggest that equality in
the absence of such common measure can only mean equality with reference to a death that is always their own, even as it provides a relation
between the two combatants. In being equally given to their own deaths—
which can never be a shared and substantive measure—the warrior and
his enemy give an immeasurable equality to each other.

This equality is especially evident where the warrior fights with the
knowledge from the beginning that he will lose. In still wagering his death
in the battle, he refuses to accept subordination to the other, and becomes
equal to his enemy. Another example: even where the warrior secures
domination over the other, he does so only by means of his "own hands
and feet," refusing to infinitize himself by acquiring or deploying whatever
weapons may be necessary to win.

The equal relation between the combatants also makes the battlefield a
site that refuses every totalization, that cannot be subsumed or dialecticized
into narratives about the victory or defeat of one of the actors. As such, this
violence, however immense and epic, is nevertheless finite and travels by
analogy and metaphor rather than by causality and the distinctive infinitude
that causality involves. And precisely because measure is impossible here,
there can be no justice of the third party. There is always only the battlefield itself—the site of a violence that cannot be subsumed, that always
persists. Indeed, this impossibility of subsumption marks the *Mahabharata*
itself, which is centered on a battlefield—Kurukshetra. In the battlefield,
the warrior does not give his life for a larger or transcendent cause. Rather,

he gives up his life because that is what constitutes a warrior. In his very prodigality with his life, in giving himself to his death, he practices the terrifyingly immeasurable reciprocity, the potlatch, that makes him a warrior.

~

Because of his equality, the warrior gives his life not as a gift to a transcendent entity or even to those whom he protects; rather, he gifts it to the one he battles against. Thus an emphasis on being and finding a worthy opponent occurs repeatedly in Gandhi's writings. Consider the remarks he makes in a speech in Dakor: "Though I criticize the English Sultanate ["British Empire"], I also call it fearless. The British love their country. It is their evil [rakshashi, demonic] tendencies which are to be shunned. I would even admire Ravana's courage. Tulsidas has said that, if one must have an enemy, let him be like Ravana. To fight against Lakshmana, one must be an Indrajit."[45]

The gift a worthy opponent gives to the warrior by engaging him— whether in battle or peace—is equality to the warrior's own death. This is not a constative and formal equality that the warrior already has. Rather, immeasurable equality has to be received from the other (beginning with the other that one oneself is) as a gift. Without receiving it from the other, even where the other seeks to kill him, the warrior cannot claim an immeasurable equality with the other. Perhaps one should say then: immeasurable equality is not something a warrior first has and then gives to his enemy— he receives it rather in fighting his enemy as an equal. This is the gift of sovereignty that warriors always give each other, that warriors can always receive only from the other who is immeasurably their equal. In the *Bhishma Parva,* which so fascinates Gandhi, Bhishma perhaps seeks that gift when he tries to goad Krishna into taking his life. Losing his life to a godly figure like Krishna would have allowed Bhishma to achieve an illustrious equality to his own death.

We arrive thus at a curious insight, one foreign to Gandhi's explicit formulations and yet in another way very faithful to them: the warrior is not only equal to his own death, but can receive his equality only from the other. This equality is the warrior's glory. Such glory must not be confused with power, even if it traverses much the same terrain. (As Bataille remarks in a related context: "*Glory,* the consequence of a superiority, is itself something different from an ability to take another's place and seize his possessions: it expresses a movement of senseless frenzy, of measureless expenditure of energy, which the fervour of combat presupposes.")[46]

The distinctiveness of the warrior's immeasurable equality with his enemy can be elicited by contrasting it with the equality purportedly practiced in modern warfare. The modern general must, in principle at least, respect the enemy combatant's human rights; these rights are laid down in protocols such as the Geneva Convention. Yet these protocols institute only a measurable and abstract equality, a baseline that must be respected under all circumstances. Beyond this abstract equality, modern generals must measure so perfectly that they master the enemy without bringing their own deaths into play, without making their opponents into equal combatants. Indeed, it is precisely the warrior's immeasurable equality that the modern generals must deny to their enemies.

To the extent that they follow these protocols, they deny immeasurable equality not only to their enemy but even to themselves. Even where modern soldiers are outmeasured and have to become heroic, wagering their own lives, their claim is not to immeasurable equality with death. Rather, they give their lives to an infinitude—the nation usually—which is greater than either themselves or the enemy. As such, to the extent that they work within a modern understanding of violence in terms of means and ends (and we shall see that it is impossible to work purely within such an understanding), what these soldiers can never give to themselves or their enemies is immeasurable equality. Even when modern warfare involves "dying for," such dying occurs for and toward an infinitude. In Gandhi's terms, the modern soldier-hero must, like Dhingra, always "give his body wrongly." As with Dhingra, the soldier-hero's courage is that of the intoxication, not of the man. Where modern soldiers are immeasurable in the sense of seeking to master measure, their fearlessness has little in common with the fearlessness that constitutes the warrior's immeasurable equality.

The warrior's protocols of immeasurable equality sustain a relationship of love between friends and respect between opponents. Respect here springs from the equality that prevails between the warrior and his enemy because both put into play their own deaths. Where there is such equality, then even when the warrior seeks to kill his enemy, there is always the possibility of another relation with the enemy—one of sovereign daya ["compassion"], forgiveness, repentance, and forgetting. Some combination of these elements, Gandhi could well have argued, organizes the suspension of the battle in the *Bhishma Parva* while Bhishma lies dying.

Gandhi's thinking of the warrior here resonates strikingly with Nietzsche's remarks in the *Genealogy*:

How much reverence has a noble man for his enemies!—and such reverence is a bridge to love. For he desires his enemy for himself, as his mark of distinction; he can endure no other enemy than one in whom there is nothing to despise and very much to honor. In contrast to this, picture "the enemy" as the man of ressentiment conceives him—and here precisely is his deed, his creation: he has conceived "the evil enemy," "the Evil One."[47]

That resonance may be amplified by a contrast with Schmitt's friend-enemy distinction. For Schmitt, the enemy may be mastered or killed without being granted equality. Despite his critique of liberalism, and of Hegel, Schmitt conceptualizes life here in a way that remains entirely within a sublative tradition. For Gandhi's or Nietzsche's warrior, by contrast, life itself emerges in an equality with death. And the enemy and friend are no longer categorically different; rather, both belong together. (As such, from the perspective opened up by Gandhi's and Nietzsche's emphasis on the warrior, Schmitt's politics appears more an authoritarian liberalism than a conservatism.)[48]

In sum, the warrior lives a life that is not after death but by death—using the word "by," to echo Isabel Hofmeyr, in its "full prepositional and adverbial range."[49] This is why the warrior never only "dies for" something: his death does not lead on to something; rather, he always already stays with his death. In this life by death, he becomes capable of relations of immeasurable equality not only with enemies but also with friends. Unlike the classical *brahmachari*, who sacrifices his life because he is repelled by it and seeks something higher, the warrior sacrifices his life even as he loves it. And he sacrifices it not for something he loves more, but because it is in sacrificing his life that he can love it. In sacrificing it, he creates a life marked by a distinctive affect and love (and relatedly enmity) for concrete persons—an affect marked by the eschewal of calculable relations, constituted by an immeasurable giving and taking. Only in an assumption of one's own death, whether massively as with the warrior or in a thousand small ways, is it possible at all to love.[50] As such, in Gandhi's writing, to love is always to have also loved one's own death, to have refused to persist in being.

(It is tempting to speculate that Gandhi is hostile to romantic love not only for the reasons he explicitly conceives, but even more because it bears the everyday possibility of simultaneously inhabiting immeasurable equality and inequality: lovers are both immeasurably equal to each other, and at the very least immeasurably exclude from this equality all those who are not their lovers. Such romantic love would be especially threatening to the conservatism that Gandhi sets out from, because romantic love is much more difficult to read in terms of the *brahmachari* or celibate. But romantic love is not necessarily opposed to the absolute equality his writing opens up to. It would be very interesting indeed to explore the dissemination that marks his descriptions of satyagrahis as "lovers": though in his explicit formulations they are certainly not romantic lovers, this is not a possibility he can consistently keep at bay.)

In the immeasurable equality of warriors and lovers, whether they be combatants or friends, we are returned also to the tropes of "true civility" and two. Does not the figure of the warrior organize the Editor's remarks noted in the previous chapter? "Our ancestors" who practiced "true civility" were certainly not satyagrahis. Could we not describe them as warrior-sovereigns? And what of this? "Two persons fight, one or both of them have their heads broken. What justice can a third party do in this? Those who fight may expect to be injured. When body hits body, there will necessarily be a wound. In this, how can there be justice?"

~

But the warrior's immeasurable equality, the gift of sovereignty that he receives from his opponents, is also, third, simultaneously an immeasurable inequality. In 1908, again referring to Lakshman and Meghnad, two key figures from the *Ramayana,* Gandhi says in a letter to his nephew Maganlal Gandhi:

> Lakshman and Indrajit were both *brahmacharis* and had conquered sleep and were therefore equally valorous. But the valour of the former was divine, while that of the latter ungodly [*asuri,* demonic]. This means that the vow of *brahmacharya* and other vows are holy and bring happiness only when they are taken as a spiritual discipline. If resorted to by a demon, they only add to misery. This is a very serious statement to make; but all the same, it is no doubt true. [*Missing in English translation: Ema shanka jaraye nathi:* There can be no doubt in this matter] Lord Patanjali has shown this very well in his Yogadarshan. This is the thing our religion teaches us.[51]

Recognizing and perhaps recoiling from the radicalism of his words, Gandhi describes his pronouncement as a "very serious statement to make" but adds that it is nevertheless "the thing our religion teaches us." And serious it is. Here an inversion occurs that he also recoils from (never before or after, to the best of my knowledge, does he make any comparable statement about *brahmacharya* or the warrior). No longer is *brahmacharya* a way to Brahman or Being, no longer does it ground the warrior's ethics, and no longer is it even a way to realize ahimsa. Equally the greatest violence and the greatest nonviolence, equally demonic and godly, *brahmacharya* now becomes preethical—a moment before and necessary to both ethics and the violation of ethics. Moreover, given that the warrior is the truth of the *brahmachari*, the warrior's immeasurable equality too becomes preethical.

Here, we should not think preethicality instrumentally, where the warrior has, through his austerity and discipline, acquired a great force to be used as a means for either good or bad ends. It is not at all the case that immeasure is a general category of which equality and inequality are merely forms. Rather, the warrior's immeasurable equality is preethical because it is also an immeasurable inequality. Warriors offer their lives to each other in the pursuit of sovereign power over each other. Even with his enemy, with whom he acknowledges an immeasurable equality, the warrior's practices must necessarily obscure that very equality. He practices equality with the enemy only momentarily. Though he stays with his own hands and feet in order to be equal to the enemy, he *wagers* his death—he fights to win or secure an immeasurable domination over the enemy.[52] Even when he has no chance of winning, in the very process of being defeated he asserts his mastery over the other who is himself, and who would prefer to die rather than accept subordination.

Here equality involves becoming equal to inequality. Consider the account in the *Mahabharata* of Bhishma's death, which Gandhi never alludes to but which he would doubtless have been aware of given his fondness for the text. Bhishma dies following a battle with Shikhandi, whom he chooses not to fight against. As a woman in a previous birth, Shikhandi is unequal to Bhishma, and Shikhandi's skill in weapons, even if it were to be greater than Bhishma's, cannot overcome this inequality. Thus, Bhishma must let himself be killed rather than fight Shikhandi—that is his way of practicing equality. By dying, he becomes equal not only to his own death, but equal also to the inequality that marks his relation with Shikhandi. Such equality of inequality is necessarily profoundly violent, as most famously illustrated in the demand that Dronacharya, teacher in the *Mahabharata* to both the Pandavas and Kauravas, makes for the thumb of his low-caste disciple, Eklavya. Bhishma's and Dronacharya's actions work with an understanding of varnadharma as an order where each caste is equal to its inequality, and relations between castes are centered around this "equality."

This, then, is the paradox that Gandhi encounters as he thinks the warrior's equality, the gift of sovereignty. Even as it exits from the instrumental or calculable logic of means and ends, and relatedly from the violence involved in abstraction and measure, that exit only opens onto another violence—an immeasurable violence and indeed inequality. This inequality is not secondary; it is coeval to and constitutive of his equality.

~

Is not this immeasurable equality-inequality at work everywhere in the traditions we describe with the shorthand "conservative"? What sets the various conservatisms apart from calculable humanisms, after all, if not an insistence that humans are immeasurably given to their finitude, to some forms of being—whether caste, class, gender, race, culture, time, or place? And that these are differences that cannot be overcome, inheritances that cannot be disavowed?

Conservatism marks the warrior's politics: his task is to conserve the incommensurable differences between groups and individuals. So it is that Dronacharya must ask for Eklavya's thumb, that Bhishma must die rather than fight Shikhandi, and so on. The warrior-*brahmachari*, in all his immeasurable equality-inequality, is also conservative in a most material sense of the word. Recall: "He who has conserved his generative fluid is known as *viryavan*, a man of strength."[53] Or again in an essay in 1944: the *brahmachari* "has so controlled his sexual instinct that he never gets erections. He does not become impotent for lack of the necessary secretions of sexual glands. But these secretions in his case are sublimated into a vital force pervading his whole being." As such, the *brahmachari's* condition should not be confused with the "pitiable state" of those who have "become impotent or are on the way to become so for loss of the necessary secretions," for the "cultivated impotency of the man, whose sexual desire has been burnt up and whose sexual secretions are being converted into vital force, is wholly different."[54]

To sustain his conservative order, the warrior makes a potlatch of his life, becomes immeasurably equal to it. But potlatch secretes its own immeasurable inequality; it sets in place a reciprocal and substantive order. As such, the warrior's potlatch is the gift of rivalry (contrary to what Bataille sometimes assumes, only the pure gift is part of the general economy—not the gift of rivalry). Through his gifts, the warrior establishes a conservative sovereignty, as distinct from the autonomous sovereignty the Reader desires.

To reprise on another register the arguments of the previous chapter: in modern civility or for that matter republican democracy, sovereignty resides in the power to decide who is excepted from the rule of law. And law is so important because here violence and inequality are conceived as marked by wrong measure or lack of measure, and the rule of law institutes an autonomous measure. For the warrior, by contrast, modern civility is violent because of its abstraction and mastery of death. The warrior's sovereignty is organized quite differently, around his equality with his own death.[55] This makes it representative and even democratic in a nonhistoricist way, where representation emerges from one's ability to have one's own death as a companion (even though the utmost self-discipline is needed to make one's own death into such a companion).

Also, because the warrior is constituted by self-sacrifice, because he is given to and beyond the point of his own death to an end, he is no longer either an instrumental or a noninstrumental means to an end. Rather, there is a togetherness of means and ends—what Gandhi sometimes describes as *kushalta*—skill or accomplishment. Here, means and ends are not external to each other and then later brought into accordance through the institution of a noninstrumental order. Relatedly, while in the problematic of calculable general responsibility the sovereign autonomously gives himself the law and exceptions to it, here, even though the warrior is sovereign, this is a sovereignty without autonomy. He does not decide his dharma or "law" for himself. His decisions are made as one immeasurably given to what is proper—he cannot and does not decide on the exception or decide autonomously.

Involved in conservative sovereignty thus is a form of domination organized around a proper to which the sovereign too is given without autonomy. Central to it is the insistence on something proper to being, which should be conserved by marginalizing improper forms of being. To insist on the proper is to inscribe on oneself and the other a certain limit. Within an order of the proper, humans have no abstract rights as humans; their rights flow from the proper performance of the duties give to them by their position. Conservatism is, in this sense, the sovereignty of the proper.

⌒

But the contrast that Gandhi often explicitly presumes between the justice of the warrior and that of modern civility, or in other words between conservative and autonomous sovereignty, also often becomes unstable in his writings. This should not be surprising. Potlatch and its immeasurable economy do not mark only the warrior. While modern civility—which articulates the ideology that Heidegger describes as the "instrumental and anthropological definition of technology"—separates out means [sadhan] and ends [sadhya], and makes them external to each other, so that they can be in an instrumental or calculable relation, this separation is always haunted by the togetherness it excludes, and constantly supplemented by an immeasurable economy.[56]

In the years after *Hind Swaraj*, Gandhi sometimes names the belonging together of *sadhan* and *sadhya* as *sadhana*. The three words—which he possibly encounters already in the Buddhist, Hindu, and Jain texts he devours—become even more prominent in his vocabulary after he reads in 1922 the English translation of Tagore's book *Sadhana*, which Gandhi describes on one occasion as, along with *Gitanjali*, "a world apart." *Sadhana*, again a recurring concern of Indian philosophical traditions, could be glossed as spiritual discipline geared toward self-realization. But in Gandhi's writing it refers also to being given to a task at hand in such a way as to no longer be either a means to an end, or even in an autonomous relation to it.

This *sadhana* marks not only *satyagraha* or even the warrior, but all action that is incalculably given. Thus, he does not only talk of his own *sadhana* of ahimsa and spinning, but also of Hitler's *sadhana* of war:

> We have to be up and doing every moment of our lives and go
> forward in our *sadhana*. We have to live and move and have our
> being in *ahimsa*, even as Hitler does in *himsa*. It is the faith and
> perseverance and single-mindedness with which he has perfected
> his weapons of destruction that commands my admiration. That
> he uses them as a monster is immaterial for our purpose. We have
> to bring to bear the same single-mindedness and perseverance in

evolving our ahimsa. Hitler is awake all the 24 hours of the day in perfecting his *sadhana*.[57]

As this dizzying passage suggests, even something as massively defined by calculability and means–end relations as the Nazi war machine (or the British Empire, that other demonic force) can for that very reason not be treated as only calculable. What Gandhi admires in Hitler and the British Empire is the way they are immeasurably and incalculably given over to the very pursuit of measurable and calculable ends. When pursued so intensely, even these ends come to be suffused with aneconomy and incalculability, even a *rakshasi* or demonic finitude.

He often uses the word "intoxication" (which we have encountered already in his characterization of the bravery of the terrorists) to describe the immeasurable pursuit of the measurable. Already in *Hind Swaraj*, the Editor notes in chapter 6:

> Those who are intoxicated by modern civility ["civilization"] are not likely to write against it. Their care will be to find out facts and arguments in support of it. And it is not even as though they do this consciously. They themselves believe what they write. A man seized by sleep, believes in the dreams that come to him. When his sleep flies away, only then does he realize his own mistake [*potani bhool*]. The same is the situation of a man seized by civilization. . . . Their writings hypnotize us. And so, one by one, we are drawn into the vortex.

Modern civilization binds and seizes those who are intoxicated by it. In Gujarati, strikingly, the chapter is titled "*Sudharana Darshan.*" The term *darshan*, as we know well, is a charged one—it insinuates a vision of the incalculable, a vision that seizes the viewer. Here the Editor beholds the demonic immeasure that marks modern civilization's claim to measure. This demonic immeasure, invisible to those intoxicated or seized by measure, makes modern civilization the moment of the greatest danger. Here, those intoxicated with sleep think they have awakened, or (to misuse a Kantian metaphor) think they have emerged from their self-imposed immaturity, have the courage now to use their own understanding. This thought is itself the dream. Trying to awaken others, they only "hypnotize us," pull us into the vortex of the hypnotic dream that is modern civility.

And yet, whether in the case of Hitler, the British Empire, or modern civility, Gandhi suspects that this intoxication is also a moment of awakening, and so the moment of the greatest hope. In chapter 2 of *Hind Swaraj*, the Editor describes the principal consequence of the partition of Bengal as the loss of fear: "They do not fear even a row, or being imprisoned." And in chapter 3, describing the "unrest" that accompanied the "real awakening" brought about by the Partition of Bengal in 1905, the Editor says,

> When a man rises from sleep, he twists his limbs and is restless. It takes some time before he is entirely awakened. Similarly, although the Partition has caused an awakening, the comatose condition has not yet disappeared. We are still twisting our limbs and are still restless, and just as the state between sleep and awakening must be considered to be necessary, so may the present unrest in India be considered a necessary and, therefore, a proper state. The knowledge that there is unrest will, it is highly probable, enable us to outgrow it.

Moreover, unrest is "in reality, discontent." "This discontent is a very useful thing. As long as a man is contented with his present lot, so long is it difficult to persuade him to come out of it. Therefore it is that every reform must be preceded by discontent." *Ashanti* (the antonym in Hindu, Jain, and Buddhist traditions of *shanti*, "peace") becomes a prelude necessary to formulate the question of *shanti*.

Similarly, even as the Editor describes the British as essentially driven by the calculable desire for profit (it is unlikely, he quotes a South African official as saying, that there is gold in the moon, since the British would otherwise have annexed it), he also emphasizes their bravery—they "will never allow their country to be lost," and are like the *rakshasi* or demonic figures of Ravana or Indrajit. This intoxicated and brave willingness to not only kill but die for their cause is in Gandhi's writing perhaps not so much part of a tradition of "Western sacrifice" as it is the distinctive *sadhana* of modern civility, which has seized both the British Empire and Hitler. In the process, the distinction between the "intoxication" of modern civility and the warrior's fearlessness becomes less clear. The warrior's fearlessness may be a mark of modern civility too, may be exercised by those who pursue measure immeasurably. The third party, the law courts, the judge, the doctors—all these figures are not merely marked by measure, calculation, and number; they partake also of the immeasurability, incalculability, and innumerability of the warrior. Indeed, if they were not, if they were purely measurable, then satyagrahis could not have addressed them, and satyagraha against them would not have been possible.[58]

Gandhi's invocation of Hitler, the British Empire, "modern civilization," or modern civility and parliament as demonic models for a *daivi* or divinely inspired satyagraha resonates strikingly with the Heinrich Hölderlin that Heidegger invokes: "But where the danger is, grows the saving power also."[59]

On the one hand, political swaraj is the moment of the greatest danger, for it is marked by the immeasurable pursuit of measure; by the insistence that humans are uniquely and incalculably given to calculation; by the inscription, through abstract equality, of an everyday calculable sovereign power on all citizens. On the other hand, it is also the moment of the greatest saving power, for this very pursuit of sovereign power provokes the most sustained fearlessness both among those who seek domination and those who resist; and that provocation secretes always also the possibility of another equality and fearlessness.

Satyagrahis are true warriors because they seek to conserve the immeasurable equality and fearlessness this moment secretes, because they discern that what is most proper to being is the relinquishment of sovereign power. But in doing so, they face further questions: How is the arms-bearing warrior's immeasurable equality and fearlessness to be appropriated? How to be a true warrior? What is the relation between the *duragrahi* and the satyagrahi? If republican democracy is relinquished, what is the place of its rights in the order of satyagraha? What rights does satyagraha claim, and how?

· II ·

The Aneconomies of Satyagraha

CHAPTER 4

The Impossible Gift of
Fearlessness, for Example

In India there is not only no love but hatred due to emasculation.
There is the strongest desire to fight and kill side by side with utter
helplessness. This desire must be satisfied by restoring the capacity
for fighting. Then comes the choice. Yes, the very act of forgiving and
loving shows superiority in the doer. But that way of putting the prop-
osition begs the question, who can love? A mouse as mouse cannot
love a cat.

—Mohandas Gandhi, "Letter to Esther Faering,"
August 3, 1917

We should speak here of the im-possible event, an im-possible that is
not merely impossible, that is not merely the opposite of possible, that
is also the condition or chance of the possible. An im-possible that is
the very experience of the possible. This means transforming the con-
ception, or the experience, or the saying of the experience of the possi-
ble and the impossible. I do not believe that this is simply a subject of
speculation for professional philosophers.

—Jacques Derrida, "A Certain Impossible Possibility
of Saying the Event"

G ANDHI'S RECASTING OF ahimsa and satyagraha as the mark and responsibility of a true warrior, as the truth of the warrior, allows him to
circumvent and sidestep one criticism of ahimsa that had been gathering
force since the late nineteenth century, when the creation of a nationalist
Hinduism got under way. As Gandhi becomes more influential, the "Lion
of the Punjab," Lala Lajpat Rai reiterates the criticism very forcefully in 1916.
"There is no religion higher than truth, nor a course of conduct nobler
than *Ahimsa Paramo Dharmah.* Rightly understood and rightly applied
to life, the latter makes a man a saint and a hero. Misunderstood and mis-
applied, it makes a man cowardly and craven, base and stupid."

> It was this perverted use or misuse of ahimsa (non-killing), or its
> exaggerated importance at the cost of everything else, that brought
> about the social, political and moral downfall of the Hindus. They
> forgot that manliness was as good a virtue as ahimsa. In fact the
> former was in no way inconsistent with the latter, if rightly applied.
> They overlooked the fact that individual as well as national
> interests made it incumbent that the weak should be protected
> against the strong, and that the aggressor and the usurper, the thief
> and the scoundrel, the lustful villain and the infamous violator of
> women's chastity, the ruffian and the cheat, should be prevented
> from inflicting injustice and doing harm.[1]

Lajpat Rai's translation of ahimsa as "nonkilling" is symptomatic of the way
ahimsa is usually read by the early twentieth century as an attenuation of
force. In nationalist accounts of the decline of India, the "pernicious doctrine" of ahimsa is often ascribed a significant role.

 But even if we would interrogate Lajpat Rai's nationalist framing, his
other concern—that ahimsa as nonkilling withdraws from the universality
involved in law and justice, from the duty of protecting the weak—remains
relevant. Akeel Bilgrami's elegant essay draws out well the distinctive universality involved in such an ahimsa. He argues that Gandhi's politics departs significantly from the "Western tradition of moral philosophy," which
tries to establish universalizable principles:

> In Gandhi's writing there is an implicit but bold proposal: "When
> one chooses for oneself, one sets an example to everyone." And
> because there is only the example and no principle, because there
> is "no generality" to the exemplar's truth, "the entire moral
> psychology of our response to others who depart from us is
> necessarily much weaker. At most we may be disappointed in
> others that they will not follow our example, and at least part of the
> disappointment is in ourselves that our example has not taken
> hold. And the crucial point is that disappointment is measurably
> weaker than criticism, it is not the paler shade of contempt,
> hostility, and eventual violence."[2]

Also, "the 'satyagrahi' or nonviolent activist has to show a certain kind of
self-restraint, in which it was not enough simply not to commit violence. It

is equally important not to bear hostility to others or even to criticize them; it is only required that one not follow these others, if conscience doesn't permit it." Thus the "distinction between the principle and the exemplar" is that the latter is "necessarily much weaker," never universalized.

What is at stake here may be elicited by contrasting Bilgrami's reading of Gandhi's ethics with the categorical imperative. The latter seeks to institutionalize an order that treats the other as an autonomous end, rather than only a means to the self's ends. The former, acting as an exemplar who "chooses for oneself," effectively withdraws from means–ends relations altogether and becomes, to use Karuna Mantena's suggestive phrase to describe Bilgrami's argument, "self-contained."[3]

If this is indeed what ahimsa and satyagraha entail, then Bilgrami's criticisms of it are very pertinent, only erring perhaps on the side of generosity: "The romance in this morality is radiant. Somehow goodness, good acts, enter the world and affect everyone else. To ask how exactly they do that is to be vulgar, to spoil the romance. Goodness is a sort of mysterious contagion. The idea is as attractive as it is romantic."[4] One might add: choosing for oneself or limiting oneself to disappointment only leads to passive participation in perhaps a greater violence, and even injustice and inequality.

But Bilgrami's critique may be misplaced in two ways. First, is satyagraha an attenuation of force? Even Gandhi's explicit formulations, with their emphasis on war and warriors, emphatically disavow any reading of ahimsa as an attenuation of force, a weaker universality, or simple nonkilling. Consider his response to a correspondent who asks him to clarify the difference between his ahimsa and the Jain principle that there "are two kinds of himsa—direct such as that involved in agriculture, and indirect as that involved in the eating of agricultural produce. Where one cannot altogether escape from either, a votary of ahimsa should try to avoid direct himsa." Refusing to accept this as a Jain principle, Gandhi argues:

Let us see, for instance, to what it [the purportedly Jain principle] leads to if pushed to its logical conclusion. You may not kill a snake but if necessary, according to this principle, you may get it killed by somebody else. You may not yourself forcibly drive away a thief but you may employ another person to do it for you. If you want to protect the life of a child entrusted to your care from the fury of a tyrant, somebody else must bear the brunt of the tyrant's fury for

you. And you thus refrain from direct action in the sacred name of
ahimsa! This in my opinion is neither religion nor ahimsa.

For Gandhi, ahimsa as unqualified nonkilling withdraws from politics in
a profoundly violent manner, a manner moreover sustained by the himsa
others practice.

Second, does satyagraha entail that one chooses for oneself, and influence others only by that example? Satyagraha, as the Introduction suggested, is not an individual politics but a minority politics—it is necessarily
marked by a sharing. Thus, he insists that ahimsa must be universalized.
And his ahimsa or satyagraha is often marked by a confrontational spirit.
To begin with, he criticizes friends and opponents forcefully. He describes
the British empire as "Satanic," "wicked," and "evil'; and Allied rhetoric
as "sanctimonious humbug"—words that almost all disciplinary scholarship today would recoil from, whether to describe the British Empire then
or American imperialism and Indian majoritarianism today. "I stand first,
these days, in using the word 'Satanic' [rakshasi]." And yet for him there
is "nothing but daya" or compassion in his use of the word, that he does it
without anger or hatred, that he is simply "observing dayadharma" or the
religion of compassion in using the word.[5]

He is also, if anything, terrifyingly celebratory of occasions where satyagrahis face violence. As David Hardiman has reminded us, in 1931 during
the Borsad satyagraha, after Gangabehn Vaidya writes to him about how
she had been "beaten till blood poured from her head," Gandhi replies: "If
I had seen your sari, wet with blood, how I would have laughed? I was
charged when I knew about this atrocity, but I did not experience the least
sorrow [dukh]. I felt happiness [harsh]."[6]

~

But how is ahimsa to be conceived, if not as attenuation of force, a weaker
universality, or simple nonkilling? One word that seizes Gandhi quite early
on is *abhaydan*. That word, conventionally the "gift of fearlessness," conjoins *abhay* or fearlessness with *dana* or the gift. The 1916 reply (originally
written in English) to Lajpat Rai says:

> Ahimsa necessarily includes truth and fearlessness. A man cannot
> deceive the loved ones; he does not fear or frighten him or her.
> *Abhaydan* (gift of life) is the greatest of all gifts. A man who gives
> it in reality disarms all hostility. He has paved the way for an

honourable understanding. And none who is himself subject to fear can bestow that gift. He must therefore be himself fearless. The practice of ahimsa calls forth the greatest courage. It is the most soldierly of a soldier's virtues.[7]

The relation between abhay and abhaydan is noted again in 1928 in his short essay discussing the vows observed at Satyagraha Ashram, and there he gives a quotation from the "Hindu Shastras" in support of each of the vows. For the vow of abhay he has this: "He alone becomes fearless who dispels fear in others." Here the gift of fearlessness is no longer something that comes after fearlessness; rather, abhaydan is the greatest and purest abhay, and true abhay is possibly only as abhaydan. Such abhaydan is also deeply religious: in 1919, he calls on protestors to offer abhaydan to the British, "the first requisite of true religion."[8]

We can trace his thinking of abhaydan by beginning with chapter 17 of *Hind Swaraj*, where the Editor is emphatic about the necessity of *abhay* or *abhayata* (also translated as "fearlessness").

Satyagraha cannot proceed a step without *abhayata*. Abhay is appropriate forever and for everything. Satyagraha is possible only where there is abhay, whether about possessions, false honour, their relatives, the government, bodily injuries or death. . . . A warrior without *abhayata* cannot be conceived of. Some may feel that he would not need it to observe the vow of satya. But where there is abhayata there *satya* ["truth"] dwells. When a person abandons satya, he does so because of fear in some form.

The Editor begins then with fearlessness, which as the previous chapter suggested is in his writing a criterion of the political shared between the satayagrahi and the *duragrahi*. But he quickly radicalizes that fearlessness by associating it with satya—being. Only where there is fearlessness can there even be a sustained care for satya. Such fearlessness takes the form especially of abandoning fear of death. Indeed, killing the enemy, especially where it emerges from a desire to persist in one's own being, itself originates usually in fear. A true warrior thus would seek not so much to kill the enemy as abandon his fear of his own death. Speaking in October 1921 to a group of Kathi Rajputs, he says that they should, for the sake of Hindustan,

abandon the thought of killing, prepare to die, and become true
[shudh] Kshatriyas [the warrior caste]. Killing is not a Kshatriya's
dharma. The Kshatriya who kills somebody weaker than his own
self is not a Kshatriya but a murderer. The one who in order to
rescue the weak fights with a strong man and kills him is forgiven,
but the one who dies in rescuing the weak, without killing even
the strong is a complete [pooro; "true"] Kshatriya. To die—to not
run away, this is his dharma. It is not his dharma to create fear of
death in the other [beeja]. Rather his dharma is to abandon fear
of death.[9]

By 1929, he extends his formulations and redefines the Kshatriya. "Readers are not unfamiliar with the liberties I have been taking with words for
many years. I have given a new definition of the word Kshatriya. The latter
is not a person who knows how to kill others but rather one who acquires
the art of sacrificing his own life so that others may live. A Kshatriya is one
who has well mastered the mantra of never retreating in the battle between
gods and demons which is raging in this world. A Kshatriya is one who is
the very embodiment of compassion."[10]

The warrior's experience of compassion thus always already makes his
practice of abhay into abhaydan, or the giving of fearlessness.

But abhaydan in what way? Gandhi would likely have been familiar,
given the classical training his ashram associates have, with the recognition
in Sanskrit texts that a certain abhaydan organizes even the arms-bearing
warrior's sovereign power. The Manusmriti, for example, says: "The king
who gives safety [abhaya] is constantly revered; for the extended sacrifice
that he performs, in which safety is the sacrificial gift, always thrives."[11]
The arms-bearing warrior-king offers the "gift of life" (to draw on Gandhi's
lexically unjustified translation of abhaydan) in two ways: he gives his subjects their lives by assuring their safety, and he is willing to offer his life in
order to do so. The sovereign's gift of life requires him to pursue power: the
greater his sovereignty, the more successfully he can accomplish the gift of
life.[12] Even if the sovereign is to "require a self-imposed constraint on one's
own activity" such as that laid down "in the Dharmasastra Nibandhas" to
desist "from abusing royal force," this is more a regulation than relinquishment of sovereign power.[13] Here abhaydan is a sovereign gift, and the injunction ahimsa paramo dharma, "ahimsa is the highest religion," bolsters
the just and life-preserving violence of the sovereign.

In contrast, the sovereign gift not only cannot erase but can also be undone by the pure gift—a gift that would bring about the most thoroughgoing destruction of the power of the sovereign. From the South Asian traditions that he makes his inheritance, Gandhi will have received two proper names as provocations with which to think this destruction: Mahabali (whose name could be glossed as "the great sacrifice/r") and Harishchandra. (As we shall see later, Gandhi claims in the *Autobiography* to have received one of his earliest intimations of satya-ahimsa when seeing a play about Harishchandra). With these two figures, sovereign power, the moment of the greatest violence, topples over into the greatest nonviolence, into the moment where sovereign power is destroyed by the pure gift of ahimsa.

Perhaps responding to and being responsible to these provocations, Gandhi's writings presume that the true warrior—the satyagrahi—does not experience a sovereign abhay. Hinduism, he argues in 1920, "teaches that the truly pure Kshatriya is he who knows not how to kill but how to die. The *Gita [Gitaji]* has taught me one most important word, *apalaayanam* [fearlessness]. He who wields the sword is likely some time to retreat. Relinquishing *[taji]* his faith *[shraddha]* in God, he puts his faith in his arms and, therefore, he is unable to abide by the duty of *apalaayanam*."[14] The arms-bearing warrior's fearlessness is fragile and prone to retreat because its faith is in only its own sovereignty. The fearlessness of the being who relinquishes arms and sovereignty can be more thoroughgoing because it involves faith in God (itself a shorthand, as chapter 6 will argue, for nonsovereign being). And in the process, he gives fearlessness to others.

It is this other abhaydan that Gandhi describes as "the first requisite of true religion." He is possibly aware of at least Jain traditions around such abhaydan. For the Svetambara Jain thinker from medieval Gujarat, Hemacandra (who is translated into English by Gandhi's close associate Anandshankar Dhruva), "positive ahimsa is expressed in the form of *karuna dana* or *abhaya dana*."[15] (*Karuna*, as noted earlier, is the Sanskrit term Gandhi translates into Gujarati as daya, and into English as love or compassion; already in the texts he works with, thus, the purest and greatest giving of love and compassion occurs in the gift of fearlessness.) By the eighteenth century, a sect of reformers splits off into their own sect on this issue: for them, conventional acts of charity were not enough, and only "the higher act of giving constituted true Jainism."[16] In the late nineteenth century, Gandhi's Jain mentor Raychandbhai (Shrimad Rajchandra) also associates ahimsa and abhaydan, remarking that abhaydan is the "highest gift" and "there is no other gift like it."[17]

Abhaydan is the highest gift, as subsequent chapters indicate, because it exemplifies and even "is" the only possible pure gift—the gift given unconditionally and aneconomically, without expectation of return, without even knowledge (among givers, receivers, or, for that matter, observers) of the gift having been given or received. In the previous chapter, we have encountered the sovereign gift given by the warrior. That gift seeks to create and sustain economic relations, whether hierarchical or nonhierarchical. But to think the gift only in terms of sovereign power and economy is also to obscure its concept. As Derrida says of Mauss: "One could go so far as to say that a work as monumental as Marcel Mauss's *The Gift* speaks of everything but the gift: It deals with economy, exchange, contract (*do ut es*), it speaks of raising the stakes, sacrifice, gift *and* counter-gift—in short, everything that in the thing itself impels the gift *and* the annulment of the gift."[18] Even if, as Mauss and in some ways Bataille too presume, the sovereign gift marginalizes the pure gift, the latter is constitutive of the concept of the gift—not even the economic gift could occur but for the specter of the aneconomic gift.

The quiet transitivity between ahimsa and the pure gift should not by now be surprising. While both most certainly are everywhere imbricated in relations of power and sovereignty, what organizes them conceptually is precisely their effraction of these relations. Both struggle to destroy and displace sovereign power. Bound together in this struggle, the two concepts constantly incite and provoke the thinking each of the other; and this to the point where the purity of the gift can only be thought in terms of ahimsa, and the purity of ahimsa only in terms of the gift. So it is that Gandhi often writes of "offering" ahimsa and satyagraha. Ahimsa itself is "our religion, the great gift of the rishis." That gift from the rishis he perhaps himself receives as he gives it: "I am convinced that I have no gift better than this for India."

～

As a pure gift, abhaydan requires the greatest fearlessness. This fearlessness the arms-bearing warrior does not possess. While the arms-bearing warrior is fearless about his own life, he fears sharing his fearlessness with others. He can have his fearlessnesss only by mastering others—whether by protecting them or giving them *bhay* or fear. In contrast, abhaydan tries to make fearlessness universal by giving it to the other, and indeed to all being. Abhaydan as the pure gift—this is to venture on an intriguing, even dizzying, path. Gandhi's writing radicalizes the traditions it inherits by making abhaydan the purest abhay. Abhaydan is the most intense criterion of the political, one that coexists with and yet also displaces that other criterion, abhay. Also, abhaydan is "the first requisite of true religion"; it is the criterion of religion. Combined with the insistence that religion is love (prem) or compassion (daya), this says: not just any love or daya, but the love involved in abhaydan is religion.

In yoking the criteria of politics and religion this way, Gandhi's writing departs also from those immense traditions that think ethics-politics together (and whether he realizes it or not, this departure is implicitly thematized in the very proliferation of the word "dharma," poised indecidably as it is between "ethics" and "religion"). In his writing, religion displaces or more precisely supplements ethics, and what it must work through rather is religion-politics together—why and how there can be "no politics without religion," to recall that declaration he makes in 1924 when accepting the "honor of presiding at the forthcoming [annual meeting of the Indian National] Congress."[19]

To understand the distinctiveness of this displacement, it may be instructive to draw a contrast with Kant and Derrida, who could well be said to describe the beginning and end points of the modern reworking of the pair ethics-politics. Kant enshrines, perhaps more than any other figure in philosophical traditions, the secular question as the ground of ethics; Derrida questions the secular question itself, undertaking a "questioning without limit and the to the depths of the axioms that appear to be the most incontestable, such as, for example, the 'human' in the rights of man."[20]

The premises of Kant's grounding of politics in "morals" or ethics emerge in the Appendix to *Towards Perpetual Peace*, which declares: "Morals is of itself practical in the objective sense, as the sum of laws commanding unconditionally, in accordance with which we *ought* to act, and it is patently absurd . . . to want to say that one nevertheless cannot do it." Two points about this ethics may be stressed. First, because this ethics commands unconditionally, it grounds and delimits politics. Thus: "Politics says, '*Be ye wise as serpents*'; morals adds (as a limiting condition) 'and guileless as doves.'"[21] Here, one might say, ethics identifies the bounds beyond which calculations and guile cannot be allowed; and politics conversely calculates and makes conditional decisions within these bounds, or in a way that does not and cannot violate the unconditional commands of ethics.

Second, Kant insists that this unconditional ethics is at the same time "practical in the objective sense," which is to say that it is an ethics of the possible: the actions it enjoins are practical in the sense of being both knowable and operable. This practicality is stressed at several points in the essay. The third definitive article for perpetual peace, for example, stipulates, "Cosmopolitan right shall be limited to conditions of universal hospitality." Such hospitality "means the right of a foreigner not to be treated with hostility because he has arrived on the land of another. . . . What he can claim is not the right to be a guest . . . but the right to visit" (8:357). On the one hand, this is a sovereign hospitality—extended by the sovereign to a visitor in a manner that does not challenge or undermine the sovereign's authority over his land. On the other hand, this sovereignty is law-governed: hospitality is here a right of the cosmopolitan visitor rather than an act of philanthropy from the sovereign, and imposes a set of clearly stipulated obligations on the sovereign.

Derrida describes himself as "ultra-Kantian. I am Kantian, but I am more than Kantian."[22] One crucial departure from the Kantian schema may be his insistence that the unconditional is not practical but hyperbolic, his insistence also on a certain "impossible possibility" that marks ethics-politics. Three implications of this insistence are especially crucial here, and we can elicit them by attending to his formulations around hospitality (a similar structure organizes his formulations around other unconditional injunctions, such as forgiveness). First, the "unconditional law of hospitality" requires hospitality without limit, in a way that not only ruins the sovereignty or even identity of the host, but because of this also exceeds knowledge and operability (which requires the sovereignty and identity of the knower). Hence: "We do not know what hospitality is."[23] Second, the unconditional law that is most at stake in ethics is heterogeneous to the various conditional laws of hospitality (among which laws Kant's cosmopolitan right too would surely number), which constitute what would conventionally be called the realm of politics. Third, there is the aporetic relation between the unconditional law and conditional laws: "the nonnegotiable, the unconditional is, as unconditional, subject to political transaction: and this political transaction of the unconditional is not an accident, a degeneration, or a last resort; it is prescribed by ethical duty itself. One should not have to negotiate between two negotiables. One must negotiate the nonnegotiable."[24] This negotiation of the nonnegotiable is at work in various concrete laws, and in various decisions organized by the law. "These two regimes of law, of the [ethical] law and [political] laws, are thus both contradictory, antinomic, and inseparable."[25]

In anticipation of later chapters, suffice here to say that Gandhi's emphasis on abhaydan and relatedly his pair, religion-politics, thinks the relation between the conditional and the unconditional in a way that departs from the arc of the modern ethics-politics problematic for which "Kant-Derrida" can serve as a conjoined proper name. Gandhi's writing presumes two modalities of law, of negotiating the nonnegotiable: abhay and abhaydan. Abhay (fearlessness), which imposes the law of sovereignty and is the domain of ethics-politics, is organized by the immeasurable equality-inequality of the warrior; it is from and with this nonnegotiable, and the sovereignty of the proper that it institutes, that the warrior conducts his sovereign negotiation (though in the sovereign decisions he makes, he transforms the aporias he begins from into problems).[26]

Abhaydan (gift of fearlessness) is the "domain" of religion-politics; it imposes the unconditional and nonnegotiable law of nonsovereignty. In the decisions that seize them, there occurs a nonsovereign negotiation— hence, as chapter 8 will argue, his insistence that satyagrahis must cipher themselves. Only nonsovereign negotiation can sustain the aporia of satyagraha, or for that matter any aporia. Nonsovereign negotiation is required because of a paradox: abhaydan is the premise for abhay, but abhaydan can only be obscured in any action organized by abhay; conversely abhaydan must begin from its coeval obscuring in abbay, but it must destroy abhay in order to "be." These two laws, abhay and abhaydan, which precede every substantive law, are in an aporetic relation with each other: there can be no transition from one to the other, each can only obscure the other. As the enactment of nonsovereign negotiation, moreover, abhaydan is the most tenacious aporia, even the only aporia (one that following the plural logic of the aporia multiples into various figures of the impossible: conscience, death, forgiveness, friendship, gift, trust, question, religion, and sacrifice among them for Gandhi).

Gandhi's writing opens up the intimation that dharma or religion precedes the concept of ethics not as its prehistory but as what is both before and after it; that if ethics is the unconditionality of the sovereign question, then perhaps religion is the unconditionality of the question that surrenders its sovereignty. As this suggests, ethics, and relatedly the pair ethics-politics, is possible only in the forgetting and obscuring of religion; conversely, religion is possible only in the relinquishing of ethics.

From the perspective enabled by the Gandhian reading of abhaydan, we might ask: Does not the Derridean aporia participate in sovereign power, and thus become nonaporectic? This participation is perhaps most marked in the way his "Force of Law" reads the "decision of a judge," stressing three aporias. First, the judge's "calculable" decision becomes "just" when it not only follows a "general law" but also reinvents the law in each case and becomes incalculable. "Each case is other, each decision is different and requires an absolutely unique interpretation, which no existing, coded rule can or ought to guarantee absolutely." Second, the judge's decision is also marked by the "undecidable," which in Derrida's formulation is "the experience of that which, though heterogeneous, foreign to the order of the calculable and the rule, is still obliged . . . to give itself up to the impossible decision, while taking account of law and rules." "The undecidable remains caught, lodged, at least as a ghost—but an essential ghost— in every decision, in every event of decision. Its ghostliness deconstructs from within any assurance of presence." Third, the "moment of decision, as such, always remains a finite moment of urgency and precipitation," always interrupts and breaks from the "theoretical and historical knowledge" that must precede it; the "instant of decision is a madness."[27]

One might say of the judgment here, to draw on Derrida's remarks in another context, that the judge's exceeds information or cognition, that it "enters the night, . . . the 'night of non-knowing,' something that's not merely ignorance, but that no longer pertains to the realm of knowledge. A non-knowing that is not lack, not sheer obscurantism, ignorance, or non-science, but simply something that is not of the same nature as knowing. A saying the event that produces the event beyond the confines of knowledge."[28]

From the perspective that Gandhi's writing enables, however, would not the instant of the judge's decision be anything but a madness? Even if the incalculability, undecidability, and nonknowing of the judge's decision is deconstructible, does not that decision remain with the problematic of sovereignty? Indeed, more still: is it not also through incalculability, undecidability, and nonknowing that sovereignty here reproduces itself, sustains an exemplarity that remains Aristotelian (to anticipate a concept that occurs later in this chapter)? Would not the judge's negotiation of and with the nonnegotiable lead back to the sovereign power it begins from?

Should one not then distinguish—though this distinction can by its very nature never be a matter of calculation, decidability, or knowledge—between two concepts of the decision as of negotiation, one sovereign (as in the figure of the warrior, or in the incalculability that comes to mark "modern civilization"), and the other nonsovereign? Is Derrida's writing marked by an indistinction between these two concepts? And to the extent that it is, does not an "unavowed theologism," even dare one say an ontotheology, both ground and rise up through his writing?[29] And would not this theologism always, despite his commitments as an intending subject, not only reinstate and justify the violence of sovereign power, perhaps even do so moreover with a good conscience? Would the judge's decision not exemplify the warrior's sovereignty, the transformation of an aporia into a problem?

And yet, as is always the case with Derrida (or Gandhi, or Heidegger, to name two of the few others of whom this can be said), in his writing this sovereignty also deconstructs itself. The "impossible possibility" involved in the Derridean unconditional constantly rives it with difference, makes it two. In this sense, to emphasize the relinquishment of sovereignty that occurs in Gandhi's writing is not to oppose Gandhi to Derrida as it is perhaps to be strenuously faithful to Derrida's thinking of a "certain impossible possibility."

~

Acutely aware of the violence of the warrior-judge, Gandhi must abandon this figure and try instead to enact satyagraha, or the decision that remains utterly estranged from sovereign power. To the question "What is ahimsa?," then, Gandhi's writing offers the schematic answer: ahimsa or satyagraha is the gift of nonsovereign fearlessness, and this gift is the only pure gift. But this answer is only a beginning. It dehisces, as we attend to it, into a sheaf of questions that Gandhi finds he must work out for himself. To begin with, there are these: What does abhaydan as the doubled criterion of the political and the religious entail? How is the pure gift that is abhaydan to be received and given? What is the negotiation that occurs here? How would a purely nonsovereign unconditional work? Or, to parse that last question: If abhaydan is neither possible and practical in the sense that we encounter in Kant, nor an impossible possible in the sense that Derrida explicitly affirms, how does abhaydan work?

The curious phrase "dying without killing" reveals some of the difficulties Gandhi encounters as he is addressed by these questions. "Everyone, therefore, who calls himself an Indian, be he a Hindu, Muslim, Parsi, Christian, Jew, or anyone else, has to learn and master this *mantra* of dying without killing. Only the man who has faith in God can learn it and act on it."[30] No phrase for "dying without killing" exists in Gandhi's Gujarati texts. In the passage above, for example, it translates *marvano mantra,* the "mantra of dying'; "without killing" is added in the English version. The addition is not an interpolation: many passages in the Gujarati texts (for instance, some in the previous chapter) are emphatic that satyagrahis should die themselves rather than kill the other.

But the gap between the Gujarati and the English is nevertheless perhaps symptomatic of the distinctive place of "dying without killing" in satyagraha. On the one hand, dying without killing is most crucial and proper to satyagraha: here nonkilling occurs through self-sacrifice, as part of a striving to relinquish sovereignty. This makes dying without killing a religious act, for where sovereignty is relinquished, there can be no knowledge that organizes the decision—it requires faith. On the other hand, dying without killing is strictly speaking impossible, and Gandhi is too tenacious and dogged a thinker to not be aware of this. In this sense, dying without killing, and by extension satyagraha or ahimsa, is an impossible possible (to draw on Derrida's invaluable phrase, but reserving it here for the free experience of nonsovereignty).

The way he thinks the impossible possibility of "dying without killing," or, in other words, the way he thinks the unavoidable killing involved in satyagraha, changes sharply over the years. In *Hind Swaraj,* the Editor remarks: "Going to the root of the matter, not one man really practices such a [nonviolent] religion because we do destroy life. We are said to follow that religion because we want to obtain freedom from liability to kill any kind of life." In such remarks, the focus is on how ahimsa is impossible because everyday life involves a residual killing—the "inevitable violence" and "unavoidable violence" of eating and drinking that not even the most rigorous practitioner of nonkilling can break from. This residual killing is external to ahimsa—occurring not because of the practice of dying without killing but because "one never completely renounces the will to live." And yet, the satyagrahi is responsible for it, and must try constantly to reduce it. Aware of this residual killing, he describes ahimsa by analogy to the Euclidean line or point: a high ideal striven for but never achieved.

Here, ahimsa is an impossible possible in the idealist sense, or in the Hegelian sense of a "bad infinity"—possible because violence is external to ahimsa, and one can know when one is engaged in ahimsa and when not; impossible because it can never be fully achieved, but one for which satyagrahis must strive. Thus he says of Raja Harishchandra: "We shall not find anywhere in the world a perfect example [*sachot namuna*] of such a person; as in geometry we require imaginary, ideal figures, so in practical affairs, too, we require ideal instances when discussing ethical issues."[31] When ahimsa is conceived in these idealist terms, then its affinities with liberal traditions of civil disobedience are all too evident.

Already by the time of *Hind Swaraj*, however, Gandhi is perhaps also inchoately aware of the inadequacy of such a reading of ahimsa. In chapter 16, defending the use of "brute force," the Reader says: "You will not find fault with a continuance of force to prevent a child from thrusting its foot into fire?" (The trope of the child who does not know what is good for it is of course a familiar one in colonial discourses.)

The Editor's reply displaces the Reader's question. In the English text, he says: "I hope you will not consider that it is still physical force, though of a low order, when you would forcibly prevent the child from rushing towards the fire if you could. That force is of a different order and we have to understand what it is." What this different order is, how it would diverge from the state's use of force to discipline those who break the law because of their immaturity—these questions *Hind Swaraj* quite glosses over. Save for this passing acknowledgment of a violence internal to ahimsa, *Hind Swaraj* presumes that satyagraha and ahimsa are innocent of coercion and the use of armed force.

~

But in June 1918, in the wake of the Kheda satyagraha, as he begins his campaign to recruit soldiers from Kheda for the British Indian army fighting the world war, he comes to another sense of ahimsa as an impossible possible. This follows from his growing recognition that ahimsa itself requires a capacity for himsa or violence. This sentiment is put especially forcefully in a letter in June to a skeptical C. F. Andrews:

> Regarding those who want to fight but will not, either out of cowardice or spite against the British, what is my duty? Must I not say, "If you can follow my path, so much the better, but if you cannot, you ought to give up cowardice or spite and fight." You cannot teach ahimsa to a man who cannot kill. You cannot make a dumb man appreciate the beauty and the merit of silence.

Although I know that silence is most excellent, I do not hesitate to take means that would enable the dumb man to regain his speech. I do not believe in any Government,—but Parliamentary Government is perhaps better than capricious rule.[32]

Here, perhaps for the first time so clearly, the duragrahi or arms-bearing warrior and the satyagrahi are intertwined in a more complex way. Now, only by first being a duragrahi can one become a satyagrahi, only by first affirming speech can silence displace it, only by first acquiring the sovereign ability to wreak violence can ahimsa emerge. Sovereign power cannot be simply rejected; it must be adopted and then relinquished. How is this adoption and relinquishment to take place?

(Another theme to be noted in the passage above, though it will not be explored in this book: silence is conceived here in a tripartite schema: dumbness–speech–silence. Satyagraha belongs not to speech, the zone of reason and logos, nor even to dumbness, the subaltern soundlessness, but to silence—a zone that comes only as a withdrawal, which is also to say, a traversal, of both speech and dumbness. Parliamentary rule and violence both belong to the speech—speech here includes writing: since parliament is a representative institution, its speech is a writing—that rejects dumbness, and the satyagrahi both affirms this speech and bursts from it into silence. But what is this silence?)

Perhaps because these questions vex Gandhi too, he adds: "If I have not made the position clear, you should try if you can to come down." Three days later, he makes a speech in a Kheda village urging listeners to join the British Army, and says: "Our mightiest weapon, satyagraha, is always with us. But he cannot be a satyagrahi who is afraid of death. The ability to use physical force is necessary for a true appreciation of satyagraha. He alone can practise ahimsa who knows how to kill, i.e., knows what himsa is."[33] Here again, killing develops the ability for satyagraha.

Or as he puts in a letter the next month to his south Indian associate Hanumantrao:

It is my practice of ahimsa and failure to get our people even to understand the first principles of ahimsa that have led to the discovery that all killing is not himsa, that, sometimes, practice of ahimsa may even necessitate killing and that we as a nation have lost the true power of killing. It is clear that he who has lost the

power to kill cannot practice non-killing. Ahimsa is a renunciation
of the highest type. A weak and an effeminate nation cannot
perform this grand act of renunciation, even as a mouse cannot be
properly said to renounce the power of killing a cat. It may look
terrible but it is true that we must, by a well-sustained, conscious
effort, regain this power, and, then, if we can only do so, deliver
the world from its travail of himsa by a continuous abdication of
this power. . . . I do believe that we shall have to teach our children
the art of self-defence. . . . I am most anxious that you should
understand this new view of ahimsa. It is not a fall but it is a rise.
The measure of love evoked by this discovery is infinitely greater
than ever it was before.[34]

At least some of his close associates, including his relative Maganlal Gandhi
(whose suggested word *sadagraha,* recall, had developed into the neologism
satyagraha), are disturbed by his insistence on the necessity of acquiring
the power for himsa before becoming capable of ahimsa. Maganlal seems
to have received a report from Raojibhai Patel that Gandhi was abandoning his faith in nonviolence, and inquires about this in a letter. Around a
week after the letter to Hanumantrao, Gandhi writes back to Maganlal:
"You have been frightened by Raojibhai. I frightened Raojibhai. He read
too much into my words. No, my ideals *[adarsh]* have not changed. . . . The
old idea has developed into something purer *[swachh]*."
   And then he goes on: "I have come to see, what I did not so clearly
before, that there is nonviolence in violence. This is the big change which
has come about. I had not fully realized the duty of restraining a drunkard
from doing evil, of taking the life of ["killing"] a dog in agony or one in-
fected with rabies. In all these instances, violence is in fact non-violence."[35]
   "Violence is in fact non-violence." Now the power of violence is no
longer acquired and then relinquished; now the very practice of violence
can be nonviolent. Even if this is a purer understanding of ahimsa, it is
also more terrifying, not least for Gandhi. Two days after that letter to
Maganlalbhai, Gandhi writes to ashram associate and philosopher Kishorelal Mashruwala about the education of the children at the ashram:

In what manner should the children learn to use their strength? It
is a difficult thing to teach them to defend themselves and yet not
be overbearing. Till now, we used to teach them not to fight back if

anyone beat them. Can we go on doing so now? What will be the effect of such teaching on a child? Will he, in his youth, be a forgiving or a timid man? My thinking fails me [*Mari akkal kam nathi karti*]. Use yours. This new aspect of ahimsa [*nava dekhata swarup*] which has revealed itself to me has enmeshed me in the web of no end of questions. I have not found one master-key for all the riddles, but it must be found. . . . These are the problems which face us if we give up the main path [*dhori marg*] of suffering two blows when one is given ["royal road of turning the other cheek"]. Is the first course [the "royal road"] the right one because it is easier to take? Or is it that we shall come upon the true path only by treading through a dangerous one? The foot-tracks which go up the Himalayas lead in all directions, sometimes even away from the destination and yet an experienced guide will take us in the end to the summit. One cannot climb the Himalayas in a straight line. Can it be that, in like fashion, the path of non-violence, too, is difficult? Save me, save me [*trahi ma, trahi ma;* "May God protect us, may He indeed"].[36]

Trahi ma, trahi ma indeed! What here lies in ruins is the understanding of violence as external to ahimsa, of the warrior's sovereignty as simply opposed to and relinquished by dying without killing. Now dying without killing or "turning the other cheek" (a translation indicative of how his universalism works—here, Jain and Hindu traditions, on the one hand, and Christian traditions, on the other, are transported into each other even as they remain singular) cannot be a rule to be always followed—to do so would make it a "blind fetish."[37]

Dying without killing is rather now the "royal road" of ahimsa. While the use of a metaphor associated with sovereign power is almost surely unintended, perhaps even inserted by later translators, it is suggestive. In dying without killing, satyagrahis do not use sovereign power to get their end, and instead trust God/satya. Dying without killing is also marked with an unknowability: satyagrahis themselves cannot know whether they are offering ahimsa or practicing violence by other means. Still, dying without killing at least has the form that is empirically knowable as ahimsa. In the very ease with which such ahimsa might claim innocence and deny its own violence, it perhaps retains a secret affinity with the sovereign; in this sense, it remains a "royal road."

Now this "royal road" needs to be supplemented by other "foot-tracks"—by another ahimsa that might involve killing. This satyagraha is "something purer" because it requires an even greater faith: it cannot have the recognizable form of ahimsa as in "dying without killing"; it is not only groundless but unknowable as ahimsa, for now satyagraha may on occasion require even killing the friend or the enemy. It is thus very apposite that at this vertiginous moment, Gandhi's thinking fails him, and he must exclaim: *trahi ma, trahi ma.*[38]

$\sim$

The acknowledgment that ahimsa might involve and even require killing and hurting is quite possibly a turning point. In later years, Gandhi often strays along this ahimsa of the foot-tracks, away from the royal road. He claims to find precedents for it in both Jain and Hindu texts. In his speech on Raychandbhai's birth anniversary in 1921, he insists: "Those persons or institutions against which we employ non-co-operation are indeed hurt by our action, but dayadharma does not teach that we may never hurt anyone. That is not the dayadharma I have learnt from the Poet."[39] Raychandbhai, he notes, was often "full of indignation over oppression and I often saw him boil over."[40]

Again in 1926, during the period when he is giving the *Gitashikshan* lectures, he writes a series of articles that explicitly explore how ahimsa might involve the use of physical force: "Merely taking life is not always himsa, one may even say that there is sometimes more himsa in not taking life."[41] In the next article in the series, he comes back to the question in terms that resonate with his discussion of the *Gitashikshan:*

> [T]he sin of himsa consists not in merely destroying other bodies ["taking life"], but in falling in love with one's own body, in taking life for the sake of one's perishable body. All destruction therefore involved in the process of eating, drinking, etc., is selfish and, therefore, himsa. But man regards it to be unavoidable and puts up with it. But the destruction of bodies of tortured creatures being for their own peace cannot be regarded as himsa, or the unavoidable destruction caused for the purpose of protecting one's wards cannot be regarded as himsa.
>
> This line of reasoning is liable to be misused but that is not because the reasoning is faulty, but because the love of body [*deha pratyena mohaney,* "inherent frailty"] leads man to catch at

whatever pretexts he can get to deceive himself. But we cannot clarify the path of ahimsa if we hide true matters because of fear of misuse.[42]

The crucial distinction here is between sovereign killing and nonsovereign killing, and the latter is ahimsa because it is done in a spirit of trembling faith, of self-sacrifice and surrender, by a being who has relinquished sovereign power. Such ahimsa is an impossible possible in a sense familiar to us from Derrida's arguments: it is possible in the sense that it is always being accomplished, perhaps even fully accomplished; it is impossible in the sense that the very nature of this ahimsa requires that nobody—neither the one who offers it, nor the one who receives it, and certainly not a third party—can ever know whether it has been offered, whether what has happened is a nonsovereign killing.[43] (It is of such a killing perhaps that Walter Benjamin writes: "The killing of a criminal can be moral—but never its legitimation.")[44]

His struggles to think this vertiginous ahimsa condense sometimes around the phrase *mariney jivavano*, which he on occasion translates as "living by dying" or "dying to live." In August 1920, he offers another formulation: the true warrior is he "who does not die killing [*maariney marto*] but who accomplishes the *mantra* of living by dying [*mariney jivavano*]."[45] That formulation is agnostic about whether satyagraha involves killing; what matters here is that satyagrahis embrace their own death in a manner that relinquishes sovereignty over their lives.

Two ahimsas, then: an unknowable ahimsa that at least conforms to the form of dying without killing, and that other, even darker night of nonknowledge—the unknowable and formless ahimsa of living by dying (though Gandhi does not to my knowledge explicitly oppose the two). The form of the latter makes it easier to follow, the royal road, less liable to lead to situations where satyagrahis mislead themselves. This may be why it is the more usual description of ahimsa. And yet, dying without killing can well conserve the sovereignty of the being who practices it. So satyagraha must nevertheless at its purest follow the more dangerous, unknowable, and formless ahimsa of the "foot-tracks"—that of living by dying.

~

At work in this pair—ahimsa that still has the form of nonkilling, and unknowable ahimsa that might even kill friend or enemy—is a very distinctive

concept of the example. Gandhi persistently invokes the quasi-concept of
the example when trying to describe how satyagraha will be universalized.
This is another of those terms that is convoked into being only in the
English text: it renders a range of Gujarati terms, perhaps also convoking
them in the process into a sharing. During the Rowlatt Satyagraha, in the
first of a series of pamphlets issued to explain satyagraha, he writes that the
"method of satyagraha is unique. In it example [*aacharan,* conduct] alone
is precept."[46] He constantly urges associates to "follow the example" [*nak-
kal,* copy] of those figures, historical and mythological, who have offered
satyagraha; he hopes to convince "by example [*kariney,* doing]"; "by per-
suasion, above all by my own example."[47]

Pure example and pure means—two ways, then, of describing satyagraha. And Gandhi's example is a curious concept. The usual lexical equivalents to it (such as *dakhlo* or *namuno*) are not as prominent in Gandhi's
Gujarati texts: while the English word "example" is often passive, the words
Gandhi translates as "example" are often active, and carry a range of additional connotations—conduct, doing, copying.

As earlier discussions should indicate, the thinking of the example
offered here cannot be conceived the way Bilgrami suggests: as a choosing
for oneself, becoming self-contained, or a sovereignty without universality. The claim here rather is that the example is another universality. In
order to prepare for engaging in later chapters with how Gandhi thinks
the example, the rest of this chapter will explore how the discourse of general responsibility conceives exemplarity and the example; this conception is articulated in *Hind Swaraj* by the Reader.

In the *Prior Analytics,* Aristotle lays the foundations for that thinking of
the example:

> to argue by example is neither like reasoning from part to whole,
> nor like reasoning from whole to part, but rather reasoning from
> part to part, when both particulars are subordinate to the same
> term, and one of them is known. It differs from induction, because
> induction starting from all the particular cases proves (as we saw)
> that the major term belongs to the middle, and does not apply the
> syllogistic conclusion to the minor term, whereas argument by
> example does make this application and does not draw its proof
> from all the particular cases.[48]

What, then, is the relation of the example with the whole, the universal, the law? In his analysis of this very passage, Giorgio Agamben points out that while here induction proceeds from the particular to the universal and deduction from the universal to the particular, the paradigm is defined by a third and paradoxical type of movement, which moves "from the particular to the particular." The domain of Aristotle's discourse, Agamben suggests, is "not logic but analogy":

> [Analogy] intervenes in the dichotomies of logic (particular/
> universal; form/content; lawfulness/exemplarity; and so on) not
> to take them up to a higher synthesis but to transform them into a
> force field traversed by polar tensions, where (as in an electromag-
> netic field) their substantial identities evaporate. But in what sense
> and what way is the third given here? The analogical third is
> attested here above all through the disidentification and neutrali-
> zation of the first two, which become indiscernible. The third is
> this indiscernibility, and if one tries to grasp it by means of bivalent
> caesurae, one necessarily runs up against an undecidable. It is
> thus impossible to clearly separate an example's paradigmatic
> character—its standing for all cases—from the fact that it is one
> case among others.

The example as the analogical third bears a distinctive relation to the exception:

> If we now ask ourselves whether the rule can be applied to the
> example, the answer is not easy. In fact, the example is excluded by
> the rule not because it does not belong to the normal case but, on
> the contrary, because it exhibits its belonging to it. The example,
> then, is the symmetrical opposite of the exception: whereas the
> exception is included through its exclusion, the example is
> excluded through the exhibition of its inclusion.[49]

We could heighten the stakes of Agamben's reading by contrasting the juridical third and the example or the analogical third. To bring together the arguments of the previous chapters: chapter 2 suggested that the jurid- ical third is in Gandhi's writing the distinguishing mark of modern civility, and is constituted by measure. And yet, chapter 3 suggested, there is no moment of pure measure; modern civility itself makes measure immeasurable. Putting these two arguments together leads us to a question: If measure is immeasurable, would this not transform the third party as a category? The analogical third, I would suggest, names the transformation the third party and its universality must undergo because measure is always already immeasurable. Put differently, the example names the impossibility of a pure induction or deduction, the way the analogical third in its impurity everywhere disidentifies and neutralizes the dichotomies of logic.

By extension, the disidentification and neutralization at work in the example as the analogical third names the way that sovereign power encounters newness, makes decisions, experiences freedom. We can briefly indicate how this work by considering the Reader, who says:

> If the education we have received be of any use, if the works of Spencer, Mill and others be of any importance, and if the English Parliament be the Mother of Parliaments, I certainly think that we should copy [nakal karvi] the English people, and this to such an extent that, just as they do not allow others to obtain a footing in their country, so we should not allow them or others to obtain it in ours.[50]

Here, to copy or follow the example of the British would already produce a difference and newness that cannot be subsumed within the phrase "English rule without the Englishman." The Reader's swaraj is thus a very emplaced one, marked by a sensible—an Indian flag and Indian navy, perhaps even by an Indian civilization. This swaraj erases its colonial origins, allows a critique of colonialism, and even assumes the sensibility of its new home. The Reader is here sovereign in relation to the very example he copies, to the rule he follows; hence he is not anxious about the derivativeness of the modernity he might establish, nor is he concerned that the swaraj he establishes will be a placeless universal.

Moreover, by following the example of the English parliament, he will establish himself as not just another sovereign example but an example of universality itself—swaraj. Neither the English parliament nor the future Indian parliament is subordinate to the universality of swaraj—rather, to draw on Agamben, they have a relation of "exclusive inclusion" with it. It is precisely the exclusive inclusion of the example that allows the Reader and Gandhi to conceive modern civilization as a restless potential simultaneously absolutely internal to and absolutely external to every socius. (As this suggests, the debates over the last few decades about the derivativeness or otherwise of modernity, nationalism, or other related phenomena is quite misplaced—symptomatic of our failure to recognize how concepts travel primarily, maybe even only since the power to conceptualize requires a certain constitutive freedom, through the sovereign example.)

One should add: the Reader also seeks to establish the Indian parliament—a rule of right means—as an example by resorting to an exception: by using any means whatsoever to drive out British. As this suggests, it is not enough to think of the example as only the reverse of the abject exception. The Reader's example is constituted by exercising a sovereign exception—by excepting himself from the law of right means. And everywhere here, the universality of the law works by example—whether the sovereign makes an exception to or enforces the law, he makes an example. In this sense, the example is the dominant term in this relation between exception and example, for the exception itself is an example of sovereign power.

And to return to a question we encountered earlier, would not the sovereignty of the example as an analogical third require us to revise our thinking of the concept the decision? Derrida writes:

A decision has to be prepared by reflection and knowledge, but the moment of the decision, and thus the moment of responsibility, supposes a rupture with knowledge, and thus an opening to the incalculable—a sort of "passive" decision. In other words, one cannot rationally distribute the part [part] that is calculable, and the part that is incalculable. One has to calculate as far as possible, but the incalculable happens [arrive] . . .[51]

In view of the centrality to sovereign power of the analogical third and the example, would not this formulation be too preliminary? Is it not necessary to distinguish more systematically between two decisions (though the two can never be kept knowably apart)—those involved in general and absolute responsibility, in sovereignty and nonsovereignty?

The Reader's experience is an example of the way general responsibility—the rule, law, or sovereign—experiences newness or the unknown. The Reader seeks a swaraj that he does not have or know, that he can anticipate only in the example of the British, and in the law that the British exemplify. Here, while what is followed is known, what the following results in—the example the follower becomes—is unknown. Nevertheless, precisely because the follower knows what he follows, the unknowability of his swaraj is experienced in such a way as to not knowably threaten the sovereignty of the follower. Recognizing the incalculability that the new always threatens to introduce, the Reader makes the most strenuous effort to remain sovereign over it. And this incalculability and unknowability will continue even after political swaraj is realized. With swaraj, the sovereign will become the judge, encounter the newness of every case by following the examples already provided by the rule of law, and thus remain sovereign through the moment of decision. Contrary to Derrida's argument, the judge calculates so that the incalculable arrives only as an analogical third.

On the other hand, there can also be another example—one that surrenders to the madness of the nonsovereign decision. To this other example and exception (which we should surely, dissenting from Schmitt's ascription of the sovereign exception to the "Protestant theologian," say is the exception-example in the Kierkegaardian sense), to this other decision, Gandhi gives the name *satyagraha*. His argument suggests: satyagraha is what is proper to the madness of the decision—a decision is not in other words properly mad unless it is an act of satyagraha.

As with Kierkegaard's example of the exceptional moment when Abraham raises his sword to kill Isaac, satyagraha is mad because it assumes absolute responsibility and in the process comes to be marked by a distinctive universality. Satyagraha is the most intense moment of universality in that it is both a potentiality borne by all being and a practice that must include all being. Because of this universality, while there can be infinite cases of satyagraha, satyagraha is nevertheless not one case among others. Moreover, satyagraha must not claim sovereignty over the other or even itself. Rather, it must practice a surrender that transforms both self and other. In all of this, it seeks to enforce a universality without sovereignty, or more precisely the universality of a freedom without sovereignty. Satyagraha is then what is proper to the other decision, the mad decision; it is the "form," so to speak, that the other decision or mad decision must have.

But what satyagraha "is"—precisely that remains to be understood. How this other example and decision works, how it ruins the sovereignty that it must begin from—all this emerges especially dramatically in the transformations that the concept of the warrior undergoes as Gandhi tries to think the satyagrahi as the true or exemplary warrior.

CHAPTER 5

The Destruction of Conservatism

I love scavenging. In my Ashram, an eighteen-year-old Brahmin lad is doing the scavenger's work in order to teach the Ashram scavenger cleanliness. The lad is no reformer. He was born and bred in ortho-doxy. He is a regular reader of the Gita *and faithfully performs san-dhyavandan. His pronunciation of Sanskrit verses is more faultless than mine. When he conducts the prayer his soft, sweet melodies melt one into love. But he felt that his accomplishments were incomplete until he had become also a perfect sweeper, and that if he wanted the Ashram sweeper to do his work well he must do it himself and set an example.*

—Mohandas Gandhi, "Speech at Suppressed Classes
Conference," April 13, 1921

But real life, composed of all sorts of expenditures, knows nothing of purely productive expenditure; in actuality, it knows nothing of purely nonproductive expenditure either.

—Georges Bataille, *The Accursed Share*

BY ASSERTING THAT Mahavira and Buddha, founders, respectively, of Jainism and Buddhism, are true Kshatriyas or warriors, that ahimsa is the truth of the warrior, Gandhi embarks on a radical conservatism—radical in the etymological sense that it uproots the figure of the arms-bearing warrior, who is its point of departure. If absolute equality and ahimsa is the truth of the warrior, then the truth of the warrior lies in the destruction of the arms-bearing warrior, and what is most proper to the concept of the warrior is that it gives itself its own destruction.[1]

But this radical conservatism is profoundly unstable and fractured in its autoimmunity. The same sentences, phrases, and words divide unde-cidably into two ways of destroying the arms-bearing warrior's conser-vatism. In the first, absolute equality is conceived as a stable order that nourishes deep-rooted and stable differences while ensuring that they remain nonhierarchical. Here, while the figure of the arms-bearing warrior is uprooted and destroyed, what is conserved and rerooted is a sovereign autoimmunity, or a sovereign order of the proper self-sacrifice. In the second, what is conserved is an absolute equality that must be accomplished by relinquishing sovereignty, by practicing a self-sacrifice that destroys the differences stabilized by the sovereign order of the proper. Here, what is most proper to conservatism is that through proper sacrifice it uproots all sovereignty, and conserves the impropriety proper to being.

Symptomatic of the way Gandhi's radical conservatism divides into two is the divergence between a Gujarati and English sentence in chapter 17 of *Hind Swaraj*. In the Gujarati version, the Editor asks: "Is he the warrior who himself [*potey*] carries his own death on his head, or he who keeps the death of the other in his own. [*Potey maathey maut lai farey tey ranvir ke beejana maut potana haath ma raakhey che te?*]." The English version is: "Who is the true warrior—he who keeps death always as a bosom-friend, or he who controls the death of others?"

The Gujarati rendering remains within the problematic of the arms-bearing warrior's sovereign self-sacrifice. Here the satygrahi carries his own death on his head (in other passages on other occasions, the satyagrahi carries his death in his fist or hands). His fearlessness is no different from that of the arms-bearing warrior—he only has more of it. Even if unlike the arms-bearing warrior he refuses to exercise sovereignty over the other, the passage seems to presume that he does so by exercising sovereignty over himself: the satyagrahi's daya-driven fearlessness is so great that he masters his fear of death. Here, willing surrender is also a willed surrender, as an act of the will over the self.

Where Gandhi conceives satyagraha within the problematic of sovereign self-sacrifice, then the warrior's fearlessness must be acquired first, and then relinquished or, in a telling word, "abdicated." Thus, to recall Gandhi's letter to Andrews in 1918: "It is clear that he who has lost the power to kill cannot practice non-killing. . . . It may look terrible but it is true that we must, by a well-sustained, conscious effort, regain this power, and, then, if we can only do so, deliver the world from its travail of himsa by a continuous abdication of this power. . . . I do believe that we shall have to teach our children the art of self-defence."[2]

Abhaydan, or the gift of fearlessness, can similarly be given by the satyagrahi in a way that remains within the problematic of the arms-bearing warrior's sovereignty. Thus, Gandhi writes in 1926:

When some sage observed man killing numberless creatures, big
and small, out of a regard for his own body, he was shocked at his
ignorance. . . . He saw that if man desired to realize himself, i.e.,
truth [atmaney, etley satyaney], he could do so only by being
completely detached from the body, i.e., by giving the gift of fearlessness to other bodies [abhaydan aapvano; "making all other
beings feel safe from him"]. That is the way of ahimsa.[3]

Here the "sage" already has abhay or fearlessness, which his desire for satya
or truth/being, then, leads him to give to all other beings. Here abhaydan
is something that the one who has abhay gives to the one who does not.

$\sim$

In contrast, the English version of the sentence above ventures a new
thought—friendship with death. That strange difference, both ventured
and concealed from Gandhi as from us, erupts more forcefully still perhaps
in the Editor's remarks about abhay or fearlessness in the same chapter.

A man with a stick suddenly came face to face with a lion and he
instinctively raised his weapon in self-defence [eni medey, was
raised of itself]. The man saw that he had only prated about fearlessness when there was none in him. That moment he dropped
the stick and found himself free from all fear.

The man in question desires the fearlessness of a satyagrahi—this is why
he would aspire to not raise his stick against even a lion, why he would not
read the raising of a stick against the lion as itself an act of fearlessness.

But he finds that two opposed automaticities sequentially seize him (he
works automatically—or in Gandhi's English translation, "instinctively,"
whether to raise or drop the stick). When he faces a lion, his stick is first
raised of itself, and the man assumes a fearlessness that allows him to face
the lion. This fearlessness is quite the converse of that at work in the satyagrahi's abhaydan: here fearlessness possibly springs from his fear of the lion,
and there is certainly no effort here to give fearlessness to the lion. Such
fearlessness enacts the machinicity and automaticity of sovereign power.
Even though he seeks to relinquish sovereign power, and has indeed perhaps successfully relinquished agency (he does not consciously raise the
stick—it is raised automatically), a sovereign power seizes him despite himself. This seizure is symptomatic of the way that sovereign power works—

it exceeds agency and cannot simply be relinquished by willing. Sovereign automaticity or machinicity constantly threatens to undermine satyagraha, makes it impossible to simply choose to be a satyagrahi—to practice a conscious, agential, or willed satyagraha.

However, another automaticity is also at work. The man begins by consciously recognizing his fear, but what follows when he drops the stick is automatic: "he found himself free of all fear." Here freedom from fear comes through an activeness that cannot be thought in terms of agency or sovereign automaticity. Here fearlessness must be received as a gift; it cannot be received through self-mastery. Even though satyagrahis take the vow of fearlessness, the vow does not itself produce fearlessness. In 1914, several years after he had been disciplining himself through the vows, including that of fearlessness, Gandhi writes to an associate: "I have not got rid of the fear of death, despite much thinking."[4] The vow of fearlessness cannot thus itself produce fearlessness even in the most famous devotee of satyagraha; devotees must be seized by fearlessness, and they cannot choose when they are seized, nor even can they know whether they have been seized. Only in this seizure do they receive from themselves—more precisely, from the other that they themselves are—the gift of fearlessness.

How is this gift of fearlessness given and received? In August 1918, Gandhi writes to C. F. Andrews and remarks: "I have always declined to work out to my satisfaction all the possible deductions. I have taken up things as they have come to me and always in trembling and fear."[5] Here, fearlessness involves not a mastery of fear but a surrender to it, a submission and openness to fear because the being feared—the lion—is also the friend; here, both fear and fearlessness spring from love. Now prem (love) and daya (compassion) no longer require fearlessness as their precondition; they call forth a fearlessness very different from that of the arms-bearing warrior.

Whether the lion receives it or not, the man gifts the lion a promise not to threaten its life; and he can do so moreover because he has also received a certain fearlessness from the lion's being. This fearlessness, to draw on a vocabulary that the next chapter will elaborate, is not unique to the lion or to the man; it is rather singularly the lion's and the man's because both share the oneness and manyness of satya or being. Here, then, abhay does not precede abhaydan; the very act of abhaydan is also the receiving and giving of abhay. Even if there is fear of the beloved or the friend (there are no enemies any longer in the conventional sense), that fear is never mastered but is tremblingly inhabited; this trembling inhabitation is itself both fearlessness and the gift of fearlessness.

Put differently, the fearlessness the satyagrahi seeks can be received only by giving it to and receiving it from others. Because seizure by fearlessness involves a gift of the self to the other, only by giving fearlessness to the other do givers receive fearlessness from themselves. Indeed, the more they give, the more they receive, and the more they have to give. Abhayadan is in this sense the gift that, in giving, there is always more to give of.

In this chapter, I will focus primarily on the first conservatism—how Gandhi's attempt to affirm the absolute equality of all being comes undone in many instances because, while this conservatism profoundly reworks the traditions that he departs from, it also often conserves the immeasurable inequalities of these traditions. Later chapters will dwell on the second, and more intriguing, conservatism—how it conceives equality, how it ruins and even destroys the immeasurable inequalities of the first conservatism, and why the tension between the two conservatisms can never be resolved in a knowable manner.

～

Symptomatic of the way the first radical conservatism works is the way the gender of the warrior-satyagrahi changes in his writings. Gandhi often envisions a social order in which men and women, to quote Sujata Patel's crisp formulation, "have separate spheres in societies and specific roles in the making of the Indian nation, for they are essentially complementary to each other."[6] In 1917, Gandhi remarks when discussing the satyagrahi-warriors: "An effeminate refusal to defend the nation, or the weak, is ever to be relinquished [tyajya]. In order to protect an innocent woman from the violence of a man, we should either offer ourselves as sacrifice and subdue him by the force of love, or if we don't have that strength we should employ all our physical strength to stop the violence of that violent man."[7] Here as in many other places in his writings, the satygrahi is male, and the innocence he protects is female.

And yet, things rarely stay that straightforward, for the innocence and feminity the satyagrahi conserves is also most proper to the satyagrahi, or what the satyagrahi must assume—satyagraha is, in one of his formulations, "innocent suffering."[8] The resultant tensions are well exemplified in the curious shuttling in his writings between the self-sacrifice of the sati [according to classical texts, the widow who immolates herself on the pyre of her husband] and the satyagrahi. The words *sati* and *satyagraha* share, of course, an etymological root: *sat*—being or truth.[9] And conceptually, both share a thinking of being as the giving of the self to the very limit— here the limit of one's own death, the nonbeing proper to one's own being. Surely because of these overlaps, Gandhi has a profoundly conflicted relation with sati.

On the one hand, he consistently attacks sati as the ideological or social practice of self-immolation. "Self-immolation [*aapghat,* suicide] at the death of the husband is not a sign of enlightenment but of gross ignorance as to the nature of the soul." This formulation avoids the colonial and national-ist contrast exemplified, for instance, among Gandhi's contemporaries by Coomaraswamy, between the forced sati, which is condemned, and the voluntary sati, which is glorified.[10] In Gandhi's writing, by contrast, the voluntary sati is even more horrifying than the forced sati, for if the latter is the moment of the most horrific subordination that is inflicted on one by others, the voluntary sati is the occasion of that most horrific subordi-nation that is inflicted on one by oneself, because of one's own "gross igno-rance," an ignorance for which one is oneself responsible.

On the other hand, he attacks voluntary sati only in order to affirm sati: "The human love that it incarnates is intended to serve as a stepping-stone to the divine or universal [*anek atmani,* of many souls] love. That is why immortal Mira sang: "God alone is my husband—none else [*Mere to gird-har gopal, dusra koi nahin]*."[11] The invocation of Mirabai (who abandons her husband for a life of devotion to Krishna) as the exemplary sati suggests that such an offering can never be made to a human. The passage returns, perhaps unconsciously, to what it presumes is the original moment of sati, where the self-immolation occurs as an offering to Shiva, or the divine. That return resonates with devotee poets like Kabir, who often describe their relation with the divine by casting themselves as satis.

This sati is simultaneously a life. The English version says: "Satihood is the acme of purity. This purity cannot be attained or realized by dying [*aap-ghat,* suicide]. It can be attained only through constant striving, constant immolation of the spirit from day to day."[12] The Gujarati version is even more emphatic: "Its difficult accomplishment is by living." Here, the con-trast of suicide with living becomes stronger, and sati more emphatically names the death and indeed the life proper to the gift of oneself to the divine.

Though these passages refuse the dying involved in the social or ideo-logical practice of sati as the self-immolation of the widow on her husband's pyre, they do so in order to affirm another death, another burnt offering, and the life that emerges from this offering. Could it be, then, that if Gandhi affirms "satihood" while refusing the social practice of sati, this is because he wishes to appropriate satihood for satyagraha, because he conceives of the satyagrahi as the true sati?

Perhaps because of this shuttling between sati and satyagraha, the qualities of "fortitude" and "forbearance" (the almost interchangeable translation into English of a wide variety of words: *dhiraj, dhairya, kshamasheelta* among them), essential for satyagraha, come to be embodied in the Kshatriya woman. "As long as we have not developed the virtue of the Kshatriya, it is difficult for us to win swaraj. That virtue is fortitude. That virtue had come to twelve-year-old Prahlad, Sudhanva, and Sita. Ravana offered tempting things to Sita, tried to frighten her, but she did not yield ever so little. That is why we regard her as a pure Kshatriya woman, a goddess, a mother.[13] Here, two children and a woman become the embodiment of Kshatriya virtue. And three years later he argues:

> Damayanti never left chanting the name of Nala, Sita could not think of anyone in the world except Rama, and Draupadi, although indignant with Yudhishthira, would never move away from him. . . . [T]he poets have depicted these three wives as more virtuous than their husbands. Rama, Nala, Dharmaraj would become insignificant without Sita, Damayanti, Draupadi. The men are impulsive, their conscience is wayward and their devotion too is not undeviating; whereas the devotion of these heroines was steady like the lustre of a gem. The patience [*kshamasheelta*] of women far surpasses that of men. Since forbearance [*kshama*] is a mark of strength, these virtuous women were not weak but strong. What is man's courage before woman's? This weakness, however, is endemic to man as such, not particularly to Nala and the rest.[14]

Being a true Kshatriya warrior now involves being a Kshatriya woman, for she exemplifies forbearance and patience. In his many formulations, it is she who suffers without resorting to violence, who practices self-sacrifice rather than sacrifice of the other. In this spirit, he claims later in life to himself have

> learnt the lesson of non-violence from my wife, when I tried to bend her to my will. Her determined resistance to my will on the

one hand, and her quiet submission to the suffering my stupidity involved on the other, ultimately made me ashamed of myself and cured me of my stupidity in thinking that I was born to rule over her, and in the end she became my teacher in non-violence. And what I did in South Africa was but an extension of the rule of satyagraha which she unwillingly practiced in her own person.[15]

The crucial role played by mothers, wives, and children is also evidence of the ordinariness of satyagraha. Now everybody can and must become a Kshatriya regardless of birth and physical prowess: "This Kshatriya spirit is possible even for a weak and handicapped child. Non-violent non-co-operation is a means of cultivating the Kshatriya virtues."[16] Giving evidence before the Disorders Inquiry Commission, in the wake of the very campaign during which he had drawn extensively in his speeches on the figure of the satyagrahi warrior, Gandhi is asked whether satyagraha does not require "extraordinary control over ordinary human passions." He replies, "It does not really require that extraordinary control for sufferings that you imagine. Every mother suffers and she is not exceptionally gifted with any great virtue."[17] He invokes in this context also the poet Dalpatram: "Let us learn to die for the country. . . . We can serve the country in this way only if we have in us the motherly love about which we learnt in our childhood from Dalpatram."[18]

Even the suffering that Indians must undergo for swaraj is the suffering of childbirth. "Nothing is ever achieved except through suffering. A mother suffers when her child is born. In the same way, India has to go through suffering at present."[19] It is perhaps symptomatic of this affirmation that from the late 1920s, Gandhi occasionally describes his relation to ashram inmates as that of a mother (thus also his niece Manu Gandhi's memoir, *Gandhi, My Mother*), the *Gita* as his mother, and urges men to develop the strength of women.

~

As we might expect, this effort to conceptualize absolute equality in terms of the life of surrender named by sati, womanhood, and childhood fails quite thoroughly. When he conceives self-sacrifice and fearlessness in terms of mother, wife, and child, that reconceptualization only reinstitutes in a more insidious and invidious form the sovereign power that his own writing elsewhere questions; in the process, it destroys also any possibility of absolute equality. To begin with, even if women exemplify satyagraha, they often seem to be only the prehistory of satyagraha—those who practice satyagraha without quite understanding it, and from whom satyagrahis must take their departure. Even more symptomatic of the reinstitution of sovereign power is the pervasiveness of the trope of the thekana—a word that names the proper or rightful place.

I have explored elsewhere how the thekana involves a policing of both self and other to keep both in their rightful places.[20] Gandhi's disquiet with the warrior is often because the latter maintains the thekana wrongly—through mastery and domination. The satyagrahi's task, then, is to maintain the thekana, or the sovereignty of the proper, in a way that is organized by daya or compassion and prem or love.

Where the thekana prevails this way, satyagraha is still thought in terms of the sovereign gift. Here satyagrahis relinquish the duragrahi's kingly sovereignty by intensifying their sovereignty over themselves: the satyagrahi asserts a sovereignty over his life through self-mastery and then makes a sovereign gift of his own life. That gift, however, necessarily conserves also an immeasurable inequality. Thus, the displacement of the male warrior is accompanied by the regulation of what is proper to womanhood and manhood, which is why Gandhi can write that "the moment the men of India realize their manhood, and the women their womanhood, India becomes free."[21]

The profound violence of the insistence on rightful places is evident in a retrospective account Gandhi provides of his educational experiment at Tolstoy Farm, conducted at a time when "my faith and courage were at their highest," a level that he has not since achieved. The experiment involved the coeducation of girls and boys, and because "my mind then used to be more innocent than it is now," and as part of it all the "boys" and "young girls" would "bathe in the same spot at the same time" and "all of us slept on an open verandah." Throughout, "my eyes followed the girls as a mother's eyes would follow a daughter." But "one day one of the young men made fun of two girls." The news made him "tremble" [dhrujyo] and he

> remonstrated with the young men, but that was not enough. I wished the two girls to have some sign on their person as a warning to every young man that no evil eye might be cast upon them, and as a lesson to every girl that no one dare assail their purity. The passionate Ravana could not so much as touch Sita with evil intent while Rama was thousands of miles away. What mark should the

girls bear so as to give them a sense of security and at the same time to sterilize the sinner's eye? This question kept me awake for the night. In the morning I gently suggested to the girls that they might let me cut off their fine long hair. . . . At first the girls would not listen to me. I had already explained the situation to the elderly women who could not bear to think of my suggestion but yet quite understood my motive, and they to had finally accorded their support to me. They were both of them noble girls. One of them is—alas!—now no more. She was very bright and intelligent. The other is living and the mistress of a household of her own. They came round after all, and at once the very hand that is narrating this incident set to cut off their hair.[22]

The "very hand that is narrating this incident set to cut off their hair": the nonviolence of satyagraha here most emphatically requires the imposition of a thekana or rightful place on the young girls—a thekana to which they are brought and kept by Gandhi, the elderly women, and their own "nobility." The violence of the thekana is all the more invidious because all those involved regard their actions, at least by Gandhi's account, as a tender and solicitous care of those protected, as nonviolence.

The violence at work here is superbly brought out in Ashwini Tambe's powerful essay, which traces how Gandhi uses "the figure of the prostitute to articulate a vision of the nationalist body politic, with the prostitute emblematizing the corruption that tested the body politic's virtue. His repeated refusals to admit prostitutes into the Congress party, in particular, are indicative of his vision of the nationalist collective." He insists that they must give up sex work before joining the Congress. He is thus marked, as Tambe points out, by an "inability, in effect, to practice a real neighbourliness towards them."

She also traces how one group of prostitutes decides to continue with sex work and remain Congress members. They were

elected as delegates, and even founded an association whose manifesto promoted helping the poor and nursing the sick, spinning and weaving, skills training among prostitutes, and adopting nonviolence. In 1925, when Gandhi encountered this group again, he reacted with intense anger that their association provided higher musical training, and declared their organization's manifesto to be "obscene." He angrily advised the women "to do humanitarian work before reforming themselves." "Let it be understood" he proclaimed, "[that] these women do know how to dance and sing. . . . Spinning must not be used as a passport to vice." He regretted that "public opinion" and their own "modesty" had not made them "refrain from seeking Congress membership." He called the women of Barisal "more dangerous than thieves, because they steal virtue," and described them as akin to "unrepentant professional murderers." Their "tremendously dangerous powers of mischief" disqualified them from being true members of the satyagraha (civil disobedience) movement.

As Tambe goes on to argue, the hostility to the figure of the prostitute is because the "sexual potency of such women represented a form of difference that crucially challenged his vision of an acceptable polity," since "being a prostitute represented the opposite of being self-sacrificial."[23]

In the spirit of Tambe's argument, we might well ask: In what conceptual sense are the prostitutes of Barisal incapable for Gandhi of offering self-sacrifice? If the assumption is that they cannot do so because sex work renders the body calculable, and that the calculable is incapable of incalculability involved in self-sacrifice, then that same assumption should also be made of landlords and industrialists—groups on whom he depends so much. As the difference in his response suggests, he works with an additional assumption: while landlords and industrialists have a thekana they abide by, prostitutes do not. (This is of course itself a reformist assumption. Historically, prostitutes too likely have a thekana. Do the Congressmen of Barisal accept participation by prostitutes because they work with an attenuated recognition of this?) The prostitutes of Barisal cannot offer self-sacrifice since they have abandoned the thekana of womanhood.

The refusal to accept the self-sacrifice offered by the prostitutes of Barisal reveals thus that satyagraha does not only involve the immeasurable and aneconomic giving of the self. That aneconomy turns out to itself be organized by an economic relation with the thekana, which is what confers the ability to offer self-sacrifice. Sacrifices offered by those who do not stay at their rightful place must be rejected even and perhaps especially if these sacrifices are aneconomic.[24]

As this example suggests, the thekana involves a profound violence. Even if all life is equal, even if the prostitutes are his "fallen sisters" (as he

calls them), they are so as his "moral unequals," to use Aishwary Kumar's
phrase (so appropriate to describe Gandhi's conservatism of the thekana)—
figures who are unfit to offer satyagraha because they have been deemed
incapable of the self-sacrifice proper to satyagrahis.[25] And precisely because
of this, Gandhi's refiguring of satyagrahis as mothers, women and children
remain within the problematic of sovereign autoimmunity, or a killing of
the self that perpetuates the sovereignty of that very self: by killing the
masculine figure of the satyagrahi-warrior, the masculine order is kept in
place. And in the process, Gandhi also maintains, as Leela Gandhi notes,
"an ideological contract with nationalist discourse through his insistence/
reassurance that the good woman in the world or on the street will never
be/become a prostitute and/or a woman with sexuality."[26]

～

Gandhi never explicitly or systematically renounces his emphasis on the
thekana or rightful place, or on the satyagrahi as having a greater degree of
the same fearlessness as the warrior. And yet, the aporetic tensions involved
in conserving absolute equality unfold in such a manner as to constantly
undo and unsay his affirmations of the thekana. That strange autoimmunity
and destruction marks especially his efforts to think caste as a proper and
complementary social order. (Perhaps this is because, beginning at least
from the time of the Vaikom satyagraha of 1924, his thinking of caste comes
to be powerfully questioned by his interlocutors and critics, above all by
Dr. Babasaheb Ambedkar, in a way that his thinking of gender is not.)

In untouchability Gandhi encounters immeasurable inequality. Untouchability is thus a "blot" [kalank] on Hinduism; he draws repeatedly
on medieval bhakti poets and other premodern sources to argue that it "is
no part of Hinduism. It is rather its excrescence to be removed by every
effort."[27] He responds by making a distinction between varnashramdharma
or varnadharma [to recall: the law or duties, dharma, of the four castes,
varna, and stages of life, ashrama] and untouchability, affirming the former
and attacking the latter emphatically (suggesting, for example, that "even
the slavery of the Negroes is better than this [untouchability]."[28]

Especially from the 1920s, as his engagement with the Gita intensifies,
varnadharma comes to him to name the equality that works across incommensurable difference. He makes this claim by reworking the Gita's
term swadharma, which he translates as "own duty" or "one's own duty."
Krishna's famous injunction to Arjuna in the Gita goes: "Better one's own
duty [swadharma], bereft of merit, than another's well-performed; better

is death in the discharge of one's duty; another's duty is fraught with danger" (III:35). He invokes this verse often, second only perhaps to another verse (II:47), again from the *Gita*.

In the traditions that he departs from, swadharma or own duty names quite the opposite of any equality. Both before and after him, these traditions identify swadharma with the duties prescribed by varnashramadharma. And swadharma is regarded as just even if it institutionalizes inequality. As the Brahmin priest of the temple that is the target of the 1924 Vaikom satyagraha says while defending the ban on untouchables entering the temple, the inequality of the various castes is just, since people are born into lower castes because of sins in their previous lives. In these conservative traditions, swadharma thus accomplishes a social hierarchy where each group is immeasurably given to its tasks, and where the immeasurable inequality that accompanies these tasks is rightful and righteous.

By the early twentieth century, many nationalist readings of the *Gita* question this conservative reading of varna, and claim that varnadharma involves only functional distinctions. Gandhi reiterates these arguments: thus his insistence in the early years that equality does not require interdining or intermarriage, that the equality of castes is entirely compatible with their separateness. But even as he does so, he inadvertently reorients these readings toward a conservatism by conceiving swadharma in terms of rooting self-sacrifice. Thus the *Gitashikshan*:

> Varnashrama had its root *[jad]* in the idea of swadharma. We
> do not see today the true idea of *varna* [no equivalent to "true
> idea of"]. It is limited now to restrictions about interdining and
> intermarriage. The idea of varna is not peculiar to Hinduism. Such
> dharma which was peculiar to one society would become narrow,
> and one need not die for it. If our dharma is universal and valid at
> all times, one should be ready to die for it.[29]

He thus argues that varnadharma does not allow for hierarchies: where all are equally marked by self-sacrifice, by a refusal to persist in being, varnadharma becomes the "truest path to equality." Again, he draws on the *Gita*:

> What may be called swadharma? The varnashrama had its origin in
> this idea. . . . In chapter 18, we were even told that following one's

swadharma one even attains perfection; that is, following one's
swadharma one attains equality with all *[eksarkhapan]*. In this
transitory world, we see equality nowhere. No two leaves are equal
[eksarkha]. But the *Gita* shows the way to equality.[30]

"No two leaves are equal"—now there is only incommensurability. Here,
as in the formulations about men and women, he struggles to think a
conservative equality—an equality that conserves incommensurability
by treating differences of caste as *swabhavik,* "natural," or of one's ownmost orientation, by treating varnadharma as the institutionalization of
finitude.[31] Varnadharma comes to name the order of an equality organized
around the thekana or rightful place:

I believe that just as everyone inherits a particular form so does
he inherit the particular characteristics and qualities of his pro-
genitors, and to make this admission is to conserve one's energy.
That frank admission, if we will act up to it, would put a legitimate
curb upon our material ambitions, and thereby our energy is set
free for extending the field of spiritual research and spiritual
evolution. It is this doctrine of varnashramadharma which I have
always accepted.[32]

Varna, he suggests, "simply means that we must treasure and conserve all
the good qualities that we inherit from our ancestors, and that therefore
each one should follow the profession of his father so long as the profession is not immoral."

The problems that this affirmation of varnadharma poses for him are nowhere more evident than in his difficult relation with what he on occasion
calls *"maryada dharma"* [the dharma of proper limits, of propriety]. The
term *maryada* is among a cluster of words that in his vocabulary names
the proper, or the proper limit. Gandhi affirms *maryada* unconditionally
and absolutely. He also regards the emphasis on *maryada* or limits as a—
maybe the—most essential element of Hinduism, as indeed of religion. This
is unsurprising, for the "concept" of finitude necessarily requires a proper,
even where the proper is conceived in terms of its own ruination. Without
maryada, there can be no critique of "modern civility," no affirmation of

"true civility" and satyagraha. By contrast, *maryada dharma* refers in his vocabulary, as is not uncommon especially among Vaishnavas in Gujarat during the period, to the customary restrictions among castes such as those around interdining, intermarriage, or intermingling. He affirms *maryada dharma* conditionally and contextually. In a speech to untouchables in 1924, he says:

> Though, however, I believe in *maryada dharma,* I do not regard it
> as an essential part of Hinduism. I can even conceive a time when
> these restrictions might be abolished with impunity. But the
> reform contemplated in the untouchability movement does not
> obliterate the restriction as to inter-dining and inter-marriage.
> I cannot recommend wholesale abolition of these restrictions to
> the public, even at the risk of being charged with hypocrisy and
> inconsistency.[33]

In this formulation, we see a tension. While *maryada dharma* is not part of satyagraha, and not an essential part of varnadharma (for the limits it imposes are not the proper limits that flow from and to from *bhog* or sacrifice), he must believe in it because he affirms the separateness of castes as substantive entities. By the late 1920s, the tension becomes more acute. Now he criticizes the restrictions on interdining, intermarriage, or intermingling among castes. In this sense, he no longer believes in *maryada dharma* (there seem to be no professions of faith in it in these later years); now his emphasis on *maryada* could itself require the relinquishment of *maryada dharma*. But things do not work that way. Instead, he continues to affirm it as a way for those upper castes who believe in untouchability to continue the practice without actively imposing social sanctions on the untouchables. He writes thus to one correspondent, who likely defended untouchability:

> To me the whole of your argument tends to show that those who
> have the ideas of physical purity that you have should treat them-
> selves as untouchables rather than treat any single human being as
> such, and this is the well-known practice followed among the
> Vaishnavas. Those who follow it do not call themselves untouch-
> ables, but they are called 'merjadees' [those who follow *maryada
> dharma*]. You know the meaning of the word.[34]

But as Gandhi would have at least unconsciously known, *maryada dharma* cannot ever be a benign disengagement: such a refusal to share a common space with other castes, especially socially subordinate ones, is itself profoundly exclusionary and violent. (Gandhi is keenly aware of this in other contexts, as instanced by his criticisms during various noncooperation movements of satyagrahis using caste boycott as a weapon against those who supported the British).[35]

That Gandhi even in later years can at best dissent only mildly from *maryada dharma,* allowing others to practice it as a compromise even if he does not practice it himself, is symptomatic of how, despite his willed opposition to untouchability, he actively participates in its perpetuation. Because he is explicitly committed to an understanding of *varna* in terms of an immeasurable equality across substantive social differences, he cannot ever consciously recognize that varnadharma or *maryada dharma* can only be experienced by Dalits as a most violent subordination. Instead, until his last years he seeks to institute a proper varnadharma—thus his emphasis on the "uplift" of lower castes, his insistence that they should abandon "unclean habits" such as eating meat or consuming alcohol.

It is surely his commitment to varnadharma as an order of conservative equality that makes him so reluctant to support temple entry movements—they demand an abstract equality.[36] His hesitation during the Vaikom satyagraha is well known. And that attitude persists into later years. Only three days before his assassination, for example, he remarks of one demand for temple entry, "Those who insist on going into the temple are not true devotees. They do not care for *deva-darshan* [beholding the gods], they are running only after their right and away from religion."[37]

⌒

But Gandhi's thinking of varnadharma cannot be entirely subsumed within the tropes of *maryada dharma* and the thekana. The challenges he faces from critics, especially Ambedkar (who so incisively and decisively points on several occasions to Gandhi's complicity in perpetuating untouchability) also threaten his conservatism profoundly. Already at Vaikom, he is compelled to accord primacy to the abstract equality he presumes is involved in temple entry. Such intense questioning ruins his efforts to root a conservative equality in concordance and complementarity. Thus, he comes to acknowledge that even if untouchability is external to varnadharma, the practitioner of varnadharma remains absolutely responsible for it. And that responsibility turns out to require nothing less than the self-sacrifice, or should one say relinquishment, of varnadharma itself.

Ironically, he comes to this argument in the very course of his efforts to affirm a varnadharma purified of untouchability. Untouchability is thus sometimes a "weedy growth fit only to be weeded out, as we weed out the weeds that we see growing in wheat fields or rice fields."[38] The branches of untouchability must be destroyed so that the tree of varnadharma can be saved: "Let us have the pruning knife and lop off those diseased branches, but let us not lay the axe at the root."[39] And to kill untouchability, he is quite willing to die: "If, in the attempt to free Hinduism of this blot, I have to lay down my life, it will be no great matter."[40] Repeatedly, he insists that varnadharma and untouchability cannot both exist—one of them must and indeed will kill the other.

This presumption of an external relation between varnadharma and untouchability is almost diametrically opposed to Ambedkar's. When in 1933 Gandhi starts the English periodical *Harijan*, he asks the latter for a message. Ambedkar writes: "The outcaste is a bye-product of the caste system. There will be outcastes as long as there are castes. Nothing can emancipate the outcaste except the destruction of the caste system."[41] The implications of Ambedkar's formulation here and elsewhere have been incisively drawn out by Anupama Rao, who reads Ambedkar to suggest: "The threat of temporary outcasting drew its force from the permanent outcasting of one community—the untouchables. This negative force held the caste order together, making structural violence integral to the molecular order of caste. Though despised, untouchables formed the glue of the caste order; while untouchability was its structuring negative principle, it was Hinduism's 'constitutive outside,' its necessary yet excised animating force."[42] Untouchability is, she writes elsewhere in her reading of Ambedkar, "the secret of the caste system."[43] For Ambedkar, thus, the killing of untouchability will also be the death of Hinduism; as he famously puts it in the reply he writes to Gandhi after the latter criticizes Ambedkar's *Annihilation of Caste:* "There can be a better or worse Hindu, but a good Hindu there cannot be."[44]

Earlier, Gandhi had written that he has "always respectfully differed from those distinguished countrymen, Dr. Ambedkar among them, who have held that untouchability will not go without the destruction of varnashramadharma."[45] But as he attempts to extirpate untouchability, some strange parallels with Ambedkar develop. It turns out that killing untouchability involves not just abolishing caste restrictions but the four varnas themselves. One register on which he conceives of this abolition is by insisting that all Indians should strive to belong to "one varna, viz., Sudras," the caste that serves others.[46] This contrasts with his statements on other occasions—in the context of the need to develop fearlessness—that all Indians are Kshatriyas. But such a displacement of the Kshatriya by the Shudra only restates the sovereign autoimmunity at work in the claim that women embody the qualities of Kshatriyas.

It is with "Harijan," ironically, that his sovereign autoimmunity, his conservatism of the thekana, both becomes most marked and eventually encounters a force that it cannot overcome. "Harijan," which can be translated as people of god, enters Gandhi's vocabulary around 1921.[47] He continues using it sporadically through the 1920s along with other terms—in Gujarati, especially *Antyaja* [last-born], and in English, especially "untouchables." Around 1931, "Harijan" becomes significantly more than a word. That year, a Dalit correspondent writes to him, in a letter reproduced in his Gujarati periodical *Navjivan,* objecting to the word *Antyaja.* Gandhi notes in his response that the words *Dhed* and *Bhangi* were formerly not liked, and now the word "Dalit," which "I think . . . was first used by the late Swami Shradhanand," is also not liked, and he concludes the article by writing: "If a better word than Antyaja or Dalit occurs to anyone he may send it to me."[48] A correspondent responds with the word "Harijan," which Gandhi is enthused by. His enthusiasm is not only because it has been used by the "father of Gujarati poetry," Narsinh Mehta, but because, "the word 'Harijana' can also be given the meaning of those who have been sacrificed [*tyagya,* 'abandoned'] by society."[49]

He explains his enthusiasm again a short while later in a speech made at the opening of the industrialist Chinubhai Ranchodlal's temple to untouchables: "The 'Antyaja' are 'Harijan'—this word is Narsinh Mehta's, and that was found for me by an unknown man, but even if Narsinh Mehta has not used it in that sense, it is still an apposite word—we are all Harijans. . . . By insulting and debasing them we have become *durijan* [bad people]. To stop being durijan and become Harijan, we have to get rid of this sin [*paap*]."[50]

⁓

Three points about this word "Harijan" must be stressed. First, within the vocabulary of general responsibility, this word is somewhat difficult to understand. The questions pile up quickly. On a secular register: Should we not respond to the abject exception-example, to the violence against "those who have been sacrificed," by instituting an abstract equality that includes the formerly excepted? On the register of secular religion: Even if the upper castes have committed a massive violence in practicing untouchability, are they still not the children of god?

"Harijan" acquires the sense it does, I suggest, because it offers redress, from within the problematic of absolute responsibility, for the sacrificial violence that created the state of abject exception. In the schema the word operationalizes, sacrifice as abandonment, as the offering of the inessential and despised, is the opposite of what bhakti poets like Narsinh Mehta, and Gandhi following them, celebrate as the only proper sacrifice: self-sacrifice, or the sacrifice of the dearest and most beloved.

And proper self-sacrifice involves an assumption by the self of absolute responsibility for an offense against the other (recall: "we are solely responsible"), where to accept culpability is to refuse to measure it out among self and others. This Gandhi who assumes absolute responsibility for untouchability would not deny the correctness of a more complex historical analysis of the phenomenon. But for him as a satyagrahi, such an analysis is irrelevant: he is concerned only with his sole responsibility. In the aloneness of this absolute responsibility for his violence, he must become the *durijan,* the *duragrahi* [the opposite of a satyagrahi]. That very process also requires that those excepted by abjection—the Dalits or untouchables—should by inversion come to exemplify the divine, or become Harijan. Those who had been guilty of violence toward untouchables cannot in this logic claim to be children of God, except by denying absolute responsibility for their violence.

Second, to stop being durijan and become Harijan, satyagrahis must atone for the sin of untouchability through what Gandhi on occasion calls *prayaschitta* or "repentance."[51] In anticipation of further discussion in chapter 9, note for now that the insistence on repentance posits a gap between Harijans on the one hand and satyagrahis as *durijans* on the other. Satyagrahis must seek to traverse this gap—which is infinite—by embodying Harijanness, as Gandhi, for instance, does by practicing scavenging. And yet, even after such embodiment, satyagrahis cannot know whether they are Harijan—they must in order to be responsible insist on an infinite gap separating them from Harijans.

He is perhaps even more aware of and troubled by this distance after the Poona Pact, when he writes: "And here I would like to recall what

Dr. Ambedkar told me. He said, 'Let there be no repetition of the old method when the reformer claimed to know more of the requirements of his victims than the victims themselves.'[52] Suggestive of his acknowledgment of that infinite and abyssal gap is his argument in 1935—which fails to persuade his associates—against having untouchables on the Harijan Sevak [service] Boards. He writes later:

> I was opposed, as I am even now, to the inclusion of Harijans in Harijan Sevak Boards. If the Harijan Sevak Sangh is a society of penitent debtors, as it has been conceived to be, it can contain no creditors. Creditors are there. They will some day or other dictate their terms. Today the vast majority are helpless. . . . The penitent caste Hindu has to render service *[seva]* in all humility. It may or may not be accepted. His repentance may be too late. But whether late or in time, he must perform it. He can't have Harijans to do for him.[53]

Thus, the figure of the Harijan is possible only where there is this abyssal gap that must be traversed and yet cannot be, for the Harijan is the figure to whom a debt is forever owed. The word "Harijan" is the acknowledgment of this debt, of the need for *prayaschitta* or repentance without end.

To the extent we can know, Gandhi's introduction of the term "Harijan" does not succeed in allowing upper castes—not even the most penitent of them, such as he himself may have been—to assume absolute responsibility for the violence of untouchability. Derrida remarks:

> At the limit, the gift as gift ought not appear as gift: either to the donee or to the donor. It cannot be gift except by not being present as gift. Neither to the "one" nor to the "other." If the other perceives or receives it, if he or she keeps it as gift, the gift is annulled. But the one who gives it must not see it or know it either; otherwise he begins, at the threshold, as soon as he intends to give, to pay himself with a symbolic recognition, to praise himself, to approve of himself, to gratify himself, to congratulate himself, to give back to himself symbolically the value of what he thinks he has given or what he is preparing to give."[54]

Derrida's reading of the pure gift allows us to indicate why "Harijan" fails to assume absolute responsibility. On the one hand: the satyagrahi gives his repentance to the Harijan. If he recognizes his repentance as no repentance at all, as inadequate given the enormity of his sins, then he has not paid himself back—he will then only be aware that no repentance has taken place. But Gandhi seems quite satisfied on several occasions (and would not even just once be enough for no gift to have occurred?) that his repentance is complete and adequate. During the Round Table talks in 1931, for instance, he presumes that his repentance has already made him a *bhangi* (a member of the sweeper caste) or Harijan, and therefore more representative of the untouchables than Ambedkar. His fast-unto-death against the Communal Award follows in 1932, and this compels Ambedkar to give up the gains the award had granted to Dalits. Nothing could be more violent than this presumption of a repentance so complete as to allow the penitent to represent the offended, to achieve union with and even teach the offended. As Anupama Rao points out: "Ambedkar noted that such penitential politics inflicted a violence of its own, and did so in two ways: first, by failing to recognize Dalits' quest for dignity and social recognition, and second, by redefining Dalits—in their quest for political autonomy— as the perpetrators of social violence rather than its historical victims."[55]

On the other hand: even if Gandhi as the penitent was to have thought of his repentance as inadequate, as not having taken place, the donees cannot but be aware of the gift they receive, and this gift must overwhelmingly be experienced by them as disempowering. Why this is so is indicated beautifully in D. R. Nagaraj's argument that "in the intensely moving romantic tragedy of self-purification . . . there was scope for only one hero, that is, Gandhiji himself."

> Babasaheb had no other option but to reject the Gandhian model. He had realized that this model had successfully transformed Harijans as objects in a ritual of self-purification, the ritual being performed by those who had larger heroic notions of their individual selves. In the theatre of history, in a play of such a script, the untouchables would never become heroes in their own right, they are just mirrors for a hero to look at his own existentialist angst and despair, maybe even glory.

Nagaraj provides a brilliantly insightful account of a moment in Gandhi's May 1933 fast, when Mahadev Desai tries to persuade a Harijan boy to come to offer orange juice to Gandhi to break the fast. The boy, Desai notes, never turned up. Why not? speculates Nagaraj. And he suggests: "the Harijan boy who took a decision not to keep the appointment with Gandhiji was reborn as a Dalit youth."[56] And he had to be so reborn, one might add, because to the extent that the term Harijan persists, it institutes the right-ful places of varnadharma (and thus inescapably of a punitive *maryada dharma,* however much Gandhi might wish this to not happen). As such, the gift it gives is economic, which is to say, not only no gift at all, but a gift that subordinates its recipient, regardless of the intentions of the giver.

~

The third point to be noted about "Harijan," however, is this: that term is overtaken by a distinctive autoimmunity. As Gandhi becomes willing to envisage the total destruction of varnadharma in the pursuit of absolute equality, the figure of the Harijan goes to a death that is no longer governed by the problematic of sovereign autoimmunity. Already in an essay in 1921 describing his abandonment of the belief that he was "a citizen of the Empire," Gandhi draws an analogy with the untouchables: "The whole sit-uation is now changed for me. . . . I can take no pride in calling the empire mine or describing myself as a citizen. On the contrary, I fully realize that I am a pariah untouchable of the empire. I must therefore constantly pray for its radical reconstruction or total destruction, even as a Hindu pariah would be fully justified in so praying about Hinduism or Hindu society."[57]

In an interview in 1927, he goes further. He is told: "So long as you do not destroy varna, untouchability cannot be destroyed." And he replies: "I do not think so. But if varnashrama goes to the dogs in the removal of untouchability, I shall not shed a tear."[58] This position parallels in striking ways Ambedkar's insistence that the destruction of untouchability requires the destruction of varnadharma. Unlike Ambedkar, of course, Gandhi comes to his argument most reluctantly, and he continues to recoil from it all his life.

And yet, by the late 1930s, as he himself assumes the identity of a *bhangi* or sweeper more emphatically, his prayers become ever more paradoxical: he must pray for varnadharma by seeking its death. His conservatism, then, must even as it affirms varnadharma make restitution for its violence by leaving itself open to its—varnadharma's—own death or killing as a self-sacrifice. In this self-sacrifice, varnadharma must be displaced by what un-touchables put in its place—"they will someday or the other dictate their terms."

Could it be then that from a Gandhian perspective the quasi-concept of "Harijan" must seek to sacrifice itself to that other quasi-concept, the

Dalit, that this very death is the destiny the concept "Harijan" must seek to receive from the concept Dalit? Is an absolute responsibility assumed in the peculiar death of the term "Harijan"? The very nature of absolute responsibility—its unknowability—precludes an answer this question.

And that vehement denunciation of the prostitutes of Barisal—what happens here? If a distinguishing mark of satyagrahis is that they give themselves aneconomically, then a paradox follows. Going by Gandhi's understanding of their lack and even refusal of thekana or rightful place, the prostitutes of Barisal would in their double abandon—abandoning their thekana and abandoning themselves to satyagraha—have given themselves more aneconomically to it than those who do not abandon the thekana. Is his vehemence, then, also an anxiety-ridden recoil from the possibility that the prostitutes of Barisal may be the true satyagrahis and true warriors, not him? And if this is so, what is the satyagraha that he does not (as we in our turn do not) know whether he ever practices? What is this other radical conservatism? How else can the figure of the arms-bearing warrior be destroyed?

· CHAPTER 6 ·

Daya Otherwise

I have not seen Him, neither have I known Him. I have made the world's faith in God my own, and as my faith is ineffaceable, I regard that faith as amounting to experience. However, as it may be said that to describe faith as experience is to tamper with truth, it may perhaps be more correct to say that I have no word for characterizing my belief in God.

—Mohandas Gandhi, *Atmakatha [Autobiography]*,
Part IV, chapter 11, *Autobiography*

To be sure, nothing is less sure than a god without sovereignty; nothing is less sure than his coming, to be sure.

—Jacques Derrida, *Rogues: Two Essays on Reason*

WRITING IN 1926, Gandhi recalls his first meeting with the Jain thinker Shrimad Rajchandra, or Raychandbhai: "I was introduced to Raychandbhai in July 1891, on the very day on which, returning from England, I landed in Bombay. At this time of the year the sea is stormy. The ship, therefore, had arrived late and it was already night. I stayed with Dr. Pranjivan Mehta, Barrister, now the well-known jeweller of Rangoon. Raychandbhai was his elder brother's son-in-law." At the time of the meeting, Gandhi is almost twenty-two and Raychandbhai almost twenty-four. Retrospectively at least, Gandhi considers that very first meeting the beginning of a certain break. Pranjivandas Mehta (whom Gandhi had already known in Britain—he is described later, recall, as the model for the Reader in *Hind Swaraj*) describes Raychandbhai to Gandhi as a poet and a *shatavadhani*—one who can pay attention to a hundred things simultaneously:

> Someone suggested that I should utter a number of words in his presence, saying that no matter to what language they belonged he would repeat them in the same order in which I had uttered them.

· 171 ·

I could not believe this. I was a young man, had just returned from England, and was a little vain, too, of my knowledge of languages; in those days I was under the powerful spell of English. Having been to England made a man feel that he was heaven-born.

So Gandhi writes down a list of words from different languages ("for how possibly could I afterwards remember them in their due order") and reads them out. Raychandbhai, who "did not know English at all," slowly repeats the words in the same order. "This was an excellent experience to break a little the binding spell of English on me." Until his death in 1900, Raychandbhai continues to play a crucial role in Gandhi's life, with the two keeping up a sporadic but intense correspondence.

Many of Gandhi's key terms occur in Raychandbhai's *Mokshamala*, written when the poet was around sixteen, and the one book by him that we know he asks Gandhi to read. Much of *Mokshamala* is devoted, as the title suggests, to the question of how to attain moksha. While that term is usually understood as salvation from the cycle of life and death, Raychandbhai emphasizes a more immanent understanding of it in his writings and reiterates this understanding in a letter to Gandhi: "While the *atman* is in the state of ignorance, characterized by anger, etc., it is under the bondage of the body, and complete cessation of such a state, deliverance from it, is described by seers as moksha."[1] But moksha is here inseparable from daya or compassion, the *"sarvamanya dharma"* or "religion accepted by all." Daya is practiced through abhaydan or the gift of fearlessness to all life.[2] And abhaydan is realized through ahimsa, which is thus the primary vow required to practice daya.

Even the form of *Hind Swaraj* resonates in some ways with *Mokshamala*, which consists of many short chapters, some of which are written as a dialogue between a seeker *[jigyasu]* and satya [truth/being]. Gandhi is also aware, perhaps because of the readings he has done at Raychandbhai's suggestion, of other sources with which to think daya—most notably the *Gita* and the *Tulsi Ramayana*.

But almost until the writing of *Hind Swaraj*, he reads these texts from within the problematic exemplified by William Salter's invocation of "ethical religion." It is only following his unconscious break with Salter, which occurs many years after Raychandbhai's death, that there is a more rigorous reworking of those Buddhist, Hindu, and Jain traditions that Raychandbhai has helped make into his inheritance.

If *daya* is one of the key terms that his reading of these traditions picks up on, that may be because the *Mokshamala* already brings it to the point where it emphasizes the equality all life. That emphasis already murmurs in some articulations of the classical Jain problematic of moksha. For example, the *Uttaradhyayana Sutra* insists that all creatures are averse to pain, and that "a man should wander about treating all creatures in the world so as he himself would be treated."[3] The equality of all life demands the renunciation of the world, for himsa is committed in the pursuit of one's worldly life. The equality of all life in this tradition is not in the inert modern sense where they all share a biological baseline defined as life, but rather in the sense that all that lives is marked by the potentiality for moksha. Even if moksha itself is possible in this tradition only from a human life, animals can be reborn as humans, and this makes for a certain equality of all life.

Mokshamala reads this equality in a way that no longer focuses only on the potentiality for moksha but on something else—love of life, worldly or not: "its own life is beloved to every living being, and [so] there is no religion higher than one that protects [*raksha*, also rescue] the lives of all living beings."[4] This recognition of the other's love of life, this equality of all loves, is the experience of daya. Daya now comes to be oriented toward two-ness, to simultaneously emphasize absolute equality and absolute difference. As Gandhi reads *Mokshamala* and other texts, he radicalizes the thinking of daya he inherits to the point where the old category destroys itself and emerges anew, otherwise.

This chapter explores three senses in which the category daya is transformed: how Gandhi questions the idea of a "kinglike God" or any concept of Being organized under the sign of sovereignty, and thinks God and Being instead under erasure; how his dayadharma articulates the simultaneous "not-ness" and "manyness" of being through its emphasis on the Upanishadic phrase *neti neti* (not this, not this) and the Jain phrase *anekantvada* (manyness of reality); and how this not-ness and manyness of being is the "living by dying" that he describes as a friendship with death.

∼

Raychandbhai sometimes insists on a hierarchy of religions and gods. In chapter 13 of *Mokshamala,* for instance, Satya [truth/being] tells the Seeker that he cannot say whether those who worship Shankar, Vishnu, Brahma, Bhavani, Mohamed, or Jesus will obtain moksha. Those whom these devotees call god [*parmeshwar*] have themselves "not attained moksha."[5] And chapter 29, after insisting that "daya is the most proper manifestation [swarup] of dharma," that "there is no dharma where there is no daya," goes on to attack "meaningless religious sects" that say it is not a sin to kill life, and which say that "at most protect human life." The followers of these religions are "fanatical" and do not know the "slightest manifestation of daya."[6] For him, relatedly, while the Vedas are better since they do at least recognize the importance of daya, only Jainism realizes dayadharma.

While here ahimsa becomes the criterion by which to assess the degree of daya in a religion, by which to create a universal hierarchy of daya and of religions, on other occasions Raychandbhai also seems uncomfortable with these hierarchies. Gandhi writes in his *Autobiography* about how he received from Raychandbhai the sense that "Hindu dharma" already had the resources to think all questions of dharma or religion. Raychandbhai also reassures him around 1894, when Gandhi is engaged intensely with "Christian friends" and "Mussalman friends" who try to persuade him to convert. "I expressed my difficulties in a letter to Raychandbhai. . . . Raychandbhai's letter somewhat pacified me. He asked me to be patient and to study Hinduism more deeply. One of his sentences was to this effect: 'On a dispassionate view of the question I am convinced that no other religion has the subtle and profound thought of Hinduism, its vision of the soul, or its daya.'"[7] Raychandbhai suggests that he read the *Gita* and other Hindu texts. "I had already been introduced to him and a close bond had grown between us. I had respect for him, and so I decided to get from him everything he could give. The result was that I gained peace of mind. I felt reassured that Hinduism could give me what I needed." The reassurance that Raychandbhai gives Gandhi is somewhat at odds with the assertion in *Mokshamala* in the previous decade about the superiority of Jainism over Hinduism. But again Gandhi is concerned more with extending the argument that Raychandbhai makes in his letters: "If we follow Raychandbhai's point of view, no one need give up his faith and embrace another."[8]

～

Picking up on these strands from Raychandbhai, Gandhi draws out another way of thinking daya-ahimsa. No longer a hierarchical universalism, it is oriented now rather around the absolute equality and unity of all being, and the absolute responsibility that this entails. His thinking of daya-ahimsa is especially difficult to read since he thinks these concepts through the term *satya*, a term that (like its translations Being or Truth, which are central to the ontotheologies and logocentrisms of Western metaphysics) is often caught up in a long history of hierarchical universalisms. Though his list of vows varies over the years, satya is always the first. Thus his formulations in the 1930 letters on the Satyagraha Ashram vows: "As a matter of fact all observances are deducible from satya and are meant to subserve it." He insists that a vow can be recognized as one only if it is organized by the desire for satya. Any vow found opposed to satya, a *rakshasi* or demonic vow, must be abandoned.

In his writing, this word steeped in the hierarchical universalisms of the Indian subcontinent comes to be reworked—though not always in his explicit formulations—to open toward another universalism. Symptomatic of this reworking is the way he thinks the relation between satya or truth/being and *Ishwar* or God. In 1929, he writes to Prabhudas Gandhi: "Usually I had been saying and writing that God is Truth. In the new manual I have deliberately improved upon that definition and I now say Truth is God. I am here thinking of that Truth which transcends even God."[9]

Now, this is not correct—he "usually" does not say any such thing during the period. Already in 1908, he writes: "Truth is God, or God is nothing but Truth. We come across this idea in every religion."[10] Through most of the teens and 1920s, he writes in a similar vein. Though the remark that satya is God is slightly more frequent than the one that God is satya, if there is anything "usual" during this period, it is a symmetric and transitive equivalence between satya and God, such that God names satya and satya names God, and both name daya. But even though his own chronology of his intellectual shift may be a bit off, the letter to Prabhudas does reveal to us that by 1929 such transitive equivalence is no longer available to him and that, in retrospect, even the apparent symmetric and transitive equivalence of previous years was governed actually by the formalization "God is Satya."

What could be at stake in refusing a symmetric and transitive equivalence between the two terms? Since Gandhi's explicit arguments do not answer this question, it remains our task to do so. In the formulation "God is satya," I would suggest, Gandhi reiterates the shift that secularists like Salter also make. They refuse to think of God as sovereign and insist instead on the sovereignty of being—whether of the highest principles (as in a performative ethical order) or the most general principles (as in a constative scientific order). In the process, they leave unchallenged the most ontotheological of concepts—sovereignty. "God is satya"—this shifts the infinite and grounding sovereignty from God to being.

The formulation "Satya is God," by contrast, segues into another think-ing of being. Already by 1913, Gandhi is hesitant about any conception of God or Being in terms of sovereignty. That year he describes apprecia-tively "the view of the *advaitvadins*" [exponents of *advaita,* the nonduality of being]: "God is no dispenser of rewards and punishments [*fal,* fruit], nor is He an active agent [*karta*] . . . . At no time and in no circumstances do we need a kinglike God [*raja jeva*]. By thinking that we do, we put a limit to the power of the *atman,* which is infinite."[11]

From the late 1920s, through his insistence that satya is God, Gandhi articulates this intriguing argument that refuses to think God in terms of sovereignty. In a letter in July 1930 on the vow of satya (the first of a series of letters, written while jailed in Yeravda, and devoted to vows that inmates of Satyagraha Ashram should observe), he writes:

> The word "satya" is derived from *sat. Sat* means that which *is* [*hovu,* emphasis original]. Satya means a state of being [*hovapan*]. Nothing is [*hasti*; English addition: "or exists in reality'] except Truth. The right name for God [*parmeshwar*] is sat, that is satya. In fact it is more correct to say that "satya" is God than to say that God is "satya." But we cannot do without a ruler [*rajyakarta*], a general [*sardar*]. That is why the name God is more current, and will remain so. However, on thinking, it will be realized that sat or satya is the only correct name, and only it conveys the full significance. . . .
>
> . . . what may appear as truth to one person will often appear as untruth to another person. But that is no reason for worry. Where there is honest [*shudh,* pure] effort, it will be realized that what appear to be different truths are like the countless and apparently different leaves of the same tree. Does not God Himself appear to different individuals in different aspects? Yet we know that He is one. But Truth is the right designation of God. Hence there is nothing wrong in every man following Truth according to his lights. Indeed it is his duty [*kartavya*] to do so. . . . Therefore the pursuit of satya requires bhakti, devotion. Such bhakti is "a bargain in which one risks one's very life." It is the path that leads to God. There is no place in it for cowardice, no place for defeat. That is the "mantra of living by dying" [*E "marine jeevvano mantra" chhe;* "It is the talisman by which death itself becomes the portal to life eternal."]

But now we have come to the shores of ahimsa. We shall discuss it next week.[12]

In these passages, first, a distinctive unity and oneness marks satya—all the various satya are leaves of one tree. Gandhi comes quite early on, presumably through his thinking of daya, to affirm the tradition of *advaita* or nonduality of being, which he glosses in English with phrases such as "the essential oneness of life." Because daya cannot know any limits, it must include all, and sustain their oneness. This "essential unity of man and for that matter of all that lives" named *advaita* makes universalism both possible and necessary.[13] "We have but one soul. The rays of the sun are many through refraction. But they have the same source. I cannot therefore detach myself from the wickedest soul (nor may I be denied identity with the most virtuous). Whether therefore I will or no, I must involve in my experiment the whole of my kind."[14]

Second, thought as daya, the *advaita* of sat or being becomes a universalism inflected with an absolute equality. "I believe in the rock-bottom doctrine of Advaita and my interpretation of Advaita excludes totally any idea of superiority at any stage whatsoever. I believe implicitly that all men are born equal."[15] And not just all men: all living beings and perhaps even inanimate things are absolutely equal because they are suffused by an immanent satya.[16]

Third, where such equality prevails, no overarching principle can hold together what is absolutely equal. Here, unity cannot be thought in terms of the infinite sovereignty usually ascribed to God. To understand God as infinitely sovereign is to conceive a God who is not Godly enough—who cannot take account of absolute equality or infinite multiplicity, whose Godly power is merely a higher form of the power of human sovereigns. But this inadequacy of the term God does not lead to the replacement of the term God with a new secular term, Being. Being too is inadequate when thought in conventional terms. Rather, now sat becomes a placeholder for daya-ahimsa, a unity riven by the irreconcilability of the absolutely equal. *Advaita* thus demands here another notion of God, where God is no longer the grounding and sovereign principle but the recognition of the impossibility of any such principle.

Fourth, bhakti or devotion must be groundless or "pure" here, for it is of the very nature of absolute equality that there can be no grounded reasons for it. "It is only if we have the faith in our hearts that we are all one, though we exist as separate beings, it is only then that we can experience equality [*samata anubhaviye*]. Otherwise, in the world there is no equality [*samaanta*] even between two leaves."[17] Involved here is a break from conservative equality-inequality, which, too, recognizes incommensurable differences, and goes on to found and make present a rooted social order and hierarchy (for Gandhi, above all varnadharma) around these differences. By contrast, at stake here is an absolute equality. Such equality, given the incommensurability of differences, cannot be made present or substantive. It can only remain a matter of faith; it can only be sustained through faith. Where satya or being is absolute equality, the groundlessness involved in faith in God is required to affirm sat; this too is why Gandhi must say not "God is Satya" but "Satya is God."

In his insistence on absolute devotion, Gandhi affirms here the very fanaticism that religion is usually charged with—religious persons must follow their own truth, even by risking their own lives, even at the risk of defying every collective ethics. But that insistence is shot through here by what the absolute devotion is toward: the absolute equality and difference of every other (which is also to say, of every other's faith and being). Absolute devotion leads here thus to an encounter with the groundlessness of one's own faith; what must be practiced therefore is the faith proper to this groundlessness.

~

This very distinctive understanding of satya brings Gandhi, as he notes, to the "shores of ahimsa" because now the devotee of satya can no longer seek to dominate or eradicate the various other satya that he encounters. How then to relate to them? How to practice a groundless faith? His letter from jail the next week is devoted to the vow of ahimsa:

But it is impossible for us to have a perfect darshan of satya ['realize perfect truth'] in this body. We can only imagine [*kalpana*] it. For this ephemeral body, a manifestation of the eternal body is not possible. That is why in the end we must depend on faith [*shraddha*].

That is why the seeker came to the appreciation of ahimsa. Should I suffer the difficulties that come my way [*marg*], or should I wreak whatever destruction is needed and cut my way? This question stood before the seeker. If he keeps destroying, then he does not cut his way but simply stays where he was—this the seeker saw. The one who suffers difficulties marches ahead ['and at times even took the others with him']. In the very first act of destruction he saw that the satya which he sought is not outside him but within. Hence the more he took to violence, the more he kept falling back, the more he receded from truth. . . .

This much everybody should know: without ahimsa the search for satya is impossible. Ahimsa and satya are as inseparable [othproth] as two sides of a coin, or rather a smooth unstamped metallic disk. Who can say which is the obverse and which the reverse? Nevertheless, ahimsa may be considered [ganiye, "is"] the means [sadhan] and satya may be considered the end [sadhya]. The means is what is within our reach, and this is why ahimsa is the supreme dharma. Satya becomes God. If we keep attending to the means, we will someday behold [darshan] satya.[18]

This formulation indicates what is proper to the groundless faith demanded by a satya that is internally marked by infinite and incommensurable multiplicity. While one person's "truth" is another's "untruth," that untruth too is a truth. The devotee must nourish the absolute equality of these other truth-untruths. Only thus are they faithful to their own faith, to the satya that is "within" rather than "without." To violate the absolute equality of others' truth-untruths would be to violate also the absolute equality given by their own truths. And yet, this nourishment of the absolute equality of other truths can never take the form of disengagement; what is affirmed here is not only absolute equality but also an absolute unity. *Advaitvadis* can be faithful to the absolute equality and unity that their own faith secretes only by constantly staging confrontations between their own and other truth-untruths in a way that sustains absolute equality between them. This confrontation Gandhi describes with the classical term *ahimsa* and his neologism *satyagraha*.

The insistence on ahimsa—which Gandhi describes on occasion as a "negative word"—inscribes a certain not-ness into satya. For while only satya or being "is" (as Gandhi says on several occasions), this "is-ness" is neither constative nor performative; rather than presencing itself as a fullness, this satya can be realized (though that word is no longer appropriate) only by practicing the not-ness that is ahimsa. Gandhi puts this suggestively in 1925, in one of his earliest essays on the *Gita*:

Satya is positive *[hakar]*, while ahimsa is negative *[nakar]*. Satya
is the witness of things *[vastunu sakshi chhe]*, nonviolence forbids
something despite its being *[vastu chhata]*. Satya is *[chhe]*, *asatya* is
not *[nathi]*. Violence is, non-violence is not. Nevertheless, the
highest dharma for us is that nothing but non-violence can be *[hovi
joiye]*. Satya is its own proof *[swayamsidh]*, and non-violence is its
supreme fruit. It is necessarily hidden in satya. But it is not evident
[vyakt] as satya is, and so humans search ['the meaning of'] the
Shastras without acknowledging it. Nevertheless, their truth will
teach them nothing but nonviolence.[19]

It may be misplaced to presume that the comparison here is "between
truth and violence as positive objects and untruth and non-violence as
negative ones."[20] I am tempted to think that the passage suggests rather
that "is-ness" in the originary sense of satya or being cannot be confused
with the is-ness of *asatya* or nonbeing; indeed, satya can be sustained only
by constantly reflecting on how to distinguish it from asatya. Asatya performs a constative—it solidifies being. To do so, asatya requires a violence
or himsa that refuses to allow for the singularity of either of the being car-
rying out asatya, or of the being on whom asatya is inflcted. The not-ness
of himsa and asatya consists in the way they dominate not just beings
on whom violence is inflicted, but even those who inflict violence. Asatya,
one might say, does not let be. This is why, from the perspective of satya-
ahimsa, one might say that asatya and himsa are not.

Relatedly, in thinking ahimsa, we need to take our cue from that striking paradox: ahimsa is not, and yet nothing but ahimsa can be. Put together,
this says: satya as being is marked by a constitutive not-ness, ahimsa. This
not-ness is very different from the not-ness of asatya and himsa. Ahimsa
involves a not-ness of being because here self-sacrifice becomes a surrender without subordination—an encounter with the other that seeks to
orient both toward satya. Here, while ahimsa is a means to realize satya, it
is not a means in the sense of being an instrument that leads to satya;
rather, ahimsa is itself the being of satya. Through ahimsa, the groundlessness of faith as well as the irreconcilability of truths is acknowledged as not
just empirical but conceptual. Indeed, satya and ahimsa are so indistinguishable that the distinction between the head and tail of a coin would not
make sense (hence Gandhi's additional remark about a "smooth unstamped
metallic disk"). But as in a disk, they are not the same—satya and ahimsa

remain constantly outside each other, each oriented to and necessitating the other without passing over into the other. Despite the insistence on darshan as a beholding, what is beheld here is not presence but absence or notness. Devotion does not and indeed must not overcome the gap between the devotee and satya. Rather, the devotee must practice ahimsa in order to properly sustain the gap; in order to provincialize the devotee's truth.

〜

The not-ness of ahimsa, of this truth that provincializes both itself and other truths, is marked by a pair of phrases that enters Gandhi's vocabulary in the teens and 1920s. One of these is the phrase *neti neti*—"not this, not this" (or perhaps: not this, not that). Gandhi notes in 1921: "The final word of the *Upanishads (Brahmavidya)* is Not. *Neti* was the best description the authors of the *Upanishads* were able to find for Brahman."[21] The phrase is associated most famously with the sage Yajnavalkya's response to a question about what the nature of Brahman is. With that phrase, which can be too easily and misleadingly collapsed into the generic category of negative theology, Yajnavalkya insists that a not-ness marks the question of being. This insistence on not-ness is taken up in the Advaitic systematization associated with Adi Shankaracharya.

Gandhi radicalizes neti neti to the point where its apophasis is not accompanied by an eventual mystical cataphasis of moksha, where the devotee achieves union with God. By 1922, he writes: "Moksha also recedes farther away from an aspirant. This fact inspired the profound expression 'neti.' A number of great *rishis* in ancient times set out to seek moksha—the *atman*. In its pursuit, they descended into many valleys and climbed many hills, jumped over thorny hedges and discovered, at the end of the journey: 'It cannot be this.'"[22] Indeed, his *Gitashikshan* lectures suggest that neti neti is not just the description of God entailed by profanity, but rather constitutive of divinity itself. "God, our selfness *[hu]* and all other things in the universe become one. Even God vanishes and we have only neti, neti."[23] Put differently, being can only be, and be thought, in its notness. What is this moksha that ends in apophasis, that resists cataphasis, that remains a mysticism and religion rather than becoming a theology? Gandhi writes in a letter again in 1922: "I am an *anekantvadi*. This is the most important thing I have learnt from Jain philosophy [darshan]. It is implicit in Vedanta. It is explicit in Jain philosophy."[24]

Anekantvada—the doctrine of manysidedness—is a central term in Jain thought, associated also with *syadvada* (the doctrine of possibilities).[25]

Whatever the source from which Gandhi picks up his understanding of anekantvada, he describes it as a form of ahimsa.[26] But his anekantvada or *syadvada*, he adds, "is not the *syadvada* of the learned, it is peculiarly my own. I cannot engage in a debate with them. It has been my experience that I am always true from my point of view, and am often wrong from the point of view of my honest critics. I know that we are both right from our respective points of view. . . . I very much like this doctrine of the manyness of reality."[27] Anekantvada, then, comes to be another name through which Gandhi thinks ahimsa. For Gandhi, what is compelling about anekantvada is that it thinks the absolute equality and irreconcilable difference involved in the not-ness of being. Symptomatic of the way this satya works through neti neti and anekantvada is Gandhi's remark: "I am an *advaitist* and yet I can support *dvaitism* (dualism)."[28] If *advaita* itself becomes compatible with "dvaitism," this is because a rigorous pursuit of *advaitism* must deal also with the irreconcilability and separation that constitutively marks *advaita*'s oneness. Here, the "neither this nor that" of neti neti leads to the "both-and" or manyness of anekantvada, where different truths can exist together. What Spivak has suggested in a related context may be relevant here: "It is not too fanciful to say that a possible *dvaita* 'structure of feeling,' if there are such structures, would be the future anteriority of every being as potentially, unanticipatably *avatar* in the general sense. It is within this general uneven, unanticipatable possibility of *avatarana* or descent—this cathexis by the ulterior, as it were, that the 'lesser' god or goddess, when fixed in devotion, is as 'great' as the greatest."[29] The stress in Gandhi's writing on simultaneously being advaitist and supporting dvaitism, it is tempting to speculate, on the equality of all being, might one say, is oriented precisely through such cathexis, where the least becomes as great as the greatest.

This coexistence of irreconcilable truths, this logic where neither–nor leads to manyness, cannot be thought in terms of sovereignty, or the justice that sovereignty involves. It has to be thought rather in terms of devotion and absolute faith. Thus he writes in a letter to Maganlal: "Where you go wrong is in expecting justice. Go on doing justice yourself. That which asks for return is not love. If you were overflowing with love yourself, where could you store the love others might give? This is the hidden significance of seeing all as in-different [*abhed*, 'one']. When Mira felt the stab of love [*premni katari*], she was one with God. This is the principle of *advaita* in actual practice."[30] When Gandhi emulates the oneness that he sees in Miraben, he finds that it does not overcome his separation from God.

Rather, separation turns out to be proper to that oneness. When satyagrahis say neti neti, in other words, they do not say it because of a dissatisfaction with what they have arrived at. That kind of dissatisfaction often retains as its horizon the possibility of a cataphatic resolution—a moment when there is no longer any neti neti. And where it explicitly avoids cataphasis, as with the modern conceit that privileges the sovereign question and infuses the questioner with the power always to negate, a certain dissatisfaction masters and rejects what it says no to; in the process, it refuses otherness and returns to itself. Here, in contrast, Gandhi's insistence on neti neti—which must extend even to ahimsa—comes from his affirmation of and oneness with ahimsa, and necessarily involves an affirmation of manyness. Here satya is no longer sovereign but is marked by an unruly (in the etymological sense of the word) equality and plurality.

Equality and plurality require that the being of *sat* can only be thought under erasure. Explaining a verse from the *Gita*, which refers to "the supreme Brahman which has no beginning, which is called neither Being nor non-Being," Gandhi suggests: "*Brahman* does not mean being, the contrary of non-being. When we use the word *sat* in connection with the *Brahman*, its meaning transcends the two opposites, and from the pair being and non-being, it is neither. It is, so to say, a neutral *[trikalabadya]* term."[31]

∼

Is it not this being marked by nonbeing, this "neither being nor nonbeing," that is at stake in the Editor's remark that the satyagrahi "keeps death always as a bosom friend"? Remarks about friendship with and love of death are not common in Gandhi's writings, but on occasions we can discern the suggestion that daya "is" a friendship with and love of death; it "is" simultaneously abhay and abhaydan. When in *Hind Swaraj*, the Reader suggests that there can be no fault in the use of force to prevent a child from thrusting its foot into fire," the Editor responds (another part of the response was discussed in chapter 5):

Now we shall take your last illustration, that of the child thrusting its foot into fire. It will not avail you. What do you ['really'] do to the child? Supposing that it can exert so much physical force that it renders you powerless and rushes into fire, then you cannot prevent it. There are only two remedies open to you—either you must kill it in order to prevent it from perishing in the flames, or you must give your own life because you do not wish to see it perish before your very eyes. You will not kill it. Unless your feeling of daya [dayabhav] is total [sampurna; "if your heart is not quite full of pity'] it is possible that you will not surrender yourself by preceding the child and going into the fire yourself.

Those spurred by a total daya and prem might thus even do what would in causal terms be futile—go into the fire so as not to see the child go into the fire. There is a paradoxical relation between what the Editor enjoins in this passage and what he says later in chapter 17:

The poet Tulsidas has sung:

Daya is the root of dharma, pride the root of the body,
Tulsi says do not leave daya as long as the body has life

I consider these verses to be canonical truth [shastragyaan, 'scientific truth']. I believe the above lines as much as I believe that two plus two is four. The force of compassion—that is the force of love, that is satyagraha.[32]

While here "Tulsi says do not leave daya, as long as the body has life," the earlier passage suggests that daya requires an embracing of death: if "your dayabal is total," then "because you cannot see it going into the fire, you give your life to it." Paradoxically, thus, though daya cannot be abandoned as long the body has life, the exercise of daya is the giving up of life.

The total dayabal required to surrender oneself by preceding the child into the fire—would not the daya involved here be quite different from the daya practiced by the satyagrahi of the thekana or "rightful place"? For the latter, abhay or fearlessness involves the mastery of his own fear of death, and it is separate from and precedes daya. For the former, the experience of daya is originary and is itself the experience of abhay, the embracing of death.

Unlike the satyagrahi of the thekana or rightful place, who assumes and intensifies the warrior's fearlessness, here the satyagrahi is made fearless by daya (compassion) and prem (love). And this fearlessness is not the warrior's mastery of fear but rather the trembling helplessness, hopefulness, and fearfulness of the one who loves. It is a surrender to fear, but a fearfulness that is nevertheless fearless in the sense that it does not close itself to or seek to master what it fears, that it remains open to what it fears.

Satyagraha involves striving for this other fearlessness. It is this sense of satyagraha perhaps which is at work in Gandhi's remark to C. F. Andrews in August 1918: "I have always declined to work out to my satisfaction all the possible deductions. I have taken up things as they have come to me and always in trembling and fear."[33]

Satyagrahis willingly give up their lives, even though this is futile. Their daya automatically (to recall the discussion of automaticity in the previous chapter, and to anticipate the one to come in chapter 8) leads to this action—their willingness to give up their lives is both their own and not their own. For this Gandhi, dare one say, to love is always to love one's own death. And making this love into a discipline, an automaticity, is precisely what constitutes dharma.

How this friendship with death comes to satyagrahis, how this friendship with death is itself an impossible death, and what this friendship entails, is articulated especially forcefully in 1928, when Gandhi provides his most extended reading of the phrase that is translated into English as "living by dying." Announcing that an ailing calf in the ashram had been killed by a doctor at his instruction, he writes that he had disagreed in this case with a friend who argued that "one had no right to take away life which one cannot create" (an argument that Gandhi himself makes sometimes), and had asked a doctor to kill the calf because he felt that "to take the life the calf was dharma, was ahimsa," that here "agony should be ended by ending life itself":

> Would I apply to human beings the principle I have enunciated in connection with the calf? Would I like it to be applied in my own case? My reply is yes; the same law [nyaya] is applicable to both. The law of yatha pinde thatha brahmande, as to one so to all, admits of no exceptions, or the killing of the calf was wrong and violent. In practice however we do not cut short the sufferings of our ailing dear ones by death because as a rule we have always means at our disposal to help [seva] them and because they have the capacity to think and decide for themselves. But suppose ["in the case of an ailing friend"; no equivalent in Gujarati] that no seva is possible, that recovery is out of the question and the patient is lying in an unconscious state in the throes of fearful agony, then I would not see any himsa in putting an end to his suffering by death.[34]

Satyagrahis may thus kill even humans—certainly the one who is nearest and dearest, and who cannot be helped anymore, and even perhaps the enemy (in which situation it would be all the more difficult for satyagrahis to know whether they are "deceiving" themselves).

And it is at this moment, as he submits to this immense and terrifying responsibility, that he draws on the hymn *Harino Margey* by the early modern Gujarati poet Kavi Pritam:

> I knew . . . that current public opinion [lokmat] would not like this act, that current public opinion would see only himsa in it. But religion does not think of public opinion. Where I see dharma, there another might see adharma, but even so I must follow what I think of as dharma. This is what I have learnt, and my experiences have established [siddh] that this is proper [barobar]. Really, what I think of as dharma could be adharma. But so often, without [first] making an unconscious error, adharma cannot be recognized. But if because I am fearful of public opinion, or because of any other fear, I don't follow what I consider to be dharma, then I will never be able to decide between dharma and adharma, and in the end will become bereft of dharma [dharmahin]. That is why the poet has sung:
>
>> The pathway of love [prempanth] is the ordeal of fire [pavakni javalla],
>> The shrinkers turn away from it.
>
> The love of *ahimsadharma* is the pathway of love. And on that path one often has to tread all alone.[35]

"Ordeal of fire"—this is also the title of the Gujarati article. If Gandhi does not name the hymn or the poem, this may be because he expects his readers to be familiar with it—it had been reproduced earlier in *Young India* and *Navjivan*, and is sung repeatedly by those around him during the twenty-one-day "Great Fast" of 1924, undertaken as penance for Hindu-Muslim violence. Kavi Pritam is one of the most prominent Gujarati early modern poets, and he is, like many other bhakti poets, concerned with the path of religion—what he calls, as is common in bhakti literature, the *prempanth* or pathway of love. In the English translation of the hymn that Gandhi uses, the last few lines are:

The pathway of love is the ordeal of fire. The shrinkers turn away
  from it
Those who take the plunge into the fire attain eternal bliss.
Those who stand afar, looking on, are scorched by the flames.
Love is a priceless thing, only to be won at the cost of death.
Those who live to die, these attain; for they have shed all thoughts
  of self.

The translation (I have not been able to ascertain whether this is an extant translation or one prepared by him or his associates) does not have a strict equivalent for the word *marjiva*, which occurs twice in the Gujarati version. Kavi Pritam compares seekers on the path of God to the *marjiva*. Etymologically, *marjiva* conjoins death *(mar)* and life *(jiva)*. In Kavi Pritam's poem, the word is poised between two senses. Most evidently, it is a reference to the divers in the ocean who go seeking pearls, who lead a life so dangerous that they always have their lives in their hands. More implicitly, it also refers to some yogic traditions of renouncing everyday concerns, and living as though dead. In Gandhi's translation, the word *marjiva* is translated in the last line as "those who live to die." It would not be surprising if it is from this hymn that Gandhi receives the word *marjiva*, as well as the related phrases translated often as "living to die" or "living by dying."

Living by dying entails a distinctive responsibility, whose contours emerge in the emphasis Kavi Pritam places on aloneness: recall the hymn—"On that path one often has to tread all alone." If aloneness is stressed this way, that could be because it condenses within it, simultaneously, singularity and absoluteness. Those on the pathway of love make the decision alone in the sense that they recognize that there can be no grounded and demonstrable way of justifying what they do. This is not to say that their decision is made without knowledge: it is rather made after knowledge, at the moment when knowledge no longer suffices. It may thus be correct but too preliminary to describe their decision as one made in nonknowledge; while that is indeed how their decision appears from within the perspective of knowledge, it may be more appropriate to describe their decision made in the solitude of a singularizing faith. Here faith is not an evacuation of reason; rather, it emerges in the very pursuit of a "line of reasoning" to the point where grounding in a community of reason is no longer possible.

Their dharma is not only a singular responsibility but also an absolute responsibility—a responsibility that is binding on them, and that they
must pursue even if it is outrageous and wrong by social and ethical criteria. It is this absolute responsibility that makes him decide to kill the
calf, or makes him to carry out controversial actions that are indefensible
by any conventional criteria. This absolute responsibility binds them so
much that they do not choose their actions: their love *compels* them to this
action—in this sense, their willingness to give up their lives is both their
own and not their own.

Whether they kill or die without killing, then, satyagrahis must do so
in keeping with the absolute and singular nature of their responsibility.
They cannot in other words kill in a "higher interest"; they cannot claim
the authority of general responsibility of law for their actions. Such a
responsibility, to be faithful to what is most proper to it, would necessarily
have to relinquish sovereign power, which everywhere enacts a general
responsibility that destroys anything absolute and singular. Even where it
kills, it does so not in the name of general responsibility, but in a surrender
without subordination to absolute responsibility.

~

If every dharma—not only the satyagrahi's—always already encounters
the thought of ahimsa, then this is because dharma is in Gandhi's writing the name for the assumption of absolute and singular responsibility,
and ahimsa is what is proper to such responsibility. Dharma (and the
ahimsa that is proper to it) in this sense simultaneously exemplifies absolute responsibility, and excepts itself from general responsibility. Thus it
may not be accidental that in describing dharma, Gandhi so often draws
on examples of Ibrahim and Ismail (the Abraham and Isaac of the Christian and Jewish tradition—the example-exception that Kierkegaard also
draws on to think sacrifice), and of Harishchandra and Satyavati. In each of
these examples, his readings suggest, involve the assumption of absolute
responsibility: the making of decisions that could not have been justified
by grounded criteria, but were nevertheless carried out in faith—through
a surrender of sovereign power. It is because of this absolute and singular
nature that satyagraha is an ordeal of fire, that the assumption of aloneness
requires a greater courage than the royal road of dying without killing.

At the same time, each of these examples runs counter to the commands of general responsibility. This is not surprising: if dharma is absolute responsibility, it cannot follow any general rule, and would have to

constantly inhabit the moment of the exception to general responsibility; it would have to make that exception the rule—no longer the sovereign exception that Schmitt discusses, but its term by term opposite which Kierkegaard is concerned with, and which Schmitt so erroneously claims continuity with. The example in Kierkegaard and Gandhi exemplifies not the rule but the exception to the rule; the exception must here universalize itself without ever becoming the general. There can be no exception to the absolute responsibility of the pure example-exception.

This exemplariness-exceptionality that is involved in satyagraha—again, do not satyagrahis receive it from their own death? If Gandhi stresses friendship with one's own death, is this because he suspects that one always experiences one's own death both exemplarily and as an exception to general responsibility? Satyagrahis, moreover, live by dying: they strive to experience their own death not at the end of their lives but in every moment of it. The suffusion of their lives with this submission to an absolute responsibility that can never be either sovereign or abject—Is this what satyagrahis receive by making their own death their dearest friend?

CHAPTER 7

The Sacrifice of the *Gita*

Only a change brought about in our political condition by pure means can lead to real progress. Gokhale not only perceived this right at the beginning of his public life but also followed the principle in action.... He firmly declared that, unless our political movement was informed with the spirit of religion, it would be barren.

—Mohandas Gandhi, "Foreword to Volume of Gokhale's Speeches," before February 19, 1918, *Akshardeha*

And the employment of the word Ge-stell [enframing] that is now required of us seems equally eerie, not to speak of the arbitrariness with which words of a mature language are thus misused. Can anything be more strange? Surely not. Yet this strangeness is an old usage of thinking. And indeed thinkers accord with this usage precisely at the point where it is a matter of thinking that which is highest. We, late born, are no longer in a position to appreciate the significance of Plato's daring to use the word eidos for that which in everything and in each particular thing endures as present. For eidos, in the common speech, meant the outward aspect [Ansicht] that a visible thing offers to the physical eye. Plato exacts of this word, however, something utterly extraordinary: that it name what precisely is not and never will be perceivable with physical eyes.

—Martin Heidegger, "The Question Concerning Technology"

IN 1919, DURING THE Rowlatt satyagraha, Gandhi writes a series of pamphlets about the issues the movement raises for him. Perhaps unsurprisingly, Leaflet 18 is devoted to the *Gita*. It tries to "answer in all humility a doubt raised by some Hindu friends regarding the meaning of the *Bhagavad Gita*. They say that in the *Bhagavad Gita*, Sri Krishna has encouraged Arjuna to slay his relations and they therefore argue that there is warrant in that work for violence and that there is no satyagraha in it."

The leaflet suggests that the *Gita* is concerned with the "universally acknowledged spiritual war" between satya, "good," and asatya, "evil." That war is the concern of all religious thought. "In Islam, Christianity, Judaism, it is a war between God and Satan, in Zoroastrianism between Aurmazd and Ahriman." To confuse the description of this universally acknowledged spiritual war with a momentary world strife is to call holy unholy." It describes the medieval poet Narsinh Mehta as one example of a devotee "nurtured in the *Bhagavad Gita* teaching." "He conquered his enemies only by love and has given through one single poem of matchless beauty the great text of their conduct to his fellow-*Vaishnavas.*" That "matchless poem" is Gandhi's favorite hymn, *Vaishnav Jan To,* which identifies the Vaishnava as among other things the one who "knows the pain of others" and sees all equally [sam-drishti].[1]

This is in all likelihood Gandhi's first extended written engagement with the *Gita,* though he has been making similar arguments since at least 1909.[2] The skepticism of Gandhi's "Hindu friends" is unsurprising, and it may be that the short Leaflet does not sway them much. The *Gita* is set in the battlefield of Kurukshetra, where the divine charioteer Krishna exhorts the warrior Arjuna to pick up his weapons and commence the battle against his kinsmen. Even the *Mahabharata,* within which the *Gita* is set, mentions ahimsa very rarely.[3]

Perhaps many respond to the leaflet like Swami Anand, a close associate, and the editor for some time of Navjivan Press, who tells Gandhi: "The meaning you give to the *Gita,* that meaning will be appreciated only when you one day translate the whole *Gita,* and add whatever notes you deem necessary, and we read the whole text. I do not think it is proper [barobar] on your part to deduce ahimsa etc. from stray verses."[4] Maybe both in response to such demands, and to answer his own questions, from around 1926 Gandhi talks and writes extensively on the *Gita.* Together, his writings explicitly devoted to it run close to a thousand pages and include both a translation of it and a gloss on the translation.[5] In these writings, moreover, the word *purushartha* occurs often—the word, recall, that is translated as "immeasurable pity" in *Hind Swaraj* and that would conventionally in classical Hindu texts refer to the four ends of human existence. It is tempting to suggest that what he articulates here is the *purushartha* that may be contrasted to that involved in "immeasurable pity."[6]

～

The implicit point of departure in these writings is the famous and, for Gandhi, originary injunction—the answer that precedes every question—

of Jain, Buddhist, and Hindu traditions and texts: *ahimsa paramo dharma,* "ahimsa is the highest religion." Gandhi insists that ahimsa is the founding historicity or being of the world. In *Hind Swaraj,* chapter 17 begins with the Reader asking: "Is there any historical evidence as to the success of what you have called soul force or truth force." The Editor's response includes the following remarks:

> The force of compassion—that is soul-force, that is satyagraha. And copious evidence of that force can be seen. If that force was not there, tthethe universe would disappear.
>
> But you ask for historical evidence *[aitihasik puravo]*. So we have to know what we call *itihaas* ['history'] The meaning ["Gujarati equivalent"] of the word *itihaas* is "thus it happened" *[aam thai gayu]*. If we work with that meaning, then [I can] give you copious evidence of satyagraha. If we interpret *itihaas* by the meaning of the English word, which concerns the chronicles *[tavarikh]* of emperors, then there can be no evidence of satyagraha. How can you expect to find silver ore in a tin mine? In "history" [English word in Gujarati text] we find only the stories of the noise *[kolahal]* of the world. . . . The fact that there are so many men still alive in the world shows that it is constituted not on the basis of the force of arms, but on satya, daya and soul-force. Therefore, the greatest and most unimpeachable *[aitihasik,* 'historical'] evidence is to be found in the fact that the world still lives on despite all the wars. Therefore, it must be constituted by some other force than the force of arms. History is really a record of every interruption of the even working of the force of love or of the soul. . . . "History" is a record of incidents that are against our ownmost orientation *[aswabhavik,* "a record of the interruption of the course of nature"]. Satyagraha is of our ownmost orientation *[swabhavik,* "natural"] so it cannot even be noted.

Ahimsa is here both an originary force and yet coevally accompanied and obscured by himsa or violence. The very term *ahimsa* can only be conceived as a negation of himsa. To follow ahimsa as the highest religion would be to work against its coeval obscuring in himsa. (This is also why Gandhi at his most intriguing begins with the figure of the arms-bearing warrior as a way of thinking immeasurable equality, rather than picking on those figures—say, the child, a figure whom Gandhi does draw on in his more communitarian formulations—who could be easily associated with an originarily noncoercive or nonviolent immeasurability.) The opposition between ahimsa and himsa accompanies that which the Editor draws in *Hind Swaraj* between *itihaas*—conventionally, history—and the English word "history," with the former, like ahimsa, naming the being that has no being, that "cannot even be noted," and yet constitutes and gives the world.[7]

Indeed, it may even be said that *ahimsa paramo dharma* is in Gandhi's writing the answer that precedes the question that every religion is. This answer or originary injunction is not ahimsa in his sense of satyagraha—not at all. As he says in the preface to the *Anasaktiyoga*: "It may be freely admitted that the *Gita* was not written to establish ahimsa. It was an accepted and primary duty even before the *Gita* age. . . . When the *Gita* was written, although people believed in ahimsa, wars were not only not taboo, but nobody observed the contradiction between them and ahimsa."[8] Or again: "We cannot improve [*sudhari*] upon the celebrated maxim, 'Ahimsa is the highest or the supreme duty" [*ahimsa paramo dharma*], but we are bound, if we would remain the inheritors of that tradition [*punji*], to keep exploring its immeasurable strength [*amap shakti*]."[9]

The injunction *ahimsa paramo dharma* is thus before the *Gita* (as indeed before every religious text) in two senses—it precedes and anticipates the *Gita,* and it does so by lying in the future of the *Gita.* It precedes and anticipates every religious text in the sense that since the "root of ahimsa" is "selflessness" [*niswarthatha*], the injunction *ahimsa paramo dharma* necessarily implies *yajna*—a word that, as we saw, Gandhi insists already by 1914 is self-sacrifice rather than simply sacrifice. And every religious text responds to this injunction to self-sacrifice. This self-sacrifice is religion; it is sacrality. "The root word [*dhatvarth*] in the English term for *yajna* had a good meaning; it meant "to sanctify" [*pavitra karvu*]. In Sanskrit, *yaj* means "to worship" [*poojvu*]. In the Old Testament, the word for yajna means "to renounce" [*tyag karvu*]. But the underlying idea, that all actions performed for the good or service of others are forms of yajna, will be accepted by everyone."[10] "The *Gita* says that he who eats without performing yajna is a thief. In the present situation here sacrifice meant, and means, self-sacrifice."[11] "Just as the word *yajna* is in our language, our religion, so too it is there in the Bible, and the Jewish holy texts." The Koran, he notes, also emphasizes sacrifice: "A father sacrifices his own son. Ibrahim does this" [a reference to Ibrahim and Ismail, or what is known in the Bible as the story of Abraham and Isaac]. And "Ramzan etc are sacrifice [*kurbani*], that is, parting with or giving something dear to us, sacrificing it." In the Bible, the meaning of the term expands after Jesus. Jesus says that "there is no sacrifice [yajna] in taking the lives of others, rather you should give your own body."[12] "We should, therefore, include two points in the definition of yajna: it is something which is done to serve others' good, but without causing suffering to any creature."

The injunction is thus originary in the sense of being the future given at the beginning. It lies in the future of the *Gita* as indeed of every religious text because each of these terms—*ahimsa, paramo, dharma*—secretes its own difficulty, and will remain to always be worked out. If Gandhi is drawn to the *Gita*, it is because he responds to the futurity of the injunction.[13]

～

Within the shared horizon of *ahimsa paramo dharma,* what distinguishes his reading of the *Gita* emerges especially forcefully when counterpointed to contemporaneous nationalist readings. These too stress self-sacrifice and *ahimsa paramo dharma,* but as Dipesh Chakrabarty and Rochona Majumdar indicate, they emphasize "action in strictly public interest." "To act for all, which is what the nationalist aspired to do, was to act in accordance with the *Gita.* Even violence, when it was strictly unselfish and was in the interest of 'all,' could constitute proper action."[14] When the *Gita* emphasizes *nishkamakarma* [desireless action] and *karmaphalatyag* [renunciation of fruits of action], then, it renounces not fruits of action or desire for these fruits, but only a selfish desire for fruits.

It is in this spirit that a "revolutionary" nationalist, writing to Gandhi in 1925, defends the use of violence by invoking the *Gita's* injunction to destroy the wicked: "The non-violence that India preaches is not nonviolence for the sake of non-violence, but non-violence for the good of humanity, and when this good for humanity will demand violence and bloodshed, India will not hesitate to shed blood just in the same way as a surgical operation necessitates the shedding of blood. To an ideal Indian violence or non-violence has the same significance provided they ultimately do good to humanity."[15] This "revolutionary" would be quite happy thus to affirm the injunction *ahimsa paramo dharma;* his objection to Gandhi's reading could well be that it misunderstands the ahimsa involved in the *Gita* as a simple abstention from killing. In this sense, the revolutionary reiterates the charges that we saw Lajpat Rai leveling against Gandhi in 1916. Bal Gangadhar Tilak, the militant leader prominent in Indian politics since the 1890s, attacks Gandhi in a similar vein during their famous exchange of

1920: "Politics is a game of worldly people and not of sadhus [renunciants], and instead of the maxim *Akkodhen jine kordh* [Conquer anger by nonanger] as preached by Buddha, I prefer to rely on the maxim of Shri Krishna *Ye yatha ma prapadante tansthaiyav bhajaamyaham....* [In whatever way men resort to Me, even so do I render to them]." "Both methods are equally honest and righteous but the one is more suited to this world than the other."[16]

Tilak and the revolutionary nationalist who writes to Gandhi would resort to "any means whatsoever" neither because they think of this moment as the exceptional violence necessary to found republican democracy (as the Reader possibly does in *Hind Swaraj*) nor because they work within a calculus of political realism (as the tradition conventionally associated with Machiavelli might), but because the means have been transformed through their sacrifice to the end. *Nishkamakarma* here names sacrifice to the "right end"—an incalculable end and higher end that is unmarked by self-interest. Such sacrificial violence, whether it is directed at self or other, is nonviolence, for it will "ultimately do good to humanity."[17] If the Reader emphasizes right means, Tilak emphasizes the right end.

Gandhi is as critical of the nationalist reading of *nishkamakarma* in terms of a self-sacrifice for the "right end" as he is of the emphasis on the "rights of man and citizen" as the right means. For him, it is likely that the difference between these two is not so great as might appear from within each of these traditions. As a colonial subject, he is acutely aware that the British civilizing mission too is not simply about right means but about the right end. This may be why he refuses to accept Tilak's claim to be opposed to "modern civilization": "He has written on the inner meaning of the *Gita*. But I have always felt that he has not understood the age-old thought [*bhavanao*, "spirit"] of India, has not understood her soul [*atman*] and that is the reason why the nation has come to this pass. Deep down in his heart, he would like us all to be what the Europeans are."[18]

Gandhi's questioning of both the liberal "rights of man and citizen" as the right means and of antiliberal attempts to marginalize these rights by insisting on the right end leads to a vexing problem. Modern politics is overwhelmingly organized within a causal or instrumental understanding of the means-end relation—emphasizing either right means or right ends. If both of these are questioned and relinquished, then what is the action proper to swaraj, to self-rule or freedom?

Gandhi turns to the Gita so obsessively because by doing so he responds—machinically and automatically, should we say?—to this question. In the process, he makes two intriguing moves.

First, his writings offer a very distinctive understanding of what would
be involved in *swachh saadhan* or "pure means."[19] Walter Benjamin—
writing around three years after that phrase enters Gandhi's vocabulary, as
critical of liberalism as Gandhi, and deeply critical at this point of the
Marxism that he will later briefly affirm—notes in "Critique of Violence"
that in "class struggles" the "strike must under certain conditions be seen
as a pure means." In contrast to the political general strike, which seeks to
replace the existing regime, the proletarian general strike, he suggests, citing Sorel, "clearly announces its indifference toward material gain through
conquest by declaring its intention to abolish the state":

> Against this deep, moral, and genuinely revolutionary conception,
> no objection can stand that seeks, on grounds of its possibly
> catastrophic consequences, to brand such a general strike as
> violent. Even if it can rightly be said that the modern economy,
> seen as a whole, resembles much less a machine that stands idle
> when abandoned by its stoker than a beast that goes berserk as
> soon as its tamer turns his back, nevertheless the violence of an
> action can be assessed no more from its effects than from its ends,
> but only from the law of its means.[20]

Later in the essay, Benjamin uses the phrase "divine violence" to name
pure means. Divine violence is itself an absolute responsibility. Thus the
injunction "Thou shalt not kill" "exists not as a criterion of judgment but
as guideline for the actions of persons or communities who have to wrestle
with it in solitude and, in exceptional cases, to take on themselves the
responsibility of ignoring it."[21]

Gandhi's arguments resonate with Benjamin's: relinquishing causal or
instrumental action, Gandhi wrestles almost continuously with the question of how to practice pure means. But he perhaps emphasizes more
systematically than Benjamin that pure means requires a distinctive self-
sacrifice—the sacrifice of the sovereign power that everywhere marks
being.[22] And it is in thinking the self-sacrifice that makes action into a gift
of the self, into pure means, that the *Gita* becomes important. He writes in

1927 in the *Autobiography* that around 1903 "Words like *aparigraha* (non-possession) and *samabhava* (equability) gripped me."[23] Whether that sense being gripped by these words is retrospective we do not know. But if in 1927 these two words grip him enough for him to single them out for mention, that is perhaps because between them, as we will see, they describe how pure means works: *aparigraha* (nonpossession or the renunciation of "mineness") enacts a relinquishment of sovereignty; *samabhava* (equal regard for and absolute equality of all being) enacts the surrender without subordination involved in such relinquishment.

Second, his writings on the *Gita* respond also to another question: How does newness come into the world? Hannah Arendt describes the "problem of the new" as the "abyss of nothingness that opens up before any deed that cannot be accounted for by a reliable chain of cause and effect and is inexplicable in Aristotelian categories of potentiality and actuality." Newness opens up because of the gap between the past and the future: with modernity, she stresses, the past is no longer a guide to the future. Moreover, newness is inseparable from the question of freedom: as Arendt again notes, Kant was already aware that "an act can only be called free if it is not affected or caused by anything preceding it."[24]

Gandhi faces a question very similar to Arendt's, but his radically different response emphasizes the pure example—the event of pure means. The pure example opens onto an experience of newness that cannot be understood in terms of causality, actuality, or potentiality. His writing secretes the provocative suggestion that only in following an example—in his case, the *Gita*, but what is followed is less important than how it is followed—through a surrender without subordination can newness and freedom at all be experienced. By so following an example, moreover, satyagrahis strive to make themselves the pure example, though they can never know whether they are such examples.

～

Gandhi's reading of the *Gita* stresses its "message of renunciation of fruit [*anasakti*]":[25]

> The matchless remedy is renunciation of fruits of action [*karmaphaltyag*].
>   This is the centre round which the *Gita* is woven. This renunciation is the central sun, round which devotion, knowledge and

the rest revolve like planets. The body has been likened to a prison *[sentence missing in Gujarati].* There must be action where there is body. Not one embodied being is exempted from labour. And yet all religions proclaim that it is possible for man, by treating the body as the temple of God, to attain freedom. Every action is tainted, be it ever so trivial. How can the body be made the temple of God? In other words how can one be free from action, i.e., from the taint of sin? The *Gita* has answered the question in decisive language: "By desireless action *[nishkamakarma]*; by renouncing fruits of action; by dedicating all activities to God, i.e., by surrendering oneself to Him body and soul.[26]

He also refers often to the verse in the second chapter of the *Gita* where Krishna tells Arjuna: "Action alone is thy province, never the fruits thereof; let not thy motive be the fruit of action, nor shouldst thou desire to avoid action."[27]

He is drawn to these arguments because he apprehends that the means-end relation is both unavoidable and unavoidably violent. The act of eating exemplifies the violence he fears: while it is necessary to eat in order to exist, to eat is yet also to master, destroy, and consume that which is eaten. In the passage above, such violence makes the body a prison. And because satya or being involves *niswarthatha* or selflessness, the act of eating itself is always the originary theft of and from satya.

How to respond to, be responsible for, this unavoidable and originary violence? From quite early on, Gandhi responds by insisting, as in the passage above, on right means. Already in chapter 15 of *Hind Swaraj,* when the Reader suggests that "any means whatsoever" may be used to drive out the British, the Editor responds: "Your belief that there is no connection between the means and the end is a great mistake. Through that mistake even men who have been considered religious have committed grievous crimes." He also says: "The means *[sadhan]* is the seed and the end *[sadhya]*—that which is to be got—is the tree. That is to say, as much relation as there is between the seed and the tree, that much is there between means and end."[28] And in later years, he returns to this emphasis, on occasion describing means and ends as "convertible terms," and seeming to suggest that the right means is the end. And in 1924, in a national appeal to Indians to not abandon satyagraha, he writes:

They say "means are after all means." I would say "means are after all everything." As the means so the end. Violent means will give violent swaraj. That would be a menace to the world and to India herself.... There is no wall of separation between means and end. Indeed, the Creator has given us control (and that too very limited) over means, none over the end. Realization of the goal is in exact proportion to that of the means. This is a proposition that admits of no exception. Holding such a belief, I have been endeavouring to keep the country to means that are purely "peaceful and legitimate."[29]

In this consistent emphasis on right means, Gandhi displaces (to recall Heidegger) "the instrumental and anthropological definition of technology." But Gandhi displaces that instrumental and anthropological understanding with one that emphasizes self-sacrifice. Now, yajna as self-sacrifice is the right means, but what must be sacrificed here is nothing less than the instrumental understanding of the means-end relation, and relatedly the humanist human of anthropology.[30]

The words *sadhan* ("means") and *sadhya* ("end"), which we have already encountered briefly, share an etymology in the profoundly generative term *sadh* or *sidh*—to accomplish. (This etymology rustles through many terms, including *sadhana* or spiritual discipline, *sadhu* or renunciant, *sidhanth* or principles.) As the shared etymology may lead us to suspect, here it becomes easier to acknowledge that *karma* or action involves simultaneously the separation and togetherness of what accomplishes, the *sadhan,* and what is accomplished, the *sadhya.*

This is in sharp contrast to the "instrumental and anthropological" understanding, which conceives means and ends as separate, with the means as a doing that stands apart from the doer and the end, a doing that can be directed to varied ends.[31] Here separateness is first, and togetherness is secondarily achieved through mechanisms such as the categorical imperative.

Such an understanding of action in terms of means and ends is never simply wrong. But it misses out on what is at stake in conceiving *sadhan* and *sadhya* as seed and tree. Here means and end are bound together by a distinctive separation from each other: the seed dies, and in this yajna or sacrifice the tree is (perhaps) born. This analogy of seed and tree comes to be crucial for Gandhi's understanding of self-sacrifice. In his 1920 essay titled "The dharma of *aapbhog*," he writes already: "Life comes out of death. A seed must disintegrate under earth and perish before it can grow into grain."[32]

Here means is the offering of the self through the not-ness of self-sacrifice: now the death of the means (which is to say, living by dying) gives life to the end. As infinitely separated and infinitely together as death and life, the concept of means and end is itself now transformed into something quite other. *Nishkamakarma* and *karmaphaltyag* transform means-end action into pure means—an offering or surrender of the self. By "surrendering oneself" in *nishkamakarma,* he hopes, the unavoidable and originary exercise of sovereign power that constitutes the self will be transformed, and eating will no longer necessarily be a theft—though, as we might expect given the unknowability of the end and even the means, it cannot be known to not be a theft.

The surrender of intentionality and the seizure by automaticity is crucial here. The example he cites of the nonviolence of *nishkamakarma* is often that of Raja Harishchandra. Yet Harishchandra is scarcely nonviolent by any conventional criteria: he lifts his sword to kill his wife Taramati because his duty requires him to do so, and only a miraculous intervention saves Taramati as the sword descends. If Harischandra is nevertheless nonviolent, this is because he does not *choose* to raise his sword on Taramati. Taramati is dearer to Harishchandra than himself—he "would certainly have preferred to put the knife to his own throat." But Harischandra is nevertheless nonviolent; this is because he does not *choose* to raise his sword on Taramati. His vow to give up attachment to the self—especially compelling here because his self is bound up with Taramati—makes him do so.

But another automaticity could well have seized his hand: if "no self-interest had been involved, if she had not been his queen, if Harishchandra had been repelled by the deed itself, then his hand would have refused to obey him, and he could have resorted to satyagraha."[33] Either way, whether his hand moves to kill Taramati or refuses to do so, he would have been doing satyagraha through a surrender of intentionality. And *nishkamakarma* or *karmaphaltyag* as pure means requires ahimsa in this sense of sacrifice as self-surrender. Already in 1919, in a letter to his associate Sakarlal Dave around two weeks after writing on the *Gita* in the Satyagraha leaflet, he associates ahimsa and *nishkamakarma*:

It is certainly the *Bhagavad Gita's* intention that one should go on working without attachment to the fruits of work. I deduce the principle of satyagraha from this. One who is free from such attachment will not kill the enemy but rather sacrifice oneself *[potano bhog]*. There is impatience in the killing of an enemy *[parkana]*, and there is attachment *[asakti]* in impatience."[34]

This point is reiterated in the *Gitashikshan* lectures in 1926:

I have felt that in trying to enforce in one's life the central teaching of the *Gita,* one is bound to follow truth and ahimsa. When there is no desire for fruit, there is no temptation for untruth or himsa. Take any instance of untruth or violence, and it will be found that at its back was the desire to attain the cherished end.[35]

Nishkamakarma, anasaktiyoga, karmaphaltyag—all of these words name in Gandhi's vocabulary "a change brought about in our political condition by pure means."

We should do no work with attachment *[mamta]*. Attachment *[asakit]* to good work, is that wrong too? Yes, it is. If we are attached to our goal of winning swaraj, we shall not hesitate to adopt bad means. Hence, we should not be attached even to a good cause. Only then will our means *[sadhan]* remain pure *[sara,* good] and our actions *[karma]* too will remain good.[36]

Here yajna or self-sacrifice becomes pure means because the end itself is self-sacrifice. In self-sacrifice, moreover, the end undoes and destroys itself, and thus cannot be an end. Yajna or self-sacrifice is pure means, then, in the sense that it is means without end.

But how is *nishkamakarma* as pure means to proceed? To recall: "Words like *aparigraha* (non-possession) and *samabhava* (equability) gripped me." Each of these two words or senses of self-sacrifice names a conceptual complex—*aparigraha* becomes associated with *atmashuddhi* or "self-purification" and "self-realization," and, properly speaking, is the sacrifice that must precede self-sacrifice. *Samabhava* becomes associated with various words that more emphatically carry the sense of self-sacrifice (*aapbhog, yajna, balidan,* and *kurbani* among them).

Precisely because these are all old words with long histories, it is easy to miss the strangeness and newness—an old newness, should one say?—that comes to him in them. But, as Sibaji Bandyopadhyay notes in a fascinating essay, "Gandhi's political lexicon is most profoundly coloured by a word which appears only once in the *Gita* .... The word was *aparigrahah*."[37] *Aparigraha* matters so much because it names what *nishkamakarma* renounces: *mamatva* [mine-ness] or *parigraha.* The *Gitashikshan* insists: "Where there is mineness [*mamatva,* 'possessiveness'], there is violence."[38] And Gandhi writes in his *Autobiography*: "I understood the *Gita*'s teaching of non-possession [*aparigraha*] to mean that those who desired salvation should act like a trustee who, though having control over great possessions, regards not an iota of them as his own."

Parigraha: etymologically, the word rhymes with satyagraha. Both are concerned with *agraha*—a taking hold, eagerness, enthusing, persistence, demanding, seizing. *Parigraha* is a persistence in being in the sense of *mamatva,* mine-ness. In this very persistence, it is a theft of and from being in the sense of satya. To practice satyagraha is to be seized by, to receive, and submit to satya, and relatedly to renounce *parihgraha.* As the novelist and literary critic Babu Suthar puts it with beautiful bivalence, the etymology of the term *pari* (round, about, around) suggests that *parigraha* involves "holding something from all directions, holding something in such a way that nothing of the thing escapes you."[39] Seeking to be faithful to the nothing of the thing that escapes *parigraha,* should we say, Gandhi practices *aparigraha?*

Such *aparigraha* is also always already self-purification or *atmashuddhi,* for here satyagrahis purify themselves of what is not the *atman* or self, and in this way achieve self-realization. "True swaraj, I repeat is impossible without self-purification. I do not know any other way. Call it my limitation, but then it is the limitation of satyagraha. If there is any other way, I do not know it, and anything won by means other than those of self-purification will not be swaraj, but something else."[40] And again: "All struggles involving satyagraha call for self-purification. A satyagrahi tries to make his truth triumph through his own purity and through his penance and he has faith in his endeavours."[41] "Non-co-operation is a vicious and corrupt doctrine, truly an "ugly" word, if it does not mean down-right self-purification."[42]

In *aparigraha*, "self-realization" and "self-purification," even good cannot be possessed as a virtue: "We say that we should offer up *[arpan]* everything to God, even evil. The two, good and evil, are inseparable, and so we should offer up both. If we wish to give up sin, we should give up virtue *[punya]* too. There is possessiveness *[parigraha]* in clinging even to virtue."[43] If good is possessed as a virtue, then *aparigraha* would involve sovereignty over the self, would itself be secured through self-possession. In contrast, when everything is offered up to God, then *aparigraha* becomes a relinquishment of sovereignty over the self.

Moreover, as relinquishment, *aparigraha* can only be the sacrifice that precedes *aapbhog* or self-sacrifice. *Aparigraha* cannot be self-sacrifice because of what it relinquishes—*mamatva* or mine-ness. *Mamatva* cannot be offered in self-sacrifice since it is saturated incalculably and indelibly by sovereign power, and as such is by its very nature incapable of the automatic surrender involved in the satyagrahi's self-sacrifice. Rajeswari Sunder Rajan's brilliant essay brings this out powerfully, focusing on the voluntary poverty usually involved in *aparigraha* (as Sunder Rajan recognizes, the adjective "voluntary" can at best be a placeholder in describing the spirit in which the satyagrahi must adopt the vow of poverty):

> voluntary poverty was for Gandhi less an act of *giving* than of *ridding oneself of things*. When he came to write at length about it, it is in these terms of self-dispossession that he primarily described it: ". . . I must *discard* all wealth, all possessions." He goes on to use other terms similar to "discard"—"give up . . . things" (note: not "give away"), "things slipped away from me." "I threw overboard things which I used to consider as mine." "a great burden fell off my shoulders." And he comes to the conclusion: "Possession seems to me to be a crime."

She adds that for Gandhi

> voluntary poverty is not charity, and it is not a redistributive project (hence his advocacy of trusteeship rather than communism); it is not about sharing one's wealth but sharing the other's poverty; not a giving *to* but a giving *up*. Its practice, as he

repeatedly emphasised, results not in (personal) deprivation but (universal) self-sufficiency, which is why he never described it as sacrificial.

The contrast between giving up and giving to is worth tarrying with, though perhaps with a very slight reformulation—*aparigraha* or nonpossession is a giving up, *aapbhog* or self-sacrifice is a giving of the self. And yet, because sovereign power is unworthy of sacrifice, the only way to create the being worthy of self-sacrifice is through nonpossession—by relinquishing sovereign power, by adopting "voluntary poverty." In their very practice of nonpossession, then, satyagrahis become beings pure enough for self-sacrifice—being marked by surrender without subordination. Self-sacrifice thus does not come after nonpossession. One might even say that *aparigraha* "is" yajna, though here the relation between them mirrors that which Gandhi describes between ahimsa and satya: like two sides of a coin or smooth metallic disc, they require, entail, and call forth each other; they are infinitely separated and yet infinitely together; they are each other even though there can be no passage from to the other. He stresses the togetherness of these two practices in a speech in 1921:

> Ever since 1921 I have been reiterating two words, purity
> [*paakeezgi*] and sacrifice [*kurbani*], self-purification [*atmashuddhi*]
> and self-sacrifice [*balidan*]. Without these satyagraha will not win,
> because without them God will not help. The world is touched by
> sacrifice. It does not then discriminate about whether the sacrifice
> is for good or bad[ ]. But God is not blind. He tests even sacrifice.
> His books take account of whether there is impurity or selfishness
> in the sacrifice. This is why if the sacrifice is not accompanied by
> self-purification then you will be stymied like me.[44]

~

"Like me": one more symptom of how satyagrahis can only know the failure of their satyagraha. Leaving that symptom aside for now: the other word that Gandhi is seized by, *samabhava*, has an even more curious relation with the *Gita*. It does not to the best of my knowledge occur even once in the *Gita*. But Gandhi's invocation of that word is an immensely productive misremembering. The text of the *Gita* is replete with words likely derived etymologically from *sama*—a word that shares an etymology with the English word "same"—and that have often been translated into English as "same," "equal," or "constant."[45]

The word *samabhava* seems to enter Gandhi's Gujarati vocabulary as a rendering of the Sanskrit word *samadarshanah*. In the *Anasaktiyoga,* his Gujarati rendering of the *Gita,* he translates *samadarshanah* in verse 18 of chapter 5 as *samadrishti.* (Mahadev Desai's English rendering of Gandhi's Gujarati rendering goes: "The men of self-realization look with an equal eye [*samadarshanah/samadrishti*] on a Brahmana possessed of learning and humility, a cow, an elephant, a dog and even a dogeater.") Gandhi goes on in his commentary to write that the verse calls for *samabhava.*

In the English version of that commentary, Mahadev Desai translates *samabhava* as treating "alike."[46] Earlier, in his translation into English of Gandhi's remark in the *Autobiography* about being seized by *aparigraha* and *samabhava,* Desai renders *samabhava* as "equability." Gandhi himself sometimes translates *samabhava* as equality, most famously and consistently in the vow of *sarva dharma samabhava,* or "equality of all religions." Other translations (for example, in the *Gitashikshan*) render *samabhava* as "sameness of attitude towards all."

He returns to the verse in a discussion with the Dalit leader M. C. Rajah in 1936, where he suggests that "Hindu religion teaches us to look at things with a spirit of equality," and that "we have been taught in the *Gita* to treat all men as equals":

> In the purest type of Hinduism a Brahmin, an ant, an elephant and
> a dog-eater are of the same status. And because our philosophy is
> so high, and we have failed to live up to it, that very philosophy
> today stinks in our nostrils. Hinduism insists on the brotherhood
> not only of all mankind but of all that lives. It is a conception which
> makes one giddy, but we have to work up to it. The moment we
> have restored real living equality between man and man, we shall
> be able to establish equality between man and the whole creation.[47]

As the passage indicates, *samabhavana* attempts to conceive the most intense equality, one that cannot have its baselines set by questions such as "can it reason," "can it suffer"? In rendering *samadarsana* as *samabhavana,* he breaks from a reading influential at least since the eleventh-century thinker Ramanuja. Gandhi mentions in passing his dissatisfaction with Ramanuja and others, but never elaborates. But it could well have been because of the way Ramanuja conceives equality in his commentary on the *Gita*, the *Gitabhashya*: "A person who has brought his *atman* into Yoga, will see similarity in all *atmans* when separated from *prakriti* (material nature); he will see that his own *atman* is in all beings and that all beings are in his own *atman*; in other words he will see that his own *atman* has the same form as the *atmans* of all other beings and contrariwise, so that he has seen all that is *atman* when he has seen one *atman*."[48] Here the ubiquity of the *atman* makes impossible the partiality that would allow for inequality: the *atman* is *sama* in the sense of in-different because its embodied beings are infinitely different, and yet in this difference there is sameness and equality of the *atman*. At the same time, here the equality of all *atmans* proceeds through a separation and formal abstraction from *prakriti*. Ramanuja also says: "Inequality is of the *prakriti*, not of the *atman*. Consequently, one will perceive that the *atmans* are the same in all creatures."[49] In other words, the *atman* is im-partial (not "impartial," another word sometimes used for *sama*, which can be misleading if it connotes a judge, third party, or outside entity) because it is everywhere, and both embodied and disembodied, and includes all the various *atmans*.

Gandhi likely regards Ramanuja's reading of the *Gita* as one more crucial moment in the working out of the injunction *ahimsa paramo dharma*. Ramanuja brings the injunction to a point where it conceives equality as a multiplicity of being that exceeds any formal equivalence (such as that involved in measure). But while Gandhi finds Ramanuja's readings provocative, he is also dissatisfied with them. He never writes why, and this may well be symptomatic of how pure means is often obscured even from him, its most rigorous thinker, by his simultaneous affirmation of the thekana or rightful place, of how he never explicitly becomes aware of the abyssal gap between these two ways of thinking immeasurable equality. Through that obscuring, he may well have suspected, without maybe being able to articulate it even to himself, that one crucial question remains unaddressed and even unthought: What is equality here? The Gandhi whose rooted conservatism is uprooted and destroyed by absolute equality could well have said to Ramanuja: "in-different, yes, but how can this in-difference become also an equality of embodied beings rather than only *atmans*?" And precisely because Ramauja's formulation does not address this question, because it abstracts from embodied beings while at the same time remaining very far from the formal equivalences of "modern civility," it can be complicit also in the greatest violence, such as that involved in caste.

Gandhi's alternative rendering of *samadarshanah* as *samabhava* emerges in a letter that, having expressed dissatisfaction with Ramanuja and others, goes on: "*Yajna, dana, tapas,* are obligatory duties, but that does not mean that the manner of performing them in this age should be the same as in ancient times. *Yajna, dana,* etc., are permanent principles. The way the traditions *[rudhiyo]* and ways *[reeto]* are put into practice may change from age to age and country to country."[50]

And the "manner of performing" yajna must change in his age so as to recognize the equality of all being (it is as a way of recognizing the equality of being that he advocates spinning as the yajna for his times.) The *Gita-shikshan* lectures emphasize the link between yajna and equality of and with all being: "No one can be like God, absolutely free of impurity and equal towards all *[sambhavi]*. One can, therefore, become *samadarshi* only by losing oneself in Him."[51] Again in a letter in 1930:

Yajna means an act *[karma]* directed to the welfare of others, done without desiring any return for it, whether of a temporal or spiritual nature. Act here must be taken in its widest sense, and includes thought and word, as well as deed. "Others" *[par]* embraces not only the human world, but all life *[jivanmatra]* . . . . Therefore, it will not be a yajna to wish or to do ill to anyone else even to serve somebody else *[koini pan sevane arthey,* "in order to serve a so-called higher interest"].[52]

No higher interest: by extrapolation, the equality of the atman can no longer comfortably coexist in separation and abstraction from the inequality of (material nature), to draw on Ramanuja's word. Rather, relations of *prakriti* themselves must be marked by the absolute equality and oneness of the *atman*. To get a sense of the distinctiveness of such equality, perhaps we can take a cue from the *Gitagitmanjari,* a collection of poems on the *Gita* published in 1945 by Jugatram Dave, a very close associate of Gandhi. (Gandhi reads the book before publication, and writes an appreciative foreword for it.) Two chapters are about *samata,* equality. The prefatory remarks to the first of these, titled "The Yoga of *Samata,*" says: "While heat and cold, joy and sorrow, victory and defeat should all be treated as equal *[sam],* this does not mean that [one/we] should not feel them. It does not mean that we should not protect ourselves from cold or heat, or that we so empty our hearts that we not experience sorrow or joy."[53] As these remarks imply, *samata* must be enacted by an *atman* that remains immersed in *prakriti* (embodied and material nature, beings and experience) rather than rising above it.

At the same time, there is also a distinctive abstraction involved in the experience of *samata*. In the letter Gandhi writes back to Jugatrambhai enclosing the foreword, he picks out the two chapters on *samata* (and these are the only two chapters the letter mentions). "You have called the ninth *manjari* 'Samata Yoga' and the 40th 'Samata.' You will observe that the word *samata* bears two different meanings in the two places. I would call the ninth 'Samata,' dropping 'Yoga,' and the 40th 'Samatva' or 'Samabhava.' The reason is plain."[54] In the published book, the chapter titles remained unchanged—perhaps the book was already in press, or perhaps Jugatrambhai disagreed.

It is unlikely that the reasons were not plain to Jugatrambhai, for there is a striking difference between the two poems. The first begins: "I will teach you golden *samata*; I will teach you the golden *samata* of the best yogis." The poem goes on to identify concrete ways in which *samata* is practiced—how to experience the equality of *prakriti*. The second begins: "The ultimate essence [*saar*] of knowledge is *samata*; That is the fully developed humanity." It goes on as a paen to *samata*, pointing to its ubiquity, asking why, then, inequality should persist, and saying also that "Arjuna's beloved Mohan [another name for Krishna] plays in each body as *samata*."[55]

In other words, the second poem performs a distinctive abstraction; this abstraction is *samatva* or *samabhava*. The latter is the orientation or disposition to *samata*, which is already borne in the world but is obscured and requires the work of *samatva* or *samabhava* to bring it forth. This orientation could be described, as Tridip Suhrud suggests, in terms of the metaphor that Gandhi uses for sacrifice—that of seed and tree, with *samabhava* as seed and *samata* as tree.[56]

Moreover, pure sacrifice inflects *samabhava* with a distinctive trajectory. In the reading that Gandhi offers to Jugatrambhai is the "fully developed humanity" that practices *samabhava* the familiar figure we know as the subject of humanism? Or would it be another human—the human who emerges at the end of humanism? This human cannot be thought by eschewing abstraction, falling back on communitarianism. But here abstraction concretizes itself in sacrifice; it is the abstraction proper to that other third party, the untranslatable *trahit manas*. How does this concrete abstraction—this other concrete abstraction, if we remember our Hegel and our Marx—work?

~

Samabhava is a strange equality, for here equality flows from a certain slavery. Taking his cue from the bhakti poets—and especially the two he is most familiar with, Narsinh Mehta and Mirabai—Gandhi conceives of *nishkamakarma* and *karmaphalatyag* as a surrender where the devotee is marked by slavery:

> The slave *[gulam]* can never conceive of his existence without his master. A person who has the name of another on his lips all the twenty-four hours becomes like that. The *atman* becomes the *paramatman* in the same way. The *atman* may be a ray of the *Paramatman*, but the ray is also the sun. Apart from God, we can have no existence at all. He who accepts his slavery to God *[gulamgiri]* becomes one with God.[57]

In Gandhi's vocabulary, as the previous chapter suggested, "God" is a charged word, one that does not allow for a sovereign being, and insists on the divinity of all being. Thus, the passage reorients (the word may be especially apposite here, given its etymology) the concept of slavery. That reorientation is one of the signature innovations of medieval bhakti traditions, whose devotee-saints often assume the suffix *das*—slave. Within the problematic of sovereignty, the slave is defined by an externally imposed subordination. Gandhi often attacks slavery in this sense.

But neither bhakti traditions nor Gandhi attack slavery in order to seek sovereign power or agency; they do so rather because they seek another slavery. As one formulation in 1910 puts it: "The servant of God will never consent to be the slave of any man."[58] Gandhi, following the bhakti tradition, conceives of the slave of God as freely surrendering sovereign power to the divine. Here free surrender is never volitional or voluntary—voluntary acts require sovereign power. Rather, devotees surrender because they are seized by the other that they themselves are. Enslaved by this free surrender, they lose themselves in the divine, and become one with it. But this absolute togetherness is also the moment of absolute difference, for it is of the very nature of devotion that devotees are only aware of an abyssal distance from the divine, of the nonidentification secreted by the very striving for identification with the divine.[59]

Yajna as surrender without subordination or pure means thus involves simultaneously absolute togetherness with and absolute difference from all other being—this implication of yajna is *samabhavana. Samabhavana* involves the equality of what seems incomparable—the human, the animal, and the thing. Such absolute equality of all being is the most crucial stake of Gandhi's satya and satyagraha; only in striving for it does satyagraha become faithful to the injunction *ahimsa paramo dharma.*

The absolute equality involved in *samabhava* necessarily leads to a reconceptualization of liberty, equality and fraternity. Now equality does not come after liberty, and fraternity does not work as the silent organizing exclusion that precedes, makes possible, and holds together liberty and equality.[60] Rather, all three are borne and displaced in a distinctive way by the term *samabhava. Samabhava* here—that is to say, where Gandhi's writing destroys its own rooted conservatism—not only refuses to dominate or disengage from the other but, acknowledging that it lacks autonomy from the other, surrenders to the other and in this very surrender becomes free of the other. With this move, *samabhava* becomes the coming together also of moksha or *mukti* and *swaraj*, two sets of words that can no longer be held apart with the first referring to a transcendent and the second to an immanent liberty; now, swaraj-moksha is always immanent, but immanence can no longer be thought in terms of theological secularism as the converse of transcendence.

Relatedly, where the satyagrahi must "own" kinship and absolute equality with "not merely the ape but the horse and the sheep, the lion and the leopard, the snake and the scorpion," with all the embodied beings of *prakriti,* then fraternity must be uprooted not only from its gendered but even its anthropological determinations. Where kinship is with all, where kinship excludes none, then what is involved in kinship must be refigured.

The absolute equality of *samabhava* is thus a shorthand also for the religious refiguring of liberty–equality–fraternity. How this refiguring works is perhaps indicated by the constant movement of Gandhi's analogy of satya as the end and ahimsa as the means. With *samabhava,* it could be said, that analogy takes on a new avatar: now *samabhava,* the means to *samata,* is also the end to which yajna or sacrifice is the means. The constant displacement of end and means itself mirrors the cascading structure of

Gandhi's vows. Gandhi starts out by affirming satya as the end and ahimsa as the means. Ahimsa requires *samabhavana*. But the means to such ahimsa is *brahmacharya*—not just celibacy but control of the senses. And the means to *brahmacharya* turns out to be *asteya* or nonstealing. And so on— the constant displacement of Gandhi's vows brings him to the vows of swadeshi [fidelity to one's own place] and swaraj, and then onward to the vows of spinning.

~

The surrender without subordination staged through *aparigraha-samabhavana* is also the moment of the pure example. When understood as the analogical third (to recall the discussion of Agamben in a previous chapter), the universality of the example comes from its distinctive sovereignty: even as it moves from part to part, it bears also the general and generality. This is why exemplarity is so important to the experience of newness and freedom, why the Reader must experience newness precisely by following the British example.

But surrender without subordination relinquishes general responsibility. Thus it becomes necessary to work toward another thinking of the example, and relatedly of newness and freedom. Gandhi stresses the exemplarity of satyagraha on several occasions. In satyagraha, "example alone is precept"; satyagrahis lead "by example"; and what they exemplify above all is how to follow the example. How satyagraha's example works—its analogy, how it moves from part to part, how it is universal—is intimated in the way his writing works out the claim that the *Gita*, as indeed all religious texts, is necessarily *rupak*. He translates this adjective usually as "allegorical" and occasionally as "metaphorical."[61]

The emphasis on the metaphorical-allegorical nature of being is quite widespread in Gandhi's times, having become marked already in the nineteenth-century writings of the Theosophists.[62] The emphasis is in a way radical: it denies the metaphysical privileging of the constative truth (briefly, a truth that is corrigible—true or false); insists that truth-being is plural, inseparable from the reader who encounters it; that concepts are always also metaphors, and thus also always performative.[63] By doing so, it privileges the hermeneutic interpretations of the sovereign reader, a reader who autonomously discerns the work of language in a text laid before him.[64]

But even if for such a reader truth is a mobile army of metaphors, to draw on Nietzsche's evocative phrase, it is still an army that the reader commands. As such, the reader's metaphor must either disengage from or dominate other metaphors. Whichever of these strategies is adopted, the reader's metaphor becomes the governing or sovereign metaphor. Such an emphasis on the sovereignty of metaphor and allegory has only become more pervasive since Gandhi's times. Today perhaps it organizes one kind of insistence in the humanities that truth is performative, rather than constative, as the social sciences sometimes presume.

Gandhi's metaphor-allegory, however, cannot be understood in terms of the hermeneut's sovereignty. Consider how he clings to his reading. He is acutely aware of the dissonance between his readings and those made even by the sympathetic associates who surround him, many of them Sanskrit scholars. As early as 1919, he notes of the reading of the *Gita* offered by his close associate and ally, the Sanskrit scholar Anandshankar Dhruva: "I very much respect Anandshankarbhai's views, but I would not give up any opinion of mine which has been tempered in my experience even if it were contested by him."[65] In the *Anasaktiyoga,* Gandhi again writes: "My knowledge of Sanskrit is limited; my knowledge of Gujarati too is in no way scholarly. How could I then dare present the public with my translation?"[66]

He nevertheless clings to his reading because of his *shraddha* or bhakti— words that he translates as faith and devotion. "It has been my endeavour, and that of many companions who have stayed with me, to conduct ourselves by my understanding of the *Gita.* The meaning which this small band has tried to implement, that meaning is there in this rendering." While he does not intend any "disrespect" to other "Gujarati renderings," and "while they all have their place," "I am not aware that these translators claim the experience of conducting their lives by the *Gita.* At the back of my reading there is the claim of an effort to enforce the meaning in my own conduct for 38 years."

This passage foregrounds another sense of *rupak*—one given to us by the immensely charged noun *rup*, usually translated as form or aspect, but in the *Gita* and elsewhere referring also to the forms of the divine. Gandhi encounters the *Gita* as a *bhakt* or devotee. Such a devotee can never remain sovereign. His *shraddha* and bhakti involve rather an attempt to follow the text, make it an example, submit and surrender to it. Gandhi thus sacrifices himself to the satya of the *Gita.* In this sacrifice and surrender, in this acceptance of the position of the figure who cannot be sovereign in relation to the *Gita,* he receives the *Gita* as a gift, by having a darshan or beholding of it.[67] To behold the *Gita* in this way is to follow it as an example, to conduct one's life by it; it is also to make oneself an example in the same way. And because darshan here can no longer be about presence, but must be about the bare faith involved in nonknowing, one can make oneself an example only by practicing ahimsa-satyagraha, a practice that is all the more difficult since satyagrahis can never know whether they exemplify ahimsa.

For Gandhi, this way of thinking darshan is itself offered by the *Gita.* He writes of Arjuna, the doubtstruck warrior whom Krishna addresses in the *Gita:* "It is only when we feel nervous like him that we shall be cured. We shall not be cured till we feel a crisis. The experience is like the pangs of childbirth. Arjuna's experience is that which overwhelms one when one feels born again; may all of us have this experience. If the feeling endures, we would be saved." These formulations offer another concept of experience to us: in darshan, experience rends the subject: Arjuna dies, and is born again.

Arjuna is not just the example that satyagrahis must follow. He "is" the pure example or exemplarity itself: after that moment when he beholds Krishna, he follows the example that Krishna offers, having sacrificed himself completely. And following his example, satyagrahis too must experience a surrender, have a darshan, act without exercising choice or agency. Indeed, as we shall see again later, some of his most famous decisions are made this way—by surrender to the *Gita,* and to the not-ness that the *Gita* exemplifies. In the *Navjivan* article published on the day *Anasaktiyoga* is released, he describes how he came to launch the Dandi March: "Trying as I do to live according to the teaching of the *Gita,* I could not avoid the present struggle. As a friend says in his telegram to me, this is a holy war for me."[68]

~

And yet, Gandhi can follow the *Gita* only by refusing the dominant readings of the *Gita.* Could it be, then, that his reading of sacrifice in the *Gita* in a sense sacrifices the *Gita?* That his absolute surrender to the *Gita* allows him to claim absolute equality with and the greatest freedom from the *Gita?* That a radical newness emerges in the experience of surrender, of following the pure example?

As is well known, Gandhi rejects the newness associated with "modern civility." In the latter, newness is conceived causally—whether in terms of continuities and breaks from what preceded it, or in terms of a general potentiality, actualized or not. Because it is constantly given over to measuring and mastering what it encounters, here newness both overcomes or erases what preceded it (thus the characteristic historicism of modernist thought), and cannot encounter the radically new (a newness, in other words, that cannot be thought in terms of its historical relation to the past, a newness that is singular).

Rejecting the concept of newness associated with modern civility, Gandhi attempts to think radical newness—a newness organized not around sovereign freedom, but around the swaraj-moksha that emerges from going back to the roots as the pure example, pure means, or surrender without subordination.[69] To claim that Gandhi attempts to think radical newness might seem odd, since he often seems to affirm the old over the new, the past over present and future. Yet, when we read more attentively, his writings also stress newness. Thus the very title of the journal he takes over from Indulal Yagnik and makes his own primary journal in Gujarati—*Navjivan* or "new life"; thus the title of the English equivalent—*Young India;* thus again the system of schooling that he promotes—*Nai Talim* or new education; thus his calls repeatedly for a *navyug,* a new age.

In exploring the newness he affirms, perhaps we can take some cues from the way he reads the *Gita* newly, audaciously:

> Non-cooperation has come to mean much more than we first intended it to mean. There is no harm in putting greater meaning on [*vadharey arth mukiye,* "enlarging the meaning of"] the *Gita's* word *yajna,* even if the new meaning we attach to the term was never imagined by Vyasa. We shall do no injustice to Vyasa. Sons should expand the inheritance of their fathers. . . . Thus we may attach to it a meaning not intended by Vyasa, and only that is appropriate.[70]

In these readings we would not be wrong in espying what Heidegger calls "eerie," the strange "arbitrariness with which words of a mature language are . . . misused." But with Heidegger, Gandhi could also have said that "this strangeness is an old usage of thinking." Indeed, he claims to learn this way of thinking newness again from Vyasa (whose very name, let us not forget, refers to the way he splits and describes the *Vedas,* even we might say by extension makes it anew): "Thus the author of the *Gita,* by extending meanings of words, has taught us to imitate him." "As the world progresses, the same terms acquire new values. Manu and the other law-givers did not lay down eternal principles of conduct."[71] And in 1936, he writes in an essay in English:

I have admitted in my introduction to the *Gita* known as *Anasakti-yoga* that it is not a treatise on non-violence nor was it written to condemn war. Hinduism as it is practised today, or has even been known to have ever been practised, has certainly not condemned war as I do.[72] What, however, I have done is to put a new but natural [*swabhavik*, proper] and logical [*tarkshuddh*] interpretation upon the whole teaching of the *Gita* and the spirit of Hinduism. Hinduism, not to speak of other religions, is ever evolving. . . . The *Gita* itself is an instance in point. It has given a new meaning to karma, sannyasa, yajna, etc. It has breathed new life into Hinduism. It has given an original [*maulik*] rule of conduct. Not that what the *Gita* has given was not implied in the previous writings, but the *Gita* put these implications in a concrete shape. I have endeavoured in the light of a prayerful study of the other faiths of the world and, what is more, in the light of my own experiences in trying to live the teaching of Hinduism as interpreted in the *Gita,* to give an extended but in no way strained meaning to Hinduism, not as buried in its ample scriptures, but as a living faith speaking like a mother to her aching child. What I have done is perfectly historical [*aitihaasik pranaalikaney anusaariney,* in accordance with historical tradition].[73]

As these arguments suggest, he does not return to some original meaning of the *Gita*. Rather, he learns from the *Gita* that the most religious readings might relinquish dominant renderings, find something new in the origins. His rendering is a rending—a tearing apart tied to what it is torn from only by a pure bhakti or faith, an uprooting that is given by the roots themselves. There is no grounding "buried in its ample scriptures" for his argument; the *Gita* gives him its arguments as a mother to a child—in faith. Only in relinquishing the readings that dominate the *Gita* in order to experience it anew is it possible to be devoted to the *Gita,* to claim continuity with it.

Could it be pure examplarity that make texts religious—*rupak* in the sense of a beholding of the divine. That word, we have seen, is not simply "allegorical"; it carries also the sense of darshan, the beholding that exceeds vision and presence. In the sacrifice that makes a text *rupak*, there is a relation of surrender and submission to the text, where the sovereignty of both the source (here, the *Gita*) and the reader is destroyed, where the unicity of each comes to be riven and ruined by a constitutive two-ness. In this destruction of unicity, the devotee receives the *Gita* as a gift. To so receive it requires a distinctive translation. Here again the translation cannot be calculable, or involve what Agamben describes as the "analogical third." In order to remain a *rup* and darshan, in order that is to say to remain a gift, the translation must seize the devotee. What is translated in the bhakti or devotion, in other words, is precisely the untranslatable—that which resists an ordered relation with its translation, that which cannot appear except as darshan.

Thus, reading the *Gita* as a devotee, Gandhi receives a freedom both from it and of it. On the one hand, he rends and uproots the *Gita* from its origin, reads it in a way that differs from and even undermines the arguments that its author as a sovereign subject may have directed for it. On the other hand, however, Gandhi as a devotee sees his freedom not as rending the *Gita* but as the way of being most faithful to it; for him, even his rending away from existing interpretations only follow the injunctions of the *Gita*.

Put differently, neither the *Gita* nor Gandhi is sovereign in this relation; more broadly, both giver and receiver receive nonsovereignty as a pure gift in the act of devotion or bhakti. (In one letter, he writes: "Don't you remember Bhoja Bhagat's lash that 'Bhakti is a bargain in which you must stake your very life, for full of danger is the path ahead'?")[74] *Bhakts* and lovers can never be coherent bodies; they are always deranged by having "staked their lives" on a "bargain" that ruins their coherence.

We can now perhaps sense better how the injunction *ahimsa paramo dharma* is both originary and futural. The scriptures speak, but they do not fully work out what they give, nor indeed can their readers. Rather, they generate a multiplicity organized by two-ness —they are separate from themselves, anterior to themselves, and no interpretation can establish a unity with this anteriority. The scriptures secrete criteria by which to consider them scriptural or not, and these criteria become equal to the scriptures themselves. And these criteria—satyagraha, ahimsa, daya, and satya among others—do not transcend the scriptures (since they are themselves scriptural), nor are they immanent in the scriptures (since they have to be produced by a reading of the scriptures.) They are rather marked by faithful rending of the scriptures.

Pure faith, then, gives devotees both an absolute submission and an absolute equality to the texts that they are devoted to; their faith may have begun from these texts, may draw on them, but it must become independent of them in its very submission to them. Such is the politics of pure means, or surrender without subordination, that must always mark bhakti or pure faith.

~

Warrior and satyagrahi, abhay and abhaydan, gift and pure gift, self-sacrifice and pure self-sacrifice, example and pure example, faith and pure faith: in thinking these pairs together, with the latter as what is most proper to the former, Gandhi, following especially the Jain tradition, goes down a path vey different from that followed by some thinkers who have tried to break from ontotheology. Jean-Luc Nancy writes, for example:

> Finitude is not a "moment" in a process or an economy. A finite existence does not have to let its meaning spring forth through a destructive explosion of its finitude. Not only does it not have to do so; in a sense it cannot even do so: thought rigorously, thought according to its Ereignis, "finitude" signifies that existence cannot be sacrificed. It cannot be sacrificed because, in itself, it is already not sacrificed, but offered to the world. There is a resemblance, and the two can be mistaken for one another; and yet, there is nothing more dissimilar.

Resemblances, then, but nothing more dissimilar than sacrifice and offering. Nancy is insistent on this: "Both Bataille and Heidegger must be relentlessly corrected. Corrected, that is, withdrawn from the slightest tendency towards sacrifice."[75] Here, the line between sacrifice and offering is, if not clear, then at least knowable enough to be corrected, and if we take one for the other, that can only be a misrecognition. There can also be no transaction between them; they remain in an external relation to each other. This external relation is possible in part because both are understood in opposition to each other: sacrifice is a destructive explosion of finite existence, and existence is the unsacrificeable, that which can only be offered.

From the perspective enabled by Gandhi's appropriation of Jain, Buddhist, and Hindu texts, one might respond: while there is "nothing more dissimilar" than sacrifice and offering, that dissimilarity itself occurs in and as a relation. That relation, which is what much of this book has been exploring, could be restated as two points.

First, offering (in Gandhi's terms, pure self-sacrifice) is originarily both borne and obscured by sovereign self-sacrifice. (In the terms I have drawn out from Gandhi, sovereign self-sacrifice, rather than being a destructive explosion of finite existence, is itself the making of a certain finitude that may be contrasted to the destructive explosions of "modern civility.") Indeed, it is in and by such bearing that sovereign sacrifice exists; this is the sense in which Gandhi can say that nothing but satya is. Nevertheless, offering can come into being only by appropriating sovereign sacrifice. This is why, to reiterate what has been said earlier, the key word in Gandhi's vocabulary must be ahimsa, and not *shanti* (peace). Ahimsa or satyagraha, as negations of himsa, must begin from what they are not: the finitude of the warrior, which even "modern civility" cannot erase. There thus no *agraha* or force that is prior to satyagraha and duragraha and can take either form; rather, *agraha* exists only as this coevalness of satyagraha and duragraha. So: yes, nothing more dissimilar, but here offering's dissimilarity to sacrifice is borne by sacrifice, is even the "potentiality" of sacrifice to become the other that only it bears; this is why offering is pure self-sacrifice.

Second, and conversely, offering can never be sure it has erased sacrifice. Offering involves a faithful and constant self-examination, a discipline of the self to expunge all sacrifice. But this self-examination, if it is not to lapse into good conscience, must constantly reveal symptoms of sacrifice. Indeed, an offering, in order to be one, must not know itself as an offering. So: yes, nothing more dissimilar, but this dissimilarity requires that offering constantly mistake itself for sacrifice.

～

The pure exemplarity of the Gita infects it with a strange universalism: "This is a work which persons belonging to all faiths can read. It does not favour any sectarian point of view. It teaches nothing but pure ethics [*shudh niti*]."[76] Moreover, when those of other faiths read the *Gita,* its teaching will not convert them to some form of Hinduism; rather, it will likely deepen their engagement with the faith that provided their point of departure. In reading the *Gita,* what travels is not some substantive argument it makes, but that absolute equality of other faiths that makes response possible. Thus it is not only the *Gita* that teaches pure ethics—which is also to say, pure means, surrender without subordination—and is universally available; every pure faith must do so. Every pure faith is in this sense at every moment marked by a conversion into its other.

Because of this, there is never any need for conversion in a social sense from one religion to another. Such social conversion would for Gandhi recoil from the absolute equality, the conversion into another pure faith, that already rends every religion. Perhaps it is in terms of this conversion that we must read Gandhi's remark in 1921:

> I hope that nobody will bring up here the history of the attempts
> by Guru Nanak and Kabir to unite Hindus and Muslims; for the
> effort today is not for uniting the religions, but for uniting hearts
> while maintaining the separateness of religions. The efforts of
> Guru Nanak and others were towards fusing the two by showing
> the basic unity of all religions. The effort today is at tolerance
> [*titiksha*]. The effort is to see how the orthodox Hindu, while
> remaining staunchly [*chusth*] Hindu, can respect and sincerely wish
> prosperity to an orthodox Muslim. True, this attempt is altogether
> new, but its spirit is there at the roots of Hindu dharma.[77]

The religion that underlies all religions, then, is not a substantive or "basic unity" marked by miscibility, fuzzy identities, or blurred boundaries; it is instead the giving of an absolute equality, which is also to say of an absolute difference. The separateness of religions also should not then be read as a constative or even a performative one. Rather, orthodox Hindus and Muslims can respect each other because their very orthodoxy gives absolute equality and absolute difference to each other, and in the process always converts each into the other. In a way very different from Raychandbhai, Gandhi too must affirm that all religions are equal, that Hinduism, Islam, and Christianity are all constitutively and originarily marked by daya. When he insists that the "comparison of religions is uncalled for," he does not simply refrain from comparison as an option available to him; rather, his insistence on absolute equality prevents him from conceptualizing comparison.

This distinctive universalism organizes also perhaps Gandhi's response, recounted by B. R. Nanda, "when told that Prophet Mohamed had prescribed use of sword under certain circumstances":

> I suppose most Muslims will agree. But I read religion in a different
> way. Khan Saheb Abdul Ghaffar Khan derives his belief in non-
> violence from the Koran, and the Bishop of London derives his
> belief in violence from the Bible. I derive my belief in non-violence

from the *Gita,* whereas there are others who read violence in it. But if the worst came of the worst and if I came to the conclusion that the Koran teaches violence, I would still reject violence, but I would not therefore say that the Bible is superior to the Koran or that Mahomed is inferior to Jesus. It is not my function to judge Mahomed and Jesus. It is enough that my non-violence is independent of the sanction of scriptures.[78]

But having received from the scriptures a faith in ahimsa that is independent of them, he must work through another question: How is the faith in ahimsa to be universalized? If absolute equality, abhaydan or ahimsa can be received only by giving it, how is it to be given?

· CHAPTER 8 ·

Ciphering the Satyagrahi

*For only mythical violence, not divine, will be recognizable as such
with certainty, unless it be in incomparable effects, because the expiatory power of violence is not visible to men.*

—Walter Benjamin, "Critique of Violence"

*The "vow" I am thinking of is a promise made by one to oneself. We
have to deal with two dwellers within: Rama and Ravana, God and
Satan, Ormuzd and Ahriman. The one binds us to make us really
free, the other only appears to free us so as to bind us tight within his
grip. A "vow" is a promise made to Rama to do or not to do a certain
thing which, if good, we want to do, but have not the strength unless
we are tied down, and which, if bad, we would avoid, but have not
the strength to avoid unless similarly tied down. This I hold to be a
condition indispensable [to] growth.*

—Mohandas Gandhi, "Letter to J. C. Kumarappa,"
October 31, 1930

A S GANDHI WRITES about the politics of pure means, he repeatedly
emphasizes the terms *yama* and *vrat,* and less often *pratignya,* words
he translates interchangeably into English as vows and pledges. His civil
disobedience campaigns are organized as vows—the vows of swadeshi,
ahimsa, of satyagraha, and so on.

The centrality of the vow should not be surprising. Gandhi is acutely
aware that the fearless relation with one's own death cannot take only the
spectacular form of the confrontation in which one offers one's own life.
Already before *Hind Swaraj,* he identifies its quiet and everyday form with
the vow—whether taken by the arms-bearing warrior, the satyagrahi, or
the devotee. By 1913 he explicitly conceptualizes this association: "If we
resolve [*agraha*] to do a thing, and are ready even to sacrifice our lives in
the process, we are said to have taken a vow" [*vrat*].[1] In other words, the

vow always presumes the death of the figure taking the vow, and opens onto the everyday life secreted by this death.

The emphasis on the vow also involves a questioning—never explicitly articulated—of the principle. This again should not be surprising. Principle and vow—these are the two forms of the promise, the first being the promise to abide by autonomous or more broadly calculable reason, and the vow being the promise to maintain a distance at least always from autonomy, if not necessarily sovereignty. As the ethical abstraction that organizes both the autonomous self and the autoimmunity of that self, the principle names the highest level of general responsibility (affirming, for example, universal human rights). It calculates how general responsibility can remain sovereign in each situation; the principle exemplifies and is even the conceptual apogee of calculable ethics, the moment when general responsibility becomes incalculable.

As such, the relation between the vow and the principle is perpetually vexed rather than oppositional. Practitioners of the principle too sacrifice their lives (Gandhi could well have been writing of the principle in the sentence above), and in this sense the principle is itself a distinctive form of the vow—it is a shearing away from the vow that is itself nevertheless given by the vow, it is the vow of autonomy.

Gandhi questions the principle in the name not just of any vow, but the vow proper to satyagraha. Stated most succinctly, the vow proper to satyagraha sustains a friendship with one's own death. And friendship with death names here the opening to that other who or which goes in Gandhi's vocabulary by several names, among them, satya, *atman* or self, God, and conscience. The vow sustains the most important friendship, even the only one necessary for a politics of pure means: "But it is difficult to retain all friendships, for instance, I have not been able to retain that of the British. The reason is that I think it necessary to preserve only one friendship in this life, namely, God's. God means the voice of conscience [*antaratman*]. If I hear it say that I must sacrifice the world's friendship; I would be ready to do so."[2]

But his path toward the vow proper to satyagraha is not easy. Though he is exposed—like everyone, he will have insisted—to that vow already as a child, his more sustained engagement with it begins only during student days in England. And the vow of satyagraha itself is articulated only much later, during the satyagraha campaign in South Africa.

~

The *Autobiography,* written as a series of columns for *Navjivan* between December 1925 and February 1929, describes how he is first exposed to the vow as an especially forceful everyday form of Putlibai's dharma:

> The outstanding impression has remained with me that my mother was a saintly woman. She was deeply religious *[bhavik]*. She would not think of taking her meals without her daily prayers. Going to *Haveli*—the Vaishnava temple—was one of her daily duties. As far as my memory can go back, I do not remember her having ever missed the *Chaturmas*. She would take the hardest vows *[vrat]* and keep them without flinching. Illness was no excuse for relaxing them. I can recall her once falling ill when she was observing the *Chandrayana* vow, but the illness was not allowed to interrupt the observance. To keep two or three consecutive fasts was nothing to her. Living on one meal a day during *Chaturmas* was a habit with her. Not content with that, she fasted every alternate day during one *Chaturmas*. During another *Chaturmas* she vowed not to have food without seeing the sun. We children on those days would stand, staring at the sky—when will the sun be seen, and when will mother eat. In the rainy season, the *darshan* ["beholding"] of the sun is intermittent, this everyone knows. And I remember days when we would rush and announce it to her, "mother, mother, the sun has been seen," but by the time she would hurry out the sun would be gone. "That does not matter," she would say ['cheerfully'] "it was not in my fate to eat today" ["God did not want me to eat today"]. And she would return to her round of duties."[3]

His own vows follow a few years later and precede any commitment to ahimsa. When he leaves for England in 1888 to study law, he takes among other things that famous vow to his mother to remain a vegetarian. Soon after arriving in England, the nineteen-year-old encounters a friend (unidentified, but introduced by Pranjivandas Mehta) who is "disgusted" with Gandhi's vegetarianism, and asks: "What is the value of a vow made before an illiterate mother, and in ignorance of conditions here? It is no vow at all. It would not be regarded as a vow in law. It is pure superstition to stick to such a promise." But Gandhi continues to be adamant:

Day in and day out the friend would argue. But I had an eternal negative to face him with [*chatrees rogno harnaar ek nanno j maari paasey hato;* I had with me one "no" that could defeat thirty-six diseases]. The more he argued, the more uncompromising I became. Daily I would pray for God's protection, and I would get it. Who God was—that I did not know. But the faith that that Rambha had given was doing its own work ['It was faith that was at work—faith of which the seed had been sown by the good nurse Rambha'].

One day, the friend began to read to me Bentham's book [Bentham's *Theory of Utility*]. He read to me about utility. I was at my wit's end. The language was difficult, I understood little. He began to expound it. I said: "Pray excuse me. These abstruse things are beyond me. I admit it is necessary to eat meat. But I cannot break my vow [*pratigny*]. I cannot argue about it. I am sure I cannot win an argument with you. But please give me up as foolish or obstinate. I appreciate your love for me. I appreciate your purpose [*hetu*]. I know you to be my well-wisher [*hittechu*]. I also know that you are telling me again and again about this because you feel sad for me. But I am helpless. A vow is a vow. It cannot be broken [*pratigny nahi tootey*]."[4]

At this point, Gandhi likely regards the vow as only a commitment made to his mother for her lifetime, one he might abandon after her death. He has not come to his own thinking of what is proper to the vow. In the positions he takes, and the conversation with his friend, we can discern the opposition that he inherits between two forms of the promise—the principle and the vow.

Gandhi's unnamed friend speaks in the name of the principle.[5] The work of reason in it is acknowledged in two words that are perhaps related: *hetu* and *hittechu*. A *hetu* is a cause or reason. A *hittechu* is one's well-wisher; he looks out for one's *hit*—one's welfare, gain, or profit. Because it is grounded in autonomous reason, practitioners of the principle must claim for it a universality—a sovereignty not only over themselves but over their interlocutors and indeed over the entire public sphere. Thus, Gandhi's well-wisher must, as a subject disciplined by the Enlightenment, claim to evaluate and shape himself and his actions by the principle.

In being so shaped, he embodies the principle in the way distinctive to it. He retains a sovereign relation with the principle itself—he retains the authority to evaluate whether the principle is appropriate for a particular context, whether it needs to be abandoned, modified, and so on. Here perhaps we encounter one register of the distinction between belief and faith. Even as Gandhi's friend believes fervently in his principles, his very embodiment of these beliefs makes him sovereign over these beliefs.

Relatedly, the principle must claim sovereignty over the other. Gandhi's friend must—he has no choice in this if he is to be principled—judge Gandhi by the principle, and if he finds Gandhi's convictions wanting, either seek to reform them or treat them as Gandhi's personal beliefs. Love only increases the force of the principle—the friend says that if Gandhi had been his own brother, he would have sent Gandhi back to India long ago.

As a principled person, then, Gandhi's friend is impatient. What offends him most about Gandhi's vow of vegetarianism is his inability to tender reasons for the vow. And a vow made before an illiterate mother—the epitome of unreason—can have no value. If only Gandhi had made a principled commitment to his mother to be a vegetarian, he could at least have either defended it rationally or reversed it in view of the new context and circumstances. Gandhi's friend hopes to make Gandhi a principled person, who will then on his own find vegetarianism wanting and abandon it. This would be the principled way to have Gandhi abandon his vegetarianism. But it is far from the only way. The friend is also willing to bully Gandhi into abandoning his vow. To do so is not unprincipled on the friend's part. When confronted with something less than the principle, the use of force to impose the principle is itself principled.

The friend's dismissiveness and impatience resonate with long-standing traditions of rational ethnocentrism: Kant's distinction between dogmatic and reflecting faith, Hegel's threefold classification with Christianity as the most developed, Tiele's distinction between "natural religions" and "world religions" or "ethical religions," or, more recently, Levinas's distinction between the sacred and the holy, and relatedly between polytheism and monotheism. Gandhi never explicitly disavows, as we have seen, these rational traditions of thinking religion. But for these rational traditions, the devotion of those like his mother can only be superstition, part of the prehistory of religion properly speaking. Caught in this bind, his affirmation of these traditions works itself out in ways that exceed them.

~

In resisting his friend's arguments, it is "the faith that that Rambha had given" which "was doing its own work." We do not know much at all about Rambha. But she may in some ways be a greater "influence," if we are to work with that vocabulary, then perhaps all the other usual "influences" combined. Earlier in the *Autobiography*, he refers to her:

> Being born in the Vaishnava faith, I had often to go to the *Haveli*. But it never appealed to me. I did not like its glitter and pomp. Also I heard rumours of immorality being practised there, and lost all interest in it. Hence I could gain nothing from the *Haveli*.
>
> But what I failed to get there I obtained from my nurse, an old servant of the family, whose affection for me I still recall. I have said before that there was in me a fear of ghosts and spirits. Rambha, for that was her name, suggested, as a remedy for this fear, the repetition of *Ramanama*. I had more faith in her than in her remedy, and so at a tender age I began repeating *Ramanama* to cure my fear of ghosts and spirits. This was of course short-lived, but the good seed sown in childhood was not sown in vain. I think it is due to the seed sown by that good woman Rambha that today *Ramanama* is an infallible remedy for me.

This is her gift to him: the injunction: repeat *Ramanama*, repeat the name of Rama over and again. That gift is the seed of faith. It is given the way faith must be given: in a singular relation. It is not her arguments that convince him, but his "faith in her." Faced many years later with the arguments of his friend, the faith given by "that Rambha" allows him to cling to his vow.

In continuing to submit to the vow made to his mother, to receive his faith from "that Rambha," Gandhi is compelled to refuse his friend's profoundly colonial hierarchies of religion. Where the possibility of dharma or religion is coeval with vows, with faith in the other, dharma becomes a possibility that marks every society and every time, not by disregarding or transcending the singularities of the societies and institutions where it occurs, but in and through them. As such, this dharma requires no particular historical background or context. (This is so because unlike a principle, which requires autonomous reason, and is therefore a historical phenomenon, the vow is coeval with the promise. It requires "only"— though this is quite an only if we recall Nietzsche's remarks in *Genealogy of Morals*—a "promising being.") It can be practiced equally by the San-thal, Putlibai, Gandhi's Jain mentor Rajchandra, or the nineteenth-century British atheist Charles Bradlaugh, whom Gandhi describes as a most religious person.

Gandhi's refusal of autonomous reason organizes his response to his friend. He tells his friend that he cannot reason or argue for vegetarianism. He even acknowledges the compelling nature of the friend's reasons—it is rationally necessary to eat meat. And yet Gandhi will not accede to that reason. He can only pray to God for strength to resist it. And then, he does not know who God is. So it is not God who works here in the vow; it is faith, *shraddha*. Only as an act of faith, given to him by Rambha but now working its own way through him independent of either her or him, does he affirm vegetarianism. Confronting the principle, all mere faith can do is be obstinate, plead foolishness. A vow thus plods along stubbornly, grounded in pure faith; in other words, it is a groundless faith. "A vow is a vow. It cannot be broken."

But this is not a refusal of or to reason; it is an offer rather of pure means, pure faith, or pure sacrifice (and these three are convertible terms here) as a reason. Observing Putlibai and Rambha as a child, Gandhi receives this reason. This reason says: to take a vow is always to surrender by freely offering oneself as self-sacrifice. In a vow, one submits to an incalculable and unconditional relation. Putlibai is bound without reserve to the vow, and a vow cannot be observed calculably or even in a sovereign manner. She accepts and experiences a tellurian vulnerability and surrender to the skies. As the children scour the skies for her, do they sense and maybe even share her experience?

In his submission to the vows given by Putlibai and Rambha, Gandhi receives, before he has even arrived at his concept of the arms-bearing warrior, an abyssal separation from that concept. The warrior too observes vows, beginning with the vow of *brahmacharya*. And yet, while the warrior's vows refuse autonomy, they do not refuse sovereignty—he is constituted by mastery, beginning with self-mastery and expanding outward to mastery of the other. By contrast, contemplated in the vows undertaken by Rambha and Putlibai is a pure self-sacrifice, a self-sacrifice that is neither a self-mastery nor a mastery of the other.

⁓

And yet, though Gandhi will have been exposed through the vows of Rambha and Putlibai to pure self-sacrifice, though he will have affirmed the vow in their spirit, at this point he is yet to arrive at his own thinking of the vow. One question especially arrests him, all the more so because he does not yet have the vocabulary to formulate it: What is the form (drawing on that word under erasure) of the decision involved in pure self-sacrifice?

However limited and precise, a vow can never escape the decision. (Later in the *Autobiography,* Gandhi gives an example of this inescapable decision: the vow he has taken to not drink milk—did it include all milk, or only cow's milk? He persuades himself, with help from Kasturba, that the vow included only cow's milk, and he can drink goat's milk.) This decision is also the moment of an unavoidable engagement with the universal, for the decision necessarily involves an other—at the very least the other that is oneself. Where the principle or "modern civilization" decides by the abstraction of the third party, by the liquefaction of the other as also the self, the arms-bearing warrior decides by a self-sacrifice that is also a sacrifice of the other. Moreover, both these decisions—whether the calculated and liquid decision of modern civilization, or the incalculable and sacrificial decision of the warrior—are made by sovereign beings. In their vows, however, Rambha and Putlibai no longer work as sovereign beings. How, then, do they make their decisions?

By the 1920s, Gandhi retrospectively senses—maybe not consciously— a machinicity and not-ness both in Putlibai's actions and in his youthful response to his friend: Putlibai thus accepts that it is not in her fate to eat that day, and she goes back to a round of duties—round and round, over and again; Gandhi himself faces his friend with an "eternal negative." Increasingly, as he describes the decision involved in pure self-sacrifice, he draws on a vocabulary of machinicity and not-ness.

~

Both the Gujarati phrase *ek nanno* and its English translation, "eternal negative," describe possibly not what he says to his unnamed friend, but what he will have said, what he can retrospectively by 1926 conceive himself as having said. Until around 1905, while Gandhi enforces vows in his own life, while these vows possibly refuse the sovereignty of both the principle and the warrior, he cannot yet think of the vow as a submission to the other of sovereignty; he cannot yet think of it as another universalism—a universalism that is the other of any universalism organized around sovereignty.

Precisely because of this, the young Gandhi's vow is profoundly inadequate as a challenge to "modern civilization." Unsurprisingly, then, while the young Gandhi holds to the vow against the conjoined assaults of his friend and Bentham, he is compelled, perhaps by that very encounter, to engage more with the principle and to finally embrace it. The chapter on his encounter with his friend ends by describing how a short while later he comes to the principle of vegetarianism: "I read Salt's book from cover to cover and was much impressed by it. From the date of reading this book I may claim to have become a vegetarian by choice." The Gujarati version emphasizes the nature of this transformation even more forcefully: "vegetarian by choice, that is, through thought [*marajiyaat etley vichaarthi*]." A principle requires a subject or agent, one who makes a choice, and operates through *vichaar,* the thought that finds reasons. From now on, Gandhi will always claim vegetarianism as a principle too, will defend and even argue for it in the public sphere. In the years before *Hind Swaraj,* and to some degree even in later years, he attacks "modern civilization" too in the name of the principle.

In the years after *Hind Swaraj,* Gandhi breaks from the sovereignty of the principle. But that anxious letter to Andrews, the letter to Mashruwala that says *trahi ma, trahi ma,* "save me, save me"—are these not signs of his continuing fear that the moment of decision and universalism requires always first the sovereignty of the warrior? Does he ever abandon this fear?

$\sim$

Already in the stubbornness of his response to his unnamed friend, the faith that Rambha has given him is also doing its work in ways that he does not comprehend. And in later years, its work continues. He goes back to India soon after adopting vegetarianism as a principle, meets Raychandbhai, and begins his plod away from the principle, his return to the vow of pure self-sacrifice.

In 1901, he takes the vow of *brahmacharya* or control of the senses; this is the first vow we know of him taking after the youthful ones to his mother. That vow, recall, he later realizes is by itself preethical. In relation to the vow, that preethicality could be restated thus: it is preethical not in the technological sense of being neutral, capable of being used for both good and evil, not in the chronological sense of being before dharma or ethics, but in the sense of being the possibility, which dharma itself must always secrete, of the destruction of dharma. Devotees of any vow necessarily sacrifice themselves—they surrender unconditionally and incalculably—to their vow. But their surrender is only to that vow, which can well exercise the most violent sovereignty over the other. Thus, while the observance of vows involves an immeasurable equality with oneself, it is also always potentially the occasion for an immeasurable inequality with both self and other. Vows can thus be either "demonic" [rakshasi] and irreligious [adharmik] or religious [dharmik]. This is why Gandhi must obsess over the questions: What are the vows proper to dharma? How can, when do, vows become dharmik? How do dharmik vows transform the being who observes these vows?

~

Gandhi is brought to the intensity of these questions on that other September 11, in 1906. If the date marks the start not only of the resistance movement to the Transvaal act but of the quasi-concept of satyagraha, this is because of the sudden and unexpected flickering of a vow that does not yet know its name. Speaking at the meeting, Sheth Haji Habib calls on all those present to pass the resolution against the act with God as their witness. Gandhi, who has already spoken, is "at once startled and put on my guard" by this invocation of the vow.

It is Sheth Haji Habib's vow, then, that convokes satyagraha into being. And when Gandhi speaks again, he stresses the significance of the vow they are about to take; how this vow makes what they do at this meeting different from what they have done at every other meeting. He reminds the audience to take the vow only if each person was willing to abide by it.[6]

By 1915, Gandhi comes up for possibly the first time with the list of vows that satyagrahis (in this case, members of the newly founded Satyagraha Ashram at Ahmedabad) must observe. From now, satyagrahis are always asked to take vows. He does not explicitly conceive of these vows as opposed to principles, nor does he treat vows as in any way uniquely Indian. In his English writings, in fact, he often uses "principle" and "vow" interchangeably as translations of vrat and other terms.[7] This is perhaps not at all surprising, for Gujarati does not easily allow for a distinction between the two. Symptomatic of that difficulty is the word that is sometimes translated as principle—siddhanth, which shares an etymology with sadhan and sadhya, means and end, and implies in a way the coming together of both.

But, as we might expect, the interchangeability conceals a radical divergence. Involved in the vow of pure self-sacrifice is a submission and a surrender that has no equivalent in the surrender to reason of the principled individual. Involved in the former is a groundless surrender, and the insistence simultaneously that groundlessness here has a proper. And this proper involves a distinctive discipline—that of *shunyata* or ciphering.

~

The trope of *shunyata* emerges during the *Gitashikshan* lectures in 1926, around the same time that Gandhi uses the phrase "eternal negative" in his *Autobiography,* and just a few years after he begins to invoke the phrase *neti neti.* One of the earliest systematic uses of the term occurs in April 1926 during the course of his discussion of two verses from the *Gita* (II:71–72). "The *nirvana* ['salvation'] of the Buddhists is *shunyata,* but the *nirvana* of the *Gita* means peace *[shanti]* and that is why it is described as *brahma-nirvana.* We need not concern ourselves with this distinction. There is no reason for supposing that there is a difference between the *nirvana* mentioned by Lord Buddha and the *nirvana* of the *Gita.*"[8]

And yet, having said this, over the next two decades he undertakes an audacious transposition: though he continues to invoke the phrases *moksha* and *nirvana,* he describes them in terms of *shunyata* and related phrases. In this displacement of moksha by *shunyata,* a cataphatic telos comes to be displaced by an "eternal negative," by the spirit of restlessness and questioning that must always mark apophaticism, unable as it is to arrive at a resolution, to find the questions proper to the answer it has always already received, and that is yet obscured from it.[9] What makes this movement constitutively apophatic is that *shunyata* is not only something humans aspire to; it is satya or being.

Perhaps the emphasis on *shunyata* can be thought of as the everyday practice of the politics involved in the simultaneous not-ness *(neti neti)* and many-ness (anekantvada) that chapter 6 discussed. Now, *shunya* is what is to be worshipped, meditated upon. "It is very difficult to meditate on *shunya.* The moment we attribute a single quality to God, we cease to worship *shunya.*"[10] Relatedly, when devotees surrender to the *atman,* they come to be marked by *shunyata.* Thus the *Gitashikshan* suggests: "We should live as ciphers *[shunya thaine].* And by 1929 he writes, "I talk about reducing oneself to zero everywhere."[11]

The distinctiveness of the vow that satyagrahis take—its inseparable relation to and departure from the vows he takes in the 1880s as a student—lies perhaps in this insistence on ciphering. An initial moment in this trajectory that leads to his thinking of the ciphering is the emphasis on the surrender involved in the vows of satyagraha. In 1919, Gandhi publishes first in *Navjivan* and then in *Young India* an essay by Saraladevi Chaudhari, which she submits at his request. The essay is titled "Bandhu," a word that can be glossed as brother or friend and is derived from *bandhan* or bond (two words that too may share an etymology). Considering the article to be exceptionally valuable and important, he reprises its themes two weeks later. In her moment of doubt,

> she remembered the *Bhagavad Gita*. She discovered in it the Ancient Being of beings, the Supreme Ruler. Only in Rama can the weak find strength]. When there is no living creature to console one in separation and lighten the grief [*dukh*], the grief-stricken one calls on Rama. So long as the elephant could struggle against the crocodile, he did not remember God; but, when his lordship was exhausted, he began to call on the servant of servants. Hence Saraladevi says: "I who used to roar, I will humbly surrender myself in love to the charioteer *bandhu* [Krishna], friend of Arjuna and yet none else but God. . . . Searching for that God, I have to look inwards to scan the heavens there and, as I do so, I realize that I am my own friend [*sakhi*] and I am also my own foe. If I would realize the *vishwatman* ['Universal Self'], I must first realize the *antaratman* ['Self in me']. Thus 'The self is its own *bandhu.*'"[12]

One reference here is to the elephant king Gajendra, who in a legend from the *Bhagavad Purana* fights a crocodile for a thousand years because he is confident of his own prowess. Where there is such effort to secure one's own prowess and sovereignty, there can for Gandhi only be enmity to the *atman*. By this criterion, "modern civilization" exemplifies enmity with the *atman*, which perhaps may be why the Editor can describe it in *Hind Swaraj* as *adharma* or irreligion.

And Saraladevi's quote glosses the *Gita* (VI:5), which says (drawing here on Mahadev Desai's rendering of Gandhi's Gujarati rendering): "By one's Self [*atman*] should one raise oneself [*atman*], and not allow oneself to fall; for *Atman* alone is the friend [*bandhu*] of self, and Self alone is self's foe."[13] Searching for the friend, Saraladevi and Gandhi can both find friendship (and enmity) only with the *atman*.

Friendship with the *atman*, by contrast, requires surrender to it. Sarala-devi says, "I will humbly surrender myself in love." Similarly, it is Gajendra's surrender to the god Vishnu that saves him. In this surrender, satyagrahis lose agency and become helpless. Already in the teens and 1920s Gandhi stresses the helplessness of the satyagrahi. Two verses are invoked especially often. "There is a *bhajan* we often sing in the Ashram; its first line runs: *Nirbalke bala Rama*. [This is glossed in the footnote as: 'He is the help of the helpless, the strength of the weak.'] One cannot pray to God for help in a spirit of pride but only if one confesses oneself as helpless."[14] He also often cites a "beautiful Tamil saying, 'God is the sole help of those who are helpless.'"[15]

Yet this intense helplessness is also an intense hopefulness and indeed empowerment. In September 1924, responding to the Hindu-Muslim riots, Gandhi announces a twenty-one-day fast: "The recent events have proved unbearable for me. My helplessness is still more unbearable. My religion teaches me that whenever there is distress which one cannot remove, one must fast and pray. I have done so in connection with my own dearest ones. Nothing evidently that I say or write can bring the two communities together. I am therefore imposing on myself a fast of 21 days."[16] After a newspaper misprints this statement as "my hopelessness is still more unbearable," Gandhi writes:

> My statement mentions "helplessness" [*nisahayata*] and not "hopelessness" [*nirash*]. A man with a grain of faith in God never loses hope. . . . On the contrary, his hope shines the brightest "amid the encircling gloom." But my helplessness is a very patent fact before me. I may not ignore it. I must ever confess it. There is a beautiful Tamil proverb which says: "God is the sole help of the helpless." The truth of this never came upon me with so much force as it has come today. Handling large masses of men, dealing with them, speaking and acting for them is no joke for a man whose capacity God has so circumscribed. One has, therefore, to be ever on the watch. And the reader may rest assured that I took the final step after I had realized to the full my utter hopelessness. And I cried out to God even like Draupadi when she seemed to be abandoned by her five brave protectors. And her cry did not ascend to the throne of the Almighty in vain. That cry must not be from the lip. It has to be from the deepest recesses of one's heart. And, therefore, such a cry is only possible when one is in anguish. Mine has expressed itself in a fast which is by no means adequate for the issues involved. My heart continually says:

> Rock of Ages cleft for me,
> Let me hide myself in Thee[17]

Here the failure to realize hope leads not to its recalibration (as would be the case with agential action, which is organized effectively—as means to an end) but to an insistence that the initial effort at self-sacrifice and self-purification was not enough. Indeed, Gandhi is insistent that faith wells hope.

> There is nothing that wastes the body like worry and one who has any faith in God should be ashamed to worry about anything whatsoever. It is a difficult rule no doubt for the simple reason, that faith in God with the majority of mankind is either an intellectual belief or a blind belief, a kind of superstitious fear of something indefinable. But to ensure absolute freedom from worry requires a living utter faith which is a plant of slow, almost unperceived, growth and requires to be constantly watered by tears that accompany genuine prayer. They are the tears of a lover who cannot brook a moment's separation from the loved one, or of the penitent who knows that it is some trace of impurity in him that keeps him away from the loved one.[18]

A distinctive kind of hope, then—the infinite hope of absolute responsibility, a hope that presumes that it is "some trace of impurity" in satyagrahis that keeps them away from the beloved; it is indeed the hope that must accompany the satyagrahi's grief. From the perspective of the satyagrahi, "I hold it to be an axiomatic truth that true ahimsa never fails to impress itself on the opponent. If it does, to that extent it is imperfect."[19]

~

In the *Gitashikshan*, a suggestive use of *shunyata* occurs in Gandhi's explication of a verse from the *Gita* (III:15) which says that Brahman—being—is founded on yajna or sacrifice. Sacrifice, he points out, involves a submission and ciphering that is carried out through labor.

> If when we have swaraj we wish to run our government like the British do, we would be behaving as masters [*sheth*]. But we wish to give up the ways of masters [*badshahi*, 'emperors'] and turn ourselves into workers [*majoor*]. If while working we can be

detached and make ourselves ciphers [shunyavat], we would come
out of our trance. This is the idea in the verse containing the phrase
"eternally founded in yajna" [nitya yajney pratishththam].[20]

As this formulation suggests, ciphering is the most proper form of self-
sacrifice because it is the other of sovereignty. Thus the contrast made
between the figure of the master (surely resonant also with the Kshatriya-
warrior) and the worker (or elsewhere servant, the one who serves). In
opposition to the arguments of the satyagrahi warrior, in opposition to
the analogy of the cat and mouse, ciphering names the relinquishment
of sovereignty that occurs because of love. "Love can only be expressed
fully when man reduces himself to a cipher. This process of reduction to
cipher is the highest effort man or woman is capable of making. It is
the only effort worth making."[21] Ciphering follows thus from daya and
prem. In 1928, Gandhi writes to Prabhudas Gandhi: "Anyone who wants
to do all work in love has no choice but to reduce himself or herself to
zero. How often have I explained this to you? Love is the utmost depth of
humility."[22]

And yet it is the nature of this ciphering that it cannot be made into a
vow. In the Autobiography in 1928, he writes that the draft constitution of
the Satyagraha Ashram, with its list of vows, was circulated in 1915 to many
interlocutors. And of the many suggestions that were received, "that of Sir
Gurudas Benerji is still in my memory." Benerji suggests that humility
[namrata] be added to the list of vows. Gandhi is tempted, but "I feared
humility's humility would be erased if it were given the status of a vow. The
full meaning of humility is nothingness ['self-effacement,' shunyata]. It is
to reach nothingness that there are other vows. Shunyata is the state of
moksha. If the acts of a mumuksh ['aspirant for salvation'] or a servant have
no humility or selflessness about them, then that person is not a mumuksh
or servant."[23]

Unlike the warrior's vows, which enact his sovereignty, here vows are
the very discipline of self-effacement and self-surrender. This vow is a politics of nothingness, of shunyata; nothingness is so constitutive of it that
there cannot be a vow of nothingness. And nothingness names not extir-
pation and extinction but that being involved in self-sacrifice, in the "living
by dying" that Gandhi describes as constitutive of daya, ahimsa, and
satyagraha. Thus it is that he can say: "To know the atman means to forget
the body, or, in other words, to become a cipher. Anybody who becomes a

cipher will have realized the *atman*."[24] Moreover, ciphering is not only the mark of human. Gandhi repeatedly describes god repeatedly as the servant of his servants; it is in servitude, the other of sovereignty, that god must be thought.

As the other of sovereignty, ciphering entails an absolute oneness and unconditional equality. "The more I live the more real the doctrine of oneness of life becomes to me. But the difficulty of practising the doctrine is also growing with me instead of diminishing. Realization of the doctrine seems to be impossible unless we could reduce the 'I' in us to a complete cipher."[25] "Who can say whether the mustard seed or the mountain is superior? In some cases we don't think in terms of superior or inferior [*unchnich*]. Similarly, we cannot compare the relative worth of one another [*ekbeejana*]. I have, therefore, suggested the easiest of easy rules—I should say, rather, that I have extracted it from Shastras—that everybody should live as a cipher."[26]

The discipline of ciphering thus responds to the question: How to sustain absolute and unconditional equality across irreconcilable difference? Where there are profoundly disparate beings—whether mountain and mustard seed as in this case, or ants, scorpions, chimpanzees, and humans, as in some of Gandhi's other examples—sovereignty-centered traditions of thinking unity and universalism cannot but hierarchize them. Ciphering refuses to reconcile in this manner; it is oriented rather toward an absolute equality.

Such equality involves also a relinquishment of rights. "We wish to establish unity [*advait*, 'rapport'] with 30 crore people. This would happen only when we make ourselves into a cipher. What have we to do with rights [*adhikaar*]? Politics of power is unreal. We must tell the people what is real politics."[27] Rights must be relinquished because they are organized around sovereignty—more specifically, autonomy. In the wake of the destruction of rights, Gandhi often emphasizes *farj*—obligation or duty. Given the emphasis on ciphering, this *farj* cannot be conceived in terms of the thekana or rightful place. Rather, the *farj* is to absolute equality and unity.

Ciphering exemplifies the finitude of ahimsa: it involves limitlessly assuming the limit, assuming finitude. "In order to be able to practice the dharma of ahimsa, man [*manushya*] must abide by the limits [*maryada*] laid down by the Shastras and custom. . . . Because there are no limits to self-control, there are no limits to ahimsa."[28] We are to observe all the *yamas* [vows] in thought as well, so that we shall grow more secure in them from day to day and come to think of fresh things to sacrifice. Sacrifice has no limit [*hadh*] to it."[29] "There is no limit to the potency of truth, as there is a limit to the power of an individual seeker. But if he is wide awake and is striving constantly, there is no limit to his power as well."[30] If there is no limit to ahimsa, to the dispelling of fear and relatedly to the receiving of fearlessness as a gift, this is because there are no limits to the assumption of limits by the self, to ciphering.

This ciphering requires the greatest abhay or fearlessness, and here, moreover, abhay can only be abhaydan or the gift of fearlessness, because ciphering forgets or relinquishes precisely the sovereign power that is ordinarily constitutive of both the warrior and of everyday life. Perhaps Gandhi has such abhay in mind when in 1913 he questions the government policy of extirpating snakes (which at the time kill around twenty thousand people a year in India—a figure Gandhi considers an underestimate), and offers the lifestyle of Saint Francis of Assisi, "a great Yogi in Europe," as a contrast:

> He used to wander in the forests among reptiles, etc., but they never harmed him. On the contrary, they were friends with him. Thousands of *yogis* and fakirs live in the forests of India. They move fearlessly among tigers, wolves, snakes, etc., and one never hears of their coming to any harm on that account. It might be argued that there must be casualties even among them through snake-bites, or predatory animals; this is very likely. We know, though, that in comparison with the great number of reptiles, etc., the *yogis* and fakirs are so few that if these deadly creatures were set on destroying them, not one of them would survive. These *yogis* and fakirs keep no weapons with which to withstand these beasts—this we know and believe. This proves that some [*ketlaak*, 'many'] dreaded beasts maintain a friendship with some *yogis* and fakirs, or, at any rate, do not touch them. I feel that when we relinquish all enmity towards every living creature, they too do not regard us with enmity. Daya or prem is man's greatest excellence. Without this he cannot worship God. Daya is the root [*mul*] of dharma, this we can see more or less in all dharma.[31]

Here, while the animals are abyssally apart, and threaten human life, an infinite love can still possibly cross this abyss. This love is abhay or fearlessness, and it involves an absolute equality that makes one named Christian holy man, as well as several unnamed Hindu yogis and Muslim fakirs, submit to the animals whose lives they could have taken if they wished to exercise sovereign power. They cannot take the lives of these animals because they experience a love that is also an absolute equality; surrendering to these animals, they receive their lives from these animals.

~

As ciphering, ahimsa opens out onto another power, one conceived in terms of a distinctive automaticity and machinicity. He perhaps reads the *Gita* already in terms of machinicity by 1917, when in explaining the phrase "free from desire" (which occurs in Edwin Arnold's translation of the *Gita, The Song Celestial*) in a letter, he remarks that this is a "technical expression" and that desire "means desire to be or possess something short of the highest. Thus, love of God is not 'a desire.' It is the natural longing. But to possess a fortune so that I may do good is a desire and therefore to be curbed. Our good acts must be as natural to us as the twinkling of our eyes. Without our desiring, they act automatically. The doing of good should be just as natural to us."[32]

"Natural longing": as noted earlier, one of the ways he translates the word *swabhavik* or own orientation is "natural." Here as elsewhere, the word "natural" must be understood not in terms of its European genealogies, where it is opposed to the cultural, civic, or social, but rather in terms of that originary orientation of being that he describes with the phrase *ahimsa paramo dharma*.

It is, however, in the 1926 *Gitashikshan* lectures, around the same time that he comes to stress ciphering, that Gandhi attends to this automaticity at length, drawing especially on the metaphor of the machine.[33] "In this age, we do not have the means with which to measure ourselves [*potanu map*]. The *Gita* was composed to help us. It says that we should work like machines and pour out our life in our work." It is the impossibility of any proper measure, then, that imposes on "us" the necessity of giving "ourselves" without measure. Here, the mark of a machine is that it is given over completely and immeasurably to its task. "We have to make ourselves conscious machines [*chetanayukt yantra*]. We should cultivate such perfect concentration that, like a man asleep, we are aware of nothing else."[34] "'Fruits of action do not cling to me, for I have no desire for them,' says Shri

Krishna. Once a machine is set in motion, every part in it works automatically. When we have learnt to function like a machine, then we can say that *purusharth* has been accomplished ['we shall have gained the true end of human effort']."[35]

Indeed, the machine exemplifies the self-sacrifice proper to ahimsa. Sacrificers must forget the sacrifice that they undertake; they must do it automatically, without thought or deliberation.

> It is the most difficult thing for an *intelligent* being to be like a machine [emphasis original]. And yet, if one is to become a zero, that is precisely what one desiring perfection has to become. The vital difference between the machine and the man is that the machine is inert, the man is all life and consciously becomes like a machine in the hands of the Master Mechanic. Krishna says in so many words that God moves all beings as if they were parts of a machine.[36]

"In most cases, we should behave as though we were inert things. The difference between purely inert matter and living matter is as good as nil. The entire world seems to be inert matter, the *atman* shines but rarely. So do the non-worldly conduct themselves. This was Raychandbhai's conduct—this I saw."[37] In formulations such as these, the machine names no longer the instrumentality and causality of the figure who masters it, as it did in *Hind Swaraj,* but submission and self-sacrifice—the epitome of the cipher.

Because of the ciphering and machinicity that marks them, satyagrahis cannot act as agents or rational actors; they cannot calculate and plan for the future; they do not seek to master the future. This makes for Gandhi's distinctive way of thinking the decision: "I really do not know future plans. You will believe me when I say that they are in God's hands."[38] Indeed, "one who is a lover of the *Gita,* i.e., who leaves the results of one's work to God, should never desire to know the future."[39] Even the event of satyagraha comes upon them. Explaining his 1932 fast to his friend Henry Polak, he says: "You will ask why it was not administered ten years ago. The answer is: God did not call me to it. He comes to wake you up when you least except Him."[40] To surrender to satya (let us not forget that in Gandhi's vocabulary God is the everyday name for satya, hence satyagrahi)—this leads to the action involved in satyagraha.

~

From within the problematic of sovereignty and agency, all this does not make sense. The satyagrahi-cipher is marked by the very qualities—submission, machinicity, and helplessness!—that would undermine the free agent who makes the sovereign decision. The satyagrahi-cipher is not marked by what Kant calls "man's emergence from his self-imposed immaturity." Instead of instituting sovereignty where there had formerly been helplessness, sataygrahis refuse both subordination to and exercise of sovereign power. As such, they cannot be either effective means to an end or ends in themselves. If there is a "limit attitude" and "permanent critique of our historical era" involved in the activities of the satyagrahi-cipher, then that critique and attitude is not organized by the Enlightenment emphasis on the principle, or (as we saw Foucault so powerfully put it) by "the principle of a critique and permanent creation of ourselves in our autonomy."

I am hesitant to read this relinquishment of agency in terms of that notion of karma where "action [is] seen to be completely determined by a chain of cause and effect which begins before the actor's birth and continues well after her or his death," in terms of a "notion of action as part of a pre-determined universe illustrated by the idea of rebirth." Such privileging of karma involves being "determined by the weight of a past rather than the ideality of a future."[41]

My hesitation is because even if Gandhi abjures the free agent, his helplessness-hopefulness is accompanied by its own power: he refers often to the "power of satyagraha," to satyagraha as a weapon that surpasses all weapons.[42] Indeed, he is by no means abjuring the decision—that choice between one and other that must be made at every moment, that it should properly be said even makes every moment. To give up on the decision would be to give up on politics and ethics; there can be no future, nor indeed any past, without the decision.

He comes rather to another concept or, strictly speaking, a quasi-concept of the decision, one that is not centered any longer around the figure of the free agent, one that is marked rather by automaticity and machinicity. "The man who knows the Truth proceeds on the belief that he himself does nothing. Whether seeing or hearing, smelling, eating, walking, lying down to sleep, breathing, speaking, parting with or accepting anything, winking—in all these he will say that his senses are doing their work. Such a person acts and yet does not act [te kam karto chhata nathi karto]."[43] Such a person "does not act"—this is so in the sense that the lover surrenders agency and calculation. "Such a person acts"—this is so in the sense that the surrender of agency and calculation opens onto non-agential and indeed nonsovereign action, a passive action. Thus, in becoming like a machine, every act is made into a gift to and from being:

> To do one's duty [kartavya karma] means to fight and struggle. Since every karma involves a choice, there is necessarily a struggle. Even though caught in this way between opposites, you will have transcended them if you dedicate every action to Krishna, do everything without attachment or aversion, have faith in God and present every karma as a gift [daan] to Him. If you put all on God ["believe God to be the author of all you do"], you will be touched neither by sin nor by virtue.[44]

In this relation of the gift, rather than in the liberal way of emphasizing "right means," Gandhi espies nonviolence or ahimsa. By its very nature, to gift is not only to refuse to dominate the other or the self; it is to give oneself to the other forcefully.

This, then, is the decision that satyagrahis have to make at every moment: how to make their action a gift to and from God, or, more precisely, to and from the not-ness that constitutes Being. Perhaps in implicit reference to the difficulty of this decision—itself necessarily a gift—Gandhi refers repeatedly to satyagrahis as always walking on "the edge of a sword." He elaborates on this analogy occasionally by referring to the acrobatic ropewalker, who must concentrate entirely on the task at hand in order to carry it out. Every decision that the satyagrahi makes must be marked by a similar concentration, and by a similar possibility of falling.

Involved in this decision is a striking relation with "free will," or the everyday exercise of sovereign power. On the one hand, Gandhi repeatedly stresses "free will" as a central difference between the human and "brute." "Man has reason, discrimination, and free will such as it is. The brute has no such thing. It is not a free agent [swatantrata], and knows no distinction between virtue and vice, good and evil. Man, being a free agent, knows these distinctions."[45] For him, the free will of humans is already given originarily in "modern civilization" everywhere, whether in ancient India or contemporary Europe.

On the other hand, Gandhi does not claim free will for himself. "I myself am subjugated [paradhin]. I am never sure of what will happen the next moment. My very freedom [*swatantrata*] seems like bondage [*partan-trata*] to me, while slavery to Satyanarayan [Truth as God] seems freedom to me. Though I didn't at all wish to undertake a fast, I had to do so. But the weight that was lifted off me after I had taken the decision is beyond description."[46]

How does Gandhi make this move where he affirms free will and sovereignty but also relinquishes it? Perhaps we can take our cue from his response in 1934 to a correspondent, presumably associated in some way with Verrier Elwin, who writes to Gandhi wondering whether he should join Gandhian work. Gandhi writes back:

> your *dharma* as yet is neither to come to me nor to go to Father Elwin. For now, remain where you are and learn to live in poverty. Save as much as you can and use the money for *seva* [service]. If you can teach students the elements of ethics, do so. So long as you do not feel full non-attachment, your dharma is to continue in your present way of life. Renunciation [*tyag*] of your present way of life before you have come to feel strong aversion to it will not be proper, nor will it endure. When intense non-attachment [*tivra vairagya*] has developed in you, nobody will be able to stop you.[47]

Posited here is a striking relation of nonrelation and nonpassage between the choice and the cipher, or between the principle and vow. It is necessary to prepare for the vow and for ciphering. The principle and the choice can, even must, be part of this preparation. The correspondent must adopt and abide by principles—use his money for *seva*, remain in poverty, and so on. These principles and indeed agency are necessary preconditions for faith. But these principles are yet abysally separated from the automaticity of "intense non-attachment," which comes both before and after it. That latter automaticity cannot be arrived at through the principle; that automaticity must seize one.

   This automaticity that supplements the principle is what he names by the synonyms "utter faith," "pure faith," and "ample faith"; he also describes this faith often with the word "prayer." Prayer is always both the work of faith and the pursuit of more faith. If he had "ample faith," Gandhi remarks on one occasion, "I should not hesitate to plunge into a blazing fire. But such faith cannot come by mechanical means. One must wait and pray for it."[48]

The principle is dominant, then, at precisely the moment when faith is not ample. By praying, satyagrahis seek to create the pure faith that marks the vow. But they cannot choose when they have that faith; they can only pray and wait for that moment. In this sense, even when satyagrahis take a vow, that vow only initiates the wait and preparation for the moment when the vow or faith takes them over. Satyagrahis, then, do not decide; they are seized by the decision.

How this seizure by the decision works is suggested in his explication of a word that Gandhi turns to often in order to describe it—*antaratman*. He invokes the word in discussing Saraladevi's account of the word "bandhu" or friend. "Where it is a question of determining the justice or otherwise of a particular act, there is no room for any other means [*sadhan*, "force"] but that of the mind [*budhhi*, "reason"] regulated by the voice of conscience [*antaratman*]."[49] He repeatedly insists that he seeks to listen and heed his *antaratman*. When *antaratman* is translated as "inner voice" or "conscience" (two of his favored translations), we might presume that it resonates with Kantian traditions around the conscience. But for Kant the conscience is the internalization of the principle and judge; it is the installation within oneself of the autonomous sovereign. In contrast, already by the teens and emphatically after the *Gitashikshan* lectures, Gandhi returns to a theme that resonates with many nonmodern religious traditions: he suggests that the *antaratman* is the

> voice of God. It is not our voice. It could be the voice of God or even of Satan [*shaitan*]. In order to ensure that it is God who speaks from within us, we should properly follow the vows [*yama-niyama*]. Crores claim to hear the inner voice, but the true inner voice is heard by only a few [*ekno*, one]. We cannot adduce proof in its support. . . . The inner voice is a force outside us, but it is not beyond us. . . . When we are one with the force of Being, then in the language of mysticism we say God is speaking through us. When we are one with *sat*, our ego becomes a cipher.[50]

~

Three points about this ciphering-machinicity should be noted here. First, in the passage above as elsewhere, the *antaratman* is the other within; it is the *dvaita* that marks Gandhi's *advaita*, to recall his simultaneous affirmation of both in chapter 6. To this other, Gandhi directs his prayers. For him, such prayer "plays a large part in a self-purificatory sacrifice. . . . A man of prayer and self-purification will shed the fear of death and think of death as a friend [*mrityuney mitra samaan lagey,* "embrace death as a boon companion"].[51] But given the way he thinks the question of God and Being, the concept of prayer too is reworked. That reworking emerges especially forcefully in his discussion with the Hungarian émigré Charles Fabri, who, Mahadev Desai notes in his introduction, "was particularly exercised about the form and content of prayer and would very much like to know what kind of prayer Gandhiji said. Could the Divine Mind be changed by prayer? Could one find it out by prayer?" Gandhi responds:

> The meaning of prayer is that I want to evoke that Divinity within me. . . . when I pray for swaraj or independence for India I pray or wish for adequate power to gain that swaraj or to make the largest contribution I can towards winning it, and I maintain that I can get that power in answer to prayer.
>
> Fabri: Then you are not justified in calling it prayer. To pray means to beg or demand.
>
> Gandhi: Yes, indeed. You may say I beg it of myself, of my Higher Self, the Real Self with which I have not yet achieved complete identification.[52]

Here, then, prayer is no longer offered to an external other, but to the other that one oneself always is, the other that is one's own *atman*. It is the *antaratman* that gives the distinction between self and other, which satyagrahis must then seek to abide by in all their actions.

> Haven't I compared the breaking of heads to the explosion of crackers [i.e., celebrations]? . . . But all this is true only with reference to oneself. So long, therefore, as our own heads are being broken, we should think that crackers are exploding. Don't ask how the *atman* can make a distinction between one's own and another's. So long as the body endures, we must assume this distinction between oneself and other in all our actions."[53]

It is of this *atman* that he says in 1930: "The salvation of a soul can be only through the *atman*. This is why it can be said that one becomes one's own friend or enemy. The one who has won over the mind has the soul for a friend, the one who has not has the soul for an enemy."[54] This friendship with the *atman,* which is also always necessarily a friendship with one's own death, involves an originary separation from oneself, for here one is given over to one's own otherness. But unlike the warrior, who seeks an immeasurable equality with his own death first, and derives his daya from that, here it is grief, prayer, and daya, which lead to friendship with death.[55]

In this friendship with the *atman,* satyagrahis make their decision. A few months before the *Gitashikshan* lectures, he writes: "The urge for satyagraha does not come from anyone. It must be spontaneous. Rama did not consult his elders and gurus before deciding to go and dwell in the forest."[56] Where Gandhi says that "future plans" are in the hands of God, it is the *antaratman* that he refers to. And for the decision made in submission to the *antaratman,* satyagrahis have an absolute, singular, and total responsibility, for here the decision cannot be grounded on knowledge. Indeed, of whether it is the *antaratman* speaking, moreover, "there can be no final proof"; satyagrahis cannot know for certain even whether it is the *antaratman* or the devil speaking. "Man himself does not know when he is deceiving himself, or when he is pretending."[57]

~

Second, precisely because "our ego becomes a cipher," as he puts in one of the passages above, the relation to the *antaratman* cannot be circumscribed by knowledge, and the decision is here marked by the nonknowledge and secrecy that is the mark of the pure gift, of pure means.

(Derrida notes in a similar vein how such nonrecognition marks the pure gift. "It is thus necessary, at the limit, that he [donee, but also the donor] not *recognize* the gift as gift." That "simple recognition suffices to annul the gift. Why? Because it gives back, in the place, let us say, of the thing itself, a symbolic equivalent." "For there to be gift, not only must the donor or donee not perceive or receive the gift as such, have no consciousness of it, no memory, no recognition.)[58]

In December 1911, in a fascinating rendering of Tolstoy's "Ivan the Fool and His Two Brothers," Gandhi articulates this nonknowledge that must mark the gift.[59] In the rendering (where Ivan is renamed "Murakhraj"—fool-king), perhaps even more forcefully than the English version that Gandhi read, Murakhraj, though a fool because he has given up on the conventional measures of success, is marked by an immense wisdom. Murakhraj's order exists automatically in the sense of being apparently without effort. When he becomes king, and his foolishness becomes clear, "the result was that the wise people left the kingdom and went away, only the ordinary [sada] people remained."[60]

As with Ivan-Murakhraj, Gandhi describes himself as a fool, eccentric, and simpleton. But he stresses by the time of the *Gitashikshan* what perhaps for him remains underemphasized in the account of Ivan-Murakhraj—that the foolishness of *satyagraha* requires the most intense effort. The *Gitashikshan* argues:

> There is no outward difference between a fool [murakh] and a wise man [gyani]. The fool has no pretensions. The wise man wants to be taken as a fool by the world. To the world, the behaviour of the two will seem alike. The man whose mind is active with intense energy [shakti] will appear dull [jad]. The earth rotates with such great speed that it seems to be stationary. This is not a matter of *shunya*. Buddha's *nirvana* was also not *shunya*. There is only a seeming inertness.[61]

This passage disavows the word *shunya* to the extent that it names the inert cipher or nullity. This remark comes two days after he suggests that there are no significant differences for the satyagrahi between Buddha's *shunyata* and *nirvana*. Buddha's *shunyata-nirvana* is not nullity; *shunyata* or ciphering is rather the most intense activity possible. But that intense activity is not easy to distinguish from the activity of the fool. The wise man wants to be taken by the world to be a fool not because he conceals his wisdom from them, or keeps it secret to himself, but because he himself does not know whether he is wise. Practicing self-sacrifice as he does in the spirit of machinicity, he must forget and perhaps not even know that he has offered self-sacrifice. Satyagrahis must act in the spirit of self-sacrifice, but they too must forget and not know their self-sacrifice. This forgetting and non-knowing renders the actions of satyagrahi secret from both themselves and others.

What makes this secret so distinctive is that its defiance of the public-private distinction emerges from the most rigorous submission to that distinction. Gandhi affirms the public-private distinction most forcefully. There are thus matters that he recognizes are private. Most often that privacy is between intimates. Thus his personal correspondence is replete with discussions that are clearly not meant for those other than the figures it is addressed to. Proper names that he refers to as examples in his discussions and talks at Satyagraha Ashram, within an intimate community, are regularly expunged in the published versions of these. Many interlocutors remain unnamed, or recognizable only for a circle of intimates—for example, the friend who tries to persuade the young Gandhi to eat meat.

Gandhi also insists that there can be no secrets in public life, that he has no secrets that he keeps from the public, and that satyagrahis must keep their transactions entirely transparent: "In the war of non-violence we walk in the fear of God, give no secret information, brook no treacherousness." Indeed, the "secret of non-violence" and satyagraha is self-sacrifice to the other, and self-sacrifice always involves giving oneself as transparently as one can to the other; in this sense, the secret of nonviolence is a nonsecret giving.

Yet this insistence on intense transparency in the public sphere secretes its own opacity and secrecy into that very sphere. Satyagrahis are seized by a force that they do not know, and that they must yet be responsible to. Even as they try to keep their actions open to scrutiny, these actions become secret from both themselves and others. So it is that he can write in 1928 about the Ashram rules: "Even I who was the author of the rules do not know their full meaning, though I am realizing it more and more clearly every day." In the *Anasaktiyoga,* the book on the *Gita* that is released on the day that the Dandi march commences (and I cite here from the official translation—done by Mahadev Desai, and reviewed by Gandhi), he suggests:

> As breathing, winking and similar processes are automatic [*potani medey*] and man claims no agency for them, he being conscious of the processes only when disease or similar cause arrests them, in a similar manner all his activities [*swabhavik karma*] should be automatic, without his arrogating to himself the agency or responsibility thereof. A man of charity [*jeno swabhav udartano chhe*] does not even know that he is doing charitable acts, it is his nature to do so, he cannot help it. This detachment can only come from tireless endeavour and God's grace.[62]

Here automaticity is a giving not only without reserve but also without knowledge; indeed, the mark of daya (here, *udarta,* a word that Gandhi uses less often than daya) must be that the practitioners of daya do not know that they are practicing it. They do not know—here we are no longer re-iterating the spontaneous nonknowledge of Ivan-Murakhraj. Unlike Ivan-Murakhraj's, satyagrahis practice a tireless discipline that makes them not know.

Indeed, even when they try to offer satyagraha, satyagrahis can never be sure that what they have offered is satyagraha. To begin with, satyagraha emerges from a suspicion of motives or intentionality. As he puts it in a letter to an early interlocutor, W. J. Wybergh,

> Nor can I hold with you that motives alone can always decide the question of a particular act being right or wrong. An ignorant mother may, from the purest motives, administer a dose of opium to her child. Her motives will not cure her of her ignorance, nor, in the moral world purge her of the offence of killing her child. A passive resister, recognising this principle and knowing that, in spite of the purity of his motives, his action may be utterly wrong, leaves judgment to the Supreme Being, and, in attempting to resist what he holds to be wrong, suffers only in his own person.[63]

The suspicion of motives and intentionality, then, leads to ahimsa. Also (even though Gandhi may not intend to say so), satyagrahis are strikingly like the ignorant mother: they too kill their own—themselves, since for this offense they can take responsibility.

And even though they offer ahimsa because they want to avoid "utterly wrong" action, they cannot be sure that what they offer is ahimsa: "Indeed, it is likely that what we believe to be an act of ahimsa is an act of himsa in the eyes of God."[64] This is not merely modesty but an acknowledgment of the unknowing at work in pure means. The pursuit of ahimsa and swaraj requires satyagrahis to constantly undertake *manthan,* churning or "self-examination."[65] Such self-examination is different from the public cit-izen's because the latter undertakes self-examination in order to become transparent. Though the latter never actually achieves transparency, the very pursuit as a utopian possibility installs public reason and the public sphere.

In contrast, Gandhi's self-examination is neither public nor private; it is "religious" and "prayerful." "In my opinion, such self-examination is only possible where there is religious perception."[66] What makes it religious is "self-purification," the relinquishment above all of the desire for "fruit," or ends. Thus self-purification relinquishes precisely the sovereign self who is capable of knowledge—the self who conducts and is visible to the most vigorous self-examination.

Here the very pursuit of transparency opens onto the moment where transparency is no longer possible, where the self is concealed and obscured from the self. Symptomatic of this concealment and obscuring is the contrapuntal "surrender to God" involved in self-purification. "No great reforms can be brought about without self-examination [manthan]. But the fact is that my fasts are not mine [mari nathi]; they are inspired by God. This is what I think."[67] Self-examination thus leads on to a freedom that no longer belongs to the order of autonomy. The rationality of their actions must be concealed from satyagrahis themselves; they must make themselves a secret from themselves. "The words which I pen or speak, come to me of their own [teni medi, "unsought"]. Only such words are true [khara], for they are living words."[68] Gandhi thus is not in control even of his speech, and the very fact that the words he utters are secret from himself makes them living.

Moreover, it is the nature of ahimsa that the more satyagrahis offer it, the more aware they are of not having offered it. Gandhi thus occasionally echoes the bhakti poet-saints Tulsidas and Surdas, both of whom insist that there is "no greater sinner" than they. In the *Ashram Bhajanavali*, which he translates into English for Mirabehn [Madeleine Slade] and which compiles the prayers sung at the Satyagraha Ashram in Ahmedabad, there are again some verses by Surdas, including the famous one that begins: "Who can be so crooked, bad or dissolute as I? I am so faithless that I have forgotten the very God who gave me this body. . . . Who can be a greater sinner than I, I am the chief among them." As Gandhi points out, "Neither Tulsidas nor Surdas was such a person, but they regarded themselves as such."

If Surdas and Tulsidas so regard themselves, however, this is because to give the gift of ahimsa is to develop precisely the power to give more, an awareness of what has not been given. As such, even as this is a giving without limit, it is a giving that, unlike the sovereign or metaphysical gift, secretes an unknowing—conceals its giving from itself. The secretion of this unknowing necessarily accompanies the relinquishment of mastery:

where is no mastery of what they encounter, satyagrahis give up the possibility of knowing whether satyagraha works or has taken place.

Thus, though daya is marked by an intense transparency, this transparency leads onto its own secrecy. This combination of transparency and secrecy-opacity involves a curious relation with the public-private distinction that founds republican democracy. Because daya is a secret from its practitioners, the mark of daya as pure means or pure faith is precisely that it cannot know itself as such. Put differently, pure faith or pure means knows only one thing—its impurity; this is both the humility and the secret of satyagraha. And since it can exclude the principle only if it knows itself to be pure, it must submit to the principle even as it opposes and questions the principle. The resistant submission involved in satyagraha is in this sense secreted already by the vow, and it requires that satyagrahis must both refuse and submit to the public-private distinction. In the process, satyagrahis become ciphers in a doubled sense—they relinquish agency, and in so doing become secret from and to themselves.

Perhaps it is symptomatic of this curious relation with the public-private distinction that Gandhi should, even as he insists on transparency, also stress the importance of silence in satyagraha. "What we expect to attain by acclamations in ordinary movements, we often gain by silence [chupkithi] in satyagraha. The human voice can never reach the distance that is covered by the still small voice of conscience [antarna unda nado]." Here silence names the impossibility of a shared language, perhaps even of a language shared with oneself. The stillness and silence of the voice responds to the specter of a speech without a shared language.

~

Third, ciphering also organizes the relation between human being and other modalities of being—animal, plant, or thing. The question of this relation troubles Gandhi's writing. While he insists repeatedly on the absolute equality and oneness of all being, he also stresses that human being is different from other being—animals, plants, or things. To refuse to acknowledge this difference, to insist too quickly on the sameness or equality of human being and other being—he is aware that this would be deeply irresponsible, a way of giving oneself a good conscience. How to think this difference, and equal relationships across this difference? This question is yet another of those knots at which his writing tears undecidably into two, with the same sentences and phrases bearing two very different senses, each of which threatens to destroy the other.

Gandhi's explicit formulations, especially those in English, seem pervaded by the presumption of both a massive distinction and a hierarchy between human being and other being. This distinction and hierarchy is already evident in the very way satyagraha is presented in the English version of *Hind Swaraj*, where its opposite is "brute force." On several occasions, he makes remarks to the effect that what "distinguishes man from all other animals is his capacity to be non-violent."[69] And he writes in 1926, to cite at greater length from the essay Mahadev Desai translates into English:

Man is higher than the brute in his moral instincts and moral institutions. The law of nature as applied to the one is different from the law of nature as applied to the other. Man has reason, discrimination, and free will such as it is. The brute has no such thing. It is not a free agent, and knows no distinction between virtue and vice, good and evil. Man, being a free agent, knows these distinctions, and when he follows his higher nature shows himself far superior to the brute, but when he follows his baser nature, can show himself lower than the brute. . . . Man being by nature more passionate than the brute, the moment all restraint is withdrawn, the lava of unbridled passion would overspread the whole earth and destroy mankind. Man is superior to the brute inasmuch as he is capable of self-restraint and sacrifice, of which the brute is incapable.[70]

This self-sacrifice that distinguishes humans from animals is again a theme in the *Gitashikshan* lectures in 1926, where he says: "Man does not live by bread alone, whereas the animal *[pashu]* needs only food to live. Men are like tigers and snakes, so Anna Kingsford used to say. Certainly, animals *[pashuo]* are our brethren *[bhaibanduo]*. We all come from the same place *[thekana]*. But they live by eating, whereas man *[manas]* lives by performing *yajna*. Everyone performs *yajna* in one way or another."[71] And in 1920, in an essay possibly written in English by him: "Non-violence is the law of our species as violence is the law of the brute. The spirit lies dormant in the brute and he knows no law but that of physical might. The dignity of man requires obedience to a higher law—to the strength of the spirit."[72]

In all these formulations, human being is higher than other forms of being, which are defined by lack. What such superiority entails is well laid out in a letter Gandhi writes in 1921 to C. F. Andrews:

The crime against the untouchables I feel, the exploitation of the dumb millions I feel, but I realize still more clearly our duty to the lower animal world. When Buddha carried that lamb on his back and chastised the Brahmins, he showed the highest measure of love. The worship of the cow in Hinduism typifies that love. And what does that love demand? Certainly not hospitals for cattle ill-treated by fellow-beings, though they are not to be destroyed, but promotion of kindness to beasts. Our love consists in our getting off the necks of our dumb fellow-creatures. The more helpless the lower life, the greater should be our pity."

Many years later, he returns to the theme in a letter to Nehru: "Cow-protection to me is infinitely more than mere protection of the cow. The cow is merely a type for all that lives. Cow-protection means protection of the weak, the helpless, the dumb and the deaf. Man becomes then not the lord and master of all creation but he is its servant. The cow to me is a sermon on pity."[73]

In formulations such as these, satyagraha seems to require a compassion organized by the logic of thekana or rightful place. This compassion would not erase or minimize the hierarchy between human being and other being. But at the same time, by serving other beings, satyagrahis seek not to take advantage of the superiority and domination involved in human being, they seek to love other being in and despite the latter's inequality. This Gandhi could well have said, with Heidegger, "The human being is the shepherd of being."[74] Such *seva* or service, offered by a higher being to a lower being, at the very least often perpetuates the very inequalities it seeks to redress. We have already seen this happen in the case of *seva* to Dalits, and if there were space, we could trace the same phenomenon with the animal, or, more precisely, with animals.[75]

And yet, closer reading reveals the ways in which these hierarchies unsay themselves, in which the emphasis on the cipher infects Gandhi's thinking of the relation between humans and animals. He writes, for example, in 1926.

Consider beasts and birds [*pashupankhiyo*]. Cattle [*dhor*] do not eat for the satisfaction of the palate, nor do they eat like gluttons. They eat when they are hungry—and just enough to satisfy that hunger. They do not cook their food. They take their portion from that which Nature proffers to them. Then, is man born to pander to his palate [*swad karva*]? Is he alone fated to be always ill? Among the animals [*dhor*] which are not domesticated, there is no starvation; they have no rich and poor, nor is there one group that eats ten times in a day and another that can scarcely eat even once. All these distinctions are to be found only in our species, yet we regard ourselves as superior in intelligence to animal. It is, however, evident from all this, that if we make our stomach our God and spend our lives in its worship, we must surely be inferior [*utarta*] to them.[76]

Here beasts and birds are no longer finite in a privative sense (as they were in the earlier formulations); rather, they are finite in the sense of having an orientation to observe limits—the limits that humans too should observe. This finitude, one might say, makes for the equality and plurality of animals. Now one can no longer simply say, "non-violence distinguishes man from all other animals"; rather, one has to say: violence distinguishes man from all other animals, and because of this, man is also distinguished by the potentiality for and orientation toward nonviolence.

But if the potentiality for violence (and *therefore* for nonviolence) is the distinctive orientation of humans, in what sense do humans use "brute force," and how are they "like" tigers and snakes? Here, I would suggest, likeness is not identity or convergence, but rather a mirroring that begins from an infinite difference, and therefore becomes infinitely different from what it mirrors. This sense of likeness as mirroring, as also the unsaying of the hierarchical relation between humans and animals, emerges especially forcefully in one curious gap between the Gujarati and English renderings of *Hind Swaraj*. In Gandhi's English translation of that book, the phrase "brute force" occurs fifteen times. But this phrase is a blanket rendering of eight words from the Gujarati—most often *maaramaari* [physical violence] *shareerbal* [bodily force], *maariney* [by beating], *hatiyarbal* [force of arms], but also *hatiyar* [arms] *darugodo* [ammunition], *talwarnabal* [force of the sword], *topbal* [force of guns]. Notable also for its absence among these Gujarati words is the word *pashubal,* the word closest to "brute force" (and one that is part of his vocabulary at least by 1920).[77]

We thus have an intriguing situation. The Gujarati words that are translated as "brute force" are so diverse that they do not bear any consistent or even necessary relation to the figure of the animal. The concept "brute force," and the connotation of animality that it bears, is convoked into being in the English version of *Hind Swaraj*. Thus, it may well be (though a more sustained reading of Gujarati and English texts together will be needed to ascertain this) that the distinction between human being and other modalities of being becomes more massive in his English writing.

Equally interesting is the concept of brute force that is at work in *Hind Swaraj*. On closer examination, it turns out that here "brute force" is not a force wielded by the animal as distinct from the human, by human become animal. It is rather a violence internal to human being, even in some ways exercised only by human being. "Man's" potentiality for and even orientation toward infinitude is precisely the moment of "brute force." "Brute force," in other words, falls away from what is proper to man, and falls away also from the finitude proper to other being. There are thus two animalities, quite abysally separated: finitude is the animality of animals and infinitude is the animality of humans.

A second sense of likeness—that of emulation across infinite difference—is at work when humans do what is most proper to their being: become finite, or offer a self-sacrifice driven by the trembling care and love that relinquishes mastery. It is for this emulation that Gandhi uses the terms "ciphers" or "like machines." This ciphering changes the daya that is felt for "helpless" "lower life," for now satyagrahis wish to become helpless like this lower life they have daya for. Daya can thus no longer be hierarchical.

This ciphering occurs perhaps in the practices of Gandhi's Saint Francis of Assisi or those various other unnamed fakirs, who live in togetherness with animals, birds, and forests. These fakirs render themselves vulnerable to other being. Indeed, the fakirs' very persistence in being depends on their receiving love from other being. This love is the originary "power," so to speak, these other modalities of being give to the fakirs. The giving of this love is also a sacrifice: they sacrifice the power to harm the fakirs. Sacrifice, moreover, is not only offered by other being to humans: recall the cases that Gandhi cites of animals protecting their young, or the seed dying so that corn can emerge. Where love and sacrifice are exercised by all being, there satyagraha and abhaydan become, contrary to Gandhi's explicit arguments to the contrary, the attribute of all being.

These fakirs can be the shepherds of being only in a very different sense from that specified by Heidegger. On the one hand, to the extent that they cipher themselves and practice an absolute equality with all beings, sat-yagrahis cannot be good shepherds in at least two senses: first, rather than possessing the power and mastery necessary to protect other beings, they themselves become vulnerable to these other beings; second, they no longer possess the knowledge that is required for shepherding. On the other hand, it is of the nature of ciphering that ciphers are acutely aware of not having ciphered themselves. Perhaps the only way they can responsi-bly bear this knowledge is by becoming shepherds of being. Here, then, the shepherding of being is the way general responsibility is inhabited and ruptured by those oriented toward absolute responsibility in the only form proper to it, abhaydan.

And where ciphering does occur, it gives rise to a very distinctive equal-ity—no longer the equality of "man" and "animal," but the equality that emerges in the disintegration of these concepts themselves as they come now to be infused with a plurality they can no longer contain. It may be symptomatic of this unsaying that Gandhi writes of various figures: of the mouse that is as mouse incapable of offering satyagraha; of the ant whose stubbornness and persistence the satyagrahi seeks to emulate; of the moth that like the revolutionaries sacrifices its life thoughtlessly; of the cow whose patient suffering the satyagrahi seeks to emulate; of the monkey whose inattentiveness is symptomatic of the mind; of how satyagrahis must deal with monkeys in their ashram; of whether the dangers of rabies justifies killing dogs; of the dog that the bhakti poet Narsinh Mehta writes about, who runs under the bullock cart and imagines, like the unciphered being, that it is pulling the cart; of the pests whom the farmer must kill in order to practice his agriculture; of the lion who like British officials charged the lamb's father with muddying the water in the river and killed the lamb; of that other "fabled lion" who like the Indians had been brought up in the company of lambs and found it impossible to feel that he was a lion; of the two buffaloes, the Durban whites and the white farmers, whose fight threatened to uproot the Indian tree, and so on.

In each of these analogies-metaphors, even that of the pest, the meta-physical and ontotheological distinction between human and animal, a distinction marked with abstract generality, is abandoned. Instead of that single massive distinction, there come to be a multitude of transactions and analogies-metaphors (not, note, a series of more nuanced distinctions, say biological ones between specific kinds of animals and humans). These transactions and analogies-metaphors cannot and perhaps must not erase the massive animal-human distinction; they do, however, perhaps fragment and rive it. Conversely, where these transactions and analogies-metaphors become attenuated and difficult to inhabit or think, as with "modern civility," then it becomes tempting to think in generalized and massive terms, such as are exemplified in the very phrase "human-animal relation."

· CHAPTER 9 ·

The Extreme Limit of Forgiveness

"When is satyagraha going to be resumed?" is the question many have been asking me. There are two answers. One is that satyagraha has not at all ceased. As long as we follow satya, and ask others to do so, so long satyagraha can never be said to have ceased.

—Mohandas Gandhi, "Satyagraha Leaflet 12," May 2, 1919, *Akshardeha*

We can imagine, and accept, that someone would never forgive, even after a process of acquittal or amnesty. The secret of this experience remains. It must remain intact, inaccessible to law, to politics, even to morals: absolute. But I would make of this trans-political principle a political principle, a political rule or position taking: it is necessary also in politics to respect the secret, that which exceeds the political or that which is no longer in the juridical domain. This is what I would call the "democracy to come."

—Jacques Derrida, *On Cosmopolitanism and Forgiveness*

IN AN ESSAY IN OCTOBER 1926, after describing Mahavira, Buddha, Rama, and Krishna as Kshatriya "votaries of ahimsa," Gandhi goes on: "Ahimsa is the extreme limit of forgiveness *[kshamani parisima]*. But forgiveness is the quality of the brave. Ahimsa is impossible without fearlessness."[1]

What could the extreme limit of forgiveness be? How would it differ from the economic concept of forgiveness, where the forgiver forgives the offender because the latter has repented, and earned the forgiver's trust? Once again, Gandhi does not explicitly answer such questions. But the economic concept forgiveness undergoes in his writing a peculiar ruination, and in that ruination it is taken to its extreme limit, beyond economy, into quasi-conceptuality.

Perhaps we can approach this thinking of the extreme limit of forgiveness elliptically, by beginning with what could well appear to be a curious puzzle about the way he thinks "mutual trust." Writing in 1918 of his effort to improve Hindu-Muslim relations, he remarks: "I want, at the end of it, to see established not mutual distrust and the law of force, but mutual trust and the law of love."[2] What he opposes here implicitly is "modern civility" or "modern civilization," which for him institutionalizes such mutual distrust and law of force—recall his remarks about "equality of sword."

We can see why he might feel this way. Not only do the institutions of republican democracy distrust those who are excepted (the noncitizen, terrorist, and animal among others); they also redress the exception by instituting the abstract trust and equality of the citizen. I say "abstract trust" because here trust is not in the other but in the calculable general responsibility—institutionalized in the law, judge, government, and so on—which binds both self and other. These institutions of modern civility can at most enforce reconciliation, clemency, abstract trust, and other related practices; they are incapable of immeasurable trust, repentance, or forgiveness.

Unable to take modern civility's abstract trust as his point of departure, Gandhi affirms trust by once again beginning from the figure of the warrior. An economy of sovereign trust is already at play in the figure of the warrior. Among other things, the warrior is a figure who trusts his friends without measure—incalculably and aneconomically, as a gift. And yet, this very aneconomy is also an economic and conditional trust: they have earned his trust through affective or intimate relations. His aneconomic and unconditional trust responds to this economy that precedes it. But he remains sovereign over his trust. His trust can thus be betrayed; he may in response to some provocations withdraw his trust. And there are also always those who do not deserve his trust. The warrior surrenders his sovereignty to those whom he trusts, but he surrenders his sovereignty precisely because he already knows that they will cherish and nourish that sovereignty, not destroy it.

Gandhi's arguments imply that the satyagrahi radicalizes the warrior's trust by relinquishing the sovereignty that marks it. Satyagrahis thus must trust everybody aneconomically, unconditionally, and absolutely, and must continue to do so even after their trust is betrayed. By trusting aneconomically, satyagrahis seek to create an economy of "mutual trust," but they cannot demand that economy. During the Khilafat movement, thus, he suggests Hindus must support the Muslim struggle, and trust—without demanding or expecting—that their support will eventually lead Muslims to abandon cow-killing.[3] Some years later, he returns to the theme:

> Trust can have no limits. It must always give the benefit of the doubt. It is better to suffer a million disappointments than not to have trusted where mistrust was a mistake. A man who permits himself to be deceived is never the loser. Indeed he is the gainer in the end, not the so-called successful deceiver. A thousand deceits would leave me unrepentant. My personal experience is that in spite of some very hard knocks which I can recall at the time of writing, I have no cause to regret the trustful nature with which the world around me has credited me. It is my conviction that I and those whom I have involved in my trustfulness have lost nothing, if we cannot prove to have always gained. A man loses only when he loses his soul and that can never be lost through another man's deceit.[4]

Or in a similar vein he insists many years later: "Ahimsa means that you have to trust those whom you have come to regard as untrustworthy. Unless you do so, you can never convert them."[5]

What might appear puzzling, however, is that Gandhi himself seems to constantly contradict his call for unlimited trust. His fellow ashram inmates betray their vows all too frequently for his liking—he cannot trust them to discipline themselves. And despite his insistence on his love for the peasants and masses of India, that love is by no means accompanied by trust in them. Thus his hesitations about whether the Indian masses are ready for satyagraha, thus his suspicion of the "mob."

Trust becomes even more difficult where satyagrahis encounter evil. "We are bound to hate evil, if we would shun it."[6] Given that "modern civilization" is evil, and must be opposed, he finds it difficult to trust British officials. In the years after 1920, he considers the behavior of British officials in India, of the Allies in the two world wars, or other representatives of "modern civilization" as "deceitful, cruel and greedy."[7] "The unfortunate position in which I find myself is that I thoroughly distrust Lloyd George. Somehow or other I distrust the Armenian case as I distrust the Arabian case and I am so prejudiced against the present British diplomacy that I scent the foul hand of the deceitful diplomat in Armenia, Arabia, Mesopotamia, Palestine, Syria."[8] In later years too, he is often vocally and sharply critical of British rule and of the motives behind the professions of colonial officials, and he continues to distrust "the word of the official world."[9]

Indeed, it turns out that satyagrahis cannot even trust themselves. This is one reason they need to take vows. "Not to take the vow is to trust one's little self. To take it is to distrust oneself and to trust only God. I know where I should have been if I had not taken the vows I have."[10]

What do we make of this tension between Gandhi's calls for unconditional trust and his deep distrust of himself, friends, associates, and opponents? It is indicative, I would suggest, of what trust cannot be for Gandhi. While satyagrahis can and must relinquish their own sovereignty, while they must trust the other, this trust cannot take the "form" of submitting without resistance and in faith to the other's sovereignty. To surrender one's sovereignty to the sovereignty of those whom the satyagrahi knows to be untrustworthy—would this not accept the gravest injustice not only against the self, but also against that other third person whom the Editor describes as the *trahit manas?* A trust that leaves the other's sovereignty unchallenged would quickly become complicit with the most profound violence.

How, then, do satyagrahis trust? It is as he struggles with this question that he comes to his arguments about the "extreme limit of forgiveness." His path to these arguments begins from the concept of sovereign forgiveness, but that concept inexorably ruins itself in his writing. And in the wake of that ruination, there emerges his thinking of the "extreme limit of forgiveness." In March 1914, Gandhi writes in a letter to his son Harilal:

> "You ask for forgiveness [*maafi*] in every letter. You put up a
> defence as well. It all seems to me sheer hypocrisy now. . . . Will
> this go on till death, with my forgiving every time? But what is the
> point of my forgiving? Forgiveness has a value only to the extent
> that the person who has apologized does not err again. My
> forgiving you all the time means that I should go on doing my duty
> [*farj*] as father though you may not do yours as son. My duty, of
> course, I shall continue to do by my understanding."[11]

In this letter we see the sovereign economy of forgiveness at work. This economy itself involves two intertwined economies. First, there is the economy of atonement or repentance. The offender gifts his repentance to the injured party, and to this gift the forgiver responds. Repentance creates the mutual trust required for forgiveness. This repentance does not occur only once—it must be continuous, so that "the person who has apologized does not err again." Harilal breaks this economy: he apparently errs repeatedly, and his apology loses meaning for Gandhi, who finds it difficult to any longer trust Harilal.[12]

Second, the economy of atonement works within, and presumes, a larger economy of sovereign power. To ask for forgiveness is to accept the sovereignty of the forgiver, and to forgive is to exercise sovereignty over the offender. This sovereignty again underpins the very assumption that to forgive is to absolve the offender. Through such absolution, the sovereign dissociates the offender from the offense, which no longer remains a wound. With absolution, relations between offender and forgiver are also transformed, with both receiving—back?—the ability to trust one another, and perhaps in some cases an immeasurable equality.

By the time of his letter to Harilal, Gandhi has already begun questioning this economic conception of forgiveness. But that conception always resurfaces, or continues to provide the palimpsest for Gandhi's argument; it is what he initially affirms and eventually ruins in reaching his other thinking of forgiveness. Thus, in the wake of the British massacre in 1919 of at least 379 (the official figure) and maybe around 1,000 (the figure arrived at by the Congress Enquiry Committee) people at a peaceful rally at Jallianwala Bagh in Amritsar, Gandhi contemplates what would be involved in forgiving General Reginald Dyer (the "Butcher of Amritsar," as he was described by many critics) and Sir Michael O'Dwyer (the governor of Punjab who is believed by congressmen to have been the principal instigator of the massacre). Forgiveness cannot be "out of weakness': "India does not yet feel strong as against British Governors and Generals. She still fears them. Forgiveness of Sir Michael O'Dwyer and General Dyer is therefore a meaningless term. But India is daily gaining strength and qualifying for forgiveness."[13] "A strong and self-reliant India will cease to hate Bosworth Smiths and Frank Johnsons, for she will have the power to punish them and therefore the power also to pity and forgive them."[14] And in an essay in 1920, he remarks:

> But I believe that non-violence is infinitely superior to violence, forgiveness is more manly than punishment. *Kshama virasyam bhushanam* [Mahavira's injunction, which he proceeds to translate into English as:] "Forgiveness adorns a soldier," But abstinence

is forgiveness only when there is the power to punish; it is meaningless when it pretends to proceed from a helpless creature. A mouse hardly forgives a cat when it allows itself to be torn to pieces by her.[15]

When Gandhi envisions Indians forgiving the British, thus, he often desires that they do by becoming warrior-sovereigns. The warrior must constantly decide when to forgive and when to punish. He must wherever possible try to forgive, since for him forgiveness is an essential virtue, even superior to punishment. Here, two senses of *kshama* are at work: a greater *kshama* in the sense of forbearance calls forth *kshama* in the sense of forgiveness. And even where offenders do not repent, even where the offenders do not accept the warrior's sovereignty (both of which would be true for the British), the warrior can forgive unilaterally, driven to do so by "pity." (In Gandhi's reading, it is tempting to speculate, this is the sense in which Mahavira can say that *kshama* adorns the warrior, that the *Gita* can describe *kshama, karuna,* and ahimsa as marks of the warrior, or that the dying Bhishma can, in the *Anusasana Parva* of the *Mahabharata,* as he advises Yudhisthira on good kingship, repeatedly remark: "*ahimsa paramo dharma,*" ahimsa is the highest duty.)

But can and should Indians forgive the British? Because forgiveness involves an absolution, the warrior-sovereign can always refuse to forgive. It is on occasion even absolutely necessary not to forgive, for we could ask the same question here as we did of a trust that relinquished sovereignty without questioning the other's sovereignty. To forgive the unforgivable—acts for which there can perhaps never be enough repentance—by absolving the offenders: Would not this itself practice an unforgiveable violence?[16] Would not Jallianwalla Bagh, and indeed British colonialism in general, be unforgivable? Can massive acts of violence—British colonialism, the Holocaust, the Nakba, American genocides, South African apartheid, to take just some massive examples—ever be forgiven? And what act of violence would not be massive? When is a massacre a massacre?[17]

Yet, in the passages above, Gandhi asks his interlocutors to forgive unforgivable acts. In doing so, he pushes the problematic of sovereign forgiveness, his point of departure, to its ruination. The satyagrahi relinquishes both sovereign punishment as the putative counterweight of forgiveness and the reciprocal demand for repentance by the offender. In the process, the satyagrahi's forgiveness becomes absolute and unconditional—not reciprocal, conditional, or prudent. Satyagrahis must forgive in every case, without exception; they must forgive the unforgivable.

Such absolute and unconditional forgiveness cannot be given by the sovereign, or can only be given by relinquishing the power to punish, by destroying—ruining—sovereignty and economy. Gandhi must therefore come to another trust and another forgiveness—a trust that accepts the ineradicability of distrust without being grounded in distrust (as the warrior and modern civilization in different ways are), that is unfounded and ungrounded; a forgiveness that forgives the unforgivable without absolving it, a forgiveness that ruins the sovereignty of both self and other. Could it be this other trust and forgiveness that is at work when he says: "People deceive me a thousand times; even so, how can I distrust them? As long as I see the slightest excuse for trusting people, I will certainly trust them. It is foolish to continue trusting after one has had definite ground for not trusting. But to distrust a person on mere suspicion is arrogance and betrays lack of faith in God. It is faith that keeps the world going."[18]

His thinking of this other trust and forgiveness gathers into the term *prayaschitta* ("repentance," "penance," "expiation," "atonement"), a word we encountered earlier in his thinking of the relation with the untouchable and the Harijan. As a broad trope, *prayaschitta* is pervasive in his writings already by the time of *Hind Swaraj:* in chapter 20, the Editor remarks that the strength to achieve swaraj "will be available only to him" who will, among other things, "know that this is a time for repentance, expiation, and mourning."

But only by around 1914, perhaps not accidentally after his difficulties in forgiving Harilal as long as he works within the problematic of sovereign forgiveness, does Gandhi more systematically connect satyagraha to *prayaschitta.* In late April that year, after an inmate of the Phoenix settlement, identified only as "J," commits some "terrible sins," Gandhi writes of his anguish. "The heart seems to have gone dry. The agony I am going through is unspeakable. I have often wanted to take out the knife from my pocket and put it through the stomach." And so "I thought I must atone for my own sin in putting my faith in one who did not deserve it."[19] The fast of seven days that follows, Gandhi describes in the *Autobiography* as a *prayaschitta* or penance. And the moment he takes the decision to adopt the fast, he reports, the "anger against the guilty parties subsided and gave place to the purest daya."[20]

After this, he quite consistently associates satyagraha and *prayaschitta*. His remarks in 1919 indicate how *prayaschitta* works:

> A fast *[upvaas]* undertaken purely for ostentation or to inflict pain on others is an unmitigated sin. Hence, it is only a prayerful fast undertaken by way of penance *[prayaschittarup]* to produce some effect on oneself which can be called a religious fast. Prayer . . . is the earnest cry of a soul in anguish. . . . When an individual or a nation suffers because of a great calamity, the true awareness of that suffering is prayer; in the presence of this purifying knowledge, physical functions like eating, etc., become less urgent. A mother suffers when her only son dies. She has no desire for eating. A nation is born when all feel the same sort of grief at the suffering of any one among them; such a nation deserves to be immortal. We are well aware that quite a large number of our brothers and sisters in India live in great suffering and so, truly speaking, we have occasion at every step for prayerful fasting. But our national life has not attained to this degree of intensity and purity. Even so, occasions arise when we suffer acutely.[21]

Etymologically, the words *prayaschitta* ["repentance"] and *upvaas* ["fast"] resonate with each other and with satyagraha. The *Bhagavadgomandal,* the etymologically oriented dictionary-encyclopedia that Gandhi so admires, traces the term *prayaschitta* to the Sanskrit roots *prayas* (which it glosses as *tap*—the discipline for the attainment of the *atmaswarup,* or most proper form of the *atman*) and *chitta* (which it associates with *nischaya,* or resolve).[22] Etymologically, then, *prayaschitta* refers to a broader orientation than the commonsensical use of the word "repentance" might suggest: it refers rather to a repentance that proceeds by a resolute attentiveness to the *atman.* Similarly, the *Bhagavadgomandal* traces the etymology of *upvaas* (fast) to the Sanskrit term *up,* which carries connotations of towardness, and which the *Bhagavadgomandal* translates into Gujarati as *paasey* or near. Here the towardness or nearness is directed at *vaas*—a phrase that it glosses as *rahetan,* or dwelling. Among the meanings it provides for *upvaas* is both "the vow *[vrat]* in which eating is abjured *[tyaag]*" and "becoming one with the atman through dedication *[dhyan]*." In the emphasis on *upvaas* and *prayaschitta,* Gandhi continues with the trajectory initiated in his insistence on the oneness of satya, on the desire and responsibility for satya. As an event organized by fasting and repentance, Gandhi can say of the noncooperation movement: "It is not protest, but purification. Through self-purification, purification of the other party."[23]

Self-purification is not protest because while protest places responsibility on the other for what the protest is against, *prayaschitta* requires satyagrahis to themselves assume absolute responsibility for the violence they encounter, confront, and possibly practice. As *prayaschitta*, fasts and prayers inscribe on oneself grief for the wound. They grieve for the violence and "horrible suffering" experienced by "brothers and sisters"—the other who is the self. And such grief must not be externalized and avoided by channeling it into action directed at another. In fasting and prayer, satyagrahis take grief upon themselves, riving the self with the other. And this riving is itself the experience of swaraj: a "nation is born when all feel the same sort of grief at the suffering [*dukh*] of any one among them."

This oneness of *prayaschitta* involves a life no longer conceived through mastery of fear of death, but rather through the longing for the self's own death that accompanies the absolute responsibility experienced for the loss or suffering of a beloved one. Freedom now involves assuming responsibility for the other—inseparable from the self—who is not free. Here friendship with death, the desire and yearning for death, is abysally separated from suicide. The satyagrahis' longing for their own death cannot lead onto privative death or suicide, which would end and thus escape grief. Perhaps indeed, *prayaschitta* is so important for Gandhi because in it the satyagrahi receives another life—a life marked by a friendship with the death brought about by grief.

～

Ahimsa is the extreme limit of forgiveness, then, not because satyagrahis absolve all offenders, but because of the way forgiveness must be conceived within the terms of *prayaschitta*. Such forgiveness has two modalities: absolute forgetting, and satyagraha as the gift of the refusal to forgive.

In *Hind Swaraj*, the Editor says, recall: "The Hindus and Musalmans have fought. A *trahit manas* ['ordinary man'] will say: now forget about it [*bhooli jao*]; both must be at fault; live in togetherness with one another." Earlier, chapter 2 dwelled on the figure of the *trahit manas*—the third person who is the second, the multiplicity that belongs to two—and on the togetherness he suggests. But we have not attended so far to something else he says: "now forget about it." Forgetting is emphasized again in chapter 17, where the Editor says of satyagraha: "Thousands, indeed tens of thousands, depend for their existence on a very active working of this force. Little quarrels of millions of families in their daily lives disappear before the exercise of this force."

How does this forgetting work? Ciphered by their love, satyagrahis take on themselves the responsibility for the wounds the other inflicts on them. Recall: the satyagrahi is "the penitent who knows that it is some trace of impurity in him that keeps him away from the loved one." They do *prayaschitta,* or repent. For example, the Editor goes on in chapter 17: "Two brothers quarrel; one of them repents and re-awakens the love that was lying dormant in him." In doing so, they forgive the other to the point of forgetting the wound the other inflicts. Here there occurs a gift of oneself to the other which forgets its own giving.

This forgetting—call it an aneconomic forgetting or, with Derrida, absolute forgetting—is the satyagraha that satyagrahis offer without their knowledge. Satyagraha as absolute forgetting radicalizes sovereign forgiveness to the point of its self-destruction. A forgiveness that forgets that it has forgiven—this is what Gandhi stresses most emphatically and repeatedly: Hindus and Muslims, thus, must fearlessly trust each other, "adjust their differences and forget past wrongs."[24] Here forgivers forget even that they have forgiven, and no wound, or mark of the old wound, remains. (And as for Gandhi—he forgets that his call for forgetting is made possible by forgetting the unconditional forgiveness that precedes it!) Such forgetting, even if it starts from reciprocity, radicalizes and even destroys reciprocity because what is forgotten here is reciprocity itself.

This forgetting makes for pure means or the pure gift. For there to be a gift, as Derrida notes, both donor and donee "must also forget it right away [a l'instant] and moreover this forgetting must be so radical that it exceeds even the psychoanalytic categoriality of forgetting." This absolute forgetting "would be in the *condition of the gift* and the gift in the *condition of forgetting.*" And yet, this forgetting is "not nothing"; it cannot be "a simple non-experience, a simple non-appearance, a self-effacement that is carried off with what it effaces." For "there to be gift, not only must the donor or donee not perceive or receive the gift as such, have no consciousness of it, no memory, no recognition; he or she must also forget it right away." And this is an "absolute forgetting."[25]

The *Mahabharata* that Gandhi reads so often could well have provoked him into the forgetting involved in the pure gift. In its *Anusasana Parva,*

"Yudhisthira asks Bhisma to name the best kinds of gifts. Bhisma answers: "An assurance unto all creatures of love and affection and abstention from every kind of injury, . . . and *whatever gifts are made without the giver's ever thinking of them as gifts made by him,* constitute the highest and best of gifts."[26]

This not-nothing, which is also a not-ness, Gandhi describes as *kshama* —a forgiving forbearance. Here *kshama* comes not from the fortitude of the warrior but from *prayaschitta,* where satyagrahis take on themselves the responsibility for the wound they have received or inflicted. To cultivate *kshama* is to constantly discipline oneself so as to acquire the ability to forget absolutely. And yet, *kshama* is not a constative act that takes place once and for all. What has been forgotten has not been erased—it remains always spectrally present, capable of becoming a wound again. In order to be sustained, absolute forgetting must take place over and again, automatically and machinically.

～

But to forget the unforgivable—this would be most profound violence. Aware of this, Gandhi abandons, when discussing Dyer, his emphasis on forgiveness as absolute forgetting, on a satyagraha that forgets it has happened. Responding to a friend who asks why Gandhi invokes Jallianwala Bagh incessantly despite his call to forgive, he says: "The answer is simple. To forgive is not to forget. There is no merit in loving an enemy when you forget him for a friend. The merit lies in loving in spite of the vivid knowledge that the one that must be loved is not a friend."[27]

A forgiveness is contemplated here, one that does not occur through absolute forgetting. Rather, what is given here as forgiveness is the refusal to forget or forgive. And this raises many questions. These, to begin with: What cannot be forgiven? How can a refusal to forgive be given as a forgiveness? How would the refusal to forgive be gifted?

Gandhi has no substantial criterion for the unforgivable. If we go by *Hind Swaraj,* every wound is unjusticiable, and therefore potentially unforgettable and unforgivable. Indeed, perhaps forgetting without reserve never happens (we would not know anyway, given the nature of satyagraha and forgetting). Moreover, satyagrahis do not choose whether to forget a wound or regard it as unforgivable. Rather, what they sedulously cultivate and yet cannot control—the ability to forget the wound, to trust or distrust, to love—governs their response. They can discipline themselves to be more capable of forgetting without reserve, but where they encounter the inability to forget or forgive, the reasons for that inability remain secret from them.

This inability to forget or forgive secretes its own politics of forgiveness. Indeed, the most visible forms of satyagraha—noncooperation, civil disobedience, fasting—are themselves the politics proper to that inability to forget or forgive. Satyagraha forgives by gifting to the other the satyagrahi's inability to forget or forgive.

The stakes of satyagraha as the enactment of such an in-ability (this nonsovereignty is another sense in which the phrase "passive resistance" is more apposite as a description of satyagraha than the later Gandhi will allow) emerge especially forcefully when counterposed to Derrida's thinking of forgiveness; once again, as with so many other quasi-concepts that Gandhi's thinking has offered to us, the two intersect only to diverge dramatically.

Derrida also stresses the aporia between unconditional or aneconomic forgiveness and "conditional forgiveness."[28] Pure and unconditional forgiveness forgives the unforgivable, which is "the only thing to forgive."[29] Yet, the unforgivable is also what must not be forgiven. Partially because of this, "pure and unconditional forgiveness, in order to have its own meaning, must have no 'meaning,' no finality, even no intelligibility. It is a madness of the impossible." Such forgiveness is "impossibility itself. It can only be possible in doing the impossible."[30] This impossibility includes the impossibility of that most inescapable third—a shared language. "[W]hen the victim and the guilty share no language, when nothing common and universal permits them to understand one another, forgiveness seems deprived of meaning; it is certainly a case of the absolutely unforgivable, that impossibility of forgiveness, of which we just said nevertheless that it was, paradoxically, the very element of all possible forgiveness."[31]

How does this impossibility, this impossible possible, work? Derrida stresses the necessity of an absolute forgiveness that is nevertheless not an absolute forgetting. "Must forgiveness saturate the abyss? Must it suture the wound in a process of reconciliation? Or rather give place to another peace, without forgetting, without amnesty, fusion, or confusion?"[32] At the same time in his writing this other forgiveness, one that neither sutures nor forgets, bears a deconstructive force and dissemination because of which it must work (as with the hospitality discussed in chapter 4) only in a supplementary manner: remaining in an aporetic relation with the laws for which it is law, constantly destabilizing and supplementing these laws, but still also needing these very laws.

Perhaps this is why Derrida must, even as he questions sovereignty, emphasize its unavoidability, and even necessity: "All the fundamental axiomatics of responsibility or decision (ethical, juridical, political) are grounded on the sovereignty of the subject, that is, the intentional auto-determination of the conscious self (which is free, autonomous, active, etc.)."[33] Relatedly, deconstruction must not affirm only a hyperbolic forgiveness:

> I remain "torn" (between a "hyberbolic" ethical vision of for-
> giveness, pure forgiveness, and the reality of a society at work in
> pragmatic processes of reconciliation). But without power, desire,
> or need to decide. The two poles are irreducible to one another,
> certainly, but they remain indissociable. In order to inflect politics,
> or what you just called the "pragmatic processes", in order to
> change the law (which, thus, finds itself between the two poles,
> the "ideal" and the "empirical" . . .), it is necessary to refer to a
> "hyperbolic" ethical vision of forgiveness.

It is here perhaps that Gandhi's divergence from Derrida becomes espe-cially acute. More perhaps than Derrida, Gandhi is oriented toward the relinquishment of sovereign power, which for him is inseparable from the greatest domination.

> The world [jagat] and the man established in samadhi [stithadhi]
> are like the west and the east. The world's night is our day and the
> world's day is our night. There is, thus, non-co-operation between
> the two. This should be our attitude if we understand the Gita
> rightly. . . . But we should have the faith that, if we succeed in
> crossing to the other shore, the world, too, will.[34]

In Gandhi's writing, therefore, the aporia between reciprocal or pragmatic forgiveness and the extreme limit of forgiveness, between sovereignty and satyagraha, becomes even more intense and fraught. Satyagraha does not only constantly remain outside, supplement, destabilize, and rework the laws of sovereign power, revealing itself to be the law of sovereign laws. It must also destroy sovereign laws while yet itself remaining without sovereignty; rather than being "without power, desire, or need to decide," satyagrahis must constantly decide against sovereign power, and make this decision moreover in a nonsovereign manner.

To do so, satyagrahis must inhabit a community where what is shared is precisely nothing. That distinctive sharing is already signaled in that curiously untranslated phrase in *Hind Swaraj* discussed in chapter 2—*trahit manas*, the other third party, the third party who is not translated into English. The *trahit manas*, we noted, is selfless. In this sense, the *trahit manas* is ciphered, is a satyagrahi. Ciphering, in other words, is the sharing that occurs where beings share, to recall Derrida "no language, . . . nothing common and universal [that] permits them to understand one another." But "no language" is not here an inert nullity; it is rather the sharing that occurs through the not-ness of a distinctive self-sacrifice that can never know itself to have happened or come to pass.

～

As he struggles to think this extreme limit of forgiveness that is satyagraha, Gandhi come to his most intense thinking of *prayaschitta*. Now *prayaschitta* involves the converse of what it does in forgetting without reserve; now it involves the refusal to forget. That refusal is at work in both the aspects of satyagraha that Gandhi usually identifies—the "terrible" and the "benign." The "terrible aspect" involves fasting and noncooperation. Fasting is the most apposite response to the unforgivable acts of those who love the satyagrahi, and who trust the satyagrahi's professions of love for them.

One of his early major public fasts is in 1918, when, in the thick of the Ahmedabad textile workers strike, some workers criticize what they perceive as the comfort in which Gandhi lives while they go hungry, and wish to break their vow to fight until their demands are met. (Of the strike, Gandhi says: it "is not merely for a 35 per cent increase; it is to show that workers are prepared to suffer for their rights.") Gandhi responds immediately by commencing a fast, to be continued until the workers' demands are met. With the fast, he hopes to repudiate any suspicions about his situation being comfortable, to "set a concrete example," and to persuade the workers to stick by their vow. Two days later, at the ashram, he explains the fast: "That a pledge once taken, at my instance, should be so lightly broken and that faith in God should decline means certain annihilation of dharma. I simply cannot live to be a witness to this in any activity to which I am a party. I must impress upon the minds of the mill-hands what it is to take a

pledge. I must show to them what I can do for a pledge."[35] There is a certain
appositeness to Gandhi fasting for the vow: he sometimes uses the same
word—*vrat*—for both (the convergence is hardly surprising, since fasts are
usually resorted to in order to carry out a vow, and the fast is in this sense
an enactment of the vow).

The centrality of fasting against the unforgivable again emerges in a
speech in Nadiad the next week, inaugurating the Kheda satyagraha:

> It is very difficult to take the pledge of satyagraha; it is still more
> difficult to carry out one. I cannot bear to think of any one
> breaking a pledge once taken, forsaking his God. It would cause
> me very great pain, indeed, if you took a pledge which you did
> not mean to keep. In the intensity of my suffering, I may take an
> extreme step. I may have to fast. I don't suffer when I fast; fasting
> hurts me less than that people should deceive me by breaking
> their pledge. In satyagraha, a pledge is the most valuable thing of
> all; it must be kept up to the very end. . . . Those who want to fight
> must make up their minds once for all. I would not mind very
> much if people just said that they would hold out as long as possi-
> ble but that they were not sure of themselves in case of severe
> repression. I would far rather that they cut my throat than that they
> break my heart by betraying their pledge. The man who cuts my
> throat, I would pray to God to forgive, but I would not forgive the
> other man.[36]

Fasting, however, can be a form of satyagraha only against the unforgivable
acts of the beloved. Writing to George Joseph in 1924 during the Vaikom
satyagraha, Gandhi argues that against an opponent whose love the satyagrahi cannot presume, only noncooperation is proper, not fasting:

> Fasting in satyagraha has well-defined limits. You cannot fast
> against a tyrant, for it will be as a piece of violence done to him.
> You invite penalty from him for disobedience of his orders, but you
> cannot inflict on yourself penalties when he refuses to punish and
> renders it impossible for you to disobey his orders so as to compel
> infliction of penalty. Fasting can only be resorted to against a lover,
> not to extort rights but to reform him, as when a son fasts for a

parent who drinks. My fast at Bombay, and then at Bardoli, was of that character. I fasted to reform those who loved me. But I will not fast to reform, say General Dyer who not only does not love me, but who regards himself as my enemy.[37]

This refusal to forget or forgive the unforgivable—whether by fasting or noncooperation—is not a failure or limitation of the satyagrahi's discipline. Even Gandhi's god, who is all-forgiving, does not forgive in the sense of forgetting or absolving. Indeed, because Gandhi's god is not a sovereign, this god cannot forgive. "God has vouchsafed to me a priceless gift in the weapon of ahimsa. I and my ahimsa are on our trial today. If, in the present crisis when the earth is being scorched by the flames of himsa and crying for deliverance, I failed to make use of the god-given talent, god will not forgive me and I shall be adjudged unworthy of the great gift."[38] This god's refusal to forgive Gandhi or itself takes the form of satyagraha—he remarks thus on occasion about God waging satyagraha.

~

Three unavoidable entailments mark *prayaschitta* in both its modality as absolute forgetting and as the forgiveness that refuses to forgive. First, *prayaschitta* gives absolute responsibility to both satyagrahis and their interlocutors. In an essay written shortly after Chauri Chaura, Gandhi announces a fast of five days:

> *Prayashchitta* should not be drummed about. But I have publicized mine, and there is a reason. My fast is *prayaschitta* for me but, for the people of Chauri Chaura, it is a punishment. The punishment inflicted by love [*prem*] is always of this nature. When a lover is hurt, he does not punish the loved one, but suffers himself; he bears the pangs of hunger and hits his own head. He is unconcerned whether or not his loved ones understand his suffering.[39]

By fasting, satyagrahis acknowledge that even though their love makes them incapable of demanding the justice of the third party, forgiveness as either absolution or forgetting is not here theirs to give either. Torn apart by the grief of and for this wound, they can neither judge nor forget—they fast. Their *prayaschitta* is so absolute that they no longer ask about the degree to which they are responsible for the wound, or think of how their assumption of absolute responsibility will affect the other.

In any rational calculus, Gandhi alone is not responsible for Chauri Chaura: responsibility can be determined only by an extensive and necessarily always incomplete historical analysis, of the sort so brilliantly worked out for Chauri Chaura by Shahid Amin in his *Event, Metaphor, Memory.* But Gandhi never attempts any such analysis. For him, he alone is responsible. The responsibility singularizes him, makes him alone; this is why he must undertake the fast himself. His fast gives pain to the people of Chauri Chaura, but that is not why he undertakes the fast, and he must both inflict and be unconcerned about their pain. In the constructive program, again, do not satyagrahis assume an absolute responsibility for untouchability, poverty, and Hindu-Muslim conflict?

This assumption of absolute responsibility by satyagrahis is baffling from a historical or sociological perspective, even a case at least in some instances of victims taking the blame on themselves? Given the immense power of the British, how does this make sense?

Because even though satyagrahis take on themselves absolute responsibility for the wound, they do so as figures who are no longer sovereigns. So in forgiving they do not and cannot give absolution to offenders (among whom the satyagrahis must count themselves)—only a sovereign could do that, we saw. Rather, what forgiveness gives here to offenders is the latter's absolute responsibility for the wounds (in this sense, absolute responsibility is never exclusive responsibility). In *prayaschitta,* then, satyagrahis not only relinquish sovereignty themselves; they strive to gift this relinquishment of sovereignty to their interlocutors.

The modality of forgetting without reserve gives absolute responsibility without the knowledge of the giver or receiver. Similarly, the modality of fasting gives absolute responsibility because here lovers bear witness to the suffering of their beloved. ("Through self-purification, purification of others.") We can see the sharing of absolute responsibility at work in Gandhi's report of the fast he undertakes in 1918 "to keep those ten thousand men [the striking millworkers of Ahmedabad] from falling [from their vow.] . . . [I]ts impact was electrifying. I had never expected this. The thousands of men present there shed tears from their eyes. They awoke to the reality of their soul, a new consciousness stirred in them and they got strength to stand by their pledge." What satyagrahis give to their interlocutors, then, is not something that satyagrahis have first and then share; rather, they give what their interlocutors always already have. The purpose of the fast, then, is to bring lovers back to their pledge—a pledge shared with others, and yet shared only by being made their own, and conversely made their own only by sharing. Similarly, explaining his 1932 fast to H.S.L. Polak, he remarks: "When a lover fasts to prevent the loved one from going astray, it is not blackmail, it is the cry of an anguished heart ascending to heaven. Of such, in your language, is the music of the spheres made. My fast was a whip administered to lethargic love."[40]

So it is also that Gandhi remarks of the fast in December 1947: "It is the last weapon in the armoury of the votary of ahimsa. When human ingenuity fails, the votary fasts. This fasting quickens the spirit of prayer, that is to say, the fasting is a spiritual act and, therefore, addressed to God. The effect of such action on the life of the people is that when the person fasting is at all known to them their sleeping conscience is awakened."[41] This thing that satyagrahis and their interlocutors already share, then, is the "conscience" or "inner voice," which is also what Gandhi describes as the *antaratman*.[42] Satyagrahis seek to gift those they love a seizure by their conscience; only in that process are satyagrahis too seized by their conscience.

In a different way, noncooperation also involves gifting this seizure by absolute responsibility to both self and other. Satygrahis refuse to cooperate with the law, or the operation of general responsibility, and invite reprisal from it. But this invitation is also a call to law to remember its own absolute responsibility—a responsibility that the general responsibility of law must always repress and disavow, for it threatens always to destabilize and even destroy law.

~

As the gift of absolute responsibility, Gandhi recognizes, *prayaschitta* is very dangerous, even terrifying. In thinking that they respond to their conscience, satyagrahis may be enacting their ressentiment; they may be coercing others or at least be perceived by others as coercive. By the very nature *(swabhav)* of satyagraha, satyagrahis must always assume responsibility for this danger, or in Gandhi's preferred metaphor, "walk on the edge of a sword." Gandhi doubts whether either he or his fellow satyagrahis confront this danger properly.[43] Thus he writes of his 1918 fast: "My fast in Ahmedabad in connection with the mill-strike of 1917 [sic] was against 'lovers'—the mill-hands, and not against the owners—'the tyrants.' I announced at the time that my fast was not flawless, because it was bound to influence the mill-owners who were personal friends."[44] In his remarks of December 1947 on how fasts seek to awaken the "sleeping conscience" of interlocutors, Gandhi goes on: "But there is the danger that the people through mistaken sympathy may act against their will in order to save the life of the loved one. This danger has got to be faced. One ought not to be deterred from right action when one is sure of the rightness. It can but promote circumspection. Such a fast is undertaken in obedience to the dictates of the inner voice and, therefore, prevents haste."[45]

And even this circumspection is not knowledge. Because of the relinquishment of agency that marks it, the gift always works in ways that are secret from both giver and recipient. Neither giver nor recipient knows whether a gift has been given, whether it has been accepted, or what its force is—this is the terrifying danger, a danger against which there can be no guarantees, that must always mark satyagraha.[46] Also, because they act without knowledge, satyagrahis can never know whether their satyagraha is coercive or "blackmail." And yet, because satyagraha is an absolute responsibility, this nonknowledge can never be reason to avoid satyagraha—satyagrahis have not chosen satyagraha in the first place.

But even where fasts are neither practiced by satyagrahis as a form of coercion nor experienced by other offenders as such, satyagraha is cruel. Already in 1914, Gandhi acknowledges this.

> I do not know what ['evil'] there is in me. I have such noncompassion [*nirdayata*, 'strain of cruelty'] in me—according to what others say—that in order to please me, people force themselves to do things beyond their capacity, even attempt the impossible. Lacking the necessary strength, they put on a false show and deceive me. Even Gokhale used to tell me: "You have so much harshness in you that you terrify the one facing you, and that person out of fear or in or in the attempt to please you, pushes himself beyond his capacity, while those who are weak put on a false show. You put an unbearable burden on people. I myself too, when doing work for you, do things beyond my capacity, even where I don't have the strength."[47]

Again, then, it turns out that ahimsa and satyagraha are not nonviolent if by that we refer to the attenuation of force. They are nonviolent only in that they reject the force of general responsibility and seek to abide instead by the force of *prayaschitta*—the forgiveness-repentance that is proper to absolute responsibility. Surrendering to this force involves giving it to one's interlocutors, who will all too often experience it as cruel and violent.

～

Second, *prayaschitta* involves another temporality—a time that does not belong to the economy of abstract time, and yet gives that time. Consider Gandhi's reformulation of the concept of patience. The emphasis on *dhiraj* or patience is already marked in *Hind Swaraj,* where in the first chapter the Editor says that the desire for swaraj gave birth to the Indian National Congress, and points to the contribution of Congress members such as Wedderburn, Hume, Tyebji, and others. The Reader responds: "Stop. Stop. . . . I have asked about swaraj and you are talking of foreign rule *[par-rajya].* I cannot stand English names, and you have started giving me English names. . . . I would like you to talk only of *swaraj."* To which the Editor says: "You have become impatient *[adheera].* I cannot afford impatience. That you stopped me and that you don't wish to hear about India's well-wishers suggests that for those like you swaraj is still far. If there are many Indians like you, then we would go halfway and fall back. This thought is worthy of your attention." Involved in this conversation, as in *Hind Swaraj* and other writings more broadly, is the claim that modern civilization is marked by "impatience." Now, it would be easy enough to dismiss any simple version of this claim. As noted in chapter 2, even though modern civilization's rule of law must make its decisions quickly (for justice delayed is justice denied), these decisions nevertheless claim to be just on the grounds that they embody infinite patience.

But in Gandhi's terms this infinite patience is still impatient because it is within the problematic of sovereignty, because it is a sovereign patience, so to speak. And in "modern civility" patience itself rests on a distinctive concept of time—that commonsensical time that Heidegger has so powerfully described: "Time is that within which events take place."[48] The swaraj that the Reader seeks is an event that occurs in abstract time. He seeks sovereignty, and the sovereign is constituted by measure—he both measures and, with modern civility, himself submits to the measure of reason. There is thus a conceptual compatibility between "modern civilization" and abstract measurable time. The modern sovereign is the end who can stride and master this abstract time, who is never a means to another end; conversely those like the Reader who lack sovereignty can only be objects in this time.

The time of modern sovereignty also organizes the way nationalists like the Reader embrace death. In June 1925, Gandhi reports on his meetings with students in Bengal: "In one of my talks with students, one of them said, 'Do you know why we do not spin? There is no excitement about the wheel. Our education has unfitted us for any such work. Many of us would prefer death to spinning. Death on the gallows we can gladly embrace, but spinning is an impossibility. Give us something grand. We love romance and there is none about spinning.'"[49] Within abstract time, death can only be thought of as either the means to an end, or as its converse, empty nullity. By dying on the gallows, the students would make themselves means to the end of sovereignty. Indeed, by dying on the gallows, the students assert their sovereignty over their own life even when it is taken away by the British; by seizing this dazzling instant when the time of the sovereign is embodied in an especially charged way, they hope to secure for India the sovereign experience of abstract time. And when India is sovereign, if we recall the Reader's words from chapter 4 of *Hind Swaraj*, "we must own our navy, our army, and we must have our own splendour, and then will India's voice ring through the world." Only as a sovereign can India participate in the abstract time that constitutes the world. Indeed, it is only sovereigns who can participate in and partake of this abstract time—that which lacks sovereignty can only be an object in this time; it cannot even quite be a "who."

The sovereign disposition of time, which in his writing reaches its highest form in "modern civility," is something that Gandhi ascribes to all humans, and especially to men. Thus it is that he can write in 1917 that compared to woman, "man is thoughtless, impatient and given to the pursuit of novelty."[50] But Gandhi is not dismissive of this sovereign patience. To the extent that he affirms the principle, and thinks that the waiting involved in the principle is itself a precursor to the satyagrahi's vow, he even respects sovereign patience. Nevertheless, from at least the time of *Hind Swaraj*, Gandhi also describes this patience as impatient.

The impatience of modern civility and sovereignty lies perhaps in this: even where it is infinitely patient in its terms, it cannot encounter newness as singularity. Where this disposition of time prevails, newness is encountered always as the uniqueness of the "analogical third," through the sovereign example. As such, newness is precisely what the sovereign cannot experience, for that experience would require a surrender of sovereignty; the sovereign must constantly search for newness precisely because the new here is what is always overcome and never found.

～

As with his formulations about *prayaschitta*, it is only in the years after *Hind Swaraj* that Gandhi arrives at his distinctive formulations about the patience of satyagrahis and their experience of time and newness. In *Hind*

Swaraj, quite apart from the reference to *The Fallacy of Speed,* there is the discussion in chapter 9: "Good travels at a snail's pace. . . . Those who want to do good are not selfish. They are not in a hurry. They know that it will take generations for good to make a mark on humans. Only evil can leap. ['But evil has wings.']"

This formulation about the slowness of satyagraha remains within the problematic of abstract and calendar time; it is only an inversion of modern civilization's emphasis on speed. Here the form of time is already naturally given, and the disagreement is only over the pace on which to proceed through that time. Here, indeed, Gandhi's arguments can be understood in a conservative spirit: as emphasizing intimacy over abstraction.[51]

But there is also another thinking of time that is only intimated in *Hind Swaraj,* but is articulated more forcefully in the years after his return to India, and condenses around the English word "plodding." And he writes by 1921 (to resort, ourselves, to calendrical time):

> Ability to plod is swaraj. It is yoga. Nor need the reader be frightened of the monotony. Monotony is the law of nature. Look at the monotonous manner in which the sun rises. And imagine the catastrophe that would befall the universe if the sun became capricious and went in for a variety of pastimes. But there is a monotony that sustains and a monotony that kills. The monotony of necessary occupations is exhilarating and life-giving. An artist never tires of his art.[52]

And in April 1925, he writes (to return on another register to a passage we encountered briefly in chapter 3):

> There is no necessary charm about death on the gallows; often such death is easier than a life of drudgery and toil in malarious tracts. I am quite satisfied that among the Swarajists and others there are men who will any day lay down their lives if they felt convinced that their death would bring deliverance to the country. I suggest to my friend, the revolutionary, that death on the gallows serves the country only when the victim is a "spotless lamb."[53]

Note the extraordinarily strong claim here—ability to plod is swaraj. Perhaps he can make this claim because for him plodding increasingly names the time of satyagraha. Satyagraha cannot occur in the abstract time that frames both revolutionary self-sacrifice and, more broadly, action within a means–end problematic. To plod is not simply to move infinitely and slowly through abstract time. The emphasis on plodding points rather to the other time that is proper to satyagraha, to the time when slowness and patience dehisce into a self-sacrifice that does not reach any end, that is never means.

Plodding especially characterizes the "benign aspect" of satygraha, its everyday forgiveness. The benign aspect for Gandhi consists mainly in the three activities of the constructive program—spinning (to redress poverty), work for Hindu-Muslim unity, and anti-untouchability work. Each of these atones for the unforgivable way Indians perpetuate poverty, Hindu-Muslim violence, and untouchability.

The most exemplary form of plodding—the context indeed in which perhaps Gandhi most often uses the term—is spinning. He arrives at his vow to spin for half an hour a day before his second meal (and skip his second meal if he does not) only in October 1921. From this time on, he consistently tries to persuade Indians—not just satyagrahis—that they should make time for spinning daily. In 1924 he succeeds for a period of nine months to persuade the Congress to adopt a spinning franchise (a requirement that Congress members spin as a condition of membership).[54] Even after the Congress abandons it, Gandhi remains deeply committed to it. Even though he cites economic reasons for promoting khadi and spinning, spinning is quintessentially an aneconomic activity. It can only be practiced where there is unconditional faith in the gift it gives and receives. As such a sacrificial activity or *yajna* organized by love, spinning for Gandhi transports its practitioners into another time; this may be why in 1929 he describes spinning as an "applied translation of the *Gita*." Gandhi's exhortations to Congressmen to make time for spinning, it is tempting to think, are also more: they are about entering and inhabiting the time of spinning.[55]

In spinning and plodding, satyagrahis sustain their friendship with death. Unlike revolutionaries, whose death occurs in the telos of mounting the gallows, satyagrahis inscribe their death in an everyday time and life, and respond to an everyday violence. Thus the striking translation of plodding often as *udhyam*—a word that could probably be translated as "effort" or "work." *Udhyam* and related words are crucial in Gandhi's vocabulary. Around September 1928, indeed, he pushes his reluctant associates to change the name of the Satyagraha Ashram at Sabarmati to *Udyog Mandir*—temple of work. This change, he suggests, is necessary because despite the best attempts of ashram inmates, they were very far from satya. "This change of name was necessary for the sake of humility and truth. The organizers will again accept the name Satyagraha Ashram when they gain self-confidence."[56]

What is accomplished by changing the name? For Gandhi, *udyog* is a word made sacred because of its association with the *Gita*. In Gandhi's reading, *udyog* is not just any work; it is work that can be performed "as a consecration, a *yajna* (sacrifice) or a *kurbani*."[57] To sacrifice is to relinquish relations of means and ends. Rather than making the task an end and themselves the means, thus placing both the task and themselves in an abstract time, satyagrahis "plod." This relinquishment is the *atmashuddhi* or self-purification, the ciphering, that Gandhi refers to in his analogy with the "spotless lamb." Through such relinquishment, satyagrahis become incapable of encountering time as a series of infinite nows to be traversed, whether in mastery or submission. *Udyog* and plodding name, in other words, a way that the ciphering of the self is performed every day and incessantly. Here the gift of being occurs in finite tasks such as spinning, anti-untouchabilility work, or the effort to promote Hindu-Muslim unity. Even when they mount the gallows, satyagrahis do so in the plodding spirit of *udyog*, rather than in the heroic spirit that seeks to vault across abstract time into the telos of the nation. Also, precisely because satyagrahis refuse to exercise sovereignty over their interlocutors, fasts and noncooperation have to be undertaken over and again to help both satyagrahis and their interlocutors assume their absolute responsibilities. Satyagrahis must, in other words, constantly practice the patience of groundless faith.

This time of plodding is also, simultaneously, the instant of novelty or newness. Indeed, newness is an especially apposite way of describing the stakes of Gandhi's plodding politics. As the discussion of the *Gita* in chapter 7 indicated, the new in Gandhi's terms cannot be encountered by "modern civility," since that civilization must always either master and stay sovereign over the new, or submit to the sovereignty of the new. Newness in Gandhi's terms is possible only where difference is accorded what is proper to it—absolute and unconditional equality. So it is that he associates newness with ciphering and plodding, writing, for example, to Mridula Sarabhai many years later in 1945 that "your individuality" can be preserved "only when you reduce yourself to a zero and remain a zero."[58] He does not indicate how ciphering intensifies individuality. But it may be because the cipher relinquishes instrumental or causal relations. Such relations, as earlier chapters argued, are premised on mastery and sovereignty, and cannot allow for the experience of newness. By ciphering themselves, satyagrahis practice absolute equality with their interlocutors, and thus encounter newness.

～

Third, the absolute responsibility of *prayaschitta*-satyagraha is simultaneously the moment of the greatest grief and the greatest joy. In Gandhi's accounts, grief marks being. Even if satyagrahis relinquish the grief involved in the experience of "mine-ness," that relinquishment itself only opens on an even more intense grief: now, grief for inequality with the other, for the unjusticiable wound. Grief marks satyagraha itself. In 1919, he says in one of the satyagraha leaflets: "hartal [strike] is an ancient Indian means [*puranu sadhan;* 'institution'] for expressing national sorrow and we can therefore demonstrate through hartal our grief."[59] And in describing a fast that satyagrahis are to undertake before commencing noncooperation, Gandhi remarks that it would be neither a hunger strike nor "designed for exerting any pressure upon the Government. It is a measure of self-discipline, it will be an expression of the anguish of the soul, and when the soul is anguished, nobody could resist."[60]

At the same time, Gandhi quite consistently emphasizes the peace and joy involved in satyagraha. Already in 1918, as Suhrud notes, Gandhi is insistent that the fast "gives me immense pleasure and, therefore, should not cause pain to anyone." That year, while on his first public fast, undertaken to persuade the striking textile workers of Ahmedabad to stick to their vrat or vow, he writes: "I am at present overflowing with joy. When, on a former occasion, I took such a vow, my mind did not enjoy the peace it does today. I also felt at that time the pull of the body. This time I experience nothing of the kind. My mind is filled with profound peace. I feel like pouring forth my soul to you all but I am beside myself with joy."

How does the greatest anguish open onto the greatest joy? Gandhi is forced to think the precise nature of this joy from at least 1921, when Tagore questions it and the noncooperation movement, suggesting that the movement involves the "fierce joy of annihilation." Tagore develops his argument through a contrast between Buddhism and the Vedic tradition:

Brahmavidya, the cult of Brahma, the infinite being, has for its object *mukti,* emancipation, while Buddhism has *Nirvana,* extinction. It may be argued that both have the same ideas in different names. But names represent attitudes of mind and emphasize particular aspects of truth. *Mukti* draws our attention to the positive and *Nirvana* to the negative side of truth. Buddha kept silence through his teachings about the truth of Om, the Everlasting Yes, his implication being that by the negative path, destroying the self, we naturally reach that Truth. Therefore he emphasized the fact of *dukha,* misery, which had to be avoided. But *Brahmavidya* emphasized the fact of *ananda,* joy which had to be attained. The latter cult also needs for its fulfillment the discipline of self-abnegation; yet it holds before its view the idea of Brahma, not only at the end, but through the process of self-realization.

Therefore the idea of life's training was different in the Vedic period than it was in the Buddhistic. In the former it was the purification of life's joy; in the latter it was the eradication of it.[61]

Already in 1921, Gandhi cites from this passage and disagrees with its terms and its contrast, pointing to the centrality of the term *neti* in the Brahmavidya tradition, and emphasizing that "mukti is as much a negative state as nirvana."[62]

But perhaps in later years Gandhi develops the vocabulary to also have disagreed with Tagore in another way—by insisting that the joy involved in satygraha's gift of being is quite different from the arms-bearing warrior's "fierce joy of annihilation." Satyagraha is the response proper to grief because it refuses to overcome grief, and makes it instead into grief for an unjusticiable wound. That wound is their relation to the *atman*—not just being but, given the unity of being, all beings. The originary wound that marks them and gives them grief is the insurmountable and constitutive separation from *atman.* For that wound, satyagrahis cannot escape responsibility and must atone by seeking oneness with *atman.* But here, where *atman* is despite Gandhi's explicit formulations thought immanently, in terms of the absolute equality of all beings. Here, the oneness of being that the etymologies of the words satyagraha and *prayaschitta* refer to cannot be that of fusion. What persists in satyagraha is the not-ness of Being, and there can be oneness only with the not-ness of being.

Thus the way that Gandhi invokes Goethe's *Faust* in 1922, after his second reading of it while in Yeravda jail:

> Margaret is sore at heart and troubled. She finds no relief from her misery save by going to the spinning-wheel and to the music of the wheel giving vent to her grief. . . . . Margaret is alone in her room torn within with doubt and despair. . . . She involuntarily goes to the wheel and finds peace in refusing to find it.
>
> > . . . . My peace is gone, and my heart is sore:
> > I have lost him, and lost him, for evermore!
> > The place, where he is not, to me is the tomb.
> > The world is sadness and sorrow and gloom!
> > My poor sick brain is crazed with pain;
> > And my poor sick heart is torn in twain!
> > My peace is gone and my heart is sore,
> > For lost is my love for evermore!
>
> You may paraphrase them a little and . . . the verses almost represent my condition. I seem to have lost my Love too and feel distracted. I feel the abiding presence of my Lover and yet he seems to be away from me. For he refuses to guide me and give clear-cut injunctions. On the contrary, like Krishna, the arch mischief-maker to the Gopis, he exasperates me by appearing, disappearing and reappearing.[63]

Marked constitutively by loss, becoming at home in not being at home, "finding peace in refusing to find it": this is the immense aloneness and solitude of the satyagrahi. This not-ness is the moment of the greatest joy for satyagrahis, for it affirms the absolute equality of satya or being. But it is also the moment of the greatest grief, for satyagrahis are acutely aware of their infinite separation from absolute equality. Here grief and joy open onto each other aporetically, incite and intensify each other.

A related dimension of this forceful emphasis on the simultaneity of grief and joy in ciphering emerges in what Gandhi writes in 1925:

> Many young men have sacrificed lucrative careers. That is certainly to their credit. But even there I should respectfully suggest that praising can well be overdone. No sacrifice is worth the name

unless it is a joy. Sacrifice and a long face go ill together. Sacrifice is "making sacred." He must be a poor specimen of humanity who is in need of sympathy for his sacrifice. Buddha renounced everything because he could not help it. To have anything was a torture to him.[64]

And in the *Gitashikshan* lectures of 1926, he argues: "Following the path of non-violence, we discovered the spinning-wheel, we discovered *brahmach-arya*. Beyond the river [Sabarmati] is *bhogabhumi* while this is *karmabhumi*. We wish to follow the path of renunciation. But no renunciation is truly such unless it gives us joy. We cannot live without joy."[65] *Karmabhumi*— land of karma. Karma often names for Gandhi by the 1920s the action that is carried out as sacrifice; karma is already *karmaphaltyag* (sacrifice of the fruits of action) and *nishkamakarma* (desireless action). Wherever there is such action, there is also joy; indeed, joy is the mark of such action.

And plodding work is so valuable to Gandhi because it is the time where grief and joy open out onto each other. In 1928, he writes to Nehru: "Let us recognize that the task before workers is not as easy as we thought at one time it was. I would like you not to lose patience and take up some plodding work with a living faith in it. Let *The Song Celestial* [Edwin Arnold's English translation of the *Gita*] be your guide-book."[66] An injunction, of course, which Nehru could only have received with puzzlement and exasperation.

· AFTERWORD ·

The Miracle of the Gift

*It is true that, as a man cannot see his back, so can he not see his
errors or insanity. But the sages have often likened a man of religion
to a lunatic. I, therefore, hug the belief that I may not be insane and
may be truly religious. Which of the two I am in truth can only be
decided after my death.*

—Mohandas Gandhi, "Some Objections Answered,"
August 10, 1924

*I have conceived no such thing as Gandhism. I am not an exponent
of any sect. I never claimed to have originated any philosophy. . . .
Well, all my philosophy, if it may be called by that pretentious name,
is contained in what I have said. You will not call it Gandhism; there
is no ism about it. And no elaborate literature is needed about it. All
that I have written is but a description of whatever I have done. And
my actions alone are the greatest exposition of truth and nonviolence.
Those who believe in these can propagate them only by following
them in practice. They call for no books. My work is there for them to
emulate. But it may be said that this, too, is not permanent.*

—Mohandas Gandhi, "Speech at Gandhi Seva Sangh Meeting,"
March 3, 1936

D URING ONE OF HIS DAILY LECTURES in 1926 on the *Gita*, Gandhi
says: "Shri . . . , the goldsmith, asked me to give him something, saying 'Else, what could I carry back with me?' I looked at him for a while,
unable to think of anything. Then I said: 'Repeat *Ramanama.*' What was it,
however, that I gave him? And what did he receive? Things don't work that
way *[aam kai thathu nathi].*"[1]

"Repeat Ramanama"—chant the name of Rama—"Rama-Rama"—
indefinitely. Could this injunction be an early gift of fearlessness or *abhaydan* to Gandhi? Recall what he writes of his youth: he could "gain nothing

from the [Vaishnava] *haveli*," and what he fails to get there he receives "from my nurse, an old servant of the family, whose affection for me I still recall. I have said before that there was in me a fear of ghosts and spirits. Rambha, for that was her name, suggested, as a remedy for this fear, the repetition of Ramanama. I had more faith in her than in her remedy, and so at a tender age I began repeating Ramanama to cure my fear of ghosts and spirits."[2] "That Rambha" again. Here, to repeat Ramanama becomes an enactment over and again of the vow of abhay or fearlessness. Only where there is abhay can one attend to satya-ahimsa—the nonbeing of being. (To recall the Editor in *Hind Swaraj:* "When a man abandons truth, he does so owing to fear [*bhay*] in some form.")

From around 1900, Gandhi comes to describe the repetition of Rama-nama as "all-sufficing" for him. Moreover, it is so not as part of some sepa-rable personal religion, but as his politics. Ramanama comes back to him at several crucial moments. It saves him when his friend tries to persuade him to break his vow abstaining from meat. When he commences satya-graha, what Rambha gave him returns with even more force:

> As I grew old, the faith weakened. My mentor, the nurse, was dead. I ceased to take the name of Rama, and my fears revived. In the jail I read the *Ramayana* with greater attention and still greater devotion than ever before, and whenever I felt lonely or felt the pride in me rising and telling me that I could do something for India, to give me due humility and to make me experience the presence of the Almighty, and thus to remove my loneliness, I used calmly to recite the name Rama with all the halo that Tulsidas has surrounded it with.[3]

Rambha dies, but she never stops giving Ramanama, and the more he receives, the more there is for him to receive and her to give. Repeating Ramanama, Gandhi surrenders to satya—perhaps. As he proceeds on his satyagraha marches, as he spins, he resorts repeatedly to the Ramanama; when he is shot, he dies saying the Ramanama. In other words, Ramanama is not just incidental to his satyagraha; it is his satyagraha.

What is it, however, that Rambha gives him? And what does he receive? And what, many years later, does Gandhi give to the unnamed goldsmith who wants something to carry back? And what does the goldsmith receive?

Gandhi remarks sometimes (as do devotees today) that a reversal of the syllables "Rama-Rama" leads to the Gujarati phrase *mara-mara*—mine, mine. *Mara-mara:* this would exemplify the everyday exercise of sovereign power. The very utterance Rama-Rama can thus, if said without faith, become its converse. Perhaps this is a threat that somebody like the unnamed goldsmith is especially exposed to, working as he does with one of the universal currencies of desire (though Gandhi is aware that this threat can certainly be overcome—Raychandbhai is a goldsmith by profession). Faith thus sustains Ramanama. "Ramanama has no independent power. It is not a quinine pill, which has a power of its own . . . , [which] destroys malaria germs wherever they may be. Ramanama has no such independent power. A mantra acquires power through devotion."[4]

This chant that Rambha gives, Rama-Rama: she must have repeated it herself. In this repetition, she is perhaps seized—enchanted—by Ramanama. To be so enchanted is to surrender to the *antaratman,* or the other within oneself, "conscience." Her surrender to her own other, her not-ness, her enchantment by Ramanama—this is what she gives the young Gandhi.

How does Gandhi receive what she gives? "I used to love [Rambha] as my mother, and in whose company much more of my time was passed in childhood than in my mother's."[5] He repeats Ramanama not because of faith in the mantra, but because of his own faith in her, his own surrender to her. Only in their singular relation—and every singular relation is one of surrender—does the giving and receiving occur.

What is it that he receives? Not Rambha's surrender to Ramanama. Gandhi gives to himself his own surrender to the injunction—this is what he receives from her. This surrender is not the same as her surrender. Even though he receives the injunction from her, it unfolds along its own path.

She gives one thing, he receives another thing, and both what is given and what is received is least of all a thing. Such is always the nature of the pure gift: giving nothing, it gives difference, singularity.

～

To all, including himself, Gandhi gives the chant: Repeat Ramanama. What does he give and what does he receive in this repetition?

Nothing. This is so in two senses, between which no one can know.

Nothing as inert nullity—no gift—has been given if those to whom Gandhi gives the injunction experience it as evasion. Similarly, nothing as inert nullity has been given if opponents experience the demands of the satyagrahi as coercion or domination. Satyagrahis, moreover, cannot perceive this experience as a lack on the part of those to whom they offer their gift; they can only perceive it as their failure to offer satyagraha rigorously enough. They must respond by a *manthan* [churning, "self-examination"] that seeks to decipher why their self-sacrifice was not enough.

But here, to decipher is also to cipher. So nothing in quite another sense—the nothing of the cipher—is given and received where the gift of ahimsa takes place. Describing satyagraha in chapter 16 of *Hind Swaraj*, the Editor says: "This force is indestructible, and he who uses it is one who understands his position perfectly [*barobar,* properly, rightly]. It is summed up in the proverb of our ancestors: "One negative cures thirty-six diseases" [*ek nanno chattris rogne harey*]. The same phrase (translated there into English as "eternal negative") occurs in Gandhi's account of his encounter with the friend who wants to make him abandon his vegetarianism. In Gandhi's negative, Ramanama becomes satyagraha.

Of course, the negative does not mark only satyagraha—it marks every demand for rights. As Gayatri Spivak has reminded us, every demand for rights also rights wrongs, says no to a wrong.[6] And not perhaps accidentally, as *Hind Swaraj* opens, the very first question the Reader asks is about the Editor's opinion on the "wave of swaraj" and the demand to "acquire rights." The Reader and the Editor share the demand for rights. In doing so, they say no to the wrong involved in colonial rule. The Reader, of course, says no in a distinctive way—the way of the autonomous self. The Reader's no is the no that marks critique—the no that has one of its earliest iterations perhaps in Socrates' discovery that he is wise precisely because he does not presume to know what he does not know, and reaches its Enlightenment culmination in Kant's insistence that the enlightened ruler "takes it to be his duty to prescribe nothing."[7]

But to that no, which is also the no of ontotheology and logocentrism, Gandhi must say no. With the Ramanama, he opens the "no" of "modern civilization" back to the "no" given by "true civilization"—the no the former comes from and obscures. So it is that his remarks, stitched together, also say: satyagraha is the perfect or proper negative. Ramanama exemplifies this ciphering. In his luminous essay on Gandhi's invocation of Ramanama, Tridip Suhrud writes: "With the disappearance of the form what remains is the Name."[8] Put differently, surrender to Ramanama is a surrender of being to nonbeing, and as such a ciphering of the self in the most radical sense possible.

How does satyagraha give nothing? Satyagrahis give their own life to the sovereign in such a manner as to destroy sovereignty. This destruction of sovereignty is the gift of satyagraha. Here surrender is the giving of absolute equality, of what can be given only by negating sovereignty. Satyagraha's gift of nothing transforms "theoretical, legal equality" so as to reveal what it both obscures and is yet given from—the finitude and abhaydhan, gift of fearlessness, of absolute equality. Satyagraha thus seeks to destroy the life of the sovereign, but only in order to gift the sovereign another life—the life of absolute equality, or the life nothing gives. Satyagrahis do not have this other life before they give it to the sovereign; rather, they receive it themselves only in giving it to the sovereign, and only if the sovereign receives it. This is the constitutive paradox of satyagraha: one receives absolute equality oneself only when the other receives absolute equality from oneself.

As the gift of absolute equality, then, satyagraha is suffused by nothing. Nothing because what satyagrahis must give is the life they receive by surrendering to their own death, the not-ness that they have made their own. Nothing because this absolute equality marks being with an originary resistance to subordination—not a resistance organized against this or that specific grievance, which will disappear once the grievance disappears, but rather a resistance that always wells anew. Nothing because not-ness is most proper to being.

This absolute equality is simultaneously a yes and a no: an originary affirmative that negates, and an originary negation that affirms. Satyagraha affirms the yes that is daya (compassion) or prem (love), but finds that such affirmation requires the no that is ahimsa. Conversely, here the no of ahimsa gives daya and prem. Ahimsa and satya thus name, respectively, the no required by a yes, and the yes required by a no—this indeed is why they are "two sides of a coin, or rather a smooth unstamped metallic disk."

～

"Things don't work that way." Gandhi gives the injunction, "Repeat Rama-nama," to the goldsmith. While givers and receivers can never know whether they have given or received the gift, they will have their suspicions. Perhaps Gandhi suspects he has given—and by extension, received—only nothing as inert nullity. Perhaps he also suspects that he has given—and again by extension received—only nothing as inert nullity during his nine-month series of lectures on the *Gita*. Is this why he says, in his fourth-from-last lecture, as he winds down the series: "Things don't work that way"?

How then do things work with the gift? Swaraj in the Reader's sense—swaraj as the sovereign right to a "theoretical, legal equality," which the British already have—is a thing that can be unilaterally given from above by the sovereign (for it is always up to the sovereign whether to treat another as an end or means), or unilaterally seized from below by subjects.

By contrast, as the ceaseless demand for absolute equality, satyagraha-ahimsa requires a swaraj that cannot be given or taken unilaterally. Gandhi writes in April 1921 of his concept of swaraj: "Such swaraj will not be a gift from anyone. It will not fall from above, nor will it be thrown up from below; we have to establish it."[9] Similarly, in an article written about a week earlier, just before the second anniversary of the Jallianwala Bagh massacre, he expresses the hope that swaraj will arrive soon, and then goes on: "But it is not in my hands. It is not even in God's hands. Even God cannot grant us swaraj. We will have to take swaraj by our own hands. There is only one way of doing so. The moment we understand it and conduct ourselves by it, swaraj will be ours.[10]

As Gandhi should have anticipated, that turns out to be a controversial thing to say. We learn from an article he writes a month later that one of his associates protests, saying "it gives the impression that I was placing limits on even the power of God." Gandhi replies:

> I count myself a religious-minded man. I believe in the reality
> of God [ishwartatva]. I have merely stated a plain fact in plain
> language and drawn attention to God's law. God has reserved no
> freedom for Himself to grant a place in heaven to a sinner. One
> can say that, after laying down His laws, God left things to take
> their own course. It is because He is Almighty that He has created
> laws which admit of no exceptions. Swaraj is a state of being of
> individuals and nations. Just as only a person who eats will have his
> hunger satisfied, so too he alone can be free [swatantra] who
> throws off unfreedom [partantra]. If we do not give up drink and
> do not discard foreign cloth, if Hindus and Muslims continue
> fighting with each other, would God make us a gift of swaraj? Can
> He? . . . Hence, even our prayer should be not for swaraj but for
> strength to win it. The very meaning of prayer is the expression of
> intense longing for a particular goal or state.[11]

No exception, then, to the law of absolute responsibility involved in the satyagrahi's swaraj: even a God cannot give it as a free gift. Rather, it has to be earned through a distinctive discipline of the self. This discipline "is" the gift of swaraj or, more properly, abhaydan, the gift of fearlessness.

~

Not a free gift, then—this pure gift. It is received back as reward for a certain discipline. The emphasis on receiving back strains at our conceptual vocabularies. We can indicate why by recalling Derrida's emphasis on the aneconomy of the gift. As he points out, the pure gift is given without knowledge of either the giver or the receiver; if reciprocated, it would no longer be a gift. And yet here, practicing satyagraha and ahimsa, the satyagrahi receives swaraj. Nor is this an exception; everywhere in Gandhi's writings, the pure gift commands a very distinctive reciprocation. Once again, a striking difference from Derrida emerges: beginning from what seem to be similar premises, Gandhi's writing moves in a radically divergent direction, a direction, moreover, that is incomprehensible within Derrida's terms.

How can there be reciprocation in the pure gift, how would it then remain a pure gift?

We could begin exploring this reciprocation by way of the life of Raja Harishchandra of Ayodhya, who figures in both the *Ramayana* and the *Mahabharata*. As a child, Gandhi notes in the *Autobiography,* he saw the play "Harischandra Akhyan" [the narrative of Harishchandra] performed by a traveling company.

> I would never tire of seeing that play. I wanted to see it again and again. But who would allow me to go repeatedly? It haunted me and I must have acted Harishchandra to myself times without number. "Why should not all be truthful like Harishchandra?" was the question I asked myself day and night. To suffer ordeals like those that befell Harishchandra and observe satya, this was true satya [kharu satya]. I literally believed that Harishchandra had suffered the ordeals written about in the play. Seeing Harishchandra's suffering [dukh], remembering them, I wept a lot. Today my common sense tells me that Harishchandra could not have been a historical character. Still both Harishchandra and Shravana are living realities for me. I am sure I should be moved as before if I were to read those plays again today.[12]

To provide the minimal detail necessary to understand the sense in which Raja Harishchandra is a living reality for Gandhi: the raja, after one formative event, vows to always keep a promise, and to always abide by satya.

Keeping a vow, the raja relinquishes his kingdom to the sage Vishvamitra, for reasons that vary in the texts. Harishchandra is thus a figure who gifts always his kingdom, and gifts it away not as munificent act, but in the observance of a vow—in this sense, he neither makes gifts to Vishvamitra, nor does Vishvamitra receive the kingdom as a gift. The vow thus reworks the gift, marks it with a forgetting.

Gandhi dwells most often on what follows, when Harishchandra must, in order to also offer a *dakshina* (a further gift) to Vishvamitra, sell his wife Taramati and son Rohit to a Brahmin householder, and himself to a low caste Chandala—in some versions, he is cursed to become a Chandala—who works at a cremation ground. (Caste is thus an unavoidable provocation that Gandhi must encounter in his accounts of Harischandra. In one of these accounts he makes a parenthetical remark that perhaps does not remain only a parenthesis, that bursts forth and refigures his accounts: "What, by the way, must be the position about untouchability in those early days?")[13] His son subsequently dies of snakebite; Taramati brings the body to the cremation grounds, but Harishchandra demands, as he is required to, the cremation ground fees from Taramati before the cremation; further events require him to execute her. This moment of execution is the one that Gandhi refers to repeatedly, as previous chapters have briefly noted. The *Gitashikshan* has this:

> Harishchandra saw the auspicious necklace round Taramati's neck
> and recognized it. He saw that he had to cut off the dear head of
> her whom he adored. You will ask me how this is an illustration of
> non-violence. Violence does not consist in the act of cutting off
> someone's head; it consists in the motive behind the act. How if we
> knew that Harishchandra would have preferred to kill himself
> rather than kill Taramati? Suppose it had been the King's order
> that, if the *Chandal* could not bring himself to kill the person
> before him, he could kill himself, Harishchandra would have
> certainly preferred to put the knife to his own throat. But he was
> given no such choice. He had actually brought down the knife and
> it was then that the gods held back his hand.[14]

"Violence . . . consists in the motive behind the act." We cannot here read "motive" in terms of agential intention—the *Gitashikshan* itself stresses the ciphering of the satyagrahi, as we have seen. Here "the motive behind the act" is motivelessness. The sense in which Harishchandra's act is nonviolent is precisely because he has renounced choice and become a cipher—a figure marked by free surrender—at the moment when he raises the sword on Taramati. Is not Taramati the offering or sacrifice precisely because of his two-ness with her: by offering her, he offers himself, ciphers himself, more radically than he would by offering himself?

And this terrifying gift is also the moment of the reciprocity where Harishchandra is given another power—the gods hold back his hand, he receives back his kingdom, and he becomes among the most venerated kings of the subcontinent. (Also: Is not the offering and its interruption marked by caste? If it is his duties as a servant of the Chandala that make Harishchandra sacrifice Taramati, could it be that when Gandhi sacrifices varnadharma, the fourfold caste order, in order to abolish untouchability, and yet prays to get varnadharma back in this very sacrifice, he acts unconsciously with Harishchandra as an example?)

This aneconomic economy of the pure gift, this other reciprocity, is the distinctive moment of Gandhi's satyagraha, dharma, or what we would usually call his politics. Consider the way he explains his participation in the Khilafat movement:

> I consider myself to be among the staunchest of Hindus. I am as eager to save the cow from the Mussulman's knife as any Hindu. But on that very account I refuse to make my support of the Mussulman claim on the khilafat conditional upon his saving the cow. The Mussulman is my neighbor. He is in distress. His grievance is legitimate and it is my bounden duty to help him to secure redress by every legitimate means in my power even to the extent of losing my life and property. That is the way I can win permanent friendship with Mussulmans. . . . The nobility of the help will be rendered nugatory if it was rendered conditionally. That the result will be the saving of the cow is a certainty. But should it turn out to be otherwise, my view will not be affected in any manner whatsoever. The test of friendship is a spirit of love and sacrifice independent of expectation of any return.[15]

Here, his support for the Khilafat movement is marked by unconditionality and in-consequence. Unlike a strategy, bargain, or economic exchange, his support will always be given, regardless of whether it is reciprocated; it is "pure means," not a means to an end. Nevertheless, there is also what might seem to be a contradictory insistence that "the result will be the saving of the cow is a certainty." This apparently contradictory insistence on both economy and unconditionality marks abhaydan, too. Speaking in 1915 at Gurukul Kangri, he says abhaydan would "pave the way for an honorable and just solution of many problems that worry us today," and goes on: "It should be remembered that in practicing ahimsa, there need not be any reciprocation, though, as a matter of fact, in its final stages, it commands reciprocation."[16]

As all these remarks should suggest, aneconomic reciprocation is not just an addition to the thinking of the pure gift. It is rather the moment that makes the pure gift possible in its impossibility. (This is not a distinction between Indic and Abrahamic traditions. Kierkegaard's powerful reading of the moment when Abraham is stopped from killing Isaac should suffice to remind us that aneconomic reciprocation is crucial to the pure gift in Abrahamic traditions, too.)[17]

This power is all the more crucial since satyagrahis relinquish causal action, whether incalculable as with the warrior, or calculable as with "modern civilization." Their action is never causally organized—this to say also that they undertake their actions without expecting return. That relinquishment makes aneconomic reciprocation or return the only form of "effectivity" (though that word again is not appropriate here, belonging as it does to the problematic of means and ends) or power that satyagrahis "have." The force of this power Gandhi is insistent on: "Giving up the desire for the fruit [fal] of one's action [karma] does not imply that no result will follow. It implies that every action brings in its result."[18]

～

How does a gift remain pure if it is reciprocated? When speaking and writing of satyagraha-ahimsa, Gandhi often draws on the word chamatkar or "miracle." Satyagraha is a "miracle," has "miraculous power," works "miraculously." Indeed, the miracle may even distinguish an Indian heritage: "This country is the treasure-house of tapascharya [penance/austerities]. In this country alone do people belonging to different religions live together in amity and the gods of all are venerated. If, despite all this bounty, we fail to work a miracle [alaukik karya, etymologically, unworldly work], bring peace to the world and conquer the British through the play of moral force in our life, we shall have disgraced our heritage."[19]

But what is the miracle of satyagraha? He writes in 1926: "I have not studied the miracles as miracles [*chamatkar tarike*, 'from the miraculous standpoint']. I neither believe nor disbelieve them. I hold that they ought not to affect our conduct one way or the other."[20] What he takes a delicate distance from here is the affirmation, common to many "customary religions," of the miracle as a supernatural intervention in a natural order of things. To that miracle, the Enlightenment has already responded with disbelief, classing it as part of superstition within the triad of superstition–religion–reason.

Outside the theologies of both "customary religion" and the Enlightenment, Gandhi does not have to believe or disbelieve in their concept of the miracle; he ventures instead another concept or quasi-concept of the miracle. Here the miracle names the experience of bare faith. And satyagraha is what is most proper to the miracle because it enacts the barest of bare faiths: limitless and unconditional daya or prem, "compassion" or "love." Gandhi will have said: satyagraha is the miracle, and the miracle is satyagraha.

The miracle of satyagraha is the love that arrives without announcement, and conversely the reciprocation that arrives without the slightest expectation. The "great yogi in Europe," Saint Francis of Assisi, and other yogis and fakirs in the "forests of India," could live with "serpents, etc" because they experienced limitless prem or love—this was their "miraculous remedy."[21] Because of their love, they command reciprocation even though their action is not intended to do so.

Gandhi is not sure that he himself has not experienced this miracle or power. "I know that I am filled with overflowing love. But is there any limit to love? I know that my love is not limitless [*aseem*]. Can I play with a serpent? I have a firm belief that even a serpent would be at peace in the presence of an incarnation [*murti*] of non-violence."[22]

In a letter in 1932, he returns implicitly to the distinction between the miracle of "customary religion" and his sense of the miracle by recalling the moment in the Mahabharata when the Pandavas' wife Draupadi is gambled away: "The protection of Draupadi's honour is not a miracle like the conversion of water into wine. The faith that God succors his devotees when they are in distress helps one, and the examples which support such faith are worth cherishing. If, however, a person cultivates devotion [*bhakti*] in expectation of such help, his devotion is of no value."[23]

Central to the miracle thus is the faith that must never be an expectation. The distinction ventured here between faith and expectation turns
on the bareness and indeed singularity of the former. To expect is to
ground in a reciprocal relation, where faith is conditional and likely to be
withdrawn if expectations are not met—where faith is everything but a
faith. Devotees by contrast experience an absolute faith—their faith cannot be withdrawn simply because it remains unreciprocated or unproven.

The bhakti traditions Gandhi inherits stress already pure, bare, and
absolute faith. If Gandhi radicalizes these traditions, he does so only—but
what an *only*!—by insisting that absolute or pure faith has some "thing"
proper to it: finitude or limits. To practice bare faith is thus to refuse to find
ontological or epistemological ground for one's faith, to make it only one's
own faith.[24] In this very observing of the limit, pure faith always already
provincializes both self and other, gives both a distinctive equality and finitude. Self: because the self's faith is here singular and ungrounded, the self
must remain open to the other's faith, acknowledge an absolute equality
with the other, because it can seek dominance over the other only by abandoning the singularity and bareness of its own faith. The other: because
even as the self submits to absolute equality with the other, it must refuse
the other's domination, as well as the other's claim to sovereign power over
either the self or any other other; it must constantly resist the other's claim
to ontological and epistemological grounds. What the self recognizes as
the other's absolute equality is the pure or absolute faith that constitutes
the other, with or without the other's knowledge.

Such finitude must, moreover, relinquish action organized by an "instrumental or anthropological definition" of means and ends.[25] But giving up the fruit of one's action does not merely lead to a situation where
the same actions can be carried out without desire for fruit. Rather, to
renounce fruit is to act so as to always and everywhere perform absolute
equality—this is the miracle of satyagraha. But that miracle and satyagraha,
if it ever happens, is only as nonviolent as Harishchandra is when he lifts
the sword to kill Taramati.

Acknowledgments

AMONG THE MOST PLEASURABLE aspects of writing this book have been the conversations that have accompanied it. It is not at all too much to say that this book would simply not have been possible but for the immense friendship and intellectual companionship that has come my way.

I have been especially lucky to have had an intense and sustained series of conversations for over a decade with a small group of friends in Minneapolis: Vinay Gidwani, Qadri Ismail, John Mowitt, and Simona Sawhney. In addition to reading and commenting on drafts, Vinay has constantly reminded me of the most urgent contemporary stakes of the project; the impress of our discussions is everywhere in the book. Conversations with Qadri helped bring me to the conceptual framings of this project, and our agreements and divergences over the years have incalculably refined and nuanced its stakes. John and Simona have often taken my thoughts, intensified them beyond recognition, and returned them to me. John, whose immense erudition is exceeded only by his generosity, also pointed me to crucial readings and debates, and offered powerful insights into many questions taken up here. Simona and I have discussed together many of the texts that figure here; she also provided critical comments on drafts of several chapters; conversations with her have repeatedly been like the shake of a kaleidoscope, leading me to recast entire arguments.

I have also been very fortunate in having a large circle of interlocutors and friends formerly or currently at the University of Minnesota, with whom I have at various points discussed some of the themes in this book. In the History Department, Chris Isett, Helena Pohlandt-McCormick, J.B. Shank, and Thomas Wolfe have been constant interlocutors. In addition, I especially thank: Bruce Braun, Cesare Casarino, Anna Clark, Lisa Disch, David Faust, Kirsten Fischer, Tamara Giles-Vernick, Francis Harvey, Allen Isaacman, Hiromi Mizuno, Patrick McNamara, Richa Nagar, and Gloria Goodwin-Raheja.

My debts to friends and interlocutors elsewhere too are immense: conversations with G. Arunima over the years have kept me alert to the ambiguities of Gandhi's arguments; but for the late Chris Bayly's insistence on the complexity and distinctiveness of Indian liberalism, I might have dealt with it with less care; Rustom Bharucha's comments helped me clarify the relation between my readings of Gandhi and those offered in other recent scholarship; the late Kirit Bhatt introduced me to Gujarati politics, and as the first militantly leftist Gandhian I knew closely, has left his own indirect impress on this book; Dipesh Chakrabarty's unstinting generosity and support helped me see the implications of the project at a time when I was not sure where it was going; an intense set of daily conversations, lubricated with plentiful single malt, over a month in 2007 in Mexico City with Ishita Bannerjee-Dube and Saurabh Dube convinced me of the centrality of religion as a concept to not just think about but think with; David Hardiman persuaded me of the importance of being attentive to the difference between Gandhi in Gujarati and English; Aishwary Kumar has read my essays since 2010, and the ensuing exchanges have been invaluable; Vinay Lal first spurred me to write about Gandhi and religion, and also provided some of the insights that led to this book; Venugopal Maddipati read the first half of the book at an early stage, and long e-mail exchanges ensued, sparking some of the questions explored in later chapters; Karuna Mantena, who read the manuscript for the Press, offered a range of incisive comments that greatly helped with the revisions; Jayant Meghani from his base in Bhavnagar constantly supplied me with books, and sometimes alerted me to works I did not know about; Dilip Menon read in 2012 the first complete version of the manuscript, and with his characteristic acuity offered comments that made me realize how much work remained to be done; discussions with Rosalind O'Hanlon many years back provided some of the kindling for what I offer here; Gyanendra Pandey's suggestions pushed me to revise many of my formulations, especially those around caste; Thomas Pantham, with whom I was fortunate enough to work with as an undergraduate, introduced me to Gandhi and insisted—years before I was willing to consider this—on the novelty of Gandhi's thinking; Rajeshwari Sundar Rajan's comments on an earlier draft of the chapter "Living by Dying" brought me to my understanding of Gandhi's radical conservatism as also of his self-sacrifice; Mrinalini Sinha (who turned out to also be the anonymous reader for the press) gave a transformative set of comments on an earlier draft of the Introduction, and her remarks have influenced several other parts of the book; Gayatri Chakravorty Spivak's comments on some of the chapters here, as well as the questions she has asked, led me to reformulate some key concerns of the book; Bina Srinivasan, before her untimely death, pressed me to think about what Gandhi's politics implied for those who were critical of his conservatism; in addition to our continuing conversation since 2005, Tridip Suhrud patiently went through the whole manuscript just before I was to send it off to the Press, and the ensuing flurry of e-mail exchanges left me clarifying some very important issues until the last possible minute; at a time when my knowledge of written Gujarati was even more rudimentary than it is now, Babu Suthar took time out from writing his novels and poetry, and helped me with the conceptual and philosophical implications of Gujarati terms, drawing out their stakes in a way that I would never have managed on my own.

My colleagues in the now-disbanded Subaltern Studies collective have been an intellectually formative influence ever since I joined the group in 1995. In addition to those mentioned above, I especially wish to thank, for many thought-provoking conversations: Shahid Amin, Partha Chatterjee, Sudipta Kaviraj, Shail Mayaram, the late M.S.S. Pandian, Gyan Prakash, and Susie Tharu.

Many other conversations and friendships over the years have also shaped this book. I especially wish to thank: Arun Agrawal, Ifthekar Ahmed, Anjali Arondekar, Prathama Banerjee, Manu Bhagavan, Ruchi Chaturvedi, Vinayak Chaturvedi, Alon Confino, Faisal Devji, Richard Drayton, Leela Gandhi, Rajkumar Hans, Walter Hauser, Patricia Hayes, Priya Kumar, Premesh Lalu, Saba Mahmood, Allan Megill, Uday Singh Mehta, Shyam Menon, Gary Minkley, Sanal Mohan, Himadeep Mupiddi, Janaki Nair, Nauman Naqvi, Akhileshwar Pathak, Anand Pandian, Mahesh Rangarajan, Anupama Rao, Ghanshyam Shah, James Scott, Janet Seed, K. Sivaramakrishnan, Sue Taylor, Ananya Vajpeyi and Milind Wakankar.

I have also benefitted incalculably from the insights that emerged in graduate seminars where the arguments offered here received some of their first iterations. I would especially like to thank: Lalit Batra, Abir Bazaz, Papori Bora, Aniruddha Dutta, Atreyee Gupta, Maria Gutierrez, Joya John, Emily Rook-Koepsel, Ketaki Jaywant, Sravanthi Kollu, Priti Misra, Ilona Moore, Quynh Pham, Sugata Ray, and Julietta Singh.

I felt extremely lucky to have been supported by the University of Minnesota in various ways during the course of this project, including: a single semester leave, the McKnight Land Grant fellowship, a Grant-in-Aid, an

Institute of Advanced Studies fellowship, and a sabbatical. The Institute of Global Studies, led by Evelyn Davidheiser, and the Department of History have also provided supportive environments where collegiality, teaching, and research seem to constantly well into each other.

I have also been fortunate to receive institutional support from elsewhere. I am especially thankful to the faculty and staff at the Center for Asian and African Studies, El Colegio de Mexico, where the book was first conceived; and the Center for Humanities Research, University of the Western Cape, where the first draft of the book was completed.

At the University of Minnesota Press, Jason Weidemann has been very enthusiastic and supportive of the project from an early stage, when I first broached the possibility of a book on Gandhi to him. I also had the extraordinary good fortune of working with Anne Carter twice—first, when, informally and as a friend, she read the entire manuscript carefully and provided extensive editorial suggestions, and, second, when the manuscript was assigned to her at the Press. I am also very lucky to have worked with Cherene Holland, whose meticulous edits to the manuscript have improved it greatly.

All thanks is perhaps inadequate, but the greater the debt the more acutely one remains aware of the inadequacy. With this awareness, I would like especially to thank: Shiney Varghese, without whom this project would not have been conceived, with whom I suspect almost every argument has been discussed threadbare at some point over the past many years, and whose own work on questions of rights has given form to this project. To my father, M. A. Skaria, for the incalculable gift of his militant atheism, his faith in knowledge; to my mother, Daisy Skaria, for her irrepressible enthusiasm for life; to Shiney's parents, the late M. A. Varughese for his gentle patience, and Santamma Varughese, for her curiosity about the faith she has; to Ramesh Desai or "Pappa" for the affectionate and heated arguments that we have had ever since I became part of his family; to Aru and Anvaya, whose childhood this project has accompanied, for their general irreverence, and also (this I am under strict injunction to mention) for their incomparable and absolutely amazing copyediting.

Notes

Preface

1. Gayatri Chakravorty Spivak, "The Politics of Translation," in *Outside in the Teaching Machine* (New York: Routledge, 1993), 190.

2. Each of these words, "dharma" and "religion," has of course a complex and storied genealogy, and at least some of the uncanniness of Gandhi's writing comes from the way these words occur there as also always translations of the other. This infection often activates and foregrounds what is usually recessive in either term by itself. For brevity's sake, I shall in this book often use only one of these words at a time, but it should be stressed that neither word can in Gandhi's writings be understood without its infection by the other.

3. The quotes around the term "concepts" are to acknowledge its simultaneous indispensability and inadequacy as a way of thinking. "Concept," with its connotation of mastery and sovereignty—of subsuming, without significant remainder, the particular under the universal—is in a sense always already ruined, for no concept ever masters its particulars. That ruination becomes especially acute where we are concerned with thinking such as Gandhi's, which at its most intriguing involves a vertiginous questioning of hierarchies of power. And yet, perhaps no questioning of power can ever erase power and domination—this is why the concept remains indispensable even where ruined; it must be drawn on under erasure. Many of the concerns of this book—for example, conscience, death, forgiveness, friendship, gift, trust, question, religion, and sacrifice—are concepts only in this ruined sense. Conversely, all these concerns are also "impossible" in the sense that they can never *knowably* occur in their purity; we can know them only in their ruined form.

4. G. W. F. Hegel, *Faith and Knowledge*, trans. and ed. Walter Cerf and H. S. Harris (Albany: State University of New York Press, 1977), 190.

5. It would be inadequate to think the apprehension of the death of God only in the terms that Hegel provides. Another and more radical sense of that apprehension rustles through the proclamation that Nietzsche's madman, who proclaims in the marketplace, "God is dead. God remains dead. And we have killed him. How shall we comfort ourselves, the murderers of all murderers?" Friedrich Nietzsche, *The Gay Science: With a Prelude in Rhymes and an Appendix of Songs*,

trans. Walter Kaufmann (New York: Vintage Books, 1974), 181. As Martin Heidegger points out, here the assertion "God is dead" is not only a "formula of unbelief" (63). Rather, "'God' and 'Christian god' in Nietzsche's thinking are used to designate the suprasensory world in general. God is the name for the realm of Ideas and ideals"—the world that since Plato has been considered to be the only true world," as more real than the sensory world. "The deposing of the suprasensory does away with the merely sensory and thus with the difference between the two." This devaluing of all values is in Heidegger's reading the nihilism that Nietzsche identifies with the death of God. Martin Heidegger, "The Word of Nietzsche: God Is Dead," in Heidegger, *The Question Concerning Technology and Other Essays,* trans. William Lovitt (New York: Garland, 1977), 63, 54, 61.

6. "Speech at Public Meeting, Vykom," March 10, 1925, *The Collected Works of Mahatma Gandhi,* 98 volumes (New Delhi: Publications Division, Government of India, 1999), available online at http://www.gandhiserve.org/cwmg/cwmg. html), 30:311; *Gandhijinu Akshardeha* [Gandhiji's Collected Works], 81 volumes (Ahmedabad: Navjivan Press, 1967–92), 26:174f. For Gandhi's writings apart from *Hind Swaraj,* citations are from his collected works in Gujarati (henceforth *Akshardeha*) and English (henceforth Gandhi, *Collected Works*). The endnotes first refer to the language in which the text is originally written, and then the language into which it is translated. Where the original is in English, I have provided a reference to the Gujarati version only if the translation (it is often impossible to know the identity of the translator) flags some interesting issues. I have also often modified the official translation of Gandhi's Gujarati writings, trying to bring the sentence structure and lexical sense closer to the Gujarati version, even if this involves sacrificing some of the apparent clarity of the English version. Interested readers should compare my translations with the official English translations available online. On some of these occasions, I have provided the original Gujarati phrase and also, where necessary, the official English translation in parentheses within quotation marks. In places where I have retained the official English translation, but sense an especially striking dissonance with the Gujarati, I have indicated the Gujarati word, and another possible translation of it, but without quotation marks. I have been especially fortunate in having extended conversations with Tridip Suhrud and Babu Suthar, which enabled me to draw on their deep knowledge of Gujarati language and literature. I have also drawn extensively on the brilliant critical edition of *Hind Swaraj,* which has been published recently: *Gandhi's Hind Swaraj: A Critical Edition,* annotated and edited by Tridip Suhrud and Suresh Sharma (Hyderabad: Orient Blackswan, 2010). Gandhi's collected writings in both Gujarati and English are now available online at https://www.gandhiheritagepor tal.org/. This website carries the first edition in English of Gandhi's *Collected Works*; my references are from the second edition, available online at the website mentioned earlier.

7. "Letter to Edmond and Yvonne Privat," February 5, 1925, Gandhi, *Collected Works,* 93:366–67.

8. For an erudite and comprehensive discussion of the relation between satya and God in Gandhi's writing, see Sushil Kumar Saxena, *Ever unto God: Essays on Gandhi and Religion* (New Delhi: Indian Council of Philosophical Research, 1988), 8–28.

9. For a discussion of the Bihar earthquake, and Gandhi's departure from the secular version of the immanent-transcendent distinction, see my "'No Politics without Religion': Of Secularism and Gandhi," in *Political Hinduism: The Religious Imagination in Public Spheres,* ed. Vinay Lal (New Delhi: Oxford University Press, 2009).

10. In this preface, my focus is on the most intriguing way—which is to say, the way that remains untimely, touching on and yet exceeding both his time and ours—that religion is articulated in Gandhi's writing. Later chapters will indicate how this untimeliness is only one possibility in his writing.

11. Heidegger, *The Question Concerning Technology and Other Essays,* 35.

12. The German sentence reads, "Denn das Fragen ist die Frömmigkeit des Denkens." This could be translated as: "Then/thus the question/questioning is the piousness of thought" (John Mowitt, personal communication).

13. Immanuel Kant, "Preface to the Second Edition," *Critique of Pure Reason,* trans. Norman Kemp Smith (New York: St. Martin's Press, 1965), 29.

14. Karl Marx, "On the Jewish Question," in *Selected Writings,* ed. David McLellan, 2nd ed. (Oxford: Oxford University Press, 2000), 55. An interesting implication of Heidegger's suggestion, noted earlier, is that Marx, because he deposes the suprasensory, can no longer be a materialist.

15. Carl Schmitt, *Political Theology* (Chicago: University of Chicago Press, 1985), 36.

16. I use the adjective "theological" in order to acknowledge that not all secularism is necessarily theological, that the commitment to the theologico-political is primarily today a mark of liberal secularism.

17. The phrase "public religion" is from José Casanova, *Public Religions in the Modern World* (Chicago: University of Chicago Press, 1994.) My concerns here are, of course, quite different from Casanova's: he is concerned with the sociological question of whether the secularization thesis is valid, while my concern here is with how the apprehension of the death of God is constitutive of modernity. Perceptions of secularization would be one factor that could provoke these apprehensions.

18. Hannah Arendt, *Love and Saint Augustine,* ed. Joanna Vecchiarelli Scott and Judith Chelius Stark (Chicago: University of Chicago Press, 1996), 57.

19. "Talk with Mars Chesley," on or before December 15, 1934, Gandhi, *Collected Works,* 65:461.

20. Gandhi sometimes resorts to the term "mystical" as a broad adjective for the religion he affirms; that resort is symptomatic of the groundless nature of his faith. He regards himself as a mystic, and satyagraha itself as closely related to mysticism. In 1942, for example, he says in an interview: "For the first time in history nonviolence instead of being confined to individuals, religious enthusiasts and mystics, has been brought down to the political field and been experimented on by vast masses of mankind." "Interview to Foreign Correspondents," July 15, 1942, Gandhi, *Collected Works*, 83:106.

21. "Satyagraha Leaflet–6," *Akshardeha*, 15:240; Gandhi, *Collected Works*, 17:448.

22. Arendt, *Love and Saint Augustine*, 94. For my limited purposes here, I accept Arendt's reading of Augustinian Christianity as adequate. It is likely that other readings may not allow for the distance I posit here between Augustine and Gandhi.

23. Ibid., 95–96.

24. *Gitashikshan, Akshardeha*, 32:180; Gandhi, *Collected Works*, 37:212. The sense of desh influential in Gandhi's time is "country" in a nationalist sense. That sense occurs in Gandhi's writings at many places, but as the passage above indicates, the term also often takes on an emphasis on place, tipping swadeshi over thus into a politics of neighborliness.

25. Ernesto Laclau reminds us that in mysticism God is "radically not representable," and that a long tradition has described this experience of the impossibility of representation as the "experience of finitude." Nonrepresentability and the associated experience of finitude are constitutive of Gandhi's religion, too. But the way these are articulated in Gandhi's writing may reveal some of the elisions of Laclau's formulations. First, for Laclau, God's ineffability requires that his name not be granted "any determinate content"; his name "has to be an empty signifier, a signifier to which no signified can be attached." At the same time, since this empty signifier names God, it also stands for the universal, for "Oneness." Second, this empty signifier of mystical discourse "reveals something belonging to the general structure of experience." The example "from the field of politics" Laclau gives of this general structure is the experience of hegemony—"a relation by which a particular content assumes, in a certain context, the function of incarnating an absent fullness." Ernesto Laclau, "On the Names of God," in *The Rhetorical Foundations of Society* (London: Verso, 2014), 46, 44, 48.

While I share Laclau's extremely important emphasis on the experience of finitude, it may be necessary to reformulate the arguments about it. Laclau's emphasis on the empty signifier may not adequately describe even his Christian examples—Meister Eckhart and Pseudo-Dionysius. Be that as it may, an emphasis on the empty signifier is especially inadequate as a way to think the religion that emerges from Gandhi's writing. In Gandhi's writing, first, the impossibility of representing God entails the destruction of God as a sovereign being, and the location of divinity instead in the immanent plurality and equality of all beings. God is thus experienced as a radical and singularizing finitude. Second, religion as such an experience of radical finitude must constantly relinquish any claim to hegemony. This is so because here oneness with the universal must be experienced in such a way as to recognize the truth of other universals, even as these universals are contested. Drawing on Gandhi's writing, we might even suggest, contrary to Laclau, that what separates groundless faith or "mysticism" from theological "forms" of religion (and these other forms could more appropriately be described as organized around an empty signifier), is precisely its relinquishment of sovereignty and hegemony.

26. Hannah Arendt, "Reflections on Little Rock," *Dissent* 6 (Winter 1959). I thank Simona Sawhney for urging me to read this essay.

27. Ibid., 50–54.

28. Ellison remarks: "I believe that one of the important clues to the meaning of experience lies in the idea, the *ideal* of sacrifice. Hannah Arendt's failure to grasp the importance of this ideal among Southern Negroes caused her to fly way off into left field" [emphasis in original]. See the interview with Ellison in Robert Penn Warren, *Who Speaks for the Negro* (New York: Random House, 1965), 343. Ellison's reading of sacrifice diverges in significant ways from that we shall see offered by Gandhi—like Gandhi's critic Dr. B. R. Ambedkar, he is much more acutely sensitive to the violence involved in the demand for sacrifice. But in the emphasis on the "ideal of sacrifice," Gandhi and Ellison also come curiously close.

29. When the three principles are conceived as "realms" that effectively exclude one another, phenomena like feminism and civil rights movements become incomprehensible (as in some ways they were to Arendt). Already by the time Arendt was writing, citizenship was recognized as not only political but also social: T. H. Marshall had made this point in a famous essay almost a decade before Arendt's intervention. See T. H. Marshall, *Citizenship and Social Class and Other Essays* (Cambridge: Cambridge University Press, 1950).

30. Étienne Balibar, *Equaliberty: Political Essays*, trans. James Ingram (Durham: Duke University Press, 2014), 3.

31. For Balibar's discussion of the mediation of the "modern, subjective remaking of right" through fraternity and property, see *Equaliberty*, 52.

32. Jacques Rancière, *Disagreement: Politics and Philosophy* (Minneapolis: University of Minnesota Press, 1999), ix–xi.

Introduction

1. *Dakshin Afrikana Satyagrahano Itihaas* [A History of the Satyagraha in South Africa], in *Akshardeha*, 29:62; *Satyagraha in South Africa*, trans. Valji Govindji Desai, in Gandhi, *Collected Works*, 34:88.

2. "Some English Words," December 28, 1907, *Akshardeha,* 7:426; Gandhi, *Collected Works,* 8:31.

3. "Johannesburg Letter," before January 10, 1908, *Akshardeha,* 8:22–23; Gandhi, *Collected Works,* 8:80.

4. Gandhi reminds his readers and listeners on several occasions that the "word *satya* comes from *sat,* which means "to be," "to exist" *[hovu].* "What Is Truth," November 20, 1921, *Akshardeha,* 21:428; Gandhi, *Collected Works,* 25:135.

5. *Hind Swaraj* is first published serially in 1909 in Gandhi's journal, *Indian Opinion.* It is then published in book form in early 1910, and is immediately banned by the British government. Gandhi then publishes an English translation by March of that year.

Given the easy availability online of at least three different editions in English, in citing passages from *Hind Swaraj,* I only indicate the relevant chapter. Since the chapters are quite short, it should not be difficult for readers to find the passage.

6. "My Notes," May 24, 1925, *Akshardeha,* 27:128; Gandhi, *Collected Works,* 31:386. I draw on the word "republican" here in the sense indicated by Kant in "Towards Perpetual Peace: A Philosophical Project." Kant writes there: "A constitution established, first on principles of the *freedom* of the members of a society (as individuals), second on principles of the *dependence* of all upon a single common legislation (as subjects), and third on the law of their *equality (as citizens of a state)*—the sole constitution that issues from the idea of the original contract, on which all rightful legislation of a people must be based—is a *republican* constitution." Kant also distinguishes the republican constitution from the democratic constitution by noting: "*Republicanism* is the political principle of separation of the executive power (the government) from the legislative power." Strictly speaking, he points out, democracy would not be republican but despotic, since here "all, who are nevertheless not all" decide "against one (who thus does not agree)." Immanuel Kant, *Practical Writings,* trans. and ed. Mary J. Gregor (Cambridge: Cambridge University Press), 322, 324. Later historical developments have revealed that, contrary to Kant's suspicion, republicanism and representative democracy are not opposed to each other. In what follows, the term "republican democracy" refers to a democracy drawing on these republican principles.

7. Gandhi translates the phrases *adhunik sudhara* or *adhunik sudharo* as "modern civilization." The word *sudhara,* which Gandhi picks up on in the phrase, becomes pervasive in nineteenth-century Gujarat, where it corresponds to and is often a translation of "reform" (and either Gandhi or his translators do so often translate it). Many *sudharak samaj* or reform societies are set up, and there are many self-styled "*sudharako*" or reformers. In Gujarat as in many other parts of India, *sudhara* was centrally about introducing a new civility. The phrase could thus equally well be translated as "modern/contemporary civility" or "modern/contemporary reform." The words "civility" and "reform" perhaps indicate better

than "civilization" the active orientation to change and self-making involved in the terms *sudhara* or *sudharo*. Tridip Suhrud writes in a personal communication (January 25, 2014): "I do however wish to think that MKG's usage [of *sudharo*] has the idea of the sanskrit root of *Dhri*, the one that holds and hence civilization. The term *adhunik* has a sense of transient, ephemeral, temporary, of today. My preference would be for transient civilization, which is closest to the sense in which MKG thought." Here I shall primarily use the translations "modern civilization" and "modern civility," but in the sense indicated here.

8. Gandhi's translation says: "Religion is dear to me and my first complaint is that India is becoming irreligious. Here I am not thinking of the Hindu or the Mahomedan or the Zoroastrian religion but of that religion which underlies all religions. We are turning away from God."

9. Partha Chatterjee, *Nationalist Thought in the Colonial World: A Derivative Discourse* (Minneapolis: University of Minnesota Press, 1983). Chatterjee stresses that Gandhi's critique emerges "from an epistemic standpoint situated *outside* [emphasis original] the standpoint of post-Enlightenment thought. As such, it . . . could have been adopted by *any member* [emphasis added] of the traditional intelligentsia in India, sharing the modes of thought of a large pre-capitalist agrarian society, and reacting to the alien economic, political and cultural institutions imposed on it by alien rule." If Gandhi's ideology acquires "tremendous power," this is because of its "relation to the historical development of peasant nationalist thought in India." Understood in this "historical context," its significance is that it achieves a "most important historical task"—that of enabling the "political appropriation of the subaltern classes by a bourgeoisie aspiring for political hegemony in the new nation-state" (99, 90, 100). Shahid Amin, in a similar vein, but focusing on the subaltern classes, points to how Gandhi's politics was appropriated to entirely different metaphors by the peasants who were supposed to be his "followers." See Shahid Amin, *Event, Metaphor, Memory: Chauri Chaura, 1922–1992* (Berkeley: University of California Press, 1995). I concur almost entirely with Amin's and Chatterjee's brilliant readings. I shall, however, be exploring the dissonant moments in Gandhi's writing—moments that remain untimely not only to the "most important historical task" they achieve but also to our present, summoning our readings even while remaining in the shadows.

10. These stakes were perhaps first signaled by Ashis Nandy in his profoundly generative book, *The Intimate Enemy: Loss and Recovery of the Self under Colonialism* (Delhi: Oxford University Press, 1982). Nandy, however, tends to read Gandhi as simply antisecular, ignoring Gandhi's participation in struggles for democracy or, in Gandhi's preferred phrases, "parliamentary swaraj," "political swaraj," and "republican form of government." Even a very partial list of those who have, in the wake of Chatterjee and Nandy, contributed to our rereading of Gandhi would include Leela Gandhi, David Hardiman, Vinay Lal, Karuna Mantena, Uday Mehta,

Faisal Devji, Aishwary Kumar, Parama Roy, and Tridip Suhrud. Where appropriate, I shall point to the resonances and departures from the arguments that these scholars make.

11. As the preface noted briefly, the link between secularism and Christianity is already stressed in an affirmative spirit by G. W. F. Hegel in the early nineteenth century, and in a more critical spirit in the late nineteenth century by thinkers as different from each other as Bruno Bauer, Karl Marx, and Friedrich Nietzsche. The way that modern religious movements are themselves the products of secularism has been indicated by many scholars; in the South Asian context, the scholarship of Gyanendra Pandey is especially relevant.

12. In an earlier essay, I had suggested that the dialogue in *Hind Swaraj* is between "a nationalist reader who is willing to use violence to drive the British out of India, and an editor who, ventriloquising Gandhi's explicit positions, argues that such violence would not bring about 'swaraj.'" I would now add: while the Reader is willing to use violence, this is not because he exemplifies the perspective of anarchists, the "extremists" in the Indian nationalist movements, or Hindu nationalists such as Savarkar. Rather, the violence the Reader envisages is that founding or revolutionary violence required to establish a parliamentary democracy. As Isabel Hofmeyr remarks in a characteristically nuanced essay: "This insistence on the Reader as a revolutionary has always struck me as slightly odd. If one were to envisage *Hind Swaraj* as a play, it would be difficult to imagine a fire-breathing revolutionary like Savarkar taking the part of the Reader, who is generally patient, polite, and biddable. Indeed, the idea of a revolutionary sitting patiently through Gandhi's speeches could almost shift the text toward comedy and parody." See Ajay Skaria, "Only One Word, Properly Altered: Gandhi and the Question of the Prostitute," *Economic and Political Weekly* 41, no. 49 (2006): 5065; and Isabel Hofmeyr, "Violent Texts, Vulnerable Ideas: *Hind Swaraj* and Its South African Audiences," *Public Culture* 23 no. 2 (2011): 287.

13. Gandhi does not use the term "autonomy" in the sense that I do here. But Gandhi's writings reveal that he is directly familiar—perhaps because of his training as a lawyer—with the works of Bentham, James Mill, John Stuart Mill, and Spencer, among others; he is also at least indirectly familiar with and sympathetic to Kant's arguments, which he encounters through the writings of William Salter, whose book *Ethical Religion* Gandhi enthusiastically translates in 1907 (see chapter 1).

14. "Open Letter to the Members of the Legislative Council and Legislative Assembly," Gandhi, *Collected Works,* before December 19, 1894, 1:202.

15. That association organizes in chapter 4 of *Hind Swaraj* his translation of the very word "rajsatta"—etymologically, kingly or sovereign *(raj)* power *(satta)*—as "self-government."

16. For a contemporary rearticulation that connects the citizen to autonomy and measure, see Jürgen Habermas, "On the Internal Relation Between Rule of Law and Democracy," *European Journal of Philosophy* 3, no. 1 (1995).

17. Immanuel Kant, *Groundwork of the Metaphysics of Morals* (Cambridge: Cambridge University Press, 1998).

18. "The Permanence of the Theologico-Political," in Claude Lefort, *Democracy and Political Theory* (Minneapolis: University of Minnesota Press, 1998). The contemporary implications of this conjoining of equality and liberty are forcefully elicited in Étienne Balibar, *Equaliberty: Political Essays,* trans. James Ingram (Durham: Duke University Press, 2014).

19. Derrida, *The Gift of Death,* trans. David Wills (Chicago: University of Chicago Press), 61.

20. The phrase is Dipesh Chakrabarty's. See his *Provincializing Europe* (Princeton: Princeton University Press, 2000), 9.

21. See her "Bonding in Difference: Interview with Alfred Arteaga, 1993–94," in *The Spivak Reader,* ed. Donna Landry and Gerald Maclean (New York: Routledge, 1996). For an intriguing further discussion of the paradox, see Wendy Brown, "Suffering Rights as Paradoxes," *Constellations* 7, no. 2 (2000).

22. "More Animal than Human," August 8, 1926, Gandhi, *Collected Works,* 36:5; *Akshardeha,* 31:97.

23. My stress on Gandhi's struggle to relinquish sovereignty sets the reading offered here apart from that ventured by Faisal Devji in *The Impossible Indian: Gandhi and the Temptation of Violence* (London: Hurst, 2013). While the book offers a plethora of sparkling insights, I cannot agree with what seems to me its founding premise—that Gandhi "fragmented sovereignty," affirming only the sovereignty involved in dying: "If we define as sovereign any authority that can ask people to kill or die in its name, then we must recognize that what Gandhi did was split the concept of sovereignty down the middle. By separating dying from killing and prizing the former as a nobler deed, he was doing nothing more than retrieving sovereignty from the state and generalizing it as a quality vested in individuals" (6).

This formulation is misplaced on two counts. First, to anticipate a theme I shall return to in chapter 3, to be sovereign is not only to have the power to kill, but even more importantly to have the power to die. This association of sovereignty with the power to offer the self as sacrifice is an ancient trope in both Western and South Asian traditions. Second, a distinctive feature of liberalism is that it generalizes this power—generalizes sovereignty—making it a quality vested in individuals, or more precisely the citizen. This is why citizens of a nation—and modern citizenship involves a claim to participation in sovereignty—are expected, unlike kingly subjects, to be willing to die for their country. In other words, Gandhi did not need to retrieve sovereignty from the state and generalize it—instead, this generalization is what he had to confront. And he confronted it, I suggest, by emphasizing a politics organized around the relinquishment of sovereignty.

24. This hostility to the majority persists in later years. See "Lokmanya," August 4, 1920, Gandhi, *Collected Works*, 21:11; "Notes," December 1, 1921, Gandhi, *Collected Works*, 25:167.

25. Gandhi uses the English words "minority" and "majority" in the Gujarati text; these are glossed into Gujarati as "minor party" and "major party," respectively. *Satyagraha in South Africa*, Part II, chapter 14.

26. A counterpoint with Gilles Deleuze and Félix Guattari might help clarify the distinctiveness of Gandhi's writing. Deleuze and Guattari write: "The three characteristics of minor literature are the deterritorialization of language, the connection of the individual to a political immediacy, and the collective assemblage of enunciation." By contrast, in Gandhi's writing the minor and minority are marked by only one criterion—the relinquishment of sovereignty (and relinquishment is neither antagonism nor overcoming). The beings who strive for such relinquishment do indeed assume characteristics that bear affinities to the three that Deleuze and Guattari identify. But these characteristics do not take the same "form," nor are they the only ones. See Gilles Deleuze and Félix Guattari, *Kafka: Towards a Minor Literature*, trans. Dana Polan (Minneapolis: University of Minnesota Press, 1986), 18.

27. "Nirbal ke Bal Ram," August 12, 1928, *Akshardeha*, 37:144; Gandhi, *Collected Works*, 42:349.

28. For Gandhi's association of self-surrender and dharma, see his "Letters on the Gita," Gandhi, *Collected Works*, 55:57.

29. This translation occurs, for example, in the leaflets that Gandhi publishes in 1919 during the Rowlatt satyagraha. After his return to India, the word *vinay* is part of the phrase *savinay bhang*—"civil disobedience."

30. Jacques Derrida, "Faith and Knowledge: The Two Sources of 'Religion' at the Limits of Reason Alone," in *Acts of Religion* (New York: Routledge, 2001), 71.

31. Because of his concern with proper sacrifice, there are immense resonances everywhere in Gandhi's writing with that other great twentieth-century thinker of sacrifice, Martin Heidegger. Heidegger writes in the postscript to "What Is Metaphysics?": "The need is for the truth of Being to be preserved, whatever may happen to human beings and all beings. The sacrifice is that of the human essence spending itself—in a manner removed from all compulsion, because it arises from the abyss of freedom—for the preservation of the truth of beings for Being. In sacrifice there occurs the concealed thanks that alone pay homage to the grace that being has bestowed upon the human essence in thinking, so that human beings may, in their relation to being, assume the guardianship of being." "Sacrifice is the departure from beings on the path to preserving the favor of being." "Sacrifice

tolerates no calculation, which can only ever miscalculate it in terms of utility of uselessness, whether the ends are placed low or set high. Such miscalculation distorts the essence of sacrifice. The obsession with ends confuses the clarity of the awe, ready for anxiety, that belongs to the courage of sacrifice which has taken upon itself the neighborhood of the indestructible." Martin Heidegger, Pathmarks, trans. William McNeill (Cambridge: Cambridge University Press, 1998), 236–37. Though I have not been able explicitly to trace the resonances and divergences between these two thinkers of sacrifice, the specter of Heidegger is never far away in the readings offered in this book.

32. Gandhi uses a range of words to describe limits and self-limitation—among them *hadh, seema, saiyam,* and *maryada.* That last adjective, *maryada* (boundary or limit, but also by implication rectitude and propriety, or the discipline necessary for sustaining these limits), is usually charged with positive valences in mainstream Hindu traditions. Rama, the eponymous hero of the *Ramayana,* for example, is often described as *maryada purush*—a phrase usually translated as perfect man or ideal man.

33. This Enlightenment contrast between finitude and infinitude has been exceedingly difficult to shake off. Even a thinker as critical of the Enlightenment as Michel Foucault finds it necessary to affirm a critique whose genealogy he traces back to Kant. In "What Is Critique?," he sees himself as refusing to accept the limits that Kant places on the Enlightenment. "[I]n relation to the *Aufklarung,* in Kant's eyes, critique will be what he is going to say to knowledge: do you know up to what point you can know? Reason as much as you want, but do you really know up to what point you can reason without it becoming dangerous? Critique will say, in short, that it is not so much a matter of what we are undertaking, more or less courageously, than it is the idea we have of our knowledge and its limits."

But these limits, Foucault stresses, must be transgressed: "Given this swinging movement, this slippage, this way of deporting the question of the *Aufklarung* into critique—might it not now be necessary to follow the opposite route? Might we not try to travel this road, but in the opposite direction? And if it is necessary to ask the question about knowledge in its relationship to domination, it would be, first and foremost, from a certain decision-making will not to be governed, the decision making will, both an individual and collective attitude which meant, as Kant said, *to get out of one's minority*" [emphasis added].

If we are to stay with the line of questioning Foucault that Spivak opened so powerfully over two decades ago, could it be that Foucault's argument, in this emphasis on the Enlightenment as the refusal of limits, not only surreptitiously reinscribes once again the autonomous subject, but makes that subject more powerful than ever? Foucault, "What Is Critique?," in *The Politics of Truth,* ed. Sylvère Lotringer and Lysa Hochroth (New York: Semiotext[e], 1997), 49, 47, 67. Gayatri Chakravorty Spivak, "Can the Subaltern Speak?," in *Marxism and the Interpretation of Culture,* ed. Cary Nelson and Lawrence Grossberg (Urbana: University of Illinois Press, 1988).

34. "Speech at Guildhouse Church," September 23, 1921, Gandhi, *Collected Works,* 53:398.

35. In his Gujarati writings, *daya* is also the translation often of the more classical Sanskrit word *karuna.* In translating verse 13 of chapter 12 of the *Bhagavad Gita,* for instance, he renders *karuna* as *daya.* See *Anasaktiyoga,* in *Akshardeha,* 41:126.

36. It will someday be appropriate to attend to how we could have largely ignored Gandhi's insistence on writing first in Gujarati whenever possible, or the divergences between the Gujarati and English texts. Almost all the scholarship on Gandhi in English has drawn on the English translations, and almost all scholarship on him in Gujarati has drawn on his Gujarati writings. And Gandhi's collected works in Gujarati are rarely available outside Gujarat—even major research libraries in India and elsewhere seem usually to have only the English collected works in their holdings.

37. My argument in what follows is anticipated in Tridip Suhrud's argument that *Hind Swaraj* is a bilingual text. See his *Reading Gandhi in Two Tongues and Other Essays* (Shimla: Indian Institute of Advanced Study, 2012).

38. "Preface to Indian Home Rule," March 20, 1910, Gandhi, *Collected Works,* 10:457.

39. I use these terms here in that Austinian spirit that doubts the stability of the distinction, but nevertheless retains it, with each—constative and performative—requiring the other for its operation.

40. For instance, he writes in a letter in 1917: "The English phrase 'passive resistance' does not suggest the power I wish to write about; 'satyagraha' is more appropriate *[barobar lagu padey chhe]*." Letter to Shankarlal, September 2, 1917, *Akshardeha,* 13:485; Gandhi, *Collected Works,* 16:6. Strikingly, he continues to be comfortable with "civil disobedience" as a translation of satyagraha, though he later introduces the translation "civil resistance." He also consistently argues that satyagraha is more than civil disobedience or civil resistance, and continues even when the latter is suspended. See Vinay Lal, "Gandhi's West and the West's Gandhi," *New Literary History* 40, no. 2 (2009): 281–313.

41. Hannah Arendt, *On Revolution* (New York: Viking Press, 1963), 19.

42. Hannah Arendt, *Crises of the Republic* (New York: Harcourt Brace Jovanovich, 1972), 66.

43. In this sense, Verity Smith's description of Arendt as "developing a contestatory constitutionalism of reverent disobedience" is perhaps even more apposite than Smith's explicit arguments might suggest. See her "Dissent in Dark Times: Hannah Arendt on Civil Disobedience and Constitutional Patriotism," in *Thinking in Dark Times: Hannah Arendt on Ethics and Politics,* ed. Roger Berkowitz, Jeffrey Katz, and Thomas Keenan (New York: Fordham University Press, 2010), 110.

44. Among those who have offered this insight are Giorgio Agamben, Wendy Brown, Dipesh Chakrabarty, Ranajit Guha, Jacques Derrida, Emmanuel Levinas, and Gayatri Chakravorty Spivak. In the chapters that follow, I engage with these thinkers where appropriate.

45. Uday Singh Mehta reads Gandhi as a conservative in the Burkean sense. Mehta suggests that patience and self-knowledge play the same role for Gandhi as tradition does for Burke. Moreover, Gandhi's India bears, in Mehta's telling, striking similarities to Burke's England. For Gandhi, India's "relevant ethos of unity preexisted the railways and was evident in a shared mode of life, which was knitted together by people traveling on foot or on bullock carts. Gandhi's suggestion is that the nation was the product of a long, slow process of social and psychic sedimentation; in contrast, nationalism is spurred by an attitude of political urgency." Uday Singh Mehta, "Patience, Inwardness, and Self-knowledge in Gandhi's *Hind Swaraj*," *Public Culture* 23, no. 2 (2011): 420–23.

46. Edmund Burke, *Reflections on the Revolution in France,* in *The Works of Edmund Burke* (Boston: Little, Brown, 1839), 3:54.

47. Speech on Swadeshi at a Missionary Conference in Madras, February 14, 1916, Gandhi, *Collected Works,* 15:159.

48. Jacques Rancière, *Disagreement,* trans. Julie Rose (Minneapolis: University of Minnesota Press, 1995), ix.

49. See, for instance, "Notes," September 29, 1919, *Akshardeha,* 16:176; Gandhi, *Collected Works,* 18:444.

50. *Gandhijinu Gitashikshan* (hereafter *Gitashikshan*), *Akshardeha,* 32:263; Gandhi, *Collected Works,* 37:311.

51. Speech at Mass Meeting in Ahmedabad, April 14, 1919, *Akshardeha,* 15:214; Gandhi, *Collected Works,* 17:422. For a discussion that touches among other things on *abhayadan* in Jain traditions, see James Laidlaw, "A Free Gift Makes No Friends," *Journal of the Royal Anthropological Institute* 6, no. 4 (2000). My argument here about the centrality of the gift to Gandhi's politics is anticipated in many ways by Rajeswari Sundar Rajan's brilliant essay, "Refusing Benevolence: Gandhi, Nehru, and the Ethics of Postcolonial Relations," in *Burden or Benefit: Imperial Benevolence and Its Legacies,* ed. Helen Gilbert (Bloomington: Indiana University Press, 2008).

52. Gayatri Chakravorty Spivak, "Scattered Speculations on the Subaltern and the Popular," *Postcolonial Studies* 8, no. 4 (2005): 476.

53. Spivak, "Can the Subaltern Speak?," 293. Spivak returns to this theme in some of her later essays. See her "Righting Wrongs," *South Atlantic Quarterly* 103, no. 2/3 (2004): 545; as well as "Responsibility," *boundary 2,* 21, no. 3 (1994).

54. Gyanendra Pandey, "In Defense of the Fragment: Writing about Hindu-Muslim Riots Today," *Representations* 37 (Winter 1992): 28–29.

55. *Provincializing Europe* (Princeton: Princeton University Press, 2000), 16.

56. Ibid., 255.

57. My arguments about Gandhi's politics clearly resonate with those that Uday Singh Mehta has ventured in a series of characteristically elegant and thoughtful articles. Mehta too thus stresses the centrality to Gandhi's "democratic ethics" of a fearless relation to one's own death. But there are divergences between our readings. The finitude Mehta sees as shared between Burke and Gandhi, as constitutive of Gandhi's conservatism, is not that of a relation to one's own death, but the somewhat different one of "self-knowledge," intimacy, and transparency. Thus Mehta's explanation of why the British were incapable of self-knowledge: "The essential form of empires was an outrage against the finitude of the city because empires, especially the Roman and later European ones, could not rely on the face-to-face encounters that gave the city its emotive stability and epistemic and institutional transparency." "As a political form, empires resist self-knowledge because such knowledge requires attending to the moral and civic integuments of the community, with its bounded contours. It is precisely such a community, that empires dilute and at their limit render impossible" (Mehta, "Patience, Inwardness, and Self-knowledge," 425, 426). I would suggest that while Gandhi certainly often sees his self-knowledge in these terms, it cannot be only so understood. Rather, self-knowledge here emerges as from friendship with one's own death, and the nonknowledge and opacity that such self-knowledge secretes.

Relatedly, it seems to me that Mehta may overstate the affinity between Burke and Gandhi. If we are to resort to a somewhat heavy-handed analogy, Burke's conservatism is closest to the politics Gandhi identifies with the figure of the arms-bearing warrior. Because of his emphasis on the absolute equality of all being, and relatedly on relinquishing everyday sovereignty, Gandhi's radical conservatism always destroys Burke's conservatism in one of the two ways noted above.

58. For a discussion of the work of the gift in *Provincializing Europe*, see my "The Project of Provincializing Europe: Reading Dipesh Chakrabarty," *Economic and Political Weekly* 44, no. 9 (2009).

1. Stumbling on Theological Secularism

1. "Shrimad Bhagavad Gita (Prastavna)," *Dharmavichar*, ed. Ramesh Shukla (Surat: Kavi Narmad Yugavart Trust, 1998), 159.

2. As Tridip Suhrud points out, Gandhi "was to later claim that he really became aware of the existence of God on that terrible night of May 5, 1891, at Portsmouth" "when he was about to surrender to his lust" but "was saved by the presence of Rama dwelling within his heart." Perhaps in the wake of that experience, the question of God, and of religion, becomes more pressing for Gandhi; and it is just three months later that he meets Raychandbhai. See Tridip Suhrud, "Gandhi's Ramanama," in *Speaking of Gandhi's Death*, ed. Peter de Souza and Tridip Suhrud (Delhi: *IIAS* and Orient BlackSwan, 2010), 133–47.

3. Speech on "Birth Centenary" of Tolstoy, September 10, 1928, Gandhi, *Collected Works*, 43:5; *Satyana Prayogo athava Atmakatha [An Autobiography, or the Story of My Experiments with Truth]*, Part IV, chapter 18. Given the number of editions available online, and given the shortness of the chapters, I shall limit myself in citing the *Autobiography* to providing the chapter numbers. For one critical edition online, see http://www.columbia.edu/itc/mealac/pritchett/oolitlinks/gandhi/index.html#part1. A downloadable copy is also available at http://www.archive.org/details/AnAutobiographyOrTheStoryOfMyExperimentsWithTruth.

4. See *Mokshamala,* chapter 29, in *Shrimad Rajchandra* (Agas: Shrimad Rajchandra Ashram, 2006), 78.

5. "Hinduism," Gandhi, *Collected Works,* 4:201f. Tridip Suhrud points out (personal communication) that Gandhi could also have interpreted the writings of Anna Kingsford and Edward Maitland, whom he is enthusiastic about during the 1890s, in terms of daya. (For an extremely helpful account of Gandhi's engagement with Kingsford, Maitland, and esoteric Christianity more broadly, see Kathyrn Tidrick, *Gandhi: A Political and Spiritual Life* (London: I. B.Tauris, 2006). Tidrick, however, treats Gandhi's religion as broadly continuous with these beginnings; my emphasis here is more on the way Gandhi inadvertently transforms even those traditions he tries to continue.

6. For an account of the way that Gandhi draws on liberal traditions of abstract equality, both in the years before *Hind Swaraj* and from a different perspective in later decades, see my "English Rule without the Englishman: Citizenship, Subalternity, and Gandhi's 'Reader,'" in *Hind Swaraj Revisted,* ed. Rajeev Bhargava (New Delhi: Routledge, forthcoming), and my "Relinquishing Republican Democracy: Gandhi's Ramarajya," *Postcolonial Studies* 14, no. 2 (2011).

7. "*Ethical Religion,* or Religious Ethics," *Akshardeha,* 6:300; "*Ethical Religion,*" Gandhi, *Collected Works,* 6:212–13.

8. For Adler's account of the society, see his *Society for Ethical Culture* (New York: Lehmaier and Bro., 1893). For an account of the founding of the Chicago branch of the society, see *The First Anniversary of the Society for Ethical Culture, Chicago, Abstract of a Lecture by William Salter* (Chicago: Radical Review Print, 1884).

9. Leonard Glick, cited in Geyla Frank, "Jews, Multiculturalism, and Boasian Anthropology," *American Anthropologist* 99, no. 4 (1997): 734.

10. Salter, *Ethical Religion,* 2nd ed. (London: Watts and Co., 1905 [originally published, Boston: Roberts Brothers, 1889]), 12.

11. Salter, *Ethical Religion,* 15.

12. William Salter, "Nietzsche's Attitude to Religion," *Journal of Philosophy* 20, no. 4 (1923): 105–6.

13. Ibid., 14, 16.

14. Ibid., 47.

15. Ibid., 16ff.

16. Ibid., 18, 65, 12, 16, 18.

17. Ibid., 66, 61, 60.

18. Schmitt, *Political Theology: Four Chapters on the Concept of Sovereignty* (Chicago: University of Chicago Press, 2006), 36.

19. Salter, *Ethical Religion,* 62.

20. Jeremy Bentham, *Introduction to the Principles of Morals and Legislation,* in his *Collected Works,* ed. John Bowring (New York: Russell and Russell, 1962), 1:143.

21. Jacques Derrida, *The Animal That I Therefore Am,* trans. David Wills (New York: Fordham University Press, 2007), 27f.

22. Jacques Derrida, *Of Grammatology,* trans. Gayatri Chakravorty Spivak (Baltimore: Johns Hopkins University Press, 1997), 120.

23. My argument here complements the one that Leela Gandhi makes—that this Benthamite position is part of a distinctive governmentality, "amplifying government activity to a vertiginous degree." See Leela Gandhi, *Affective Communities: Anticolonial Thought, Fin-de-Siècle Radicalism, and the Politics of Friendship* (Durham: Duke University Press, 2006), 91.

24. Ibid., 95f. It is this kind of responsibility that Spivak describes as "'the "duty of the fitter self' towards less fortunate others (rather than the predication of being-human as being called by the other, before will)." Spivak, "Righting Wrongs," *South Atlantic Quarterly* 103, no. 2/3 (2004): 535.

25. John Stuart Mill, *On Liberty,* 2nd ed. (London: Parker and Sons, 1859), 23.

26. Jeremy Bentham, "Letter to the Editor of the *Morning Chronicle,*" in *Collected Works,* ed. John Bowring (Edinburgh: William Tait, 1843), 10:549–50.

27. This emphasis on liberating those suffering from their own barbarism continues today—consider, for example, the desire of a certain Eurocentric French feminism to free Muslim women from the veil.

28. Open letter to the members of the Legislative Council and Legislative Assembly, before December 19, 1894, Gandhi, *Collected Works,* 1:193; Speech at a Public Meeting, Bombay, September 26, 1896, Gandhi, *Collected Works,* 1:410. He sought through various petitions to ensure that Indians and Kaffirs were treated differently. But by 1905, this attitude was changing. See "The Kaffirs of Natal," September 2, 1905, Gandhi, *Collected Works,* 4:398.

29. Speech at a Public Meeting, Bombay, September 26, 1896, Gandhi, *Collected Works,* 1:410.

30. "Indians in the O.R.C.," January 6, 1906, Gandhi, *Collected Works,* 5:59.

31. Johannesburg Letter, May 26, 1906, Gandhi, *Akshardeha,* 5:363; Gandhi, *Collected Works,* 5:235.

32. See, for instance, Letter to W. T. Stead, November 16, 1906, Gandhi, *Collected Works,* 6:95.

33. "Blue Book," February 29, 1908, Gandhi, *Akshardeha,* 8:50; Gandhi, *Collected Works,* 8:167.

34. "My Experiences in Gaol," March 7, 1908, Gandhi, *Collected Works,* 8:199.

35. "My Gaol Experiences–I," March 7, 1908, Gandhi, *Collected Works,* 8:182.

36. Ashwin Desai and Goolam Vahed, *The South African Gandhi: Stretcher Bearer of Empire* (Stanford: Stanford University Press, 2015), 61, 22.

37. R. Srivatsan has reminded us of Ambedkar's critique of upper-caste attempts at "Harijan reform." See his "From Ambedkar to Thakkar and Beyond," *Economic and Political Weekly* 43, no. 9 (2008).

38. Jacques Derrida, *On Cosmopolitanism and Forgiveness,* trans. Mark Dooley and Michael Hughes (London: Routledge, 2005), 28, 30. For now, suffice to note that the young Marx's very different understanding of the relation between Christianity and secularism, one that is in its way not as Eurocentric, and one that has yet remained surprisingly neglected in our readings of the relation between Christianity and secularism. For Marx, recall, the perfect Christian state is the atheistic state. But he comes to this argument by drawing on Ludwig Feuerbach to invert Hegel, and the relation between Christianity and secularism turns out to be a spectral one. "What makes a political democracy Christian is the fact that in it man, not only a single man but every man, counts as a sovereign being; but it is man as he appears uncultivated and unsocial, man in his accidental existence, man as he comes and goes, man as he is corrupted by the whole organization of our society, lost to himself, sold, given over to the domination of inhuman conditions and elements—in a word, man who is no longer a real species-being. The fantasy, dream, and postulate of Christianity, the sovereignty of man, but of man as an alien being separate from actual man, is present in democracy as a tangible reality and is its secular motto." Karl Marx, "On the Jewish Question," in *Selected Writings,* ed. David McLellan, 2nd ed. (Oxford: Oxford University Press, 2000), 57. For a further discussion of the distinctive spectrality that marks Marx's essay, see my "Ambedkar, Marx, and the Buddhist Question," *South Asia* 38, no. 3 (2015).

39. Gandhi is scarcely alone in this effort to identify a universal religion. For other examples, and for an account of the fascination with universal religion among many modern thinkers reworking Hinduism, see Arvind Sharma, *The Concept of Universal Religion in Modern Hindu Thought* (New York: St. Martin's Press, 1998).

40. *Atmakatha* or *Autobiography,* Part I, chapter 10.

41. Ibid., chapter 20.

42. See, for instance, "Letter to "The Natal Advertiser," September 29, 1893, Gandhi, *Collected Works,* 1:62.

43. *Atmakatha* or *Autobiography,* Part II, chapter 11.

44. Ibid., chapter 15.

45. For a discussion of the emergence of the category "religion," "world religion," and Tiele's role in the process, see Jonathan Smith, "Religion, Religions, Religious," reprinted in his *Relating Religion: Essays in the Study of Religion* (Chicago: University of Chicago Press, 2004), 189ff. This affirmation of "world religions" occurs within a framework that places Christianity at the top. See Tomoko Masuzawa, *The Invention of World Religions, or, How European Universalism Was Preserved in the Language of Pluralism* (Chicago: University of Chicago Press, 2005).

46. Discussion with C. F. Andrews, November 28, 1936, Gandhi, *Collected Works,* 70:60.

47. "Hindu-Muslim Tension: Its Cause and Cure," May 29, 1924, Gandhi, *Collected Works,* 28:61.

48. "Notes," September 29, 1921, Gandhi, *Collected Works,* 24:341.

49. To this extent, it may be necessary to qualify Tomoko Masuzawa's argument, indicated already in the title of her book—*The Invention of World Religions, or, How European Universalism Was Preserved in the Language of Pluralism*. While a profoundly exclusionary universalism certainly continues to be at work in the anticolonial deployment of terms such as "world religion," this universalism is in its anticolonial iteration no longer either Christian or European. If the discourses of secularism and universalism can be so easily adopted by elite Indian nationalists, it is because they can draw also on South Asian traditions to produce their own exclusionary and formal universalisms that appropriate and rework European categories.

50. "Open Letter to the Members of the Legislative Council and Legislative Assembly," before December 19, 1894, Gandhi, *Collected Works,* 1:193.

51. It is through his engagements with the suffragette movement, perhaps more than with Thoreau or Tolstoy, that Gandhi develops his understanding of liberal civil disobedience and passive resistance. See James Hunt, "Suffragettes and Satyagraha: Gandhi and the British Women's Suffrage Movement," in *An American Looks at Gandhi: Essays in Satyagraha, Civil Rights, and Peace* (New Delhi: Promilla Publishing, 2005). (I thank Karuna Mantena for pressing me to explore the genealogies of Gandhi's engagement with liberal civil disobedience.)

52. Jürgen Habermas, "Civil Disobedience: Litmus Test for the Democratic Constitutional State," in *Berkeley Journal of Sociology* 30 (1985).

53. John Rawls, *A Theory of Justice* (Cambridge: Harvard University Press, 1971), 363. For a review of the liberal debate on civil disobedience, see Jean Cohen and Andrew Arato, *Civil Society and Political Theory* (Cambridge: MIT Press, 1994).

54. "The Great Trial," March 23, 1922, Gandhi, *Collected Works,* 26:381.

55. *Satyagraha in South Africa,* chapter 12, Gandhi, *Akshardeha,* 29:62; Gandhi, *Collected Works,* 34:87.

56. "The Laws of Reflection," in his *Psyche,* vol. 2 (Stanford: Stanford University Press, 2008). It is ironic that thinkers as different as Charles Taylor, Jacques

Derrida, and Samuel Huntington should work with the same massive presumption of an autochthonous West—or, in the case of Derrida, the autochthonous world of Abrahamic religions—from where the phenomenon of modernity erupts. (For one influential statement of this presumption, see Charles Taylor, "Two Theories of Modernity," *Public Culture* 11, no. 1 [1999]: 153–74). What sets Derrida abysally apart from the other two, of course, is that his own writings provide the resources to question that presumption, even if this presumption does not always deconstruct itself in his writing.

57. "Speech in Reply to Students' Address," *Trivandrum*, March 13, 1925, Gandhi, *Collected Works*, 30:411.

58. Derrida often explicitly assumes a European origin for law and modernity, as in the passage above. That assumption is all the more surprising since, if we were to read his text beyond what he "as a controlling subject has directed in it," it would be possible to argue that his writing does not require the assumption. Gayatri Spivak, "Translator's Preface," in Jacques Derrida, *Of Grammatology* (Baltimore: Johns Hopkins University Press, 1998), lxxxvii.

59. *Dakshin Afrikana Satyagrahano Itihaas [A History of the Satyagraha in South Africa]*, in Gandhi, *Akshardeha*, 29:69; translated into English as *Satyagraha in South Africa*, trans. Valji Govindji Desai, in Gandhi, *Collected Works*, 34:93.

60. Perhaps unsurprisingly, President Barack Obama articulates the logical converse of this Rawlsian emphasis on perfect democracies, when in his Nobel Prize address he cites the example of Hitler and Al Qaeda to argue that "evil does exist in this world" and that a just violence is needed to confront evil. Quite clearly, given that Obama also here expresses admiration for Gandhi and King, a consistent pursuit of this argument would need to make one of two mutually exclusive arguments: either that racism, colonialism, imperialism, and apartheid are not as evil as fascism and terrorism (a familiar imperial excuse), or that violence against the former is as justified as against fascism (the rejuvenation of a revolutionary program).

61. "The Natal Rebellion," Gandhi, *Collected Works*, 5:179.

62. Gandhi, *Atmakatha* or *Autobiography*, Part IV, chapter 24.

63. Ibid.

64. "Interview to Tingfang Lew, Y. T. Wu, and P. C. Hsu," January 1, 1939, Gandhi, *Collected Works*, 74:384. See also his interview the same day with S. A. Tema, a member of the African Congress who was visiting from Johannesburg. "Interview to S. S. Tema," January 1, 1939, in ibid., 389.

65. "South Africa Resolution," June 26, 1939, Gandhi, *Collected Works*, 76:66.

66. No English translation of the adaptation is published in *Indian Opinion*, though there seems to have been an unauthorized translation later (which may be the one reproduced in the *Collected Works*). Gandhi does not seem to have been enthusiastic about the English translation of his adaptation. He writes in 1925:

"The Gujarati itself as the preface makes it clear is not an original effort but an adaptation from an American publication called *Ethical Religion* by Mr. Salter. The translation came under my notice in Yeravda Jail and I regretted to notice the absence of any mention of the source from which I had borrowed. The translator himself I understand did not rely upon the original Gujarati but a Hindi translation. The English rendering therefore is a round-about thing." "God and Congress" March 5, 1925, Gandhi, *Collected Works*, 30:335.

67. "Niti Dharma or Dharma Niti," January 5, 1907, *Akshardeha*, 6:352–53; Gandhi, *Collected Works*, 6:214.

68. "Niti Dharma or Dharma Niti," February 16, 1907, *Akshardeha*, 6:367; Gandhi, *Collected Works*, 6:283f.

69. Given the paucity of his remarks on the subject, we can only speculate on the connections between this rejection of the *purushartha* of immeasurable pity and his questioning of that strand of Christianity that, in its insistence that Christ dies for the sins of humans, portrays Christ as the first and primary practitioner of immeasurable pity. Gandhi encounters several Christians who make this claim in order to argue that only Christianity can offer salvation. These arguments, he reports, leave him dissatisfied; he feels that their arguments misrepresent Christ. To seek *purushartha* through immeasurable pity, then, is to become Christ-like, at least by this reading of Christ. See his *Atmakatha* or *Autobiography*, Part II, chapter 15, for one account of such a meeting.

70. The terms "general responsibility" and "absolute responsibility" are discussed at greater length in chapter 2, and they implicitly frame the discussion of satyagraha in later chapters. Though drawn from Derrida, later chapters will imbue these terms with valences that diverge somewhat from those that Derrida foregrounds. See Jacques Derrida, *The Gift of Death*, trans. David Wills (Chicago: University of Chicago Press, 1995), chapter 3.

71. For a different reading of the phrase "immeasurable pity," see Aishwary Kumar, "The Ellipsis of Touch: Gandhi's Unequals," *Public Culture* 23, no. 2 (2011).

72. Jacques Derrida, "Faith and Knowledge: The Two Sources of 'Religion' at the Limits of Reason Alone," in *Acts of Religion*, ed. Gil Anidjar (London: Routledge, 2002), 43, 62.

73. Jacques Derrida, *Rogues: Two Essays on Reason*, trans. Pascale-Anne Brault and Michael Naas (Stanford: Stanford University Press, 2005), 142.

74. Derrida, "Faith and Knowledge," 47, 53.

75. Derrida, *Rogues*, 82.

76. Derrida, "Faith and Knowledge," 49, 57. See also Immanuel Kant, *Religion within the Limits of Mere Reason, and Other Writings*, trans. and ed. Allen Wood and George Di Giovanni (Cambridge: Cambridge University Press, 1998), 71.

77. Derrida, *Rogues*, 150f.

78. Ibid., 153.

79. Derrida, "Faith and Knowledge," 47.

80. Derrida, *Rogues,* 36, 72.

81. The phrases are from "Force of Law," 11 *Cardozo Law Review* (1990): 993.

82. Derrida, *Rogues,* 30f.

83. Ibid., 33.

84. Ibid.

85. Ibid., 31.

86. Derrida, "Faith and Knowledge," 95.

87. Ibid., 85f.

2. Between Two and Three

1. Jacques Derrida, "White Mythology: Metaphor in the Text of Philosophy," *New Literary History* 6, no. 1 (1974): 7.

2. Dipesh Chakrabarty, *Provincializing Europe: Postcolonial Thought and Historical Difference* (Princeton: Princeton University Press, 2000), 30; Partha Chatterjee, *Nationalist Thought in the Colonial World: A Derivative Discourse* (London: Zed Books, 1986).

3. Perhaps it is this offer of daya that so infuriates racists like Winston Churchill—as Ashis Nandy pointed out long back, domination is perhaps most severely threatened when it encounters such "non-players." See Ashis Nandy, *The Intimate Enemy: Loss and Recovery of Self under Colonialism* (Delhi: Oxford University Press, 1982).

4. Gandhi recognizes the emergence of the concept of abstract equality, and the brotherhood this presumes, as a crucial moment in the consolidation of "modern civilization," and he quite often associates this emergence with the French Revolution. During a tour to the French-influenced areas of South India in 1934, for instance, he says that it was France that first gave the world the three significant words "Liberty, Equality, Fraternity" *[swatantrata, samaanta, aney bandhuta.]* Speaking just a day later in Pondicherry, he again remarks: "Equality *[samaanta]* and brotherhood were brought into France several hundred years before people began to realize that there was anything like brotherhood of man. The bravest of them fought and bled for that realization." Gandhi, "Speech at Public Meeting," Karaikal, February 16, 1934, *Collected Works,* 63:167; *Akshardeha,* 57:171. Gandhi, "Speech at Public Meeting," Pondicherry, February 17, 1934, *Collected Works,* 63:172–73; *Akshardeha,* 57:177.

5. It would be fascinating to explore the resonances between Gandhi's relinquishment of sovereignty and Heiddeger's questioning of "onto-theo-logy." That neologism names in Heidegger's writings the way the dominant metaphysical tradition conceives the unity of being as the unity of the "ontologic and theologic: beings as such in the universal and primal *at one with* beings as such in the highest

and ultimate." This unity necessarily entails also a distinctive way of conceiving difference: it "represents beings in respect of what differs in the difference, and without heeding the difference as difference. What differs shows itself as the Being of beings in general, and as the Being of beings in the Highest." Heidegger, "The Onto-theo-logical Constitution of Metaphysics," 61, 72.

6. "*Ladshe te ghavaashe pan khara. Shareer shareer afdaye tyare teni nishani rahej. Tema nyaya sho hoi shake?*" The last two sentences are missing in the English translation. I will return later in the chapter to this curious omission.

7. Aristotle, *The Nicomachean Ethics,* trans. J. A. K. Thomson (Harmondsworth: Penguin, 1953), 177.

8. "Modern Science, Metaphysics, and Mathematics," in Martin Heidegger, *Basic Writings,* ed. David Farrell Krell (New York: HarperCollins, 1977), 253.

9. For a discussion of this revolt, and why Bhils could never become men, see my "Shades of Wildness: Tribe, Caste, and Gender in Western India," *Journal of Asian Studies* 56, no. 3 (1997).

10. Since the Reader is willing to adopt "any means whatsoever" to secure swaraj, it has been easy to presume that the Reader argues that the right end (here, swaraj in his sense) justifies any means, while the Editor insists on right means, or a noninstrumental relation between means and ends. But such a reading would be misplaced for reasons both contextual and textual. Contextually, the Reader is modeled on Pranjivandas Mehta, a jeweler who remains a close friend of Gandhi in later decades too, and who is a staunch liberal. Textually, the parliamentary democracy the Reader seeks is one of the most comprehensive institutional orderings possible of right means in the sense that this term acquires with the Kantian categorical imperative.

11. Jawaharlal Nehru, *The Discovery of India* (Delhi: Oxford University Press, 1981), 60.

12. "The Great Trial," Gandhi, *Collected Works,* 26:381. As will be evident, my reading of Gandhi's liberalism differs from that offered by Faisal Devji in *The Impossible Indian.* Devji contrasts the "liberal regime of contending interests" to friendship, which "has to remain disinterested to be itself" (69). Relatedly, Devji presumes that "the Mahatma's vision was a deeply liberal one, not least because he thought that liberalism could only achieve perfection in an imperial order, where interests might appear in their naked abstraction without having to appeal to the prejudices of the greater number for success" (46–47). I have been suggesting, rather, that while Gandhi is indeed a liberal in the years before *Hind Swaraj,* his liberalism is organized not around contending or individual interests or self-ownership (as in the Lockean tradition) but around an almost deontological emphasis on abstract equality. (These two traditions are not, of course, opposed to each other, as the young Marx brilliantly demonstrates in "The Jewish Question.") Abstract equality, Gandhi remains convinced almost until 1906, is the best

way of conceiving the rights of the minor, and of protecting these rights. And even after he abandons this conviction, he remains convinced almost until 1920 that the British imperial order is adequate to protect abstract equality.

13. "Preface to 'Indian Home Rule,'" March 20, 1910, Gandhi, *Collected Works*, 10:459.

14. Socrates engages with his interlocutors by eliciting the presumptions of their arguments, showing that these presumptions are contradictory or otherwise untenable, and leading them to Socrates' arguments. In this sense, the Socratic dialogue is a monologue, with the other posited only in order to be overcome. This dialogue's truth and totality can allow little legitimate space for another argument or position. Gilles Deleuze and Félix Guattari, *What Is Philosophy?* (New York: Columbia University Press, 1994), 29; for the antidemocratic spirit of Socrates' questioning, see Rancière, *The Ignorant Schoolmaster* (Stanford: Stanford University Press, 1991).

15. Sawhney, *The Modernity of Sanskrit* (Minneapolis: University of Minnesota Press, 2009), 94ff. The way the *Gita* can be read as the affirmation of a general responsibility may provide a clue to why so many Indian nationalists turn to it in the late nineteenth and early twentieth centuries. Quite apart from the crucial historical contingencies that made the *Gita* available, perhaps it also accorded conceptually with their needs. These thinkers battled a colonial civilizing mission that claimed its legitimacy from the general responsibility of humanism. Could it be that in claiming and producing an alternative to this, they sought another text that could provide a framework for general responsibility? And could the decline of nationalist interpretations of the *Gita* from the second half of the twentieth century be connected to the fact of political independence and the way this transformed debates over general responsibility, making them more specific, linked to the law of the land?

16. Coursing through his dissatisfaction again is the question of what is proper to the ownmost—the word *potani* or "own" is repeated twice in the Gujarati, though the emphasis on the "own" is more obscured both times in the English.

17. The word *sanchakam* could be a neologism—I have not been able to find it in standard dictionaries of Gandhi's time. It is translated into English as "machinery," but this translation glosses over the conceptuality of the phrase.

18. Friedrich Nietzsche, "On the Genealogy of Morals," in *On the Genealogy of Morals and Ecce Homo*, trans. Walter Kaufmann and R. J. Hollingdale (New York: Vintage Books, 1989), 45.

19. In all of this, there are striking if entirely momentary resonances between the way *Hind Swaraj* questions "modern civilization" and the questioning of the Enlightenment that Max Horkheimer and Theodor Adorno undertake in *Dialectic of Enlightenment*. It would be an interesting project indeed to track the fundamental divergences between these two texts.

20. This affirmation of the violence of the two also starts out on a register that might be read as affirming the colonial fantasy of a measure that, internal to two, refuses three. Thus, in the passage above, the criterion of vengeance is own-ness ("own hands," *panch* of own kin), and the "own" is never very far from the one that segues into three. But this register is destabilized by the centrality of one's own death.

21. The Editor attacks life in this sense most systematically in chapter 12, where he deals with doctors and modern medicine. "The European doctors know no bounds. For the sake of a wrong care of only the body, they take annually lakhs of lives; they conduct trials on *jeevto jeev* [living lives]. No religion tolerates this. Hindu, Musalman, Parsi, Christian all say that we need not kill so many *jeevo* [lives] for the sake of the human body." Here he does not pick on vivisection episodically, as an objectionable but separable feature of modern medicine; rather, it is symptomatically constitutive of modern medicine. As a practice, vivisection is revealing of the inclusionary transcendence that marks the life that modern medicine seeks to sustain. It is concerned with animals solely because of their common biological life with humans—this is what makes experiments on animals relevant for the human body. And yet, in making animals into objects that could be experimented on in order to develop medicines that treated the human body, it also makes clear the particular nature of that common biological life: this is a life that is both included within and transcended by the life of the human. Medicine thus produces the human not as a singular category, but as a specific one. For the Editor, this common or specific life is not at work only in the human relation with animals; it is also at work in colonial rule and other forms of domination, including those named by the logic of the "third party." See Ajay Skaria, "The Strange Violence of *Satyagraha*: Gandhi, *itihaas,* and History," in *Heterotopias: Nationalism and the Possibility of History in South Asia,* ed. Manu Bhagavan (Delhi: Oxford University Press, 2010).

22. For a fascinating discussion of *asuras* and *rakshasas,* and the distinction between them (which Gandhi does not seem to note), see Sanjay Palshikar, "The Asura and the Gita," *Seminar* 608 (2010).

23. "My Notes," April 4, 1921, *Akshardeha,* 21:476; Gandhi, *Collected Works,* 25:191.

24. Emmanuel Levinas, *Entre Nous: Thinking of the Other* (New York: Columbia University Press, 2000), 143–44.

25. Emmanuel Levinas et al., "The Paradox of Morality: An Interview with Emmanuel Levinas," trans. Andrew Benjamin and Tamra Wright, in *The Provocation of Levinas: Rethinking the Other,* ed. Robert Bernasconi and David Wood (London: Routledge, 1988), 178.

26. This profound racism is by now recognized more widely than it was until the 1990s. See, for instance, Howard Caygill, *Levinas and the Political* (London:

Routledge, 2002); and Simon Critchley, "Five Problems in Levinas's View of Politics and the Sketch of a Solution to Them," *Political Theory* 32, no. 2 (April 2004).

27. "Talk with a Pacifist," before March 12, 1938, Gandhi, *Collected Works*, 73:15.

28. To note a trope that I shall not be attending to systematically in this book: both here and elsewhere, Gandhi thinks the limit by emphasizing hands and feet. For two interventions that thoughtfully reflect respectively on Gandhi's "spiritual and political ideology of walking," and on "the hand [for Gandhi] as an instrument of thought," see Javed Majeed, *Autobiography, Travel, and Postnational Identity: Gandhi, Nehru, and Iqbal* (London: Palgrave Macmillan, 2007), 96; and Aishwary Kumar, *Radical Equality: Ambedkar, Gandhi, and the Risk of Democracy* (Stanford: Stanford University Press, 2015), 101–2. In anticipation of further exploration on some other occasion, I would, however, add a supplementary remark to these essays: what is most interesting about feet and hands (especially hands) in Gandhi's writing is their doubleness: they exemplify not only finitude, as these books note, but also the moment that transforms finitude—for example, when machines become part of hands and feet.

29. "Discussion with G Ramachandran," October 21, 22, 1924, Gandhi, *Collected Works*, 29:270.

30. The term "aporia" is especially apposite to describe the stakes of satyagraha. Derrida contrasts the "problem," which is marked by a certain shielding and protection (and, one should say, sovereignty), with the "aporia," which encounters the impossibility of such shielding and protection. See Jacques Derrida, *Aporias*, trans. Thomas Dutoit (Stanford: Stanford University Press, 1993), 11–14.

31. Personal communications from Tridip Suhrud, October 28 and 29, 2014.

32. I have not been able to ascertain whether there was a lexical or philosophical Gujarati tradition that opposed the three of *trahit* to the three of the concept of number. It is certainly striking that Gandhi here presumes a contrast between the *treeja* and the *trahit* as though readers would be already familiar with its stakes, and did not need further explication.

3. The Warrior's Sovereign Gift

1. "The Dharma of *Aapbhog*," June 20, 1920, *Akshardeha*, 17:474; Gandhi, *Collected Works*, 20:404.

2. "Self-sacrifice," Gandhi, *Collected Works*, 3:407. For his exposure in the early 1900s to the theme of self-sacrifice in Annie Beasant's readings of the *Gita*, see Kathryn Tidrick, *Gandhi: A Political and Spiritual Life* (New York: I. B. Tauris, 2006), 60ff.

3. Gandhi's translation: "That nation is great which rests its head upon death as its pillow. Those who defy death are free from all fear."

4. "Letter to C. F. Andrews," July 18, 1918, Gandhi, *Collected Works*, 17:157.

5. "The Fear of Death [*Maranbhay*]," August 14, 1921, *Akshardeha*, 20:471; Gandhi, *Collected Works*, 24:85. For some beautifully made and analogous arguments about Gandhi's insistence on a fearless relation with one's own death, see Uday Mehta, "Gandhi and the Burden of Civility," *Raritan: A Quarterly Review* (June 2013).

6. John Locke, *Two Treatises on Government*, book 2, chapter 5, section 27.

7. "Speech at Gurukul Anniversary," March 20, 1916, Gandhi, *Collected Works*, 15:203–4.

8. "Message of Gokhale's Life," before February 4, 1916, Gandhi, *Collected Works*, 15:145. The reference is to Book 16:1–3, in the *Bhagavad Gita*.

9. One of the earliest systematic arguments that Gandhi makes about self-sacrifice is in 1920 in an essay that begins with a verse from the *Gita* (IV, 31) and a passage from the *Tulsi Ramayana*. See "The Dharma of *Aapbhog*," *Akshardeha*, 17:474–75; Gandhi, *Collected Works*, June 20, 1920, 20:404. He comes back to this theme in the *Gitashikshan*, his lectures on the *Gita*. See especially the passages from the *Gitashikshan* in *Akshardeha*, 32:127–37; Gandhi, *Collected Works*, 37:132–47.

10. "At It Again," May 7, 1925, Gandhi, *Collected Works*, 31:285; *Akshardeha*, 27:36.

11. "Speech at Prayer Meeting," August 24, 1946, Gandhi, *Collected Works*, 92:62.

12. "Nagpur Congress," January 9, 1921, *Akshardeha*, 19:183–84; Gandhi, *Collected Works*, 22:190.

13. This translation seems to be in 1910. See "Our Publications," May 7, 1910, Gandhi, *Collected Works*, 11:35.

14. In his speeches around this time, Gandhi stresses that the Dharalas, Vaghris, and Patidars have the "qualities of Kshatriyas" in common.

15. "Speech at Public Meeting," Dakor, October 27, 1920, *Akshardeha*, 18:361; Gandhi, *Collected Works*, 21:401.

16. "Letter to Maganlal Gandhi," July 15, 1918, Gandhi, *Collected Works*, 17:150.

17. "Is This Humanity–III," November 4, 1926, "Ahimsa–III," October 24, 1926, Akshardeha, 31:491; Gandhi, *Collected Works*, 36:428f.

18. "Tangled Business," May 15, 1921, *Akshardeha*, 20:87; Gandhi, *Collected Works*, 23:147.

19. "The Meaning of the Moplah Rising," October 10, 1921, Gandhi, *Collected Works*, 24:448.

20. "Speech at Gujarati Political Conference," November 4, 1917, *Akshardeha*, 14:59; Gandhi, *Collected Works*, 16:128–29. The relation with death involved in self-sacrifice resonates with Heidegger's emphasis on Dasein's being-toward-death. Saving for another occasion a more sustained exploration of these resonances, suffice here to note: first, that the trope of self-sacrifice, whether by the satyagrahi or *duragrahi*, activates the being-toward-death that already marks all being; second,

the emphasis on self-sacrifice foregrounds a line of thinking what sometimes remains obscured, though very much there, in Heidegger's writing: that the only way to experience love for the other is through one's own death. As such, the Levinasian claim that in Heidegger's writing the deaths of others are secondary to one's own death is quite thoroughly misplaced. Drawing on Heidegger's arguments, one could say: I experience grief at the death of others only because in loving them I have already died, and live a life that is after that death (to say this is quite different from saying that I love them so much that when they die, I too die).

21. "The Story of a Warrior for Truth [satyavir]," Akshardeha, 8:204; Gandhi, Collected Works, 8:288. In the Appendix to Hind Swaraj, Gandhi recommends several books for further reading. Among them is The Defence and Death of Socrates— presumably a reference to a translation by that name by Henry Cary, published in 1905. Very likely this is the source for Gandhi's translation. For a discussion of Gandhi's relation with Plato, see also Phiroze Vasunia, "Gandhi and Socrates," African Studies 74, no. 2 (2015).

22. G. W. F. Hegel, Phenomenology of Spirit, trans. A. V. Miller (Oxford: Oxford University Press, 1976), sec. 194, p. 117.

23. Hannah Arendt, The Origins of Totalitarianism (New York: Harcourt Brace, 1951), 478.

24. "Speech on Deshbandhu's Shraadh Day," July 12, 1925, Akshardeha, 27:282; Gandhi, Collected Works, 32:73.

25. "Speech at Ras," June 26, 1918, Gandhi, Collected Works, 17:100.

26. Georges Bataille, The Accursed Share, trans. Robert Hurley (New York: Zone Books, 1991), see esp. "Preface," "Theoretical Introduction."

27. Hegel articulates this ontotheology of sacrifice, as well as the distinctiveness of modern sacrifice, across several of his works. As Bataille notes, citing also Alexander Kojeve, "On the level of Hegel's philosophy, Man has, in a sense, revealed and founded human truth by sacrificing; in sacrifice he destroyed the animal in himself, allowing himself and the animal to survive only as that noncorporeal truth which Hegel describes and which makes of man—in Heidegger's words—a being unto death (Seinz um Tode), or—in the words of Kojeve himself—'death which lives a human life.'" (See Georges Bataille, "Hegel, Death, and Sacrifice," trans. Jonathan Strauss, Yale French Studies no. 78 [1990]: 18.) This ontotheology remains extremely difficult to shake off. For example, while Jean-Luc Nancy provides a critical account of it, he does not question the trope— itself ontotheological, surely—of "Western sacrifice." All the four characteristics that Nancy attributes to "Western sacrifice" could be attributed—as contentiously in both cases—to another equally ontotheological tradition called Hindu or Indic sacrifice; in both cases, the adjectives "Western" and "Indic" perform the ontotheology. Jean-Luc Nancy, "The Unsacrificeable," Yale French Studies no. 79 (1991).

28. "Confusion of Thought," February 6, 1930, Gandhi, *Collected Works,* 48:299.

29. "My Friend, the Revolutionary," April 9, 1925, Gandhi, *Collected Works,* 31:138.

30. *Atmakatha* or *Autobiography,* Part IV, chapter 25.

31. "Letter to Narandas Gandhi," August 3–5, 1930, *Akshardeha,* 44:70; Gandhi, *Collected Works,* 49:422.

32. "Letter to Narandas Gandhi," July 18–22, 1930, *Akshardeha,* 44:42; Gandhi, *Collected Works,* 49:384.

33. "General Knowledge about Health–17," April 26, 1913, Gandhi, *Collected Works,* 13:92.

34. *Satyagraha in South Africa,* chapter 13; "Satyagraha v. Passive Resistance," Gandhi, *Collected Works,* 34:94f.

35. Gandhi possibly arrives at this formulation through his exposure to the correspondence between F. W. Maitland and Anna Kingsford. Maitland makes some very similar remarks about the Women's Suffrage Bill in a letter to Anna Kingsford around 1876. Edward Maitland, *Anna Kingsford: Her Life, Letters, Diary and Work,* 2 vols., 2nd ed. (London: George Redway, 1896), 76. While we have no evidence that Gandhi read this book, it would surprising if he had not, considering that we have records of his stocking other books by Maitland and Kingsford.

36. "Fight Square If You Must," February 23, 1928, Gandhi, *Collected Works,* 41:214. In a similar vein, another title, "A Shortage of the Kshatriya Spirit" [*kshatrivatni khami*], is translated in 1924 from the Gujarati as "Below the Belt. See *Akshardeha,* 24:476; Gandhi, *Collected Works,* 28:428.

37. Letter to Jamnadas Gandhi, around May 30, 1913, *Akshardeha,* 12:77; Gandhi, *Collected Works,* 13:154.

38. Levinas, *Time and the Other,* trans. Richard A. Cohen (Pittsburgh: Duquesne University Press, 1987), 73.

39. I have placed quotes around the "is" to indicate the not-ness and erasure that marks being here; these quotes may be presumed wherever the warrior's and satyagrahi's being is discussed.

40. Jacques Derrida, *Given Time: Counterfeit Money I,* trans. Peggy Kamuf (Chicago: University of Chicago Press, 1992), 7, 12.

41. Marcel Mauss, *The Gift: Forms and Functions of Exchange in Primitive Societies,* trans. Ian Cunnison (London: Cohen and West, 1966), 1. For a suggestive reading of Mauss's argument, see also Jonathan Parry, "The Gift, the Indian Gift, the 'Indian Gift,'" *Man (n.s.)* 21, no. 3 (1986).

42. Bataille, *The Accursed Share,* 69, 67.

43. This is brought out very powerfully in Bama's short story "Pongal," where a Dalit father comes to realize the force of his son's refusal to accept ceremonial gifts from the landlord, and throws away the pongal he has received. Bama, *Harum*

Scarum Saar and Other Stories, trans. N. Ravi Shanker (New Delhi: Women Unlimited/Kali for Women, 2006).

44. "London," August 14, 1909, *Akshardeha,* 9:361; Gandhi, *Collected Works,* 9:428.

45. "Speech at General Meeting," Dakor, October 27, 1920, November 3, 1920, *Akshardeha,* 18:361; Gandhi, *Collected Works,* 21:401. Ravana is the demon-king who abducts Sita, the wife of Rama, the eponymous hero of the *Ramayana.* Lakshmana is Rama's brother and Indrajit is Ravana's son, who is powerful because of his ascetic practices. Tulsidas is the composer of the *Ramcharitmanas,* the version of the Ramayana of which Gandhi was especially fond.

46. Bataille, *The Accursed Share,* 71.

47. Friedrich Nietzsche, "On the Genealogy of Morals," 39.

48. Carl Schmitt, *The Concept of the Political,* trans. George Schwab (Chicago: University of Chicago Press, 2007). Richard Wolin argues that Schmitt participated in a "conservative revolutionary habitus," which made a distinction between the "hero" (or "soldier") and the "bourgeois." "Whereas the hero thrives on risk, danger, and uncertainty, the life of the bourgeois is devoted to petty calculations of utility and security." Wolin suggests that unlike their "traditional conservative" counterparts, who longed for a restoration of the imagined glories of the earlier Germanic Reichs and generally stressed the desirability of a return to premodern forms of social order (e.g., Tonnies's *Gemeinschaft*) based on the aristocratic considerations of rank and privilege," the conservative revolutionaries felt that "what was necessary was "modernization," yet a form of modernization that was at the same time compatible with the (albeit mythologized) traditional German values of heroism, "will" (as opposed to "reason"), *Kultur,* and hierarchy. In sum, what was desired was a *modern community.* Richard Wolin, "Carl Schmitt: The Conservative Revolutionary Habitus and the Aesthetics of Horror," *Political Theory* 20, no. 3 (August 1992): 428.

If Wolin's reading is correct, then there would be striking analogies between Schmitt and Gandhi's figure (exemplified for him by Bal Gangadhar Tilak) of the modern armed warrior who seeks to overthrow the British. But it may be more plausible, given Schmitt's sublative moves, to read him as a theorist of authoritarian liberalism. For a suggestive argument along the latter lines, see Renato Cristi, *Carl Schmitt and Authoritarian Liberalism: Strong State, Free Economy* (Cardiff: University of Wales Press, 1998).

49. Isabel Hofmeyr, *Gandhi's Printing Press* (Cambridge: Harvard University Press, 2013).

50. I say a thousand small ways because Gandhi is insistent that "the sacrifices involved in noncooperation are easy to make and not impossible for ordinary human nature and it is because of this, I believe, that the people have welcomed the movement. The main principles are Hindu-Muslim unity, preserving peace

even under provocation, total boycott of foreign cloth, daily spinning for a fixed period, contributing money according to one's capacity, treating the Bhangi as one's brother and giving up addictions, immorality, etc. . . . I have demanded nothing which other nations have not shown themselves capable of." "Tangled Business," May 15, 1921, *Akshardeha*, 20:87; Gandhi, *Collected Works*, 23:147.

Putting such remarks together with his remarks on other occasions about the necessity of a fearless relation with one's own death, it could be argued that the ordinary and easy self-sacrifices are marked also by the specter of that death, even that they are part of the everyday and "easy" discipline of that death, perhaps the discipline that both flows from and prepares its practitioners for the self-sacrifice involved in embracing their own death.

51. "Letter to Maganlal Gandhi," December 28, 1908, *Akshardeha*, 9:118; Gandhi, *Collected Works*, 9:222.

52. In this sense, it is certainly correct to say that the warrior seizes the last chance before his own death—but note that this chance is after he has assumed his own death.

53. That essay is part of a series in *Indian Opinion*, "General Knowledge about Health," which is later published in India in an English translation, *Guide to Health*, though Gandhi does not learn of the translation until many years later. The *Collected Works* draws on this translation.

54. These remarks are in his book *Key to Health*, written and published in 1944. In the preface, he refers to the "General Knowledge about Health" (which by now he thinks he has written in 1906—a significant forgetting, since that is the year he takes the vow of *brahmacharya*) and says that he would now like to revise the arguments about health he made there, though he does not have the original in front of him.

55. This relation to death is one difference between the warrior and the citizen of modern civilization. In the latter, even as a certain askesis—the "civilizing process" was Elias's phrase for it, strangely paralleling Gandhi's "modern civilization"—produces the autonomous self, sovereignty over the self involves mastery of rather than equality with death.

56. Martin Heidegger, "The Question Concerning Technology," 5.

57. "Speech at Meeting of Gandhi Seva Sangh and Charkha Sangh," July 21, 1940, Gandhi, *Collected Works*, 78:350.

58. One of the many superb observations that Faisal Devji makes is about precisely this threat to satyagraha: "The atom bomb, moreover, separated assailants from victims by such a distance as to nullify . . . the relations it [satyagraha] sought to create between violence and nonviolence. . . . Not fascism, then, but its defeat posed the greatest challenge to Gandhi's belief in the universal applicability of nonviolence" (Devji, *The Impossible Indian*, 148). In a similar vein, in our contemporary moment by far the more inhuman violence from a Gandhian perspective

would be that of drones rather than that of the terrorist, since the former dehumanizes more thoroughly both those who deploy drones and those who are its victims; it threatens to make both so thoroughly calculable as to require an even greater satyagraha.

59. Heidegger, "The Question Concerning Technology," 28.

4. The Impossible Gift of Fearlessness, for Example

1. Lala Lajpat Rai, "'Ahimsa Paramo Dharmah'—A Truth or a Fad?" *Modern Review* (July 1916): 19–21; reprinted in Gandhi, *Collected Works*, 15:516ff.

2. Akeel Bilgrami, "Gandhi's Integrity: The Philosophy behind the Politics," *Postcolonial Studies* 5, no. 1 (2002).

3. For a reading of Bilgrami's emphasis on exemplarity in these terms, see also Karuna Mantena's fascinating essay, "Gandhi and the Means-End Question in Politics," Paper no. 46 (Princeton: School of Sciences Occasional Papers, Institute of Advanced Studies, June 2012), available at https://www.sss.ias.edu/files/papers/paper46.pdf.

4. Bilgrami, "Gandhi's Integrity," 88.

5. "Dayadharma: Speech on the Birth Anniversary of Shrimad Rajchandra," November 16, 1921, *Akshardeha*, 21:384; *Collected Works*, 25:90.

6. "Letter to Gangabehn Vaidya," February 2, 1931, *Akshardeha*, 45:146; Gandhi, *Collected Works*, 51:94. For a searching discussion and contextualization of this episode, see David Hardiman, *Gandhi in His Time and Ours* (New York: Columbia University Press, 2004).

7. The reply also stresses that there is no "historical warrant" for the suggestion that adherence to ahimsa "synchronized with our becoming bereft of many virtues." "On Ahimsa: Reply to Lala Lajpat Rai," October 1916, *Akshardeha*, 13:273; *Collected Works*, 15:252. See also, a few months earlier, "Speech at Gurukul Kangri Anniversary," March 20, 1916, *Akshardeha*, 13:242; Gandhi, *Collected Works*, 15:205.

8. "Speech at Mass Meeting in Ahmedabad," April 14, 1919, *Akshardeha*, 15:214; Gandhi, *Collected Works*, 17:422.

9. "Understanding as Distinct from Literacy," October 30, 1921, *Akshardeha*, 21:328; Gandhi, *Collected Works*, 25:28.

10. "Carding or Archery," September 1, 1929, *Akshardeha*, 41:338; Gandhi, *Collected Works*, 47:1.

11. Cited in Ariel Glucklich, "What's in a List: A Rule of Response for Hindu Dharma Offered in Response to Maria Hibbets," *Journal of Religious Ethics* 27, no. 3 (Fall 1999): 466.

12. The pervasiveness of the characterization of the king as "giving life" may also be a salutary caution against generalizing Foucault's contrast between premodern sovereign power as letting live and making die and modern sovereign power as a making live and letting die.

13. Maria Hibbets, "Saving Them from Yourself: An Inquiry into the South Asian Gift of Fearlesseness," *Journal of Religious Ethics* 27, no. 3 (Fall 1999): 446. See also Maria Heim, "Dana as a Moral Category," in *Indian Ethics: Classical Traditions and Contemporary Challenges,* ed. Purshottam Billimoria, Joseph Prabhu, and Renuka M. Sharma (Aldershot: Ashgate, 2007).

14. "Speech at a Meeting in Wai," November 6, 1920, *Akshardeha,* 18:408; Gandhi, *Collected Works,* 21:458.

15. R. Williams, *Jaina Yoga: A Survey of the Medieval Srvakacaras* (Delhi: Motilal Banarasidass, 1963/1983), 71f. Because Williams does not recognize the conceptual logic that ties the gift and ahimsa to each other, he suggests abhaydan is "only in name a form of dana and belongs properly to the sphere of ahimsa (158).

16. Maria Hibbets, "Saving Them from Yourself," 445–46.

17. *Shrimad Rajchandra* (Agas: Shrimad Rajchandra Ashram, 2006), 24.

18. Derrida, *Given Time: I, Counterfeit Money,* trans. Peggy Kamuf (Chicago: University of Chicago Press, 1992), 24.

19. "May God Help," November 27, Gandhi, *Collected Works,* 29:374.

20. "Ethics and Politics Today," in Jacques Derrida, *Negotiations: Interventions and Interviews, 1971–2001,* trans. Elizabeth Rottenberg (Stanford: Stanford University Press, 2002), 296.

21. "Towards Perpetual Peace," in Immanuel Kant, *Practical Philosophy,* trans. Mary J. Gregor (Cambridge: Cambridge University Press, 1996), 338. In making the arguments in this and the next paragraph, I have drawn also on Marguerite La Caze, "At the Intersection: Kant, Derrida, and the Relation between Ethics and Politics," *Political Theory* 35, no. 6 (2007).

22. "On Forgiveness: A Roundtable Discussion with Jacques Derrida," moderated by Richard Kearney, in *Questioning God,* ed. John Caputo, Mark Dooley, and Michael J. Scanlon (Bloomington: Indiana University Press, 2001), 66.

23. Jacques Derrida, "Hostipitality," *Angelaki: A Journal of the Theoretical Humanities* 5, no. 3 (2000): 6.

24. Derrida, "Ethics and Politics Today," 304.

25. Anne Dufourmantelle and Jacques Derrida, *Of Hospitality,* trans. Rachel Bowlby (Stanford: Stanford University Press, 2000), 79–80. See also Jacques Derrida, "The Principle of Hospitality," *parallax* 11, no. 1 (2005). It should be noted, however, that Derrida both affirms and is cautious about the association of the unconditional law with ethics and conditional laws with politics: see "Ethics and Politics Today," 301.

26. I draw here on the contrast, noted in chapter 2, that Derrida makes between the aporia and the problem. See *Aporias,* 11–12.

27. Derrida, "Force of Law," 961, 963, 967.

28. Jacques Derrida, "A Certain Impossible Possibility of Saying the Event," 448.

29. Derrida uses the phrase "unavowed theologism" to reflect on the possibility of some affinity between his emphasis on a democracy to come and Heidegger's remark, "Only a God Can Save Us Now." As should be evident, it is not that theologism which is the concern of my remarks here. Derrida, *Rogues*, 110.

30. "Test," November 13, 1921, *Akshardeha*, 21:382; Gandhi, *Collected Works*, 25:88.

31. "Gitashikshan," *Akshardeha*, 32:271; Gandhi, *Collected Works*, 37:318.

32. "Letter to C. F. Andrews," before June 23, 1918, Gandhi, *Collected Works*, 17:88.

33. "Speech at Ras," June 26, 1918, Gandhi, *Collected Works*, 17:101.

34. "Letter to Hanumantrao," July 17, 1918, Gandhi, *Collected Works*, 17:131f; *Akshardeha*, 14:432;

35. "Letter to Maganlal Gandhi," July 25, 1918, *Akshardeha*, 14:449; Gandhi, *Collected Works*, 17:150.

36. "Letter to Kishorelal Mashruwala," July 29, 1918, *Akshardeha*, 14:460; Gandhi, *Collected Works*, 17:163.

37. "Fiery Ordeal," September 30, 1929, *Akshardeha*, 37:294; Gandhi, *Collected Works*, 43:59.

38. It is perhaps because of the impossibility of affirming ahimsa as an exclusive dying without killing that he must derive ahimsa from satya rather than the other way round. See, for example, "Letter to Jamnalal Bajaj," March 16, 1922, *Akshardeha*, 23:91; Gandhi, *Collected Works*, 26:364.

39. "Dayadharma: Speech on the Birth Anniversary of Shrimad Rajchandra," November 16, 1921, *Akshardeha*, 21:384; Gandhi, *Collected Works*, 25:90.

40. Ibid., *Akshardeha*, 21:387; Gandhi, *Collected Works*, 25:93.

41. The articles, suggestively, are titled "Ahimsa" in Gujarati and "Is This Humanity" in English. As that transposition should remind us, ahimsa is always also a question of thinking what is most proper to being human. "Ahimsa–III," October 24, 1926, *Akshardeha*, 31:491; "Is This Humanity–III," Gandhi, *Collected Works*, 36:429.

42. "Ahimsa–IV," October 24, 1926, *Akshardeha*, 31:491; "Is This Humanity-IV," Gandhi, *Collected Works*, 36:449–50.

43. Walter Benjamin's remarks about divine violence as distinct from mythic violence resonate strikingly here: "For only mythical violence, not divine, will be recognizable as such with certainty, unless it be in incomparable effects, because the expiatory power of violence is not visible to men." Walter Benjamin, "Critique of Violence," in *Reflections: Essays, Aphorisms, Autobiographical Writings*, trans. Edmund Jephcott (New York: Schocken Books, 1986), 300.

44. Walter Benjamin, *Selected Writings: 1913–1926*, vol. 1 (Cambridge: Harvard University Press, 2004), 481.

45. "The *Nyaya* [justice] of the Sword," August 15,1920, *Akshardeha*, 18:145; "The Doctrine of the Sword," August 11, 1920, Gandhi, *Collected Works,* 21:133. There is no equivalent to this phrase in the English version. This is one of the many essays in which the Gujarati and the English diverge dramatically, despite being published almost simultaneously. In this case, the English version was published in *Young India* before the Gujarati version was published in *Navjivan.* We do not know whether both versions were written by Gandhi, or whether one (which one?) is a translation by an associate.

46. "Satyagrahi–I," April 7, 1919, *Akshardeha*, 15:183; Gandhi, *Collected Works,* 17:390.

47. "Royeppen Sentenced," February 5, 1910, *Akshardeha*, 12:167; "Speech to Ahmedabad Millhands," March 15, 1918, 14:223; "Speech to Villagers," Segaon, after April 17, 1936, Gandhi, *Collected Works,* 68:366.

48. Aristotle, *Prior Analytics and Posterior Analytics,* trans. A. J. Jenkinson and G. R. G. Mure (Oxford: Oxford University Press, 1928), B23, 71.

49. Giorgio Agamben, "What Is a Paradigm," in *The Signature of All Things: On Method* (New York: Zone Books, 2009), 19–20.

50. In the passage above, the phrase *nakal karvi* is translated as "copy." Elsewhere, however, *nakal karvi* is translated as "follow the example" or "emulate." We do not know whether the word *nakal* enters his vocabulary initially as a translation of "follow the example," or whether the movement is the other way round. But that may be, in his writing, it is through a copying and following of the example that universalization occurs both in modern civilization and in satyagraha. However, he does not seem to consciously acknowledge that copying and following the example proceeds very differently in the two. *Hind Swaraj,* chapter 4; "Our Duty," October 28, 1905, *Akshardeha*, 5:124; Gandhi, *Collected Works,* 4:470; "London," before October 1, 1909, *Akshardeha*, 9:507.

51. Jacques Derrida and Maurizio Ferraris, *A Taste for the Secret,* trans. Giacomo Donis, ed. Giacomo Donis and David Webb (Oxford: Blackwell, 2001), 61.

5. The Destruction of Conservatism

1. "Ahimsa–III," October 24, 1926, *Akshardeha*, 31:491; translated into English as "Is This Humanity–III," Gandhi, *Collected Works,* 36:429. This passage is quoted at greater length in chapter 3.

2. "Letter to Hanumantrao," July 17, 1918, Gandhi, *Collected Works,* 17:131f; *Akshardeha*, 14:432.

3. "Ahimsa–IV," October 24, 1926, *Akshardeha*, 31:491; "Is This Humanity–IV," Gandhi, *Collected Works,* 36:449–50.

4. "Letter to Raojibhai Patel," March 7, 1914, Gandhi, *Collected Works,* 14:103.

5. "Letter to C. F. Andrews," August 6, 1918, Gandhi, *Collected Works,* 17:177.

6. Sujata Patel, "Construction and Reconstruction of Women in Gandhi," *Economic and Political Weekly* 23, no. 8 (February 20, 1988): 378.

7. "Speech at Gujarati Political Conference," November 4, 1917, *Akshardeha*, 14:59; Gandhi, *Collected Works,* 16:128f.

8. "Civil Disobedience," August 4, 1921, Gandhi, *Collected Works,* 24:47.

9. This is noted in Gayatri Chakravorty Spivak, "Can the Subaltern Speak?," in *Marxism and the Interpretation of Culture,* ed. Cary Nelson and Lawrence Grossberg (Urbana: University of Illinois Press, 1988), 302.

10. See, for instance, Ananda Coomaraswamy, *The Dance of Shiva: Fourteen Indian Essays* (New York: The Sunwise Turn), 1918. Gandhi's distance from Coomaraswamy is also evident in his insistence: "We have never heard of a husband mounting the funeral pyre of his deceased wife. It may therefore be taken for granted that the practice of the widow immolating herself at the death of her husband had its origin in superstitious ignorance and the blind egotism of man." "'Twentieth Century Sati,'" May 3, 1931, *Akshardeha,* 46:78; Gandhi, *Collected Works,* 52:28. The Gujarati and English versions of this essay vary significantly, with the English being among other things somewhat longer. Pyarelal, Gandhi's secretary, translates this essay—we do not know whether Gandhi reviews the translation.

11. "'Twentieth-Century Sati,'" May 3, 1931, *Akshardeha,* 46:77; Gandhi, *Collected Works,* 52:26–28.

12. Ibid.

13. "Speech at a Public Meeting," Vadtal, January 19, 1921, *Akshardeha,* 19:224; Gandhi, *Collected Works,* 22:234.

14. "My Notes," August 17, 1924, *Akshardeha,* 25:6; Gandhi, *Collected Works,* 29:7.

15. "Discussion with Christian Missionaries," December 24, 1928, Gandhi, *Collected Works,* 74:311.

16. "My Notes," May 1, 1921, Gandhi, *Collected Works,* 23:103.

17. "Evidence before the Disorders Inquiry Committee," January 9, 1920, Gandhi, *Collected Works,* 19:250.

18. "Speech at the Gujarat Mahavidyalaya," August 8, 1924, *Akshardeha,* 24:494; Gandhi, *Collected Works,* 28:448.

19. "Speeches at the Natal Indian Patriotic Union," *Akshardeha,* 10:104; Gandhi, *Collected Works,* 10:357.

20. "Only One Word, Properly Altered: Gandhi and the Question of the Prostitute," *Economic and Political Weekly* 41, no. 49 (December 9, 2006). Aishwary Kumar provides an insightful reading of this moral superiority in his essay, "The Ellipsis of Touch: Gandhi's Unequals," *Public Culture* 23, no. 2 (2011).

21. "Notes," July 28, 1921, Gandhi, *Collected Works,* 24:11.

22. History of the Satyagraha in South Africa, *Akshardeha,* 29:147–48; Gandhi, *Collected Works,* 34:

23. Ashwini Tambe, "Gandhi's 'Fallen' Sisters: Difference and the National Body Politic," *Social Scientist* 37, no. 1–2 (2009): 21–38.

24. For a sustained and thoughtful consideration of the way that Gandhian satyagraha is "frequently disempowering for those who fail to meet the Gandhian standard of goodness," see especially Leela Gandhi, "Concerning Violence: The Limits and Circulations of Gandhian 'Ahimsa' or Passive Resistance, *Cultural Critique*, no. 35 (Winter 1996–97): 114.

25. Aishwary Kumar, "The Ellipsis of Touch."

26. Leela Gandhi, "Concerning Violence," 112.

27. "'Depressed' Classes," October 27, 1920, Gandhi, *Collected Works*, 20:388. The English word "excrescence" seems to have entered his vocabulary in relation to untouchability as a translation of the seventeenth-century poet Akho Bhagat, whose verse he cites several times: "As Akha has sung: 'That one may be defiled by touch of others, like a superfluous limb is this notion.'" ("Letter to Maganlal Gandhi," May, 1917, *Akshardeha*, 13:402). He translates "superfluous limb" into English as "excrescence." ["Removal of Untouchability," September 9, 1930, Gandhi, *Collected Works*, 50:41.]

28. "A Stain on India's Forehead," after November 5, 1917, Gandhi, *Collected Works*, 16:138. Where Gandhi thinks equality in these conservative terms, Faisal Devji's argument seems especially appropriate: that Gandhi's "co-operative commonwealth" . . . "can be seen as a trader's society writ large. It was precisely by means of such co-operative arrangements between groups that neither dined nor married, after all, that migrant traders had settled in South Africa." See Devji, *The Impossible Indian*, 54.

29. *Gandhijinu Gitashikshan, Akshardeha*, 32:292; Gandhi, *Collected Works*, 37:346.

30. *Gandhijinu Gitashikshan, Akshardeha*, 32:291–92; Gandhi, *Collected Works*, 37:345.

31. For a careful working out of how Gandhi thinks varnadharma along these lines, see Sanjay Palshikar, *Evil and the Philosophy of Retribution: Modern Commentaries on the* Bhagavad Gita (New Delhi: Routledge, 2014), 140–45.

32. See, for instance, "Speech at Public Meeting," Rajapalayam, October 4, 1927, Gandhi, *Collected Works*, 40:203ff.

33. "Speech at Untouchability Conference," Belgaum, December 27, 1924, Gandhi, *Collected Works*, 30:16.

34. Letter to Nagardas Bhambania, January 3, 1933, Gandhi, *Collected Works*, 58:356.

35. Aishwary Kumar in his *Radical Equality* provides a somewhat different understanding of the role of *maryada dharma* in Gandhi's writing. The difference between us may be because while Kumar's essay makes no significant distinction between *maryada* and *maryada dharma*, my reading stresses the tension between

Gandhi's explicit commitments to a substantive order of thekana and *maryada dharma* (the latter term referring also to a specific Vaishnava Gujarati cultural complex), on the one hand, and the seizure of his thinking, on the other hand, by an autoimmune concept of *maryada* or *hadh*—a "concept" that can only work through a certain ruination, uprooting, autoimmunity, or self-sacrifice of every substantive or rooted limit.

36. Ambedkar's questioning of liberal equality from a radical perspective may, similarly, account for his relative disinterest in temple entry movements—his treatment of the right to temple entry as both necessary and yet secondary.

37. "Harijans and Temple Entry," January 27, 1948, Gandhi, *Collected Works*, 98:307.

38. "Speech at Trivandrum," on or before October 10, 1927, Gandhi, *Collected Works*, 40:230.

39. "Discussion on Varnadharma," October 3, 1927, Gandhi, *Collected Works*, 40:297.

40. "A Stain on India's Forehead," after November 5, 1917, Gandhi, *Collected Works*, 16:141.

41. "Dr Ambedkar and Caste," February 11, 1933, Gandhi, *Collected Works*, 59:227–29.

42. Anupama Rao, *The Caste Question: Dalits and the Politics of Modern India* (Berkeley: University of California Press, 2009), 127.

43. Anupama Rao, "Stigma and the Political Subject," manuscript.

44. Ambedkar, "A Reply to the Mahatma," available at http://ccnmtl.columbia .edu/projects/mmt/ambedkar/web/index.html.

45. "Dr Ambedkar and Caste," February 11, 1933, Gandhi, *Collected Works*, 59:227–29.

46. "Varnashrama and Its Distortion," November 17, 1927, Gandhi, *Collected Works*, 40:383ff.

47. See, for example, Letter to Mathuradas Trikumji, October 27, 1921, *Akshardeha*, 21:321; Gandhi, *Collected Works*, 25:18.

48. "Use Another Name," June 7, 1931, *Akshardeha*, 46:355; Gandhi, *Collected Works*, 52:298. It is intriguing that by 1931 he thinks that the first use of "Dalit" was by Swami Shradhanand. In 1920, he writes an essay titled "'Dalit' vargo" [The Dalit Classes] which notes: "Vivekananda called the panchamas [the fifth caste, a name common in Gujarat at the time for Dalits] the Dalit classes. Vivekananda's adjective is more accurate, this there is no doubt about." (The term "Dalit" is replaced in the English translation, published at the time in the magazine Gandhi edited, Young India, by the phrase "Suppressed" in the text, and by "Depressed" in the title.) See "'Dalit' Classes," *Akshardeha*, 18:349; "'Depressed' Classes," Gandhi, *Collected Works*, 21:387. The term "Dalit" continues after this year to figure sporadically in Gandhi's writings.

49. "My Notes," July 2, 1931, *Akshardeha*, 47:160; Gandhi, *Collected Works*, 53:166.

50. "Harijan and Durijan," August 2, 1931, *Akshardeha*, 47:264; translated as "Speech at Ahmedabad," Gandhi, *Collected Works*, 53:170. This is the text of a speech given by Gandhi at an occasion in Ahmedabad when Sir Chinubhai Ranchodlal throws his family's personal temple open to untouchables. The footnote to the English translation by Mahadev Desai correctly describes it as a "condensed summary." See also "Why Harijan," February 11, 1933, Gandhi, *Collected Works*, 59:234.

51. The Gujarati text of Gandhi's speech at Chinubhai Ranchodlal's temple does not mention repentence, but Mahadev Desai's rendering of the last sentence referred to in note 50 is: "It is still open to us to be *harijana* ourselves, but we can only do so by heartily repenting of our sin." "Harijan and Durijan," August 2, 1931, *Akshardeha*, 47:264; translated as "Speech at Ahmedabad," Gandhi, *Collected Works*, 53:170.

52. "Statement on Untouchability–II," November 5, 1932, Gandhi, *Collected Works*, 57:333.

53. "Meaning of 'Status,'" February 15, 1935, Gandhi, *Collected Works*, 66:231.

54. Jacques Derrida, *Given Time: Counterfeit Money I* (Chicago: University of Chicago Press, 1992), 13, 16. Later chapters draw both implicitly and explicitly on the axiomatics of the pure gift laid out so powerfully in Derrida's writings.

55. Anupama Rao, *The Caste Question*, 165. Also, as Rupa Viswanath notes about Gandhi's claim to represent the untouchables: "What is significant stems rather from what Gandhi does not say, and which goes without saying: that he represents not only untouchables but also caste Hindus. For in claiming to represent both untouchable and caste Hindu, Gandhi asserts the nationalist dogma that there is no fundamental antagonism between the two, that there *is* a 'whole' capable of being represented, and that this encompassing whole is in some fundamental but unspoken way a Hindu one." See her "The Commission as Form: The 2007 Mishra Report and Representative Governance in Modern India," *South Asia* 38, no. 3 (2015).

56. D. R. Nagaraj, *The Flaming Feet* (Bangalore: South Forum Press, 1993), 17, 18, 22–23. For a fascinating discussion of *seva*, see R. Srivatsan, "Concept of "Seva" and "Sevak" in the Freedom Movement," *Economic and Political Weekly* 41, no. 5 (February 4, 2006).

57. "Notes," November 17, 1921, Gandhi, *Collected Works*, 25:102.

58. "Brahmin–Non-Brahmin Question," November 24, 1927, Gandhi, *Collected Works*, 40:486.

6. Daya Otherwise

1. "Gandhi's Questions to Raychandbhai, and the Latter's Answers," *Akshardeha*, 32:496; Gandhi, *Collected Works*, 36:502.

2. See *Mokshamala,* in *Shrimad Rajchandra* (Agas: Shrimad Rajchandra Ashram, 2006), 59. See also, in the same volume, *"Jainsidhanto"* or "Jain Principles," where abhaydan is discussed as the first principle (24).

3. *Uttaradhyayana Sutra,* in *Gaina Sutras,* trans. and ed. from Prakrit by Hermann Jacobi (Oxford: Oxford University Press, 1895), 314.

4. See *Mokshamala,* chapter 30, in *Shrimad Rajchandra* (Agas: Shrimad Rajchandra Ashram, 2006), 80.

5. Ibid., 66.

6. Ibid., 78.

7. *Atmakatha* or *Autobiography,* Part II, chapter 15.

8. "Memories of Raychandbhai," November 5, 1926, *Akshardeha,* 32:9; Gandhi, *Collected Works,* 36:477.

9. "Letter to Prabhudas Gandhi," December 2, 1929, Gandhi, *Collected Works,* 48:48. See also "Letter to Purshottam Gandhi," April 18, 1932, *Akshardeha,* 49:303; Gandhi, *Collected Works,* 55:256.

10. "Triumph of Truth," February 8, 1908, *Collected Works,* 8:120.

11. "Letter to Jamnadas Gandhi," May 30, 1913, *Akshardeha,* 12:76f; Gandhi, *Collected Works,* 13:153.

12. "Letter to Narandas Gandhi," July 18/22, 1930, *Akhshardeha,* 44:41–42; Gandhi, *Collected Works,* 49:383–84. These letters are written while he is jailed at Yeravda, to be read out to ashram inmates. The Gandhian press Navjivan collects and publishes the letters that same year under the title *Mangalprabhat.* Valji Govindji Desai translates the letters into English; Gandhi goes over this translation, which is published by 1932 under the title *From Yeravda Mandir.* I have made versions of the arguments in the next few paragraphs in: "Gandhi's Politics: Liberalism and the Question of the Ashram," *South Atlantic Quarterly* 101, no. 4 (Fall 2002); "'No Politics without Religion': Of Secularism and Gandhi," in *Political Hinduism: The Religious Imagination in Public Spheres,* ed. Vinay Lal (New Delhi: Oxford University Press, 2009).

13. "Not Even Half-mast," December 4, 1924, Gandhi, *Collected Works,* 29:408. Or as he puts it on another occasion: "You ask me to differentiate between *Advaitism* and *Dwaitism.* The former derived evidence from God who alone exists and therefore, contemplates identity between God and His creation. The latter attempts to show that the two can be never one." "Letter to E. H. James," May 12, 1926, Gandhi, *Collected Works,* 35:220.

14. "All about the Fast," September 25, 1924, Gandhi, *Collected Works,* 29:210.

15. "Speech at Tanjore," July 29, 1927, Gandhi, *Collected Works,* 40:121.

16. See, for example "Trees, Our Brothers and Sisters," January 12, 1930, *Akshardeha* 42:235; Gandhi, *Collected Works,* 48:52. Similarly, he describes Mirabai as having " travelled all alone in Egypt, Persia and Europe befriending trees and animals." "Notes," February 20, 1930, Gandhi, *Collected Works.* Intriguingly, these

seem to be among the earliest explicit references to kinship and friendship with trees. The question of Gandhi's thinking of trees and things, and the transformations of this thinking, remains to be taken up.

17. *Gandhijnu Gitashikshan, Akshardeha,* 32:105; Gandhi, *Collected Works,* 37:100f.

18. "Letter to Narandas Gandhi," July 28–31, 1930, *Akshardeha,* 44:59; Gandhi, *Collected Works,* 49:407ff.

19. "The Meaning of the *Gita,*" October 11, 1925, *Akshardeha,* 28:280; Gandhi, *Collected Works,* 33:85f. The disjunctions between the Gujarati and the English versions are especially striking in this passage, as indeed in other sections of this essay. The official translation is: "Truth is a positive value, while non-violence is a negative value. Truth affirms. Non-violence forbids something which is real enough. Truth exists, untruth does not exist. Violence exists, nonviolence does not. Even so, the highest dharma for us is that nothing but non-violence can be. Truth is its own proof, and non-violence is its supreme fruit. The latter is necessarily contained in the former. Since, however, it is not evident as truth is, one may try to discover the meaning of the Shastras without believing in it. But the spirit of non-violence alone will reveal to one the true meaning of the Shastras."

20. Faisal Devji, "Morality in the Shadow of Politics," *Modern Intellectual History,* 7, no. 2 (2010): 377; Devji, *The Impossible Indian,* 99. Devji reads this passage as symptomatic of the "mutual entanglement" for Gandhi of "truth and violence," "untruth and non-violence." While it is entirely correct to stress the entanglement, it seems to me that, as in the remark cited above, Devji sometimes reads entanglement as indistinction. It may be that Devji discerns this indistinction in part because he draws on an incorrect transcription of Gandhi's essay. According to both the *Akshardeha* and *Collected Works,* Gandhi writes, "Following the path of non-violence *[ahimsana margma],* we discovered the spinning-wheel..." *Gitashikshan, Akshardeha,* 32:282; Gandhi, *Collected Works,* 37:330. The Orient Books edition (1980), which Devji cites, however, apparently transcribes this as: "Following the death of ahimsa..." (Devji, "Morality in the Shadow of Politics," 377; Devji, *The Impossible Indian,* 98.) I discuss this passage at greater length in chapter 9.

21. "The Poet's Anxiety," June 1, 1921, Gandhi, *Collected Works,* 23:220.

22. "Divine Warning," February 19, 1922, *Akshardeha,* 22:383; Gandhi, *Collected Works,* 26:185.

23. *Gandhijnu Gitashikshan, Akshardeha,* 32:170; Gandhi, *Collected Works,* 37:199.

24. "Letter to Mathuradas Trikumji," March 6, 1922, *Akshardeha,* 23:16; Gandhi, *Collected Works,* 26:288.

25. For an introduction to some of these debates, see *Ahimsa, Anekanta, and Jainism,* ed. Tara Sethi (Delhi: Motilal Banarasidass, 2004). Perhaps one day more research will help trace the genealogies of Gandhi's anekantvada. For now, suffice

to note that the modern articulation of anekantvada as ahimsa is usually associated with Anandshankar Dhruva, the great scholar of Sanskrit, Hinduism, and Jainism, born in the same year as Gandhi, and an associate of Gandhi from at least 1917 (when he serves as a negotiator between Gandhi and the industrialists during the Ahmedabad mill strike). Dhruva is also the figure more associated with the phrase "intellectual ahimsa." See John Cort, "'Intellectual Ahimsa' Revisited: Jain Tolerance and Intolerance of Others," *Philosophy East and West* 50, no. 3 (2000).

26. Gandhi's association of anekantvada with ahimsa occurs before the first documented public use of the phrase "intellectual ahimsa" by Anandshankarbhai as a description of anekantvada. But Anandshankarbhai seems to have been associated with Gandhi since at least 1917, and we cannot rule out the possibility that Gandhi arrives at the association through his conversations with Anandshankarbhai.

27. "Three Vital Questions," January 21, 1926, Gandhi, *Collected Works,* 33:409.

28. Ibid., 408.

29. For a fascinating discussion of the "dvaita structure of feeling," see Gayatri Chakravorty Spivak, "Moving Devi," *Cultural Critique,* no. 47 (Winter 2001): 123.

30. "Letter to Maganlal Gandhi," May 18, 1918, *Akshardeha,* 14:353; Gandhi, *Collected Works,* 17:33.

31. *Gandhijnu Gitashikshan, Akshardeha,* 32:242; Gandhi, *Collected Works,* 37:287.

32. As Antony Parel notes in his erudite edition of the English version of *Hind Swaraj,* the original *doha* from Tulsidas says *"pap mool abhiman"*—the root of sin in pride. In Gandhi's account, "sin" is replaced by "body." This substitution remains curiously (deliberately, given the number of people in his inner circle who would have known the correct version of the *doha?*) uncorrected in later editions. See Gandhi, *Hind Swaraj and Other Writings,* ed. Antony Parel (Cambridge: Cambridge University Press, 1997), 88.

33. "Letter to C. F. Andrews," August 6, 1918, Gandhi, *Collected Works,* 17:177.

34. "The Fiery Ordeal," September 30, 1928, *Akshardeha,* 37:293–94; Gandhi, *Collected Works,* 43:58. The translation of this piece into English is prefaced by the remark that it presents "the substance" of the Gujarati essay.

35. "The Fiery Ordeal," September 30, 1928, *Akshardeha,* 37:293; Gandhi, *Collected Works,* 43:58; see also "My Notes," Gandhi, *Collected Works,* 48:87.

7. The Sacrifice of the *Gita*

1. "Satyagraha Leaflet No. 18," May 8, 1919, *Akshardeha,* 15:277; Gandhi, *Collected Works,* 18:26.

2. Retrospectively, by 1919, he writes that "as far back as 1889, when I had my first contact with the *Gita,* it gave me a hint of satyagraha and, as I read it more and more, the hint developed into a pure revelation *[shudh darshan]* of satyagraha."

"Letter to Sakarlal Dave," May 19, 1919, *Akshardeha*, 15:300; Gandhi, *Collected Works*, 18:50–51.) The process may have been more drawn out than this remark indicates. In 1889, as a student in London, he famously encounters the *Gita* in Edwin Arnold's English translation, *The Song Celestial*. (For a thought-provoking discussion of the Arnold translation, Gandhi's relation to it, and more broadly of colonial translations of the *Gita*, see Javed Majeed, "Gandhi, 'Truth,' and Translatability," *Modern Asian Studies* 40, no. 2 [2006].) In the 1890s, spurred by Raychandbhai, he reads the *Gita* in Gujarati and Sanskrit. By around 1903 (according to what he writes in the *Autobiography* in 1927), he sticks "slips of paper on which were written the *Gita* verses" on the wall, and memorizes them while doing his "morning ablutions." And "the *Gita* became an infallible guide of conduct. It became my dictionary of daily reference. Just as I turned to the English dictionary for the meanings of English words that I did not understand, I turned to this dictionary of conduct for a ready solution of all my troubles and trials" (*Autobiography*, Part IV, chapter 5).

Still, this association of ahimsa with the *Gita* is likely retrospective. Joseph Doke reports in his biography of Gandhi in 1909 that Gandhi tells him that he first comes to appreciate "passive resistance" through a Gujarati hymn, and then the Sermon on the Mount, and that the *Gita* only deepened this appreciation. (See Joseph J. Doke, *Indian Patriot in South Africa: M. K. Gandhi* [London: London Indian Chronicle, 1909], 84.) By 1925, however, Gandhi has come to think of his philosophy as faithful especially to the *Gita*. That year he writes: "I do not believe that 'my philosophy' is an indifferent mixture of Tolstoy and Buddha. I do not know what it is except that it is what I feel to be true. It sustains me. I owe much to Tolstoy and much to Buddha. I still somehow or other fancy that 'my philosophy' represents the true meaning of the teaching of the *Gita*." "A Revolutionary's Defense," February 12, 1925, Gandhi, *Collected Works*, 30:248. Increasingly, he cites the *Gita* as the principal influence for his ahimsa, far more important than the usual suspects we name—Tolstoy, Raychandbhai, Ruskin, or Thoreau.

3. Sibaji Bandopadhyay notes that Alf Hiltbeitel's book *Rethinking the Mahabharata* "prepares a tally sheet for the phrase *paramo dharmo* and demonstrates that out of the 54 times it occurs in the Mahābhārata, it is conjoined with the word ahimsa only *four* times." "A Critique of Non-Violence," *Seminar* (2010), no. 608.

4. *Anasaktiyoga*, *Akshardeha*, 41:83; Gandhi, *Collected Works*, 46:164. In putting forth his arguments, Gandhi must also engage with all the other close associates who too think with the *Gita*. To my knowledge, at least the following ashram inmates write commentaries on it in later years: Kakasaheb Kalelkar, Vinoba Bhave, Mahadev Desai, Kishorelal Mashruwala, and Swami Anand. Since Gandhi is acutely aware of the limitations of his Sanskrit, it would be surprising if he did

not run his translation by at least the four of these who are fluent in Sanskrit—Kakasaheb, Vinoba, Kishorelalbhai, and Mahadevbhai.

5. In 1926, over a period of nine months between February and November, during morning prayers at Satyagraha Ashram, he gives a series of almost daily talks on the *Gita*. These lectures are an especially sustained engagement with the *Gita*—together, they are longer than all his other writings explicitly on the Gita combined. These are published posthumously in 1955 under the title *Gandhijinu Gitashikshan* ["Gandhi's Teaching of the *Gita*."] Their nonpublication during Gandhi's lifetime is puzzling since the lectures are transcribed by his trusted associates, Mahadev Desai and Punjabhai Shah. With some editing Gandhi could surely have produced a manuscript for publication, as he so often does with some of his lectures and letters to ashram inmates. Perhaps the lectures—which to the best of our knowledge were given without notes—were not published during his lifetime, because they have a more pronounced paratactical quality than his written materials or even his speeches. (As Sanjay Palshikar notes in his meticulous and erudite essay: "Gandhi's discussion of the Gita can occasionally frustrate the reader if she is looking for a tight, well-argued, logically impeccable commentary. See his *Evil and the Philosophy of Retribution*, 132.) What comes to be published in his own lifetime are his more condensed formulations about the *Gita*, where the parataxis is not as evident. *Gandhijinu Gitashikshan* (hereafter *Gitashikshan*) seems to have been translated into English by the editors of the *Collected Works*, who title it "Discourses on the Gita." It is later published in English as a book: *The Bhagavadgita* (New Delhi: Orient Paperbacks, 1980).

The first book-length work by him on the *Gita* to be published in his own lifetime is *Anasaktiyoga* [Yoga of Non-Attachment] in 1930, a "rendering" of the *Gita* into Gujarati, with short glosses on some passages and an additional preface. That book is released (surely not by accident?) by Navjivan Press on March 12, 1930—the day that the Dandi satyagraha begins. We do not know when the copies arrive at Sabarmati Ashram, where much of the sixty-thousand-strong crowd that had gathered the previous evening to listen to Gandhi speak at the evening prayers before the satyagraha has stayed on until the morning, chanting bhajans. We do, however, know this: when the band of seventy-eight marchers (all men—Gandhi's insistence on a *thekana* or rightful place is clearly at work) sets off on the satyagraha that morning, each is armed with a copy of *Anasaktiyoga*. The book is translated into English in 1931 by Mahadev Desai and published initially in the periodical *Young India* and later as a separate book by Navjivan Press under the title *The Gita According to Gandhi*. (The English translations of the *Gita* that I provide in this book are from Desai's translation of Gandhi's rendering of that text into Gujarati. Desai's translation is available online from several websites.)

Two other publications follow in quick succession. Faced with complaints from ashram inmates that *Anasaktiyoga* is too difficult to follow, later that year he writes from the Yeravda Jail (where he is imprisoned following his arrest during the Dandi satyagraha) a series of letters on the *Gita*; these are collected together soon afterward and published as *Gitabodh*. To help readers further understand *Anasaktiyoga*, he prepares a glossary to the terms in it, which is published in 1936 as the *Gitapadarthkosh*.

6. For a helpful account of the role of *purushartha* in Gandhi's thought, see Antony Parel, *Gandhi's Philosophy and the Quest for Harmony* (Cambridge: Cambridge University Press, 2006).

7. For an extended reading of the work of history and *itihaas* in this passage and Gandhi's writing, see my "The Strange Violence of *Satyagraha*."

8. *Anasaktiyoga, Akshardeha,* 41:88; Gandhi, *Collected Works,* 46:173.

9. "Jain Ahimsa," October 21, 1928, *Akshardeha,* 37:361; Gandhi, *Collected Works,* 48:128. The English translation of this passage, done by Pyarelal, diverges quite significantly from the one I have provided above.

10. *Gitashikshan, Akshardeha,* 32:127; Gandhi, *Collected Works,* 37:132–33.

11. "Letter to Pragji Desai," November 15, 1914, *Akshardeha,* 12:484; Gandhi, *Collected Works,* 14:313. He invokes this verse often in the years that follow. The reference is to the *Bhagavad Gita,* chapter III, verses 12, 13.

12. Ibid. He ventures also a provocative reading of the injunction "resist not evil" (Matthew 5:39) as an intimation to satyagraha.

13. The futurity involved here resonates curiously with Arendt's emphasis on the distinctive futurity of thinking. Her arguments emerge especially clearly in *The Life of the Mind,* which introduces a distinction between thinking and cognition. The former is concerned with meaning and the latter with producing "certain and verifiable knowledge." Even though cognition "constantly corrects itself by discarding the answers and reformulating the questions," here questioning occurs as a means to an end. Cognition, Arendt suggests, is the method of the sciences (and, I might add, the social sciences). By contrast, thinking "does not ask what something is . . . but what it means for it to be." Its questions are "unanswerable" in positive terms. Thinking "is done for its own sake"; it produces "no positive results," though by asking these unanswerable questions "men establish themselves as question-asking beings." Arendt's futurity and thinking of course seem entirely secular, and in this sense are quite distinct from Gandhi's turn to the *Gita.* And yet, even this distinction is less stable than it might appear—for Arendt, newness and even thinking is a "miracle," and for Gandhi, as the preface suggested, religion itself begins with a certain death of God. See Hannah Arendt, *The Life of the Mind* (New York: Harcourt Brace, 1978), 14, 62–65.

14. Dipesh Chakrabarty and Rochona Majumdar, "Gandhi's *Gita* and Politics as Such." *Modern Intellectual History* 7, no. 2 (2010): 341.

15. "A Revolutionary's Defense," February 12, 1925, Gandhi, *Collected Works,* 30:244.

16. Tilak refers here to the *Gita,* IV:11, and to the Buddha's famed dictum: *"Akkodhena jine kodham, asadhum sadhuna jine"* ["Conquer anger by the power of nonanger and evil by the power of good"]. (The translation of the Buddha is from Tagore's letter to Gandhi, *Collected Works,* 16:464.) As Gandhi notes in his reply, Tilak accompanies this often with the injunction, *shat prati shaatyam,* or "wickedness unto the wicked." "Letter from Tilak to Gandhi," January 18, 1920; "Note on Tilak's Letter," January 28, 1920, Gandhi, *Collected Works,* 19:331. For a discussion of Tilak's interpretation of the *Gita,* and of the exchange between Tilak and Gandhi, see Sanjay Palshikar, *Evil and the Philosophy of Retribution.*

17. For a discussion of the trope of sacrifice with reference especially to Tilak, see Shruti Kapila, "A History of Violence," *Modern Intellectual History* 7, no. 2 (2010).

18. "Prayer Discourse [*pravachan*] in Ashram," March 17, 1918, *Akshardeha,* 14:226; Gandhi, *Collected Works,* 16:340.

19. "Foreword to Volume of Gokhale's Speeches," before February 19, 1918, *Akshardeha,* 14:173; Gandhi, *Collected Works,* 16:268. Though to my knowledge this is the first time that Gandhi uses the phrase *swachh saadhan* or "pure means," the insistence on right means is already marked in *Hind Swaraj,* as is the insistence on purity. To my mind, it would not be out of place to suggest that *Hind Swaraj* already works within the problematic of "pure means," which he articulates more forcefully later.

20. Walter Benjamin, "Critique of Violence," *Reflections: Essays, Aphorisms, Autobiographical Writings,* trans. Edmund Jephcott (New York: Schocken Books, 1986), 291–92.

21. Ibid., 298.

22. It is partially because Benjamin does not systematically distinguish divine violence or pure means from sovereign power that Derrida can raise the questions he does: that what is almost "intolerable in this text" is the temptation it leaves open "to think the holocaust as an uninterpretable manifestation of divine violence insofar as this divine violence would be at the same time nihilating, expiatory and bloodless." "One is terrified at the idea of an interpretation that would make of the holocaust an expiation and an indecipherable signature of the just and violent anger of God." See Jacques Derrida, "Force of Law," *Cardozo Law Review* 11 (1990)· 1044–45. Where sovereign power is relinquished, the nature of pure means and divine violence as absolute responsibility becomes more marked, and it becomes ever more difficult to read events such as the Holocaust as examples of "divine violence."

Indeed, a careful reading of "Critique of Violence" would suggest that it already deconstructs and relinquishes sovereign power. As such, the difference between Gandhi and Benjamin on this question is not immense. Derrida's questions may thus be symptomatic more of his own proclivity to affirm general responsibility over absolute responsibility, his "taste for republican democracy."

23. *Autobiography*, Part IV, chapter 5.

24. Arendt, *The Life of the Mind*, 208–10.

25. *Anasaktiyoga, Akshardeha*, 41:88; Gandhi, *Collected Works*, 46:173.

26. I have depended on Gandhi's 1931 translation of his 1929 preface. The Gujarati preface is completed in June 1929; the English translation is published in August 1931. "Prastavna," *Anasaktiyoga, Akshardeha*, 41:86; Gandhi, *Collected Works*, 46:169. The emphasis on desireless action also organizes Gandhi's invocation of another term from the *Gita*, *stithpragnyasa*, or a steadiness of insight. See Tridip Suhrud, "Satyagrahi as Stithpragnya: Gandhi's Reading of the Gita," in *Reading Gandhi in Two Tongues and Other Essays*.

27. Gandhi, *Collected Works*, 46:178.

28. Gandhi's English translation goes: "The means may be likened to a seed, the end to a tree; and there is just the same inviolable connection between the means and the end as there is between the seed and the tree."

29. "An Appeal to the Nation," July 17, 1924, Gandhi, *Collected Works*, 28:310.

30. Heidegger, "The Question Concerning Technology," 5.

31. Nietzsche, *Geneaology of Morals*, First Essay, section 13.

32. "The Dharma of Aapbhog" *Akshardeha*, 17:474; Gandhi, *Collected Works*, June 20, 1920, 20:404. The title of the English translation is "The Duty of Self-Sacrifice."

33. *Gitashikshan, Akshardeha*, 32:270; Gandhi, *Collected Works*, 37:95.

34. "Letter to Sakarlal Dave," May 19, 1919, *Akshardeha*, 15:300; Gandhi, *Collected Works*, 18:50f.

35. And the preface to the *Anasaktiyoga* in 1930 says: "Let it be granted that according to the letter of the *Gita* it is possible to say that warfare is consistent with renunciation of fruit. But after 40 years' unremitting endeavour fully to enforce the teaching of the *Gita* in my own life, I have, in all humility, felt that perfect renunciation is impossible without perfect observance of ahimsa in every shape and form."

36. *Gitashikshan, Akshardeha*, 32:108; Gandhi, *Collected Works*, 37:105.

37. Sibaji Bandyopadhyay, "A Critique of Non-Violence," *Seminar* (2010), no. 608.

38. *Gitashikshan, Akshardeha*, 32:101; Gandhi, *Collected Works*, 37:95.

39. Personal communication, February 12, 2012.

40. "Speech at Surat," August 12, 1928, Gandhi, *Collected Works*, 42:369.

41. "Bardoli Day," June 10, 1928, Gandhi, *Collected Works*, 42:95.

42. "Violence in the Camp," February 9, 1922, Gandhi, *Collected Works*, 26:134.

43. *Gitashikshan, Akshardeha*, 32:199; Gandhi, *Collected Works*, 37:237.

44. "Speech at Bharuch," March 26, 1930, *Akshardeha*, 43:149f.; Gandhi, *Collected Works*, 48:478. There are clearly four words here, not two. It may not be

insignificant that *pakeezgi* and *kurbani* are words shared between Urdu and Gujarati, while *atmashuddhi* and *balidan* are words shared between Gujarati and Sanskrit.

45. To list some: there are warriors on the field who are *sama yudhi* (equal in battle) to Bhima and Arjuna [I:4]; the one who is *samadukhasukham* (constant in pain and pleasure, for whom these are alike) is ready for immortality (II:15); *samatvam* (evenness of mind, equanimity or equability) is yoga [II:48]; the one who is free from attachment is *samah siddhau asiddhau ca* (constant in success and failure) [IV:22]; the wise are *samadarshanah* (see the same; see impartially or equally) in or between a cultivated Brahmin, a cow, an elephant, a dog, and a *swapaka* (dog-cooker, outcaste) [V:18]; even here on earth, rebirth is conquered by those who are established in *sama* (sameness, impartiality, equality) [V:19]; the highest Self of him who has conquered himself and is peaceful, is *samahitah* (steadfast, composed, collected) in cold, heat, pleasure, and pain, as also in honor and dishonor (VI:7); he is to be distinguished among men who is *samabuddhir* (impartial or equal-minded) toward friend, companion, and enemy, toward to the good and toward the evil [VI:9]; the yoga disciplined self, being *sarvatra samadarshanah* (seeing equally or the same at all times), sees the Self present in all beings, and all beings present in the Self [VI:29]; Krishna says: "I am the *samo* (same) in all beings, there is none disliked or near to me [IX:29]; he is dear to Krishna who is *sama mitra cha shatru cha* (alike to friend and enemy) [XII:18]; knowledge involves constant *samacittatvam* (even-mindedness) toward desired and undesired events [XIII:9]; and he who is absorbed in Brahman is *sama* (impartial) among all beings [XVIII:54].

46. *Anasaktiyoga, Akshardeha,* 41:107; Gandhi, *Collected Works,* 46:191.

47. "Interview with M. C. Rajah," March 22, 1936, 68:320.

48. J.A.B. Van Buitenen, *Ramanuja on the Bhagavadgita: A Condensed Rendering of His Gitabhasya with Copious Notes and an Introduction* (Delhi: Motilala Banarasidass, 1968), 95.

49. Ibid, 89.

50. "Letter to Santoji Maharaj," July 2, 1927, *Akshardeha,* 34:87f; Gandhi, *Collected Works,* 39:146.

51. *Gitashikshan, Akshardeha,* 32:180; Gandhi, *Collected Works,* 37:211f.

52. "Letter to Narandas Gandhi," October 21, 1930, *Akshardeha,* 44:236–37; Gandhi, *Collected Works,* 50:160.

53. Jugatram Dave, *Gitagitmunjari* (Ahmedabad: Navjivan Press, 1945), 19. I thank Babu Suthar for helping me translate and read the two poems.

54. Letter to Jugatram Dave, May 27, 1945, Gandhi, *Collected Works,* 86:426.

55. *Gitagitmanjari,* 93.

56. Personal communication, Tridip Suhrud.

57. *Gitashikshan, Akshardeha,* 32:111; Gandhi, *Collected Works,* 37:109.

58. "Paris Havoc," February 5, 1910, *Akshardeha*, 10:166; Gandhi, *Collected Works*, 10:410.

59. "How to Keep Health," September 1, 1927, Gandhi, *Collected Works*, 39:491.

60. Étienne Balibar elegantly traces the way dominant traditions privilege liberty over equality, and provides a powerful thinking of equality and liberty together. However, it is striking also that he has relatively little to say about the exclusion that precedes equaliberty—fraternity. See his *Equaliberty: Political Essays*, trans. James Ingram (Durham: Duke University Press, 2014).

61. Babu Suthar points out (personal communication) that there is no sharp distinction between metaphor and allegory in Gujarati. My reading of Gandhi's allegory here owes much to conversations with Simona Sawhney, and to her essay on Gandhi's reading of the Gita in *The Modernity of Sanskrit* (Minneapolis: University of Minnesota Press, 2009.)

62. Dipesh Chakrabarty and Rochona Majumdar, "Gandhi's *Gita* and Politics as Such," *Modern Intellectual History* 7, no. 2 (2010): 335–55 (347).

63. I refer here to the invocation of the term "performative" in the sense that it carries in the work of J. L. Austin, where the performative is opposed to the constative. That sense is very different from what either Jacques Derrida or Judith Butler does with the term. Very often, even where essays present themselves as drawing on the concept of the performative as articulated by the latter two, they continue to work effectively with the Austinian concept.

64. This hermeneutic tradition, which is sensitive to the allegorical-metaphorical nature of truth-being, is beautifully articulated in Hans Georg Gadamer's *Truth and Method*, 2nd ed. (London: Sheed and Ward, 1989).

65. "Letter to Sakarlal Dave," May 19, 1919, *Akshardeha*, 15:300; Gandhi, *Collected Works*, 18:50f.

66. *Anasaktiyoga*, *Akshardeha*, 41:83; Gandhi, *Collected Works*, 46:164.

67. I thank Gayatri Chakravorty Spivak for comments on the discussion of the term *rupak* in an earlier draft.

68. "Bhagavad Gita or Anasaktiyoga," March 16, 1930, *Akshardeha*, 43:98; Gandhi, *Collected Works*, 48:439.

69. The argument in what follows resonates in part with that offered by Uday Mehta in his "The Burden of Civility," *Raritan: A Quarterly Review* 33, no. 1 (2013): 44.

70. *Gitashiksan*, *Akshardeha*, 32:128; *Gandhi, Collected Works*, 37:133–34.

71. "At It Again," May 7, 1925, Gandhi, *Collected Works*, 31:288.

72. "Teaching of Hinduism," October 3, 1936, Gandhi, *Collected Works*, 69:420; *Akshardeha*, 63:331.

73. Ibid.

74. "Letter to Moolchand Parekh," May 24, 1932, *Akshardeha*, 49:437; Gandhi, *Collected Works*, 55:417.

75. Jean-Luc Nancy, "The Unsacrificeable," *Yale French Studies* no. 79 (1991): 35–36.

76. *Gandhijinu Gitashikshan, Akshardeha,* 32:281; Gandhi, *Collected Works,* 37:328.

77. "Some Questions," January 30, 1921, in *Akshardeha,* 19:270; Gandhi, *Collected Works,* 22:289.

78. Cited in B. R. Nanda, "Gandhi and Religion," in *Gandhian Alternatives: Socio-Political Thoughts,* ed. Anil Dutta Mishra and Sushma Yadav (New Delhi: Concept Publishing Company, 2005), 36. Nanda draws here on Gandhi's interview with an American missionary. "Interview with Dr. Crane," Gandhi, *Collected Works,* 71:3.

8. Ciphering the Satyagrahi

1. "Importance of Vows," October 8, 1913, *Akshardeha,* 12:201, Gandhi, *Collected Works,* 13:363.

2. "Speech in Reply to Welcome Address," Porbandar, March 1, 1925, *Akshardeha,* 26:147; Gandhi, *Collected Works,* 30:280.

3. Gandhi, *Autobiography,* Part I, chapter 1.

4. Ibid., chapter 14.

5. It would be quite inadequate to cast the principle as abstract and constative, and the vow as concrete and performative. To observe a principle is to promise to regularly repeat a certain act and commitment. Thus, the principle is already in the realm of the performative rather than constative.

6. *Satyagraha in South Africa,* chapter 13. Both Gujarati and English editions of this book are available at https://www.gandhiheritageportal.org/.

7. See, for instance, "Letter to Esther Faering," January 25, 1919, Gandhi, *Collected Works,* 17:263.

8. *Gitashikshan, Akshardeha,* 32:122; Gandhi, *Collected Works,* 37:125.

9. "Statement on Untouchability–VIII," November 17, 1932, Gandhi, *Collected Works,* 58:10.

10. In the passage above, as elsewhere, Gandhi also thinks *shunya* through a term prominent in the *Gita*—the unmanifest (*avyakt*). Now the unmanifest comes to describe the "real essence" *[kharu swarup]* of being. "Those who have fixed their minds on the Unmanifest, that is, who worship the formless Brahman experience greater difficulty in their effort, for it is extremely difficult for us, embodied souls, to know the unmanifest state. *Gandhijinu Gitashikshan, Akshardeha,* 32:235f.; Gandhi, *Collected Works,* 37:279; for the discussion of the "real essence" of being, see also *Gandhijinu Gitashikshan, Akshardeha,* 32:202f.; Gandhi, *Collected Works,* 37:241.

11. "Letter to Kishorelal Mashruwala," around May 18, 1929, Gandhi, *Collected Works*, 46:29. See also "Speech at Praja Parishad Workers Meeting," Rajkot, April 23, 1939, *Akshardeha*, 69:184; Gandhi, *Collected Works*, 75:293. There is no equivalent in the Gujarati text to the emphasis on zero.

12. "Meaning of 'Bandhu,'" before March 30, 1920, *Akshardeha*, 17:284, Gandhi, *Collected Works*, 20:190.

13. *Anasaktiyoga*, *Akshardeha*, 41:109; Gandhi, *Collected Works*, 46:194.

14. "Letter to Harilal Gandhi," November 26, 1918, *Akshardeha*, 15:63; Gandhi, *Collected Works*, 17:248.

15. "Letter to a Bereaved Father," June 28, 1924, Gandhi, *Collected Works*, 28:219.

16. "Statement Announcing 21 Day Fast," September 18, 1924, Gandhi, *Collected Works*, 29:180.

17. "Note," September 21, 1924, Gandhi, *Collected Works*, 29:198. In addition to this popular Christian hymn, Gandhi also draws on the Philippians to make this argument. "When we work purely as His instrument with an absolute self-surrender there can be no cause for anxiety or fretfulness whatever the result or however black may be the horizon for the time being. Jesus summed up the same lesson in one sentence: "Be careful of [for] nothing." Puzzlingly, in the Gujarati translation of this essay, the phrase "utter hopelessness" is rendered again as *nisahayata* or helplessness—the very translation that this essay criticizes. We do not know who translates this piece.

18. "How to Keep Health," September 1, 1927; Gandhi, *Collected Works*, 39:491.

19. "Speech at Praja Parishad Worker's Meeting," Rajkot, April 23, 1929, Gandhi, *Collected Works*, 75:290.

20. *Gandhijinu Gitashikshan*, *Akshardeha*, 32:133; Gandhi, *Collected Works*, 37:142. This portion of the passage is prefaced by an argument that insists that masters *[sheth]* and workers are both workers, and that if workers claim to be masters, then they will "come to grief." In its remarks about workers, the passage is again divided between a rooted conservatism that accepts workers' subordination (and such quiescent acceptance, as Sujata Patel has shown, often characterizes the workings of the Majoor Mahajan, the labor union that Gandhi founds) and the murmuring refusal to accept any hierarchy at all. The latter possibility is heightened in the insistence on ciphering that occurs in the portion cited above. See Sujata Patel, *The Making of Industrial Relations: The Ahmedabad Textile Industry, 1918–1939* (Delhi: Oxford University Press, 1988).

21. "Letter to Basil Matthew," June 8, 1927, Gandhi, *Collected Works*, 39:24.

22. "Letter to Prabhudas Gandhi," November 12, 1928, Gandhi, *Collected Works*, 43:216..

23. Gandhi, *Atmakatha* or *Autobiography*, Part 5, chapter 9. The English translation (in all likelihood by Mahadev Desai, though approved by Gandhi) of this passage is strikingly different from the Gujarati text.

24. "Letter to Babbaldas Mehta," August 4, 1932, *Akshardeha*, 50:330; Gandhi, *Collected Works*, 56:26.

25. "Letter to Lies Burzas," July 20, 1927, Gandhi, *Collected Works*, 39:260.

26. "Letter to Narandas Gandhi," June 16–19, 1932, *Akshardeha*, 50:68; Gandhi, *Collected Works*, 56:26.

27. "Speech at Gandhi Seva Sangh Meeting–III," February 22, 1940, *Akshardeha*, 71:268; Gandhi, *Collected Works*, 77:379, original Hindi.

28. "Problems of Ahimsa," August 9, 1925, *Akshardeha*, 28:43; Gandhi, *Collected Works*, 32:273. The Shastras and customs would, of course, have also called for *maryada* or limits to intermixing of castes. The way Gandhi affirms *maryada* here is again symptomatic of how his radical conservatism remains undecidably poised between a rerooting and an uprooting, tipping now into one and now into the other.

29. "Letter to Maganlal Gandhi," after March 14, 1915, *Akshardeha*, 13:37; Gandhi, *Collected Works*, 14:384.

30. "History of the Satyagraha Ashram," July 11, 1932, Gandhi, *Collected Works*, 56:152.

31. "General Knowledge about Health–XXXII," August 9, 1913, *Akshardeha*, 12:131; Gandhi, *Collected Works*, 13:240–41.

32. "Letter to Esther Faering," September 6, 1917, Gandhi, *Collected Works*, 16:17. See also Edwin Arnold, *The Song Celestial, or, Bhagavad Gita* (London: Trubner and Co., 1886), 37.

33. He claims again to take his inspiration from the *Gita*, as, for instance, from the verse: "God, O Arjuna, dwells in the heart of every being and to His delusive mystery whirls them all, (as though) set on a machine [*yantra*]. *Gitashikshan*, *Akshardeha*, 32:96; Gandhi, *Collected Works*, 37:326.

34. *Gitashikshan*, *Akshardeha*, 32:96; Gandhi, *Collected Works*, 37:89.

35. *Gitashikshan*, *Akshardeha*, 32:159; Gandhi, *Collected Works*, 37:89.

36. "Letter to Mirabehn," January 19, 1933, Gandhi, *Collected Works*, 59:54. The footnote here refers to the *Gita*, 18:61. An intriguing reformulation of the *Gita*'s arguments takes place here. Even if God moves all beings as if they are parts of the machine, that becomes secondary to the need to consciously become like a mechanic.

37. "*Dayadharma*: Speech on the Birth Anniversary of Shrimad Rajchandra," November 16, 1921, *Akshardeha*, 21:387; Gandhi, *Collected Works*, 25:93.

38. "Interview to Peggy Durdin," after August 17, 1944, Gandhi, *Collected Works*, 84:304.

39. "Letter to Parshuram Mehrotra," June 1, 1932, *Akshardeha*, 50:2.

40. "Letter to H.S.L. Polak," October 17, 1932, Gandhi, *Collected Works*, 57:235.

41. Devji, *The Impossible Indian*, 101–2.

42. Involved in these formulations is a helplessness quite in contrast to the "mistaken feeling of helplessness" that he discerns among Indians. This "mistaken

feeling" he decries: he attacks the idea that Indians "are powerless to do anything which may end their suffering." "Swaraj in a Year," September 22, 1920, *Akshardeha*, 18:252; Gandhi, *Collected Works*, 21:279.

43. *Gitashikshan, Akshardeha*, 32:175; Gandhi, *Collected Works*, 37:137; for the implications of this fascinating machinicity, see also *Akshardeha*, 32:219; Gandhi, *Collected Works*, 37:263.

44. *Gitashikshan, Akshardeha*, 32:154; Gandhi, *Collected Works*, 37:160.

45. "Sudharo or Kudharo," *Akshardeha* 30:353, April 25, 1926; "Reformation or Deformation," Gandhi, *Collected Works*, 35:144. I have adhered to Mahadev Desai's rendering into English—in all likelihood with Gandhi's approval—of the Gujarati text. A more literal rendering of the Gujarati text would be: "God has given humans [*manushya*] discrimination. The brute is merely without agency [*paradhin*]. This is why brutes have no such thing as autonomy [*swatantrata*], that is to say choice [*pasandgi*]. In contrast humans have choice, they can think moral thoughts, and because they are autonomous can think of virtue and vice."

46. "Letter to Anasuyabehn Sarabhai," May 6, 1933, *Akshardeha*, 55:127; Gandhi, *Collected Works*, 61:99.

47. "Letter to Driver," February 2, 1934, *Akshardeha*, 57:100; Gandhi, *Collected Works*, 63:92f.

48. "Speech at Praja Parishad Worker's Meeting," Rajkot, May 12, 1939, Gandhi, *Collected Works*, 75:381 [summary by Pyarelal]; *Akshardeha*, 69:281.

49. "Satyagraha Leaflet 17," May 7, 1919, *Akshardeha*, 15:274; Gandhi, *Collected Works*, 18:23.

50. "Discussion with a Friend," January 13, 1933, *Akshardeha*, 53:540; Gandhi, *Collected Works*, 59:493.

51. "Speech to Prayer Meeting," January 3, 1932, *Akshardeha*, 38:499; Gandhi, *Collected Works*,

52. "Discussion with Charles Fabri," on or before July 26, 1939. Gandhi, *Collected Works*, 76:165–67.

53. "Letter to Premabehn Kantak," January 30, 1932, *Akshardeha*, 49:51; Gandhi, *Collected Works*, 52:430.

54. *Gitabodh, Akshardeha*, 49:119; Gandhi, *Collected Works*, 55:46.

55. And this friendship requires ciphering. When Fabri asks what Gandhi would say to those "who cannot pray," Gandhi responds: "'Be humble,' I would say to them. . . . if someone puts a conundrum before me, I say to him: 'You are not going to know the meaning of God or prayer unless you reduce yourself to a cipher.'" When Fabri suggests that Buddhism does not require prayer, only meditation, Gandhi responds that Buddhism is "one long prayer," and refuses any distinction between meditation and prayer. "Discussion with Charles Fabri," on or before July 26, 1939. Gandhi, *Collected Works*, 76:165–67.

56. "Difficult Situations," July 5, 1925, *Akshardeha*, 27:298; Gandhi, *Collected Works*, 32:89.

57. "Discussion with a Friend," January 13, 1933, *Akshardeha*, 53:540; Gandhi, *Collected Works*, 59:493.

58. Jacques Derrida, *Given Time: Counterfeit Money I* (Chicago: University of Chicago Press, 1992), 13, 16.

59. Gandhi specifies that he does not provide a "literal translation" *[shabdarth tarjumo]* but rather a "free rendering" that brings out its "proper significance" *[rahasya barobar],* and so that "it appear right in our language." "Murakhraj and His Two Brothers," *Akshardeha*, 11:176–95. Gandhi's translation has not been translated back into English in the *Collected Works*.

60. Ibid., 189.

61. April 9, 1926, *Gitashikshan, Akshardeha,* 32:125–26; Gandhi, *Collected Works*, 37:130.

62. *Anasaktiyoga, Akshardeha,* 41:99, Gandhi, *Collected Works*, 46:182.

63. "Letter to W. J. Wybergh," May 10, 1910, Gandhi, *Collected Works*, 11:40.

64. "Discussion with Bharatanand," before September 2, 1940, Gandhi, *Collected Works*, 79:174.

65. "Speech at Gurukul Anniversary," March 20, 1916, Gandhi, *Collected Works*, 15:206.

66. "The Swadeshi Vow–II," April 8, 1919, Gandhi, *Collected Works*, 17:398.

67. "Letter to Jamnadas and Khushalchand Gandhi," November 27, 1932, *Akshardeha*, 52:83f.; Gandhi, *Collected Works*, 58:51f.

68. "Letter to Premaben Kanthak," February 25, 1932, *Akshardeha*, 49:145; Gandhi, *Collected Works*, 55:78.

69. "Non-Violence: the Greatest Force," November 8, 1926, Gandhi, *Collected Works*, 36:45.

70. "Sudharo or Kudharo," *Akshardeha* 30:353, April 25, 1926; "Reformation or Deformation," Gandhi, *Collected Works*, 35:144.

71. *Gitashikshan, Akshardeha,* 32:171; Gandhi, *Collected Works,* 37:199–200. Here as in many other places the official translation offered in the *Collected Works* can be misleading: *pashu,* for example, is rendered as "lower creatures."

72. "The Doctrine of the Sword," August 11, 1920, Gandhi, *Collected Works,* 21:133; "The *Nyaya* of the Sword," August 15, 1920, *Akshardeha*, 18:145. There is no equivalent passage in the Gujarati essay of the same title published the next week in *Navjivan*.

73. "Letter to Jawaharlal Nehru," April 26, 1925, Gandhi, *Collected Works,* 31:199.

74. Martin Heidegger, "Letter on Humanism," trans. Frank A. Capuzzi, in Martin Heidegger, *Pathmarks*, ed. William H. McNeill (Cambridge: Cambridge University Press, 1998), 252.

75. For an essay that foregrounds primarily these hierarchies in Gandhi's thinking of the animal, see Aishwary Kumar, "Satyagraha and the Place of the Animal: Gandhi's Distinctions," *Social History* 29, no. 3 (2014).

76. "Non-Violence: The Greatest Force," November 8, 1926, Gandhi, *Collected Works*, 36:45.

77. "The *Nyaya* of the Sword," August 15,1920, *Akshardeha*, 18:146; "The Doctrine of the Sword," August 11, 1920, Gandhi, *Collected Works*, 21:133. The Gujarati version says: "When *pashubal* ['animal force'] is dominant in India, then the distinctions between ancient and modern, east and west may be counted as nonexistent [*nabud*]."

"Non-violence: The Greatest Force," November 8, 1926, Gandhi, *Collected Works*, 36:45.

9. The Extreme Limit of Forgiveness

1. "Ahimsa–III," October 24, 1926, *Akshardeha*, 31:491; translated as "Is This Humanity–III," Gandhi, *Collected Works*, 36:429.

2. "Letter to F. G. Pratt," February 28, 1918, Gandhi, *Collected Works*, 16:296.

3. For a discussion of this aneconomic friendship, see my "Gandhi's Politics," and Faisal Devji, *The Impossible Indian: Gandhi and the Temptation of Violence* (London: Hurst and Co., 2012), chapter 3.

4. "Ajmal Jamia Fund," November 22, 1928, Gandhi, *Collected Works*, 43:247–48.

5. "Speech at Public Meeting," Rajkot, May 23, 1939, Gandhi, *Collected Works*, 75:421.

6. "Notes," December 15, 1920, in Gandhi, *Collected Works*, 22:96.

7. "Speech on Non-cooperation Resolution at Calcutta Congress," September 8, 1920, Gandhi, *Collected Works*, 21:254.

8. "Letter to C. F. Andrews," June 20, 1920, Gandhi, *Collected Works*, 20:410.

9. "Not Lonely," February 24, 1946, Gandhi, *Collected Works*, 89:444.

10. He goes on to note, however, that Andrews disagrees with him on the matter of vows. Andrews argues, he notes: "'What I may hold to be right today may be found to be wrong tomorrow. I must therefore hold myself free to do the will of God as I discover it from moment to moment.' This attitude has answered his purpose. I should be undone. I see a fallacy behind A's argument. He does not. So it sustains him. Fallacy, error and the like are relative terms." Note, however, that Andrews too does not trust himself, and trusts God instead, and that in this sense both Andrews and Gandhi are within the same problematic. "Letter to Mirabehn," February 28, 1927, Gandhi, *Collected Works*, 38:171.

11. "Letter to Harilal Gandhi," March 4, 1914, *Akshardeha*, 12:319; Gandhi, *Collected Works*, 14:95. For a superb account of Harilal's relation with Gandhi, see

Chandulal Dalal, *Harilal Gandhi: A Life,* trans. Tridip Suhrud (New Delhi: Orient Longman, 2007).

12. This economy of forgiveness is stressed by many of the most influential recent texts on forgiveness, though they usually focus on the first of the two economies discussed here—that of repentance or atonement. That economy provides the framework for Charles Griswold's classic work, *Forgiveness: A Philosophical Exploration* (Cambridge: Cambridge University Press, 2007). His scholarship is a fascinating exploration of what forgiveness as a virtue has conceptually entailed in ancient Greek and modern Western contexts. See also his "Debating Forgiveness: A Reply to My Critics," *Philosophia* 38 (2010): 457–73. See also V. Jankélévitch, *Forgiveness,* trans. A. Kelly (Chicago: University of Chicago Press, 2005).

13. "Notes," March 16, 1921, Gandhi, *Collected Works,* 22:414.

14. "Notes," December 8, 1920, Gandhi, *Collected Works,* 22:64. In Gandhi's vocabulary, as I will suggest later, the power to punish is not only possessed by the sovereign but also the lover. In this context, as in many others where he addresses those who are not persuaded of satyagraha, his conviction is that the satyagrahi's "power to punish" has nothing in common with the sovereign, since satyagrahis punish the beloved by suffering themselves.

In his 1921 message after the Nankana Sahib massacre, he returns to some of these themes: "The purest way of seeking justice against the murderers is not to seek it. . . . [P]unishment cannot recall the dead to life. I would ask those whose hearts are lacerated to forgive them, not out of their weakness—for they are able in every way to have them punished—but out of their immeasurable strength. Only the strong can forgive." Message to Lahore Sikhs on Nankana tragedy, March 4, 1921, Gandhi, *Collected Works,* 22:386. See also the discussion of this essay later in "Notes," Gandhi, *Collected Works,* 22:412f.

15. "The *Nyaya* [justice] of the Sword," August 15, 1920, *Akshardeha,* 18:145; "The Doctrine of the Sword," August 11, 1920, Gandhi, *Collected Works,* 21:133.

16. It is perhaps partially because of questions like this that conventional theories of forgiveness, such as that laid out by Griswold, have little patience for unconditional forgiveness. He, for instance, treats it as a categorical mistake, and suggests that there can be no such thing. Discussing the case of the Amish forgiveness in 2006 of a killer who kills ten Amish girls in a school, he writes: "It would seem that the Amish ideal is proleptic, universal, and unconditional forgiveness and the forswearing of anger altogether, such that not only all past evil but all future evil is forgiven. The goal is apparently a life entirely free from moral anger no matter what." Indeed, the Amish act is even unrecognizable to Griswold as forgiveness: "substantively it may not be a case of forgiveness at all, so much as of excusing, or forgetting, or of not feeling moral hatred" ("Debating Forgiveness," 5). I do not wish to go here in the nature of Amish forgiveness, about which I know little. All I wish to stress is that Griswold's categories make unconditional

forgiveness not only impossible but invisible, perhaps much in the same way that immeasurable equality is invisible to mainstream political theory. Jankélévitch, similarly, insists that forgiveness is possible only where there is repentance. Exhibiting the unconscious (and therefore perhaps more virulent) racism that characterizes so much of the Western response to the Holocaust (racism because European violence toward nonwhites that both preceded and followed the Holocaust is implicitly treated here as forgivable), he also declares that forgiveness died in the death camps, and that Germans never asked for forgiveness.

17. I was acutely reminded of this question in Cape Town in 2012, at the memorial to the "Trojan Horse Massacre," where three children were killed by the forces of the South African apartheid state. In the name given to the event, there is the insistence that three is not too small a number to count as a massacre. Is there a number or being too small?—this is never only a rhetorical question.

18. "Hopes Held Out," February 5, 1922, 22:303; Gandhi, *Collected Works,* 26:92.

19. "Fragment of a Letter," April 22, 1914, *Akshardeha,* 12:355; Gandhi, *Collected Works,* 14:154.

20. *Atmakatha* or *Autobiography,* part IV, chapter 36.

21. "Fasting and Prayer," October 12, 1919, *Akshardeha,* 16:220; Gandhi, *Collected Works,* 19:47.

22. A searchable *Bhagavadgomandal* is available online at http://www.bhagavad gomandalonline.com.

23. "Discussion Aboard 'The Gurkha,'" Gandhi, *Collected Works,* 22:111. The centrality of the relation with the other is foregrounded in Rustom Bharucha's *Terror and Performance* (New Delhi: Routledge, 2014).

24. "Notes," September 4, 1924, Gandhi, *Collected Works,* 29:82.

25. Jacques Derrida, *Given Time: Counterfeit Money I* (Chicago: University of Chicago Press, 1992), 17–18.

26. Cited in Maria Hibbets, "Saving Them from Yourself: An Inquiry into the South Asian Gift of Fearlessness," *Journal of Religious Ethics* 27, no. 3 (1999): 455.

27. "Notes," March 16, 1921, Gandhi, *Collected Works,* 22:413.

28. Jacques Derrida, *On Cosmopolitanism and Forgiveness* (London: Routledge, 2005), 34f.

29. Ibid., 32f.

30. Ibid., 33.

31. Ibid., 44, 45, 48, 49.

32. Ibid., 50.

33. Jacques Derrida, *Without Alibi,* trans. and ed. Peggy Kamuf (Stanford: Stanford University Press, 2002), xix.

34. Gandhi, *Gitashikshan, Akshardeha,* 32:120; .Gandhi, *Collected Works,* 37:122.

35. For a powerful account of that fast, see Tridip Suhrud, "Emptied of All but Love: Gandhiji's First Public Fast," in *Rethinking Gandhi and Non-violent*

Relationality: Global Perspectives, ed. Debjani Ganguly and John Docker (London: Routledge, 2007).

36. "Speech at Nadiad," March 22, 1918, Gandhi, *Collected Works,* 16:357.

37. "Letter to George Joseph," April 12, 1924, Gandhi, *Collected Works,* 27:225. Joseph, as is well known, is not quite convinced by these arguments and parts ways initially with Gandhi and later with the Congress.

38. "Letter to Additional Secretary, Home Department, Government of India," July 15, 1943, Gandhi, *Collected Works,* 83:371.

39. "Divine Warning," February 19, 1922, *Akshardeha,* 22:384; Gandhi, *Collected Works,* 26:187.

40. "Letter to H.S.L. Polak," October 17, 1932, Gandhi, *Collected Works,* 57:235.

41. "Question Box," December 10, 1947, Gandhi, *Collected Works,* 98:21f.

42. For an extended discussion of Gandhi's conscience, see Tridip Suhrud, "A Small, Still, Voice," in *Reading Gandhi in Two Tongues and Other Essays.*

43. So it is that he considers fasting an especially dangerous weapon—far more dangerous than either noncooperation or the constructive program—and insists on several occasions that only he is qualified for it. "Fasting for a public cause also has its shastra and I am the only one adequately versed in it." "Speech at Prayer Meeting," New Delhi, June 17, 1947, Gandhi, *Collected Works,* 95:293; original in Hindi. An unacknowledged specter haunts this claim: when made as part of satyagraha, it must provincialize itself even as it is made, and thus acknowledge that it cannot know itself to be correct.

44. "Notes," July 31, 1924, Gandhi, *Collected Works,* 95:293.

45. "Question Box," December 10, 1947, Gandhi, *Collected Works,* 98:21f.

46. For a provocative discussion of what would be entailed in a politics without guarantee, and relatedly a "history without warranty," see Saurabh Dube, *Stitches on Time: Colonial Textures and Postcolonial Tangles* (Durham: Duke University Press, 2004).

47. "Fragment of a Letter," April 22, 1914, *Akshardeha,* 12:355; Gandhi, *Collected Works,* 14:154.

48. Heidegger, *The Concept of Time,* trans. William McNeill (Oxford: Blackwell, 1992), 3E.

49. "Notes," June 4, 1925, Gandhi, *Collected Works,* 31:434.

50. "Message to Gujarati Hindu Stri Mandal," on or before November 14, 1917, *Akshardeha,* 14:76, Gandhi, *Collected Works,* 16:150f.

51. My reading here clearly reveals the impress of Uday Mehta's deeply thoughtful account of Gandhi's concept of patience in his "Patience, Inwardness, and Self-knowledge in Gandhi's *Hind Swaraj,*" *Public Culture* 23, no. 2 (2011). It differs from Mehta's, however, in two crucial ways, each of which entails a cascading set of further differences. First, for Mehta, "With respect neither to principles nor to virtues is there an independent value placed on time and hence on patience"

(418). In contrast, what I have been suggesting here is that a distinctive time and indeed patience is constitutive of liberalism, republican democracy, rule of law— of the social order that Gandhi describes as "modern civilization." Second, for Mehta Gandhi's concept of patience not only "abjures abstraction," but "urges patience in an almost intimate voice" (422). My sense is that while there is certainly textual warrant for reading Gandhi in this Burkean spirit, the fissures in Gandhi's argument cannot be contained within such a reading. I return rather to the spirit of the inaugural gesture of Mehta's essay, where he points to Job's patience, and suggests that this is not a "pure expression" of patience, since Job works with the "theological certainty" that God will redeem him.

52. "A Confession of Error," August 18, 1921, Gandhi, *Collected Works*, 24:111; Gandhi, *Akshardeha*, 20:493f.

53. "My Friend, the Revolutionary," April 9, 1925, Gandhi, *Collected Works*, 31:138f.

54. In explaining his vision of a spinning franchise, Gandhi makes an analogy with the French requirement for "military training." Spinning is thus conceived as an alternative discipline to precisely the discipline of the warrior. The Congress abandons the spinning franchise within nine months. For an extended account of Gandhi's and the nationalist engagement with spinning and khadi, see Lisa Trivedi, *Clothing Gandhi's Nation: Homespun and Modern India* (Bloomington: Indiana University Press, 2007).

55. Uday Singh Mehta provides a brilliant analysis of the time of spinning in his "Patience, Inwardness, and Self-knowledge in Gandhi's *Hind Swaraj*."

56. "Satyagraha Ashram," November 4, 1928, 38:22, Gandhi, *Collected Works*, 43:191.

57. "Handicap of Mahatmaship," November 8, 1928, Gandhi, *Collected Works*, 43:203.

58. "Letter to Mridula Sarabhai," October 31, 1945, Gandhi, *Collected Works*, 88:248.

59. "Satyagraha Leaflet No. 16," May 6, 1919, Gandhi, *Akshardeha*, 15:268; Gandhi, *Collected Works*, 18:16. The reference is to the deportation of Benjamin Horniman, a British sympathizer of the Indian nationalist movement and editor of the *Bombay Chronicle*.

60. "Speech on Satyagraha Movement," Trichinopoly, March 25, 1919, Gandhi, *Collected Works*, 17:352.

61. "Letter to a Friend," March 5, 1921, in Rabindranath Tagore, *A Miscellany: The English Writings of Rabindranath Tagore*, vol. 3, ed. Sisir Kumar Das (New Delhi: Sahitya Akademi, 1996), 285–86. These letters were addressed to C. F. Andrews, one of the closest friends of both Tagore and Gandhi, and were published at the time in *Modern Review*.

62. "The Poet's Anxiety," June 1, 1921, Gandhi, *Collected Works*, 23:220.

63. "Notes," September 4, 1924, Gandhi, *Collected Works,* 29:81.

64. "Notes," June 25, 1925, Gandhi, *Collected Works,* 32:40. Describing the khadi worker Satish Babu, Gandhi again remarks: "I praise Satish Babu's work because, though he has sacrificed his business worth millions and dedicated his intelligence, the services of the members of his family and his resources to the propagation of khadi, he is not in the least conscious of his self-sacrifice [*tyag*], or rather he has no trace of pride for having done all this. This is because he has found joy in self-sacrifice. Without that sacrifice he cannot live ['It would be impossible for him to live without it']." "Khadi Pratishthan," July 12, 1925, *Akshardeha,* 27:330; Gandhi, *Collected Works,* 32:126.

65. *Gitashikshan, Akshardeha,* 32:282; Gandhi, *Collected Works,* 37:330. For an intriguing discussion of this passage, see Sanjay Palshikar, *Evil and the Philosophy of Retribution,* 133.

66. "Letter to Jawaharlal Nehru," July 3, 1928, Gandhi, *Collected Works,* 42:201; *Akshardeha,* 37:15.

Afterword

1. Gandhi, *Gitashikshan, Akshardeha,* 32:286; Gandhi, *Collected Works,* 37:336. The discussion here draws heavily on Tridip Suhrud's essay "Ramanama," in *Reading Gandhi in Two Tongues and Other Essays.*

2. Gandhi, *Autobiography,* Part I, chapter 10.

3. "Letter to D. R. Majli," March 23, 1924, Gandhi, *Collected Works,* 27:111.

4. "Answers to Questions at Gandhi Seva Sangh, Brindaban–I," May 5, 1939, Gandhi, *Collected Works,* 75:341.

5. "Letter to D. R. Majli," March 23, 1924, Gandhi, *Collected Works,* 27:111; *Autobiography,* Part I, chapter 10.

6. Gayatri Chakravorty Spivak, "Righting Wrongs," *South Atlantic Quarterly* 103, no. 2/3 (2004): 523–81.

7. Immanuel Kant, "What Is Enlightenment," in *Perpetual Peace, and Other Essays on Politics, History, and Morals,* trans. Ted Humphrey (Indianapolis: Hackett, 1983).

8. Tridip Suhrud, "Emptied of All but Love: Gandhiji on 30th January, 1948," *Nehru Memorial Museum and Library Occasional Paper 18,* New Delhi, 2013.

9. "Speech at Meeting in Bulsar," April 20, 1921, *Akshardeha,* 20:22; Gandhi, *Collected Works,* 23:71f.

10. "Message for Last Day of Satyagraha Week," *Akshardeha,* 19:491; Gandhi, *Collected Works,* 23:27.

11. "My Notes," May 15, 1921, *Akshardeha,* 20:90; Gandhi, *Collected Works,* 23:251.

12. Gandhi, *Autobiography*, Part I, chapter 2.

13. "What Is Truth," November 20, 1921, *Akshardeha*, 21:427; Gandhi, *Collected Works*, 25:135.

14. Gandhi, *Gandhijinu Gitashikshan, Akshardeha*, 32:152; Gandhi, *Collected Works*, 37:158f.

15. "Cow Protection," August 4, 1920, Gandhi, *Collected Works*, 21:119.

16. "Speech at Gurukul Kangri Anniversary," March 20, 1916, Gandhi, *Collected Works*, 15:205; *Akshardeha*, 13:242.

17. Søren Kierkegaard, *Fear and Trembling/Repetition*, trans. and ed. Howard and Edna Hong (Princeton: Princeton University Press, 1983).

18. "In Search of Knowledge," March 15, 1925, *Akshardeha*, 26:277; Gandhi, *Collected Works*, 30:418. The Gujarati text is inflected somewhat differently. "To not retain desire for the fruit of action does not mean that no fruit is obtained. The meaning of not keeping expectation is that no action will go fruitless."

19. "Speech at Gujarat Political Conference," November 3, 1917, *Akshardeha*, 14:60; Gandhi, *Collected Works*, 16:129.

20. "Letter to Sevakram Karamchand," September 17, 1926, *Akshardeha*, 31:393; Gandhi, *Collected Works*, 36:324.

21. "General Knowledge about Health–XXXII," August 9, 1913, *Akshardeha*, 12:131; Gandhi, *Collected Works*, 13:240–41.

22. "Readers!," September 24, 1924, *Akshardeha*, 25:200; Gandhi, *Collected Works*, 29:219.

23. "Letter to Premaben Kanthak," April 22, 1932, *Akshardeha*, 49:318; Gandhi, *Collected Works*, 55:279.

24. This is why, to reiterate an argument made elsewhere, such faith is always a "guess" made by the believer. See my "No Politics without Religion."

25. Martin Heidegger, "The Question Concerning Technology," 5.

Index

aapbhog ("self-sacrifice"), 87, 91, 93, 201, 203–5. See also *bhog;* self-sacrifice

abhay ("fearlessness"), 92–93, 223; and abhaydan (gift of fearlessness), 22–24, 124–31, 133, 148–51, 183–85, 218, 239–40, 259, 268, 287–88, 334n15; and animals, 88; and death, 92, 97, 102, 106, 125, 327n3, 332n50; and modern civility, 116–17; and the political, 95; and the question, 96–97; and self-sacrifice, 99; and sovereign power, 95–96; and the warrior, 22–24, 102, 106–8, 116, 124–27, 148–51, 158, 164, 183–84. *See also* abhaydan

abhaydan ("gift of life"), 22–27, 124–33, 148–51, 287, 293, 334n15; and abhay, 124–25, 128–31, 183, 218, 239; and ahimsa, 127; and daya, 172, 183; in Hindu and Jain traditions, 126–27, 315n51, 341n2; and the political, 26, 125, 129–31; as pure gift, 26, 127–29, 133, 149–51, 221, 296; and satyagraha, 124–31, 256–57, and sovereignty, 126–27, 131, 148–50; and warriors, 126–28. *See also* abhay; gift

Abraham, 145, 188, 194, 296; Ibrahim, 188, 194–95

Abrahamic traditions, 41, 57, 296, 321n56

absolute equality. *See* unconditional or absolute equality

absolute responsibility, 55, 72–74, 82, 247, 267, 283–84, 292, 322n70; aloneness of, 186–88, 197; and the animal, 252–57; of daya, 174; and the decision, 144–46; and divine violence, 197, 347n22; and equality, 174–75; and the example, 141, 188–89; and forgiveness, 269; and general responsibility, 55–58, 72–74, 83–89, 101, 144, 188–89, 212, 276, 277; and the Harijan, 165–67; and hope, 236; gift of, 275–76, 282; and killing, 185–88, 197; and knowledge, 247–50, 275–77; and Levinas, 81–83; and repentance, 274–77, 283–84; satyagraha as gift of, 267–69, 274–77, 282; and sovereignty, 144, 347n22; and the true warrior, 121, 127; and varnadharma, 162–63, 165–69. *See also* general responsibility; responsibility

abstract or measurable equality, 3–4, 6–7, 20, 63–64, 89, 206, 317n6, 323n4, 324n12; and Ambedkar, 339n36; and the animal, 37–38; and colonialism, 38–40, 69–71; and death, 332n; demonic immeasurability of, 115–17; and the enemy, 108; Gandhi's questioning of, 47, 51–53; and general responsibility, 55, 69, 73; and the Harijan, 165; and immeasurable pity, 55, 85; and incommensurability, 159–60, 178;

Burke, Edmund, 6, 19–20, 315n45, 316n57, 360n51

calculability, and colonialism, 39, 71, 99; and general responsibility or modern civility, 7–8, 18–19, 70–71, 77–79, 101, 112–17, 129, 132–33, 224, 230, 260, 275, 296, 332–33n58; incalculability of, 7–8, 18, 57–59, 67, 70, 77–78, 81, 84–85, 112–17, 129, 132, 144–45, 224; of prostitutes, 157; and religion, 57–59, 67; and sacrifice, 312–13n31; and satyagraha, 85–86, 101, 133, 241–43; and translation, 217; and warrior, 103–5, 109, 112–17. *See also* measure
Cape Town, 358n17
caste, 206, 340n55. *See also* Harijan; untouchability; *varnadharma*
cataphasis, 181–83, 233
categorical imperative. *See* Kant, Immanuel
causality, 106, 184, 196–98, 214–15; relinquishing, 197–98, 241, 283, 296
celibacy. See *brahmacharya*
Chakrabarty, Dipesh, 25, 66, 195, 315n44, 316n58
Chatterjee, Partha, 309n9
Chaudhari, Saraladevi, 233, 234, 245
Chauri Chaura, 274, 275, 309n9
child, 53–55, 123, 135, 183–84
childhood, Gandhi's, 42, 225, 228–29, 289, 293
children, 23; as satyagrahis, 10, 153–55, 158, 193–94, 216; and self-defense, 137–38, 148. *See also* mothers
Christ, Jesus, xii, 91, 173, 195, 221, 322n69, 352n17
Christianity, viii, 54, 134, 138, 192, 220, 227, 352n17; Augustinian, xiii, 306n22; and finitude, 13, 326n21; and

mysticism, 306–7n25; for Nietzsche, 306n22; and sacrifice, 188; and Salter, 34; as secular religion, 41–43; and secularism, xi, 5, 56–57, 61, 310n11, 319n38; as world religion, 44–45, 320n45
ciphering, 24–25, 27, 352n20, 354n55; and abhaydan, 239; and animals, 254, 256; and the atman, 233, 237–38, 247, 257, 282; and choice, 244; and finitude, 238–39; and forgetting, 268; and the gift, 268; and joy, 285; and language, 272; and love, 237; and machinicity, 88, 240–41; and motivelessness, 294–95; and newness, 282–83; and nullity, 248; and the proper, 233; and Ramanama, 290; and sacrifice, 236–37, 241; and secrecy, 251–52; and sovereignty, 131, 242, 244; and *trahit manas*, 272; and the vow, 233, 237–38. *See also* unconditional or absolute equality; pure means; *shunya*; surrender without subordination
citizen, xi, xiv, xv, 3, 25, 117; and autonomy, 7–8, 13, 47, 55, 71–72, 77, 311n16; and Burke, 20; and empire, 72–73, 168; and equality, 308n6; and exception, xv, 260; and instrumentality, 67, 77; and man, 71; and nation, 72–73, 311n23; and public sphere, 98–99, 256; and satyagraha, 117; and warriors, 21, 332n55. *See also* autonomy; modern civility; rights
civil disobedience, 312n29, 320n51; in liberal traditions, 4, 17, 45–49, 320n53; and satyagraha, 55, 135, 270, 314n40; and vows, 223
civil society, 17, 45–46, 96
civility ("civilization"). *See* modern civility

principle, 227; and the question, 96–97; and reciprocity, 182, 295; and religion, xii; and republican democracy, 101; romantic, 109–10; and sati, 152; and satyagraha-ahimsa, 3, 14, 22–23, 50, 100, 186–88, 254–56, 269, 272–77, 297, 357n14; and self-sacrifice, 151, 165, 281; and surrender, 10, 234, 237, 242–43, 268; and trust, 260–61; and the warrior, 103, 108–10. *See also* daya; prem

Macaulay, Thomas Babington, 6
machines, 325n17, 327–28n23; and ciphering, 87–88, 197, 230, 240–45, 248, 256, 269, 353n33, 353n36, 354n43; and sovereignty, 67, 76–77, 86–88, 115, 149, 197, 240–43
machinicity. *See* machines
madness, 4, 58, 132, 142, 145–46
Mahabali, 127
Mahabharata, 94, 97, 101, 102, 106, 111, 112, 192, 264, 268, 293, 297, 344n3
Mahavira, 94, 147, 259, 263, 264
Majeed, Javed, 327–28n23, 343–44n2
Majoor Mahajan, 352n20
Majumdar, Rochona, 195
Malabar riots, 79
mamatva ("possessiveness"), 203, 204, 283
Mandela, Nelson, 47–48, 49
Mantena, Karuna, 123, 309n10, 320n51, 333n3
Manusmriti, 43, 126
Mapilla uprising, 79, 80
Marx, Karl, xi, 197, 210, 305n14, 310n11, 319n38, 324–25n12
maryada, 12, 160–62, 238, 313n32, 338–39n, 353n28
maryada dharma, 160–62, 168, 338–39n35, 353n28

Mashruwala, Kishorelal, 137, 231, 344n4
Masuzawa, Tomoko, 320n49
Mauss, Marcel, 26, 104, 128, 330n41
means, 35–36, 38, 197, 243, 245; abstract, 77–79; and abstract time, 278–79; ahimsa as, 179–80, 211; any means whatsoever, 71, 144, 196, 324n10; calculable, 101, 103, 108, 112, 115; and finitude, 106; instrumental, 103, 112, 196, 200; primacy over ends, 46; and questioning, 346n13, 347n22; rational, 35–36, right, 18, 46, 67, 71, 144, 196, 243, 324n10; as sacrifice, 199–203; and technology, 113–14; togetherness with ends, 113–14, 199–200; and violence, 199. *See also* end or ends; means–end problematic; pure means; *sadhana*
means–end problematic, 18, 108, 111–15, 123, 251, 296, 298, 348n28; and abstract time, 279–81; instrumental understanding of, 18, 46, 67, 77, 103, 111–14, 196–97, 200, 283, 298, 324n10; sacrifice of the, 199–200, 241–42, 280–82, 312–13n31; and violence, 18, 108; and warrior, 103, 111. *See also* means
measure, 7–8, 68–70, 78–81, 91; and absolute responsibility, 165; and citizenship, 18, 21, 311n16; colonial, 60–71; and equality, 7–9, 18, 63–64, 102, 106, 108; and general responsibility, 69–70, 78, 83; and the gift, 104; and immeasure, 7–8, 78, 84–85, 115–17; and machinicity, 240; and modern civility, 13, 78–81, 108, 142–43, 230, 296; nationalist, 71–72; and satyagraha, 11–12; and sovereignty, 278; and the third party, 67–74, 79–80, 116, 143, 326n21; two forms

241; and measure, 240; and nonbeing, 152; and pure gift, 26, 152;
ruination of, 160; and satyagraha,
xii, 11, 12, 23–24, 27, 63, 87, 117, 134,
145–46, 151, 297; and self-sacrifice,
12, 63, 148, 158, 161, 165, 202–3, 237,
241, 312–13n31; and sovereignty, or
propriety, 21, 23, 24, 113–14, 131, 134,
148, 155; and swaraj, 3, 27, 196; and
varnadharma, 158–62; and the vow,
226, 232; and the warrior, 21–22, 113–
14, 148. See also ciphering; gift;
thekana
Propriety. See proper and sovereignty
prostitutes, 24–25, 156–58, 169
public sphere, and civil disobedience,
17; and the judge, 75, 80; and the
principle, 226; and the private
sphere, x–xi, 5, 32, 98–99; and the
question, x; and religion, 5, 7–8, 73,
305n17; and the secret, 75, 248–51;
and the wound, 78–79. See also
private sphere; religion
pure faith, 217–20, 229, 244–45, 252,
298
pure forgiveness. See aneconomy;
forgiveness
pure means, xiv, 9, 6, 18, 26, 141, 191,
223, 229, 296, 347n19; and Walter
Benjamin, 197–98, 347n22; and the
destruction of conservatism, 24;
and forgetting, 268; impurity of,
252; and nonknowledge, 247, 250,
252; obscuring of, 207; as self-
surrender, 198, 201–2, 211, 215, 218–
19, 223
pure or aneconomic gift, 6, 11, 24, 113,
217–18, 289; and death, 37, 63; and
the decision, 243, 247; and fearlessness, 26–27, 128–29, 133; and
forgetting, 268; and the impossible,

37–38, 63; and nonknowledge, 247;
and reciprocation, 293–96; and the
sovereign gift, 103–4, 127–28, 243,
247, 251–52, 289, 293–95, 340n54
pure sacrifice, 93, 209, 229
purushartha, 14, 54, 55, 192, 322n69,
346n6. See also immeasurable pity
Putlibai, 42, 225–26, 227, 228, 231, 289

question, vii–ix, 346n13; mantra as,
93; as piety of thought, ix, 305n12;
religion of the, or nonsovereign, xi–
xii, xvi, 67, 131, 194, 233, 252;
satyagraha as, xvi; and secularism,
32, 129; sovereign, x–xii, 32, 59,
96–97, 131, 183; and the vow, 224.
See also answer

racism, 321n60, 357–58n16; anticolo-
nial, 41–43; British, 50–51, 323n3;
Gandhi's, 40–43, 45, 49–51; and
Levinas, 39, 83, 326–27n26; and
republican democracy, 62
Rajah, M. C., 206
rakshasi ("monstrous," "evil"), 80–81,
107, 115, 116, 124, 175, 232, 326n22
Rama, 42, 153, 223, 247, 313n32; as
Kshatriya, 94, 259; and Sita, 73–
74, 155, 331n45; surrender to,
234–35
Ramanama, 228, 287–91, 316n2, 328n9,
361n1
Ramanuja, 206–8
Ramayana, 110, 172, 293, 313n32, 328n9,
331n45
Rambha, 226, 228–29, 230, 231, 288,
289
Rancière, Jacques, xv, 21, 26, 74, 325n14
Rao, Anupama, 163, 167
Ravana, 107, 116, 153, 155, 223, 331n45
Rawls, John, 4, 46, 47, 49, 321n60

theological secularism, x– xi, 17, 71–72, 79, 211, 305n16; Gandhi's, 40, 44–46; Salter's, 32–37, 45–46, 53

theology, x, 45, 305n16, 307n25, 323–34n5, 335n29, 360n51; of civil disobedience, 46; in Derrida, 133; and religion, 5, 63, 181, 297; of the third party, 71–72, 79

third party, 15, 207, 326n21; and immeasurability, 80–82, 116–17, 143; and modern civility, 67–75, 78–82; and republican democracy, 308n6; and satyagraha-ahimsa, 140, 274; and two-ness, 85, 87–89, 110, 210, 272; and the warrior, 106, 110, 230; 278. See also justice; three-ness

three-ness, 67–68, 70; and general responsibility, 72; and law, 78–79; and one, 74–76, 326n; and two-ness in Levinas, 81–83. See also third party; trahit manas; two-ness

Tidrick, Kathryn, 317n5

Tiele, Cornelius Petrus, 44, 45, 227, 320n45

Tilak, Bal Gangadhar, 99, 195–96, 331n48, 347n16, 347n17

time, 57, 228, 278–83, 286, 305n10, 309n9, 359–60n51

Tolstoy, 32, 33, 247, 320n51, 344n2

Tolstoy Farm, 155

trahit manas ("ordinary man"), 15, 267; as the other third party, 87–89, 210, 262, 272, 327n32. See also three-ness

translation, vii, 3, 14–15; and the untranslatable, 217

transparency, 249–52, 316n57

Transvaal, 1, 45, 232

Trojan Horse massacre, 358n17

trust, 21, 131; abstract, 260; aneconomy, 261–65, 268–69, 272; Derrida on, 56, 58; economy of, 259–61; in God,

138; and modern civility, 260; and the warrior, 260–61; and vows, 356n10

trusteeship, 203–4

truth, 79–80, 329n, 342n19, 342n20, 350n64; constative, 75, 212–13; and Hegel, 329n27; and the minor, 9; and Socrates, 325n14; and universals, 307n25. See also satya

Tulsidas, 107, 184, 251, 288, 331n45, 343n32

two-ness, 67–68, 89, 92–93, 295; and absolute responsibility, 72; and ahimsa, 217; and daya, 173; and death, 78; and finitude, 78, 80; inhabiting, 85–86; in Levinas, 81–83; obscuring of, 74–75, 84–85; and surrender, 216; and violence, 326n20; and the warrior, 96

unconditional or absolute equality, xiv, 4–6, 12, 17, 64, 211; and abstract equality, 230, 291, 292; and anekantvada, 182; with animals, 252–58; and ciphering, 238, 257, 283; and daya, 174–78; and death, 12; destruction of, 154–68; as duty, 238; and finitude, 298, 338–39n35; and the Gita, 192, 196, 206–10, 214, 219–20; and the Harijan, 168–69; and immeasurable equality, 22–23, 110, 147–48, 207, 247; and incommensurability, 178–79, 238, 282; and love, 240; and the miracle, 298; and newness, 282–83; and not-ness of being, 285, 291–93; obscuring of, xiv–xvi; and religions, 219–21; and relinquishment of sovereignty, 291; and satya-ahimsa, 178–80, 183; and self-sacrifice, 208–11; and slavery, 210–11; and varnadharma, 168.

AJAY SKARIA is professor of history at the University of Minnesota. He is author of *Hybrid Histories: Forests, Frontiers, and Wildness in Western India* and coeditor of *Subaltern Studies XII: Muslims, Dalits, and the Fabrications of History*.